'A major intervention in theory and analysis, this generative collection, featuring first-rank senior and junior scholars, deploys intermediality as the historiographic key to open up the secret chambers of Brazilian cinema, revealing the cross-fertilisation of arts and media as a springboard for creativity. Cumulatively, the text reveals Brazilian cinema and media to be extraordinarily avant-garde friendly, manifested in a cornucopia of nested arts and genres (music video, vaudeville, carnival, painting). The corpus is Brazilian, but the theories and methods are transnational and relevant to all cinemas.'
Robert Stam, New York University

'This volume sheds much-needed light on the complex and wide-ranging dialogues with the other arts and media that have always characterised Brazilian cinema. Bringing together work by established scholars and emerging academic "stars", it furthermore illustrates how the intermedial method can be used to interrogate and nuance traditional approaches to the study of any cinema culture.'
Lisa Shaw, University of Liverpool

'With its focus on intermediality, this excellent volume offers new, multifaceted and innovative perspectives on the dynamic and creative relationship between Brazilian cinema and different areas of cultural and artistic practice from almost the beginning of film production in the country until the present. An important contribution to the field.'
Randal Johnson, University of California Los Angeles

Edinburgh Studies in Film and Intermediality

Series editors: Martine Beugnet and Kriss Ravetto
Founding editor: John Orr

A series of scholarly research intended to challenge and expand on the various approaches to film studies, bringing together film theory and film aesthetics with the intermedial aspects of the field. The volumes combine critical theoretical interventions with a consideration of specific contexts, aesthetic qualities, and a strong sense of the medium's ability to appropriate current technological developments in its practice and form as well as in its distribution.

Advisory board
Duncan Petrie (University of Auckland)
John Caughie (University of Glasgow)
Dina Iordanova (University of St Andrews)
Elizabeth Ezra (University of Stirling)
Gina Marchetti (University of Hong Kong)
Jolyon Mitchell (University of Edinburgh)
Judith Mayne (The Ohio State University)
Dominique Bluher (Harvard University)

Titles in the series include:

Romantics and Modernists in British Cinema
John Orr

Framing Pictures: Film and the Visual Arts
Steven Jacobs

The Sense of Film Narration
Ian Garwood

The Feel-Bad Film
Nikolaj Lübecker

American Independent Cinema: Rites of Passage and the Crisis Image
Anna Backman Rogers

The Incurable-Image: Curating Post-Mexican Film and Media Arts
Tarek Elhaik

Screen Presence: Cinema Culture and the Art of Warhol, Rauschenberg, Hatoum and Gordon
Stephen Monteiro

Indefinite Visions: Cinema and the Attractions of Uncertainty
Martine Beugnet, Allan Cameron and Arild Fetveit (eds)

Screening Statues: Sculpture and Cinema
Steven Jacobs, Susan Felleman, Vito Adriaensens and Lisa Colpaert

Drawn From Life: Issues and Themes in Animated Documentary Cinema
Jonathan Murray and Nea Ehrlich (eds)

Intermedial Dialogues: The French New Wave and the Other Arts
Marion Schmid

The Museum as a Cinematic Space: The Display of Moving Images in Exhibitions
Elisa Mandelli

Theatre Through the Camera Eye: The Poetics of an Intermedial Encounter
Laura Sava

Caught In-Between: Intermediality in Contemporary Eastern Europe and Russian Cinema
Ágnes Pethő (ed.)

No Power Without an Image: Icons Between Photography and Film
Libby Saxton

Cinematic Intermediality: Theory and Practice
Kim Knowles and Marion Schmid (eds)

Animating Truth: Documentary and Visual Culture in the 21st Century
Nea Ehrlich

Derivative Images: Financial Derivatives in French Film, Literature and Thought
Calum Watt

Towards an Intermedial History of Brazilian Cinema
Lúcia Nagib, Luciana Corrêa de Araújo and Tiago de Luca (eds)

edinburghuniversitypress.com/series/esif

Towards an Intermedial History of Brazilian Cinema

Edited by Lúcia Nagib, Luciana Corrêa de Araújo and Tiago de Luca

EDINBURGH
University Press

Edinburgh University Press is one of the leading university presses in the UK. We publish academic books and journals in our selected subject areas across the humanities and social sciences, combining cutting-edge scholarship with high editorial and production values to produce academic works of lasting importance. For more information visit our website: edinburghuniversitypress.com

© editorial matter and organisation Lúcia Nagib, Luciana Corrêa de Araújo and Tiago de Luca, 2022, 2025
© the chapters their several authors, 2022, 2025

Edinburgh University Press Ltd
13 Infirmary Street, Edinburgh, EH1 1LT

First published in hardback by Edinburgh University Press 2022

Typeset in Garamond MT Pro by
Cheshire Typesetting Ltd, Cuddington, Cheshire

A CIP record for this book is available from the British Library

ISBN 978 1 4744 5298 4 (hardback)
ISBN 978 1 4744 5299 1 (paperback)
ISBN 978 1 4744 5300 4 (webready PDF)
ISBN 978 1 4744 5301 1 (epub)

The right of Lúcia Nagib, Luciana Corrêa de Araújo and Tiago de Luca to be identified as editors of this work has been asserted in accordance with the Copyright, Designs and Patents Act 1988 and the Copyright and Related Rights Regulations 2003 (SI No. 2498).

Contents

List of Figures	vii
The Contributors	xii
Acknowledgements	xviii
Introduction Lúcia Nagib, Luciana Corrêa de Araújo and Tiago de Luca	1

Part I Intervisuality

1 Traffic in Images: Visual Spectacle before Cinema in Brazil Ian Christie	17
2 Intermedial Landscapes in the Work of Cao Guimarães Alison Butler	39
3 'The most innocent film of the year': Comic Books, Sex and Cinema Marginal Stefan Solomon	51
4 Photographs of the Invisible: Intermedial Figurations of Social Exclusion in *Babás* and *Aquarius* Tiago de Luca	71
5 Exploring the Cinematic Imaginary: Carlos Adriano, André Parente and the Precision of the Vague Martine Beugnet	94

Part II The Empire of Music

6 Watson Macedo's *Aviso aos navegantes* (1950): Reflections on the Musical Numbers of a Brazilian *Chanchada* Flávia Cesarino Costa	113
7 (In)Visible Musicians: Supporting Instrumentalists and their Intermedial Vocation Suzana Reck Miranda	131

8   Music-video Aesthetics in Pernambucan Cinema   144
    Samuel Paiva

9   Possessing Archival Images: Ghosts, Songs and Films in *Cartola –
    música para os olhos* (2007)   159
    Albert Elduque

Part III   Entertainment Circuits

10 Intermediality in Brazilian Silent Cinema: Luiz de Barros's Works
    and Intermedial Strategies   177
    Luciana Corrêa de Araújo

11 'Synchronised Film Fever' amid the 'Gramophonoradiomania':
    Record, Radio and Cinema at the Dawn of the 'Talkies' in Rio de
    Janeiro   194
    Rafael de Luna Freire

12 The Singer, the Acrobats and the Bands: A Study of Three
    Brazilian Films and their Intermedial Characters   215
    Alfredo Suppia

13 Gilda de Abreu's *O Ébrio* as a Unique Intermedial Project   228
    Margarida Maria Adamatti

14 *Chanchada*, Samba and Beyond: From the Cinema of Radio to the
    Cinema of Television (1930s–1960s)   243
    João Luiz Vieira

Part IV   From Impure Cinema to Cosmopoetics

15 Impure Cinema as Method: The Last Films of Eduardo Coutinho   261
    Consuelo Lins

16 Queering Intermediality in Brazilian Cinema   274
    Ramayana Lira de Sousa and Alessandra Soares Brandão

17 The Humiliation of the Father: Theatrical Melodrama and Cinema
    Novo's Critique of Conservative Modernisation   288
    Ismail Xavier

18 Intermedial Territories: Maps and the Amazonian Moving Image   307
    Gustavo Procopio Furtado

19 An Intermedial Reading of Glauber Rocha's Cosmogony   323
    Lúcia Nagib

Index   345

Figures

1.1 Booklet accompanying Burford's large-scale Panorama of the Bay of Rio Janeiro, exhibited at the London Panorama in 1827–8   20

1.2 Panorama Building in Leicester Square, London. Aquatint published in 1801, showing the scale of this display, where Rio de Janeiro was later exhibited   21

1.3 Lithograph by Agostino Aglio of the 'Modern Mexico' exhibition held at London's Egyptian Hall in 1824, which displayed objects collected by William Bullock and his son on their visit in 1821   21

1.4 Photographer Revert Henrique Klumb introduced stereography to Brazil during the 1850s. He produced this popular stereograph of the Emperor Pedro II   23

1.5 Part of a stereoscopic view of Porto Alegre by Klumb, probably shown in the National Exhibition of 1866 among his landscape studies   24

1.6 Church at Poços de Caldas, Minas Gerais, from a set of lantern slides archived by the American Southern Methodist Episcopal Mission   25

1.7 Teatro São Pedro in 1875, photographed by Luigi Terragano   28

1.8 A 1901 programme of films shown daily at the Teatro São Pedro on the 'Grand-Prix marvellous cinematograph' by Henrique Sastro. Films seem to have been mainly from the Lumière brothers, with *Guilherme Tell* and *Morte de Chocolat* featuring two famous clowns filmed at a Paris circus in 1897   30

1.9 Alice Guy's 1905 *Life of Christ* (Gaumont) was a big Christmas success at the Teatro São Pedro in Porto Alegre   31

1.10	*Os estranguladores* (*The Stranglers*, 1908) reconstructed a notorious recent crime in Rio de Janeiro, inaugurating a series of 'true crime' dramas that launched early Brazilian cinema into an international genre	32
3.1	While trying on a dress, Luciana (Helena Ignez) is amused by a panel from Jean-Claude Forest's *Barbarella* (1962–4) in *Cara a Cara* (1967)	55
3.2	A sample of Carlos Zéfiro's *catecismos* concealed inside a bible in *Os anos dourados da sacanagem* (1986)	60
3.3	Elsa Bannister (Rita Hayworth) attempts to explain her actions in the funhouse hall of mirrors in *The Lady from Shanghai* (1947)	63
3.4	The life and death of Miguel Metralha (Stênio Garcia) depicted across four comic-book panels in the final sequence of *O pornógrafo* (1970)	65
4.1	A silent film in *Babás* reveals the mutilation effected by the framing, as the nanny is partially cut off	76
4.2	By pausing an early film, *Babás* centralises and makes visible a black nanny in the background	76
4.3	A digitally composed mosaic of portraits at the end of *Babás* materialises the film's quest to become photography	79
4.4	Clara poses for a snap with her maid Ladjane (beside her) at the latter's birthday party, in *Aquarius*	83
4.5 and 4.6	A faceless maid, accidentally captured in family photographs, functions as a Barthesian punctum, in *Aquarius*	85
4.7 and 4.8	A focus pull enables *Aquarius* to bring the maid Juvenita into visibility	86
4.9	Now in the foreground of the image, Juvenita haunts an enfeebled Clara, in *Aquarius*	88
4.10 and 4.11	A profusion of maids in the background finally become prominent in *Aquarius*	90
4.12	A pause on a still photograph, in *Aquarius*'s opening slideshow, suddenly reveals hidden secrets	91
5.1	Carlos Adriano's *Remanescências* (*Remainiscences*, 1997), based on José Roberto Cunha Salles's *Ancoradouro de pescadores na Baía de Guanabara* (*Fishing Pier at Guanabara Bay*, 1897). Courtesy of the artist	97

5.2	View of André Parente's installation *Figuras na paisagem* (*Figures in a Landscape*, 2010). Courtesy of the artist	101
6.1	Eliana sings and dances in the musical number 'Bate o bombo' (Hit the Bass Drum) in *Aviso aos navegantes* (1950)	122
6.2	The façade of Teatro Recreio in Rio de Janeiro, where the revue *Muié macho sim sinhô* was shown between 1950 and 1951. Image from Walter Pinto Archives. Courtesy of the Centre of Documentation and Art/National Foundation of Arts (Cedoc/Funarte), Brazil	126
6.3	Oscarito and Juliana Yanakiewa rehearse for the theatrical revue *Muié macho sim sinhô* (1950). Image by Walter Pinto Archives. Courtesy of the Centre of Documentation and Art / National Foundation of Arts (Cedoc/Funarte), Brazil	127
9.1	Cartola is shot dead in Moisés Kendler's episode 'Papo amarelo', in *Os marginais* (1968)	159
9.2	Cartola in *Rio, carnaval da vida* (Leon Hirszman, 1978)	170
10.1	Prologue to *Orphans of the Storm* (D. W. Griffith, 1921), staged by Luiz de Barros in 1926 at the Gloria theatre. Courtesy of Cinemateca do Museu de Arte Moderna do Rio de Janeiro	185
10.2	Prologue to *The Lost World* (Harry O. Hoyt, 1925), which was subjected to censorship. Courtesy BRASIL. Ministério da Justiça e Segurança Pública. Arquivo Nacional. Fundo Delegacia Auxiliar de Polícia, BR_RJANRIO_6E_CPR_PTE_0826	186
11.1	A humorous cartoon comments on the noise produced by modern electrical sound technologies. Source National Library, Brazil	195
11.2	'Gramophonoradiomania': a comic strip depicts Rio de Janeiro's noisy soundscape. Source National Library, Brazil	196
11.3	Rio de Janeiro's Odeon showing its first 'talkie': *Fox Movietone Follies of 1929*. Author's private collection	204
12.1	In *Areias escaldantes* (1985) the 'terrorists', Vinícius

	Kishi ('Vini', Diogo Vilela) and Verônica Pinheiro ('Verrô', Regina Casé), carry out subversive actions	221
13.1 and 13.2	Gilberto (Vicente Celestino) borrows a guitar and plays to the audience in the bar scene	233
13.3 and 13.4	Vicente Celestino as the drunkard and the replica of his costume at the Museu Vicente Celestino	234
13.5	Mesmerised children watch Gilberto/Celestino's performance	236
13.6	A little girl sitting on the floor breaks the fourth wall as she stares at the camera, reinforcing the documentary dimension of the film	237
13.7	Singing on the radio or at open-air concerts, Vicente Celestino was always surrounded by a young audience	237
13.8	Vicente Celestino and Ricardo Nóvoa (who plays the drunkard in the TV version of *O Ébrio*) board a flight dressed as alcoholic tramps	240
14.1	Newspaper advert for the *chanchada Quem roubou meu samba* (1958), which was shown across twenty cinemas in Rio de Janeiro in advance of the 1959 carnival	254
16.1	Book cover of Cassandra Rios's *Ariella, a paranóica* (*Ariella, The Paranoid*, 1980), 2nd edition. Authors' private collection	280
17.1	Herculano in his car, with Piazzola's tango on the soundtrack	291
17.2	Geni sings at the brothel in *Toda nudez será castigada*	293
17.3	Geni at Herculano's second family home, or the 'haunted house'	294
17.4	Serginho and the 'Bolivian thief' go away together	295
17.5	*Toda nudez será castigada* ends with a close-up shot of Geni's face, who is now dead	297
17.6	A lost doll in a Rio de Janeiro summer flood at the opening of *O casamento*	299
17.7	Sabino and his daughter in *O casamento*	300
17.8	With a smile on his face, Sabino allows himself to be arrested in *O casamento*	302
18.1	Following their anticlimactic arrival in Altamira, *Bye bye Brasil*'s troupe and their indigenous passengers gather in front of a map of Brazil and	

	a television set, establishing an 'intermedial figuration'	307
18.2	While Lorde searches for a map, a shot displays the painted mountain on the vehicle's door and the stickers of hands pressed against its windshield, suggesting alternative forms of representing and experiencing space	313
18.3	Tonacci's indigenous contact film establishes a reflexive dialogue between several media including the national map, photography and the television, thus placing itself in an intermedial territory	320
19.1	Faustino's verses appear *as* poetry: that is, as handwriting on the white page of the sand dunes	324
19.2 to 19.6	Cross iconography prevails in *Deus e o diabo na terra do sol*	328
19.7	The camera's vertical gesture splits Corisco in two	330
19.8 and 19.9	The cross is weaponised in *Deus e o diabo na terra do sol*	331
19.10	*Cordel* booklets hang on strings in dedicated shops	332
19.11	Sebastião forces his followers into gruelling acts of penitence	333
19.12	Júlio, in his blindness, is able to 'see', in the real landscape, the whole history of the *sertão*	335
19.13	The cosmogonic sea in the opening of *Terra em transe*	337
19.14	The re-enactment of Brazil's legendary First Mass, in 1500, in *Terra em transe*	338
19.15 and 19.16	Characters in carnivalesque costumes pose stony-faced, as if they were decorative props on an opera stage	339

The Contributors

Margarida Maria Adamatti holds a PhD degree in Audiovisual Media and Processes from the School of Communication and Arts, University of São Paulo, Brazil. She has been developing her CAPES-funded postdoctoral research at the Federal University of São Carlos (UFSCar), Brazil, where she also lectures in the Image and Sound Postgraduate Programme. She has been a postdoctoral researcher on the IntermIdia Project. She is author of the book *Crítica de cinema e repressão – estética e política no jornal alternativo Opinião* (2019).

Luciana Corrêa de Araújo is Assistant Professor at the Federal University of São Carlos (UFSCar), Brazil. Her research on Brazilian silent cinema focuses mainly on intermedial relations, women's activities, and cinema in the state of Pernambuco. She is author of *A crônica de cinema no Recife dos anos 50* (1997) and *Joaquim Pedro de Andrade: primeiros tempos* (2013), and has published in journals and edited collections including *Nova história do cinema brasileiro* (Sheila Schvarzman and Fernão Pessoa Ramos, eds, 2018) and *Stars and Stardom in Brazilian Cinema* (Tim Bergfelder, Lisa Shaw and João Luiz Vieira, eds, 2016).

Martine Beugnet is Professor in Visual Studies at the Université de Paris, France, and a member of the LARCA Research Institute. She has curated exhibitions and written articles on a wide range of film and media topics and authored several books on contemporary cinema, including *Claire Denis* (2004); *Proust at the Movies* (2005), with Marion Schmid; *Cinema and Sensation: French Film and the Art of Transgression* (2007, 2012); and *L'Attrait du flou* (2017), on the history and aesthetics of blur in film. Her latest monograph, entitled *Le Cinéma et ses doubles: l'image de film à l'ère du foundfootage numérisé et des écrans de poche*, was published in 2021. She co-edited the book *Indefinite Visions: Cinema and the Attractions of Uncertainty* with Allan Cameron and Arild Fetveit (2017).

Alessandra Soares Brandão is a Professor of Film and Literary Studies in the Graduate Programme in Literature at the Universidade Federal de Santa

Catarina, Brazil. She has written on Brazilian and Latin American cinemas for a number of journals and has contributed to the book *Human Rights, Social Movements and Activism in Contemporary Latin American Cinema* (2018). Her recent research, 'Women on the Move and Women's Movements: Narratives of Im/mobility and In/visibility', focuses on issues of domestic labour and lesbian desire in cinema and literature from a decolonial perspective.

Alison Butler was Associate Professor in Film at the University of Reading, UK, until 2021. She has published widely on artists' film and video and women's cinema.

Ian Christie is a film scholar and curator who has worked on many aspects of historic and contemporary cinema, especially the once-neglected figures of Michael Powell and Emeric Pressburger, the peripatetic Chilean exile Raúl Ruiz and, most recently, the founding pioneer of English cinema, Robert Paul. A Fellow of the British Academy and Professor at Birkbeck College, University of London, UK, he was the 2006 Slade Professor of Fine Art at Cambridge University, UK, and has curated major exhibitions about Sergei Eisenstein, avant-garde film and early cinema. He has a strong interest in pre-cinematic visual technologies and their culture, especially the magic lantern, panoramas and stereoscopy, which informs his contribution to this book. He blogs at https://paulsanimatographworks.wordpress.com/. His website is www.ianchristie.org.

Flávia Cesarino Costa teaches Film History and Theory at the Department of Art and Communication at the Federal University of São Carlos (UFSCar), Brazil. Her research and publications focus on early and silent cinema, melodrama, and Brazilian musical cinema from the 1930s to 1950s, as well as its connections with theatre, radio, TV and popular music. She is author of the book *O primeiro cinema: espetáculo, narração, domesticação* (Early Cinema: Spectacle, Narration, Domestication) (2000). She has a PhD in Semiotics and Communication Studies at Pontifícia Universidade Católica de São Paulo, Brazil. She participates in Cinemídia – Research Group on Theory and History of Audiovisual Media at UFSCar (https://cinemidiaufscar.wordpress.com/apresentacao) and worked as a co-investigator on the IntermIdia Project (http://www.reading.ac.uk/intermidia/ip-IntermIdia-Project-Staff.aspx).

Albert Elduque is a Lecturer in Film Studies at Universitat Pompeu Fabra (Barcelona, Spain). His PhD dissertation, completed at Pompeu Fabra in 2014, dealt with the concepts of hunger, consumption and vomit in modern political cinema, focusing on the cases of Europe and Brazil and on filmmakers such as Pier Paolo Pasolini, Marco Ferreri, Glauber Rocha and Nelson Pereira dos Santos. From 2016 to 2019 he was a postdoctoral researcher at the University of Reading, UK, attached to the IntermIdia Project. His current research areas are intermediality and film, political cinema, and representations of national identities in film and music documentaries, with a focus on Spanish and Brazilian cinemas. He is co-editor of the journal *Comparative Cinema*, published by the Universitat Pompeu Fabra.

Rafael de Luna Freire is Associate Professor in the Film and Video Department and in the Cinema and Audiovisual PhD Programme at Fluminense Federal University, Brazil, where he coordinates the Audiovisual Preservation Laboratory (LUPA-UFF). His works are situated at the intersection between film history and audiovisual preservation. He was responsible for the project to restore the feature film *Antes, o verão* (1968) and for the reconstruction of the first Brazilian sound feature film, *Acabaram-se os otários* (Luiz de Barros, 1929), together with Reinaldo Cardenuto. Among his published works on Brazilian cinema history are *Cinematographo em Nictheroy: história das salas de cinema de Niterói*. He is the author of *O negócio do filme: a distribuição cinematográfica no Brasil, 1907–1915* (2022).

Gustavo Procopio Furtado is associate professor of Romance Studies and Art, Art History, and Visual Studies at Duke University, USA. His research and teaching interests include Latin American literature and cinema; film and media theory; modernity and modernism in the Global South; travel writing; ecocriticism and ecocultural studies; and ethnographic and indigenous film. His book *Documentary Filmmaking in Contemporary Brazil: Cinematic Archives of the Present* (2019) examines forms of documentary-making that emerged during Brazil's most recent period of democratisation (roughly from 1985 to 2016). The book won the 2019 Antonio Candido Prize for Best Book in the Humanities (awarded by the Brazil section of the Latin American Studies Association). He is currently working on several projects, including a book-length manuscript on questions of territoriality, film and visual media in the Amazon.

Consuelo Lins is a researcher, essayist and full professor in the School of Communication of UFRJ (Federal University at Rio de Janeiro), Brazil. She holds a doctorate and post-doctorate in Cinema and Audiovisual from the Université de Paris 3 (Sorbonne Nouvelle), France, and was a postdoctoral researcher in the Department of Film, Media and Cultural Studies at Birkbeck College, University of London, UK (2014/2015). Lins is the author of *O* *documentário de Eduardo Coutinho: televisão, cinema e vídeo* (2004) and *Cao Guimarães: arte, documentário, ficção* (2019), and co-author, with Cláudia Mesquita, of *Filmar o real*, on contemporary Brazilian documentary (2008). As a documentary filmmaker, she has directed *Lectures* (2005), *Leituras Cariocas* (2009) and *Babás* (2010), among other films. She worked as an interview researcher for two of Eduardo Coutinho's films: *Babilônia 2000* and *Edifício Master*.

Tiago de Luca is Reader in Film Studies at the University of Warwick, UK. He is the author of *Planetary Cinema: Film, Media and the Earth* (2022) and *Realism of the Senses in World Cinema: The Experience of Physical Reality* (2014), and the editor (with Nuno Barradas Jorge) of *Slow Cinema* (Edinburgh University Press, 2016).

Suzana Reck Miranda is Associate Professor of Film and Music Studies at the Federal University of São Carlos (UFSCar), Brazil. Her research interests include music in film and television, film sound, close textual analysis and Brazilian cinema history. She is author of several articles on the relationship between film and music, and was a co-investigator on the IntermIdia Project.

Lúcia Nagib is Professor of Film at the University of Reading, UK. Her research has focused on polycentric approaches to world cinema, new waves and new cinemas, cinematic realism and intermediality, among other subjects. She is the author of many books, including *Realist Cinema as World Cinema: Non-cinema, Intermedial Passages, Total Cinema* (2020), *World Cinema and the Ethics of Realism* (2011) and *Brazil on Screen: Cinema Novo, New Cinema, Utopia* (2007). Her edited books include *Impure Cinema: Intermedial and Intercultural Approaches to Film* (with Anne Jerslev, 2014), *Theorizing World Cinema* (with Chris Perriam and Rajinder Dudrah, 2011), *Realism and the Audiovisual Media* (with Cecília Mello, 2009) and *The New Brazilian Cinema* (2003). She is the writer and director, with Samuel Paiva, of the award-winning feature-length documentary *Passages* (2019).

Samuel Paiva is lecturer in Film History in the Department of Arts and Communication, Federal University of São Carlos (UFSCar), Brazil. Born in Recife, Pernambuco, he contributed to Pernambucan short films and the feature *Baile perfumado* (*Perfumed Ball*, 1996). Between 1999 and 2005 he directed television programmes for the São Paulo University Channel. He obtained his MA and PhD degrees from the School of Communications and Arts, University of São Paulo, with research on the relationship between cinema and the other arts. His PhD thesis, *A figura de Orson Welles no cinema de Rogério Sganzerla*, was published in 2018. Paiva's work also includes the co-edited book *Viagem ao cinema silencioso do Brasil* (2011) and the essay film *Passages: Travelling In and Out of Film Through Brazilian Geography* (Lúcia Nagib and Samuel Paiva, 2019).

Stefan Solomon is Senior Lecturer in Media Studies at Macquarie University, Australia. He is the author of *William Faulkner in Hollywood: Screenwriting for the Studios* (2017), co-editor with Julian Murphet of *William Faulkner in the Media Ecology* (2015), editor of *Tropicália and Beyond: Dialogues in Brazilian Film History* (2017), and curator of a film series of the same name held at Tate Modern in 2017. With Albert Elduque, he is co-editor of the journal *Comparative Cinema*.

Ramayana Lira de Sousa is Professor of Film and Literary Studies in the Graduate Programme in Language Sciences at the Universidade do Sul de Santa Catarina, Brazil. She has written on Brazilian and Latin American cinemas and on issues of gender and feminist theory for a number of journals, and has contributed to the book *Human Rights, Social Movements and Activism in Contemporary Latin American Cinema* (2018). Her recent research, 'Political images: crossings [gender, race and sexuality]', investigates the politics of lesbian desire in contemporary cinema. She is also a curator.

Alfredo Suppia holds a PhD in Multimedia and coordinates the Research Group on Film and Audiovisual Genres (GENECINE). He is an Assistant Professor of Film Studies at the State University of Campinas (Unicamp), Brazil. He is the author of *Rarefied Atmosphere: Science Fiction in Brazilian Cinema* (*Atmosfera rarefeita: a ficção científica no cinema Brasileiro*, 2013), and his research interests include world cinema, Latin American cinemas, screenplay, and science fiction film and literature, among other topics.

João Luiz Vieira is Professor in the Department of Film and Video at the Fluminense Federal University in Niterói, Rio de Janeiro. He has a PhD in Cinema Studies from New York University in the USA (1984) and has done post-doctoral research in Film and Television Studies at the University of Warwick, UK (1997–8). In 1996 he was a Fulbright Visiting Scholar at the Media Arts Department of the University of New Mexico, USA, and in 2002 in the Department of Cinema and Comparative Literature at the University of Iowa, USA. He is author and editor of a number of works, including *Cinema Novo and Beyond* (1998) and *Câmera-faca, o cinema de Sérgio Bianchi* (2004), and has contributed book chapters to *World Cinemas, Transnational Perspectives* (2010) and *Nova história do cinema Brasileiro* (2018). He also co-edited, with B. Ruby Rich, a dossier on contemporary Brazilian cinema for *Film Quarterly*

(74, Winter 2020–1). He is currently researching histories of film theatres and cinema-going.

Ismail Xavier is Professor of Audiovisual Studies at the University of São Paulo, Brazil. He has been Visiting Professor at NYU (1995) and University of Iowa (1998) in the USA, Université de Paris III, France (1999), University of Leeds, UK (2007), University of Chicago, USA (2008) and Universidad de Buenos Aires, Argentina (2011). He is the author of *Allegories of Underdevelopment: Aesthetics and Politics in Modern Brazilian Cinema* (1997), *O olhar e a cena: Hollywood, melodrama, Cinema Novo, Nelson Rodrigues* (2003) and *Sertão mar – Glauber Rocha e a estética da fome* (2007), among other books. He has contributed to: *Mediating Two Worlds: Cinematic Encounters in the Americas*, edited by John King, Ana López and Manuel Alvarado (1993); *A Companion to Film Theory*, edited by Toby Miller and Robert Stam (1999); *The New Brazilian Cinema*, edited by Lúcia Nagib (2003); *Realism and the Audiovisual Media*, edited by Lúcia Nagib and Cecília Mello (2009); and *Theorizing World Cinema*, edited by Lúcia Nagib, Chris Perriam and Rajinder Dudrah (2012). He is the editor of *On Cinema – Glauber Rocha* (2018).

Acknowledgements

Most of the chapters in this volume were initially presented at the I IntermIdia Conference/II Encontro Cinemídia, 'Towards an Intermedial History of Brazilian Cinema', organised by the research group Cinemídia, which took place at the Federal University of São Carlos (UFSCar), Brazil, on 9–11 November 2016. We wish to acknowledge the invaluable support of the following UFSCar offices: the Pro-Rectory for Postgraduate Studies and Research (ProPG); the Pro-Rectory for Research (ProPq); the Research Support Office (PAPq); the Education and Human Sciences Centre (CECH); the Department of Arts and Communication (DAC); and the Postgraduate Programme in Image and Sound (PPGIS). Special thanks are also due to the Student Organising Committee, in particular Debora Taño, Sancler Ebert and Danielle Ribeiro, who contributed to the conference organisation with passion and impeccable logistics.

This conference and the ensuing publication are outputs of the IntermIdia Project, funded by the AHRC-Arts and Humanities Research Council (AH/M008363/1), in the UK, and FAPESP-São Paulo Research Foundation (2014/50821–3), in São Paulo, Brazil, to whom we express our gratitude. The chapters by Alison Butler, Stefan Solomon, Albert Elduque, Lúcia Nagib, Flávia Cesarino Costa, Suzana Reck Miranda, Samuel Paiva, Margarida Maria Adamatti and Luciana Corrêa de Araújo result from this project. Thanks are also due to the University of Reading and its Department of Film, Theatre and Television, the generous host of the IntermIdia Project in the UK.

Finally, heartfelt thanks go to our EUP editors, Gillian Leslie and Richard Strachan, as well as to the editors of the Edinburgh Studies in Film and Intermediality series, Martine Beugnet and Kriss Ravetto, for their patience and unstinting support.

Introduction
Lúcia Nagib, Luciana Corrêa de Araújo and Tiago de Luca

This volume's ambitious aim, as well as major challenge, is to reconstruct the history of Brazilian cinema by means of an intermedial method: that is, by focusing on the ways in which it has commingled with other arts and media from its early stages to today. We argue that artists and practices from theatre, opera, dance, music, circus, radio, television and the plastic arts left a distinctive mark on the country's cinematic production, which can be observed, for example, in ventures that combined the theatre stage, screen programmes, radio shows and the trends of the phonographic industry between the 1920s and 1930s (Chapters 10 and 11); in the *chanchada* musical comedies produced on an industrial scale in Rio between the 1940s and 1960s, drawing on radio, theatre and carnival hits (Chapters 6 and 14); in the Tropicália, Cinema Novo and Cinema Marginal outputs from the 1960s onwards, which emerged from and 'cannibalised' other cultural and artistic forms (Chapters 3 and 19); in the highly popular films of Os Trapalhões (The Goofies), a television troupe relying on circus acrobatics and slapstick stunts, in the 1980s (Chapter 12); in the music documentaries and fiction films that boomed from the 1990s onwards (Chapter 9); in contemporary experimental films crossing borders with the visual arts (Chapters 2 and 5); and in other representative cases in focus here. This book proposes that these intermedial encounters entail the blurring of boundaries between local and imported traditions, high and popular cultures, and avant-garde and commercial practices, thus constituting a democratic space par excellence for artistic and social expression. The intermedial method allows us, moreover, to move away from chronological or hierarchical approaches to these phenomena, framing them instead as comparable and interrelated creative practices.

In his influential book, *Historiografia clássica do cinema brasileiro* (*Classical Historiography of Brazilian Cinema*, 1995), Jean-Claude Bernardet questions the pride of place usually given to processes of production to the detriment of exhibition and distribution. More emphatically, he challenges the 'myth of origin' in film historical accounts for ascribing a subaltern position to non-mainstream cinemas of the world. In this book, we have attempted to offer an advantageous substitute for this model by embracing a non-chronological approach to the history of Brazilian cinema, whilst extending Bernardet's challenge of primacies to the film medium itself. In so doing, we echo Ian Christie, who, drawing on Huhtamo and Parikka (2011) in Chapter 1, proposes to move the emphasis away from the 'firstness' of cinema as a technological invention to a more encompassing media-archaeological vision, which recognises that media rarely arise or die, but instead recede and reappear under new guises. Thus, this book is organised around intermedial constellations based on four categories, each of them bringing together productions from various periods and places: 'Intervisuality', where the panorama, the photographic base of cinema, and its relation with painting and other visual arts connect experiments from pre- through to post-cinema periods; 'The Empire of Music', which demonstrates the overwhelming importance of music in Brazilian culture, including cinema, of all times; 'Entertainment Circuits', which highlights the participation of theatre, radio, television and the phonographic industry in the aesthetics elicited by popular cinema in Brazil throughout history; and 'From Impure Cinema to Cosmopoetics', focusing on works that purposely embrace the film medium's impurities through a self-reflexive recourse to theatre, literature, opera and even cartography, bringing them close to a Wagnerian total artwork. By doing this, we hope to provide the reader with a panoramic as much as an in-depth understanding of the vast array of arts, mediums, traditions and industries that participate in the creation of a strong and multifaceted national cinema.

Since the mid-1990s and the so-called Retomada do Cinema Brasileiro (Brazilian Cinema Revival), Brazil's film industry has experienced a continuous process of expansion, in both numbers and genres, reaching and maintaining an average of over 100 features a year. This development suggests that the model of boom-and-bust or cycles at the basis of traditional historical approaches has become insufficient to account for such a burgeoning and varied production. It also shows the limits of the sociological model, hinging on questions of imperialism and colonial occupation, and leading to what foundational film critic Paulo Emilio Salles Gomes ([1986] 2018) once described as 'a trajectory in underdevelopment', apropos of the history of Brazilian cinema. Intermediality offers a more productive alternative to this, as well as to evolutionist views which posit 'modernity' as an aesthetic and/or political pinnacle in film history, as propounded by André Bazin's (1967a) influential model that defines Italian neo-realism post-World War II as the modern apex in the 'evolution of the language of cinema'. Following a similar approach, Salles Gomes (1986) had divided Brazilian film history into five phases, culminating in the 1960s Cinema Novo movement, an idea subsequently adapted by Ismail Xavier (1997) into the 'allegories of underdevelopment' found in Cinema Novo and Cinema Marginal films, which, for him, marked Brazilian cinema's entrance into modernity. However, as the case studies in this book evidence, so-called 'modern' features, such as medium awareness, self-parody, and a disregard for narrative suture and closure, were readily available in films deemed 'naïve' or purely commercial, such as the musical dramas and comedies that prevailed on Brazilian screens between the 1920s and 1950s. On the other hand, as narratologists such as Gaudreault (1997) and Gunning (1997) have argued, cinema's most daring avant-garde experiments are entirely comparable to, and often draw on, the very first cinematic forays, which can also be observed in the case studies carried out in Part I of this book. This approach has been aptly described by Pethő (2010b: 55ff) as 'parallax historiography', for placing historical phenomena side by side and in correlation with each other, rather than in an evolutionary line. In this, she concurs with Russell (2002: 552), for whom 'new media technologies have created new theoretical "passages" back to the first decades of film history'. Thus, rather than privileging some forms over others, intermediality has given us here the opportunity to place a variety of styles and genres on an equal footing, resulting in a kaleidoscope that more accurately reflects a national cinema's cultural richness and aesthetic complexity.

First applied by Higgins (1966) to the plastic arts, the concept of intermediality has expanded into a vast research field, in the wake of the celebration, in recent decades, of notions of 'hybridisation', 'transnationalism', 'multiculturalism' and cross-fertilisations of all kinds (Nagib 2014). As regards cinema, an even earlier herald of intermediality can be found, once again, in Bazin, who in 1951 published a visionary essay titled 'Pour un cinéma impur: défense de l'adaptation' (1981), staunchly rejecting the remnants of a self-defined purist avant-garde. Tamely translated by Hugh Gray as 'In Defense of Mixed Cinema' (1967b) and then more accurately by Timothy Barnard as 'For an Impure Cinema: In Defence of Adaptation' (2009), the article is a provocative call for cinematic hybridisation in light of the theatrical and literary adaptations sweeping through French cinema between the 1940s and 1950s. It could not be more topical today, in the face of the spiralling mixture of media and arts that pervades our virtual space. Moreover, given that Bazin's ultimate preoccupation is always realism, cinema's 'impurities' constitute, for him, a tear in the film's fabric through which the spectator can identify, for example, the actual theatrical or literary 'reality' at its base (see Arnaud 2011: 85 in this respect). Thus, 'impure cinema' can also be productively applied to radically realist ventures, such as the self-reflexive work of Brazil's foremost documentarian, Eduardo Coutinho, in its incursions into television, theatre and music, studied by Lins in Chapter 15.

Taxonomies on intermediality have multiplied in recent times, including categories such as 'ekphrasis' and 'metalepsis' (Pethő 2010a; 2020), which proved useful for Elduque in Chapter 9, in his study of composer Cartola's intermedial biopic; 'remediation' (Bolter and Grusin 2000), applied by Paiva in Chapter 8, to explain the precedence of music, and music video, in Pernambuco's Árido Movie production; 'overt/covert intermediality' (Wolf 1999), resorted to by Nagib in Chapter 19, in relation to Glauber Rocha's totalising cinematic impulse; and 'wave/vague', launched by Martine Beugnet (2017) with reference to the film medium's inherent and unsurmountable instability, to which she returns in Chapter 5. Particularly inspirational for the authors in this volume has been the notion of 'in-betweenness', passionately argued for by Pethő ([2011] 2020), for whom the space in between media constitutes the route through which film finds its ground in haptic reality. For its wider premise that keeps the interrogation into the properties of the medium constantly on the critic's horizon (Rajewsky 2010), intermediality has also increasingly been preferred over more established approaches to film, such as comparative, intertextual, adaptation and genre-based studies. The fact remains, however, that it has never before been applied to cinema as a *historiographic method*, which is being proposed in this collection as an entirely new and fruitful avenue.

In the same spirit, the book looks back at, and builds upon, previous historical accounts, including their various intermedial inklings. Salles Gomes (1966; 1986), for example, had already pointed towards the intense and extensively transnational interbreeding of arts and cultures that took place in Brazilian cinema from the moment Italian Afonso Segreto used a movie camera to record views of Rio de Janeiro in 1898. Likewise, Vicente de Paula Araújo, in his classic *A bela época do cinema brasileiro* (*Brazilian Cinema's Belle Époque*, 1976), documents the profusion of spectacles and media that surrounded and inflected the use of the *cinématographe* and other movie-making machines in Brazil in the late nineteenth century, including theatre, opera, circus and even gambling, an approach expanded upon in Part III of this book. Xavier has also been acutely aware of cinema's multimedial dialogues, as evidenced in two of his books, *O cinema no século* (*Cinema in the Century*, 1996), devoted to an interdisciplinary approach to cinema and film theory, and *O olhar e a cena* (*The Gaze and the Scene*, 2003), focusing mostly on screen adaptations of Nelson Rodrigues's theatre plays, to which he returns here in Chapter 17. In his celebrated book *Tropical Multiculturalism: A Comparative History of Race in Brazilian Cinema & Culture* (1997), Robert Stam privileges processes of inter-racial and cross-cultural mixtures in Brazilian cinema which have recently culminated in his theory of a 'transartistic commons', a utopian realm that acknowledges no borders across the various arts and media (Stam 2019: 33ff).[1]

Though self-standing and covering a wide spectrum of time and space, this book must also be understood as part of a large bilateral research project, entitled 'Towards an Intermedial History of Brazilian Cinema: Exploring Intermediality as a Historiographic Method' (short title: 'IntermIdia', 2015–19), funded by the Arts and Humanities Research Council (AHRC) in the UK and the Fundação de Amparo à Pesquisa do Estado de São Paulo (FAPESP) in Brazil, which produced over 100 publications and audiovisual works devoted to the intermedial analysis of Brazilian film history.[2] Even before joining this project, its team of researchers had been busy identifying the multimedia transactions that mark Brazilian film production throughout its history. Most notably, project members contributing to this book, such as Luciana Corrêa de Araújo (2009) and Flávia Cesarino Costa (1995), had launched innovative explorations of early to mid-twentieth-century cinema from an intermedial perspective that involves theatre, music and carnival, the same applying to Samuel Paiva (2012) and Suzana Reck Miranda (2013), in relation to Brazilian film and music throughout the twentieth century. IntermIdia's publications, analysing Brazilian cinema in light of the country's other arts and media, include the hefty volume edited by Stefan Solomon, *Tropicália and Beyond: Dialogues in Brazilian Film History* (2017), and the *Screen* journal dossier 'Intermediality in Brazilian Cinema' (Nagib 2019; Solomon 2019; Elduque 2019; Butler 2019), both focusing on the highly intermedial Tropicália movement, which originated in the plastic arts, boomed in music and generated some of Brazil's most radical films.[3]

Building on this thriving and ever-growing scholarship, though fully aware that we can only move 'towards' an encompassing history that is permanently in the making, this book hopes to finally enshrine intermediality as a historiographic method applied to Brazilian cinema as a whole.

FROM INTERVISUALITY TO COSMOPOETICS

As befits a non-linear, non-evolutionist and non-hierarchical approach to film history, we have opted to form clusters of films, filmmakers and cinematic phenomena according to the specific kind of intermedial relations at their base. Thus, Part I brings together chapters in which the visual element takes centre stage. Borrowing the term 'intervisuality' from Ivo Blom (2017), who applies it to the influence of painting and other visual arts in the work of Luchino Visconti, we have expanded it to include film's interactions with photography and pre-cinematic visual mediums. In Chapter 1, Ian Christie describes a trajectory from painting to panoramas that denotes Portugal's censorious attempts to 'hide' Brazil from the world, as Latin American images became prime examples of the exotic for nineteenth-century audiences.

A trajectory across photographic mediums also permeates Alison Butler's approach to the artist, photographer and filmmaker Cao Guimarães, in Chapter 2. Working first with photography, then with video and film, Butler argues that Guimarães has produced works that are intermedial due to the exploration of the formal qualities and traditions of photography and video contained within them.

Stefan Solomon, in Chapter 3, expands intervisuality into the realm of comics and the way they regularly feature in Brazil's Cinema Marginal in the late 1960s, from the *Barbarella* wallpaper in *Cara a cara* (*Face to Face*, Júlio Bressane, 1967) to the live-action parodies of Batman and Tarzan in André Luiz Oliveira's *Meteorango Kid: o herói intergalático* (*Meteorango Kid: Intergalactic Hero*, 1969), to Rogério Sganzerla's short documentary *História em quadrinhos* (*Comics*, 1969). The possibilities of this intermedial phenomenon are perhaps embraced most fully in two instances: the 'Coffin Joe' film series by José Mojica Marins, and João Callegaro's lesser-known work, *O pornógrafo* (*The Pornographer*, 1970). The chapter focuses on these particular case studies in its appreciation of the fascination with graphic narratives in Cinema Marginal.

Drawing on Laura Mulvey's (2006) study of the photographic stillness at the base of film, Tiago de Luca, in Chapter 4, demonstrates the revelatory power of photography and its intermedial use in two recent Brazilian films: the essayistic documentary *Babás* (*Nannies*, Consuelo Lins, 2010) and the fiction film *Aquarius* (Kleber Mendonça Filho, 2016), both of which he situates within a prolific recent trend in Brazilian cinema interested in exploring domestic socio-economic relations in Brazil, including the figure of the housemaid and the country's slave-holding past. De Luca argues that photography functions in both films as an in-between device to provoke reflection on what is almost invisible, at the edge of the frame, thus making visible structural marginalisation and social exclusion.

In Chapter 5, Martine Beugnet ties photography and technology together in an exploration of the ways in which a persistent interest in the fusion of art and the machine promotes a deeper understanding of the medium of the moving image as a means of both perception and expression. To that end, she draws on the assumption that film's immense contribution to the recent development of visuality continues to be born out of the moving image's paradoxical standing at the intersection between photographic precision and visual uncertainty, as encapsulated in the idea of the *vague* (meaning both 'wave' and 'vague'). Two works provide the basis for her discussion of intermediality seen in this light: *Remanescências* (*Remainiscences*, 1997), a short experimental film by Carlos Adriano, and *Figures in a Landscape* (2010), a multimedia installation by André Parente.

Part II moves away from the ocular-centric approach towards what we call 'The Empire of Music', Brazil's most outstanding and influential art, according to filmmakers themselves.[4] It is not mere coincidence that music was at the base of the country's most popular cinematic genre ever, the *chanchadas*, or musical comedies produced in Brazil between the 1940s and 1960s. Chapter 6, by Flávia Cesarino Costa, explores the Brazilian *chanchada* film *Aviso aos navegantes* (*Calling All Sailors*, Watson Macedo, 1950) as an emblematic production of the heyday of musical comedies. Costa's analysis focuses on the ties between the film's musical numbers and other Brazilian cultural traditions, industries and practices, including theatre, carnival, the music industry and radio performances.

In Chapter 7, Suzana Reck Miranda focuses, in turn, on Brazilian (film) music as export product, by discussing the career of Brazilian multi-instrumentalist Zezinho/Joe Carioca (José do Patrocínio Oliveira, 1902–87). After widespread appearances on local radio and in the national music industry, and starring in *Coisas nossas* (*Our Things*, Wallace Downey, 1930), one of the first Brazilian musical sound films, Oliveira worked as a supporting musician in several musical numbers featuring in Hollywood films of the 1940s and 1950s. Something similar occurred with singer and guitarist Nestor Amaral, Oliveira's partner. Both musicians were members of Bando da Lua, the musical ensemble that became internationally known for playing with Carmen Miranda in films, concerts and records. Intermediality here allows the author to focus on the performance of secondary and often overlooked musicians from the late 1930s to the early 1950s.

In Chapter 8, the empire of music expands to Recife in the state of Pernambuco, where the Manguebeat musical movement ruled the day from the 1990s onwards. Here, Samuel Paiva examines how many films produced in the region in that period present aesthetic features associated with Manguebeat, especially those by filmmakers from the so-called Árido Movie movement. In particular, Paiva examines musical moments in Pernambucan films that result from a cinematic dialogue with music videos. Another two filmmakers from Recife, Lírio Ferreira and Hilton Lacerda, are the focus of Chapter 9, now with reference to a legendary Rio composer, Cartola (1908–80), the subject of their documentary *Cartola: música para os olhos* (*Cartola: Music for the Eyes*, 2007). Albert Elduque approaches this film from an intermedial perspective that entwines its repurposing of archival images with its use of the lyrics of the Cartola songs as narrative agents. Drawing on Ágnes Pethő ([2011] 2020), the chapter suggests that intermedial occurrences in the film are the result of a 'metalepsis', or a leap between different narrative mediums.

Part III, 'Entertainment Circuits', widens the spectrum to encompass not only intermedial films, but the media industries from which these are born, intertwining theatre, casinos, radio, carnival and later television. An early skilful navigator of this complex network is Luiz 'Lulu' de Barros, studied by Luciana Corrêa de Araújo in Chapter 10. Barros not only was one of Brazil's most prolific filmmakers, having produced over 100 films, but also worked extensively with theatre and scenography, as director, set designer, playwright and impresario, in theatres, casinos and other entertainment venues. His constant transit across different types of media and forms of entertainment contributed to the construction and viability of a career that spanned no fewer than seven decades. The chapter focuses on the period between the 1910s and 1920s, which enlightens us on some significant intermedial dynamics pertaining to Brazilian silent cinema as a whole.

Rafael de Luna Freire, in Chapter 11, focuses on the relationship between the so-called 'synchronised film fever' and the 'gramophonoradiomania' in Rio, resulting from technological, social and political networks connecting radio broadcast, the record industry and the various technologies of sound film between the 1920s and 1930s. By contextualising these phenomena, the chapter provides a deep understanding of the reception and diffusion of the talking pictures in Brazil, together with its adaptations, resistances and specificities. In a jump to the period between the late 1960s and mid-1980s, Alfredo Suppia identifies, in Chapter 12, another batch of films resulting from an entertainment circuit, this time involving television as well as popular singers, rock bands and showbiz artists. This is the case of Brazilian adventure films targeting juvenile audiences, as represented by Roberto Farias's *Roberto Carlos em ritmo de aventura* (*Roberto Carlos at Adventure Rhythm*, 1968), Adriano Stuart's *O incrível monstro trapalhão* (*The Incredible Goofy Monster*, 1981) and Francisco de Paula's *Areias escaldantes* (*Scalding Sands*, 1985). As Suppia's analysis demonstrates, these films are of particular interest for an intermedial approach, given that their hybridity lured generations of young spectators until the shutdown of the state production and distribution company Embrafilme, in 1990, entailing a major crisis in Brazil's film industry.

In Chapter 13, Margarida Maria Adamatti discusses the unique case of performer Vicente Celestino and his film-director wife, Gilda de Abreu, who together constituted an entertainment circuit of their own. An intermedial artist par excellence, Celestino was active in radio, revue theatre, cinema, opera and operetta. One of his greatest successes was the song 'O Ébrio' (The Drunkard), released on Guanabara Radio in 1935. Over thirty years, he and Abreu adapted 'O Ébrio' to different media – radio, record, theatre, cinema and literature – and it also came out in a TV soap opera version. The chapter analyses the film *O Ébrio* (1946), directed by Abreu, in light of the song's multimedia transpositions, with special attention to the film's musical sequences, where the frontiers between actor and character are shattered.

In Chapter 14, João Luiz Vieira brings the *chanchada* phenomenon all the way up to the launch of television in Brazil, with echoes in today's commercial film production. The chapter investigates the negotiation between Brazilian cinema and television from the introduction of synchronised sound to the late 1950s, when television gradually became the most popular form of audiovisual contact with audiences. It concludes with an examination of how television gradually replaced radio, defining a 'cinema of television'.

Finally, Part IV, 'From Impure Cinema to Cosmopoetics', describes how the covert and overt impurities of film can lead to a kind of 'transartistic commons' (Stam 2019) via a cosmopoetics that welcomes the interface of all artforms. In Chapter 15, Consuelo Lins demonstrates how Eduardo Coutinho gradually moved from documentary making to a systematic exercise in intermediality in the last phase of his production, which includes *Jogo de cena* (*Playing*, 2007), *Moscou* (*Moscow*, 2009), *Um dia na vida* (*A Day in Life*, 2010) and *As canções* (*Songs*, 2011). Unlike his filming on real locations, which had come to a close with *O fim e o princípio* (*The End and the Beginning*, 2005), these last four works were shot in closed spaces, three of them in stage settings and based on unique strategies of interweaving artistic media and forms, as well as intensifying reflexive procedures already present in his previous work. Lins argues that the interpenetration of Coutinho's last films with theatre, television and music is so radical that it is possible to revisit his entire career based on the notion of 'impure cinema', to use André Bazin's (2009) famous expression.

Chapter 16, authored by Alessandra Soares Brandão and Ramayana Lira de Sousa, resorts to Pethő's notion of in-betweenness to address queerness in film in light of the wave of erotic films in the 1970s and 1980s, commonly known as *pornochanchadas*, which allowed the subversive literature of Cassandra Rios to reach the screens. Rios's books helped imagine sex when this imagination was socially interdicted. Patriarchal morality conferred on her the dubious status of the 'most prohibited writer in Brazil', an epithet often used as a marketing strategy on her book covers. The chapter's engagement with popular Brazilian cinema and Cassandra Rios's literature offers a novel way to evaluate their aesthetic and political potential and contribution.

In Chapter 17, Ismail Xavier addresses Nelson Rodrigues's work, which is the most prolific example of film and theatre intermediality in Brazil. His plays have been adapted for the screen more than twenty times. An equally notable feature of some Rodrigues's plays is their incorporation of spatio-temporal structures borrowed from cinema. His play *Toda nudez será castigada* (*All Nudity Shall Be Punished*), written in 1965, is a good example of the use of space–time organisational devices typical of cinema and an instance of his intermedial process of creation. Arnaldo Jabor, a leading Cinema Novo figure, adapted *Toda nudez será castigada* for the screen in 1972, and Rodrigues's serial novel, *O casamento* (*The Wedding*, 1966), became an eponymous 1975 film. Xavier examines these two Rodrigues adaptations in chronological order to highlight the gradual process of dramatic and theatrical amplification within Jabor's filmmaking style. The focus on family dramas allows Xavier to analyse the way middle-class males handle their private traumas in that specific historical moment of Brazilian political life.

In Chapter 18, Gustavo Procopio Furtado expands the intermedial approach to the hitherto unexplored field of maps and mapping. His case studies are drawn from films shot in the Amazon, a multicultural region that has resisted appropriation by imperial and national projects and endured successive waves of colonisation, a site where the movement of populations occurs in conjunction with shifting territorial configurations. During the 1970s and 1980s, a period marked by massive governmental projects of national integration and their consequences for the region, a diverse group of filmmakers located their audiovisual practice at the frayed borders of the Amazonian territory. Two films are chosen for close analysis, Carlos Diegues's *Bye bye Brasil* (*Bye bye, Brazil*, 1980), a classic road movie, and Andrea Tonacci's *Os Arara* (*The Arara*, 1980–2), an unfinished three-part documentary made for television about an indigenous contact expedition. Special attention is paid to the manner in which these films incorporate television sets and maps into the profilmic space, enacting an intermedial mise-en-scène that distils the specificities of the Amazonian moving image.

The book closes with Lúcia Nagib's examination of Glauber Rocha's intermedial cosmogony, in Chapter 19. The famous leader of Cinema Novo and the most iconic Brazilian filmmaker of all time, Rocha was extremely proficient in poetry, fiction writing, theatre, drawing, journalism and television, all of which found expression in his cinema. Though obsessed with Brazil and national identity, Rocha's films were also attempts at universalising the national experience into the condition of the entire Earth, most notably in his '*trilogia da terra*', or 'Earth trilogy', including *Deus e o diabo na terra do sol* (*Black God, White Devil*, 1964), *Terra em transe* (*Entranced Earth*, 1967) and *A idade da Terra* (*The Age of the Earth*, 1981). In all three, the reiteration of the term '*terra*', meaning both 'Earth' and 'land' in Portuguese, announces their planetary ambition. Focusing on the former two, as they mark the rise and fall of 1960s revolutionary hopes through radically innovative aesthetics, the chapter analyses cosmogonic intermediality in Rocha's work according to the totalising and strongly intermedial figures of the cross and trance.

With these four intermedial constellations covering a significant part of the history of Brazilian cinema, this book hopes to do justice to Brazil's national cinema as much as to the cultural and artistic traditions that have enabled it. As we write, Brazil is facing not only the terrible consequences of the Covid-19 pandemic, but also the nefarious actions of one of its most disastrous governments. Cinema is sadly included among its victims. We hope that this book will serve as testament to our love and support for Brazilian cinema and arts, as well as to all the artists who ever contributed to their existence.

Notes

1. Other interdisciplinary approaches to Brazilian cinema include studies of the intersection between cinema and history by Eduardo Morettin et al. (2011); Lisa Shaw's (2012; 2015) important research on the *chanchada* phenomenon in its entanglement with revue theatre, popular music and stardom; and Stephanie Dennison's (2017; 2019) extensive scholarship on the relations between cinema, popular culture and medial forms such as television and theatre in Brazil. Equally relevant to our approach is Maite Conde's (2012) contribution, in particular as refers to cinema and writing in early twentieth-century Brazil. Other historical approaches include the significant work of Fernão Ramos, the editor of a history (1987); an encyclopaedia of Brazilian cinema (with Luiz Felipe Miranda, 2012); and a new history of Brazilian cinema (with Sheila Schvarzman, (2018).
2. More information on the IntermIdia Project can be found at <https://research.reading.ac.uk/intermidia/> (last accessed 21 January 2022).
3. Another dossier, edited by Tamara Courage and Albert Elduque (2020), focuses on 'Performing Intermediality in Brazilian Cinema', highlighting the huge importance of music and theatrical performances in films, from the 1940s–1950s *chanchadas* to the numerous fiction and documentary works on music from the 1990s onwards. The latter subject was also addressed in a comprehensive catalogue on Brazilian music films edited by Elduque (2017), including a contribution on the original topic of the rock scene by Lisa Purse (2017). Aside from the printed word, the project also produced audiovisual works, such as video essays (Solomon 2016; Elduque 2016; Gibbs and Miranda 2018; Gibbs 2019; Costa and Gibbs 2020), through which viewers are able not only to see but also to hear intermedial interactions, brought to the fore by means of close film analysis.
4. Another important IntermIdia Project output is the feature-length documentary film *Passages*, directed by Lúcia Nagib and Samuel Paiva (UK, 2019), focusing on intermediality in Brazilian films from São Paulo and Pernambuco, from the 1990s onwards. Filmmakers interviewed in this documentary, such as Paulo Caldas and Marcelo Gomes, do not hesitate to confirm music as the greatest Brazilian art, superior even to cinema.

References

Araújo, Luciana Corrêa de (2009), 'Prólogos envenenados: cinema e teatro nos palcos da Cinelândia carioca', *Travessias*, available at <http://www.compos.org.br/data/biblioteca_1155.pdf> (last accessed 16 April 2021).
Araújo, Vicente de Paula (1976), *A bela época do cinema brasileiro*. São Paulo: Perspectiva.
Arnaud, Diane (2011), 'From Bazin to Deleuze: A Matter of Depth', in Dudley Andrew and Hervé Joubert-Laurencin (eds), *Opening Bazin*. Oxford and New York: Oxford University Press, pp. 85–94.
Bazin, André (1967a), 'The Evolution of the Language of Cinema', in *What Is Cinema*, vol. 1, essays selected and translated by Hugh Gray. Berkeley, Los Angeles and London: University of California Press, pp. 23–40.
Bazin, André (1967b), 'In Defense of Mixed Cinema', in *What Is Cinema*, vol. 1, essays selected and translated by Hugh Gray. Berkeley, Los Angeles and London: University of California Press, pp. 53–75.
Bazin, André (1981), 'Pour un cinéma impur: défense de l'adaptation', in *Qu'est-ce que le cinéma?*, definitive edn. Paris: Cerf, pp. 81–106.
Bazin, André (2009), 'For an Impure Cinema: In Defence of Adaptation', in *What Is Cinema?*, translation and annotations by Timothy Barnard. Montreal: caboose, pp. 107–38.
Bernardet, Jean-Claude (1995), *Historiografia clássica do cinema brasileiro*. São Paulo: Annablume.
Beugnet, Martine (2017), 'Introduction', in Martine Beugnet, Allan Cameron and Arild Fetveit (eds), *Indefinite Visions: Cinema and the Attractions of Uncertainty*. Edinburgh: Edinburgh University Press, pp. 1–16.
Blom, Ivo (2017), *Reframing Luchino Visconti: Film and Art*. Leiden: Sidestone Press.
Bolter, Jay David and Richard Grusin (2000), *Remediation: Understanding New Media*. Cambridge, MA: MIT Press.
Butler, Alison (2019), 'Devouring Images: Hélio Oiticica's Anthropophagic Quasi-Cinema', *Screen*, 60:1, Spring, pp. 128–36.
Conde, Maite (2012), *Consuming Visions. Cinema, Writing and Modernity in Brazil*. Charlottesville: University of Virginia Press.
Costa, Flávia Cesarino (1995), *O primeiro cinema*. São Paulo: Scritta.
Costa, Flávia Cesarino and John Gibbs (2020), 'Chanchadas and Intermediality: On Musical Numbers of *Aviso aos Navegantes* (Watson Macedo, Brazil, 1950)', *Alphaville: Journal of Film and Screen Media*, 19, pp. 28–30. DOI: <https://doi.org/10.33178/alpha.19.03, available at <https://vimeo.com/430520955> (last accessed 17 April 2021).
Courage, Tamara and Albert Elduque (2020), 'Performing the Intermedial Across Brazilian Cinema', *Alphaville Journal of Film and Screen Media*, 19. DOI: 10.33178/alpha.19.01.
Dennison, Stephanie (2019), *Remapping Brazilian Film Culture in the Twenty-First Century*. Abingdon: Routledge.
Dennison, Stephanie and Alessandra Meleiro (2017), 'Brazil, Soft Power and Film Culture', *New Cinema*, 14:1, pp. 17–30.
Elduque, Albert (2016), 'Hunger and Rotten Flesh: Cinema Novo, Pasolini, Eisenstein', *[in]Transition*, 3:3, available at <http://mediacommons.org/intransition/2016/hunger-and-rotten-flesh> (last accessed 17 April 2021).
Elduque, Albert (ed.) (2017), *Contemporary Brazilian Music Film*. Reading: University of Reading.
Elduque, Albert (2019), 'Between Film and Photography: The Bubble of Blood in *The Family of Disorder*', *Screen*, 60:1, Spring, pp. 148–59.

Gaudreault, André (1997), 'Film, Narrative, Narration: The Cinema of the Lumière Brothers', in Thomas Elsaesser (ed.), *Early Cinema: Space, Frame, Narrative*. London: BFI, pp. 68–75.
Gibbs, John (2019), '"Say, have you seen the Carioca?": An Experiment in Non-linear, Non-hierarchical Approaches to Film History', *Movie: A Journal of Film Criticism*, 8. Available at <https://warwick.ac.uk/fac/arts/film/movie/carioca.pdf> and <https://vimeo.com/335268992> (last accessed 17 April 2021).
Gibbs, John and Suzana Reck Miranda (2018), 'Playing at the margins', *[in]Transition*, 5:2, available at <http://mediacommons.org/intransition/2018/05/01/playing-margins>, <https://vimeo.com/208110507> and <https://vimeo.com/243270641> (last accessed 17 April 2021).
Gunning, Tom (1997), 'The Cinema of Attractions: Early Film, its Spectator and the Avant-Garde', in Thomas Elsaesser (ed.), *Early Cinema: Space, Frame, Narrative*. London: BFI, pp. 56–62.
Higgins, Dick (1966), 'Intermedia', *Something Else Press Newsletter*, 1:1 (February), pp. 1–3.
Huhtamo, Erkki and Jussi Parikka (eds) (2011), *Media Archaeology: Approaches, Applications, and Implications*. Berkeley, Los Angeles and London: University of California Press.
Miranda, Suzana Reck (2013), 'A invasão do cotidiano em *O invasor*: música popular como referente legitimador do "real"', *Revista Mídia e Cotidiano*, 1:1, pp. 5–23.
Morettin, Eduardo, Maria Helena Capelato, Marcos Napolitano and Elias Thomé Saliba (eds) (2011), *História e Cinema: Dimensões Históricas do Audiovisual*. São Paulo: Alameda.
Mulvey, Laura (2006), *Death 24× a Second: Stillness and the Moving Image*. London: Reaktion.
Nagib, Lúcia (2014), 'The Politics of Impurity', in Lúcia Nagib and Anne Jerslev (eds), *Impure Cinema: Intermedial and Intercultural Approaches to Film*. London and New York: I. B. Tauris, pp. 21–40.
Nagib, Lúcia (2019), 'Multimedia Identities: An Analysis of *How Tasty Was My Little Frenchman*', *Screen*, 60:1, Spring, pp. 160–71.
Nagib, Lúcia and Stefan Solomon (2019), 'Intermediality in Brazilian Cinema: The Case of Tropicália: Introduction.' *Screen*, 60:1, Spring, pp. 122–7.
Paiva, Samuel (2012), 'Árido Movie: da morte do pai ao nascimento de uma nova mídia', in Alessandra Brandão, Dilma Juliano and Ramayana Lira (eds), *Políticas dos cinemas latino-americanos contemporâneos*. Palhoça: Unisul.
Pethő, Ágnes (2010a), 'Media in the Cinematic Imagination: Ekphrasis and the Poetics of the In-Between in Jean-Luc Godard's Cinema', in Lars Elleström (ed.), *Media Borders, Multimodality and Intermediality*. Basingstoke: Palgrave, pp. 211–22.
Pethő, Ágnes (2010b), 'Intermediality in Film: A Historiography of Methodologies', *Film and Media Studies*, Acta Univ. Sapientiae, 2, pp. 39–72.
Pethő, Ágnes. (2011), *Cinema and Intermediality: The Passion for the In-Between*. Newcastle-Upon-Tyne: Cambridge Scholars Publishing.
Pethő, Ágnes (2020), *Cinema and Intermediality: The Passion for the In-Between*, 2nd enlarged edn. Newcastle-Upon-Tyne: Cambridge Scholars Publishing.
Purse, Lisa (2017), 'Between Phonographic Perfection and Resistance: Titãs, life even looks like a party', in Albert Elduque (ed.), *Contemporary Brazilian Music Film*. Reading: University of Reading, pp. 91–8.
Rajewsky, Irina O. (2010), 'Border Talks: The Problematic Status of Media Borders in the Current Debate about Intermediality', in Lars Elleström (ed.), *Media Borders, Multimodality and Intermediality*. Basingstoke: Palgrave, pp. 51–68.
Ramos, Fernão (ed.) (1987), *História do cinema brasileiro*. São Paulo: Art.

Ramos, Fernão and Luiz Felipe Miranda (eds) (2012), *Enciclopédia do cinema brasileiro*. São Paulo: Sesc.
Ramos, Fernão and Sheila Schvarzman (eds) (2018), *Nova história do cinema brasileiro*, vols 1 and 2, São Paulo: Sesc.
Russell, Catherine (2002), 'Parallax Historiography: The Flâneuse as Cyberfeminist', in Jennifer M. Bean and Diane Negra (eds), *A Feminist Reader in Early Cinema*. Durham, NC: Duke University Press, pp. 552–71.
Salles Gomes, Paulo Emilio (1986), *Cinema: trajetória no subdesenvolvimento*. São Paulo: Paz e Terra.
Salles Gomes, Paulo Emilio (2018), *Paulo Emílio Salles Gomes on Brazil and Global Cinema*, ed. Maite Conde and Stephanie Dennison. Cardiff: University of Wales Press.
Salles Gomes, Paulo Emilio and Adhemar Gonzaga (1966), *70 anos de cinema brasileiro*. Rio de Janeiro: Expressão e Cultura.
Shaw, Lisa (2012), 'The Brazilian "Chanchada's" Musical Moments and the Performance of Identity', in Lisa Shaw and Rob Stone (eds), *Screening Songs in Hispanic and Lusophone Cinema*. Manchester: Manchester University Press, pp. 283–97.
Shaw, Lisa (2015), 'The Teatro de Revista in Rio de Janeiro in the Long 1920s: Transnational Dialogues and Popular Cosmopolitanism', *Luso-Brazilian Review*, 52, pp. 73–98. DOI: 10.3368/lbr.52.2.73.
Solomon, Stefan (2016), 'Still Brazil', *[in]Transition: Journal of Videographic Film and Moving Image Studies*, 3:3, available at <http://mediacommons.org/intransition/2016/still-brazil> and <https://vimeo.com/181277090> (last accessed 17 April 2021).
Solomon, Stefan (ed.) (2017), *Tropicália and Beyond: Dialogues in Brazilian Film History*. Berlin: Archive Books.
Solomon, Stefan (2019), '"The Cloak of Technicolor": Intermedial Colour in *Antônio das Mortes*', *Screen*, 60:1, Spring, pp. 137–47.
Stam, Robert (1997), *Tropical Multiculturalism: A Comparative History of Race in Brazilian Cinema & Culture*. Durham, NC, and London: Duke University Press.
Stam, Robert (2019), *World Literature, Transnational Cinema, and Global Media*. London and New York: Routledge.
Wolf, Werner (1999), *The Musicalization of Fiction: A Study in the Theory and History of Intermediality*. Amsterdam and Atlanta, GA: Rodopi.
Xavier, Ismail (ed.) (1996), *O cinema no século*. Rio de Janeiro: Imago.
Xavier, Ismail (1997), *Allegories of Underdevelopment: Aesthetics and Politics in Modern Brazilian Cinema*. Minneapolis and London: University of Minnesota Press.
Xavier, Ismail (2003), *O olhar e a cena: melodrama, Hollywood, Cinema Novo, Nelson Rodrigues*. São Paulo: Cosac & Naify.

Part I

Intervisuality

CHAPTER 1

Traffic in Images: Visual Spectacle before Cinema in Brazil
Ian Christie

Past generations of film historians, especially those exploring the early years of their national cinemas, tended understandably to focus on the birth of indigenous production. They strove to discover the first films made by native filmmakers as distinct from those by visitors – often roving Lumière operators capturing local scenes for encyclopaedic catalogues of, from our perspective, a somewhat 'imperial' character. Revealingly, the memoir of one of the Lumière cameramen was subtitled 'Memories of an Image-hunter' (Souvenirs d'un chasseur d'images) (Mesguich 1933). But the preoccupation with 'firsts' has had a damaging effect on more ambitious histories of image-making and consumption that are increasingly relevant in today's multiplatform environment.

A media archaeological approach urges us to avoid teleological assumptions about media 'succession', considering instead the diverse factors that influence innovation, and recognising that media rarely 'die', even if they may be temporarily eclipsed, before reappearing in new modes (Huhtamo and Parikka 2011: 3). Perhaps the most productive concept to explain the dynamic of innovation has been Jay Bolter and Richard Grusin's 'remediation', proposed as 'the logic of new media' in their landmark book (Bolter and Grusin 2000). In place of succession, Bolter and Grusin showed how new media have self-consciously paid homage to and refashioned earlier media, demonstrating how these could be enhanced by new technologies – as in the familiar 'desktop' of computer interfaces. So the earliest popular successes of 'animated photography' in Brazil, as in many other predominantly Catholic countries, would be established subjects such as the 'life of Christ', and religiously themed melodramas. Remediation, in turn, has fed into the currency of 'intermediality', now used in a variety of senses to discuss relations between parallel media (Rajewsky 2005: 43). But the other overarching consideration that needs to be borne in mind in rewriting 'national' film histories is the inherent *globality* of technological media, whereby these were widely exported and welcomed as tokens of modernity and interconnection throughout the nineteenth century.

Traditionally, histories of Brazilian cinema have begun by recording that an 'Omniographo' was exhibited in Rio de Janeiro on 8 July 1896 (see Johnson and Stam 1995: 19). However, with more scrupulous early film studies under way, Ana López recorded that this was actually preceded by Edison's Kinetoscope making its debut eighteen months earlier, in December 1894, as it did during that year in many parts of the world, including an even earlier appearance in Buenos Aires in September 1894 (López 2005: 82; Newman 2005: 37). The eighteen-month period between mid-1894 and early 1896, which saw the remarkable success of the Kinetoscope, remains one of the least appreciated and unresearched in early moving-image history; and yet it was the audience appeal of these devices, shown in 'parlours' or arcades around the world, that persuaded many – including Antoine Lumière and Robert Paul – to develop equipment for the projection era, inaugurated by such devices as the Lumière Cinématographe and Paul's Theatrograph (Christie 2019). Kinetoscope films of dancers, performers and everyday scenes, and especially of sporting figures, were all initially produced at Edison's 'Black Maria' studio in New Jersey, but by mid-1895, there were also other suppliers of both machines and films, including Robert Paul. We know that the entrepreneurs Frank Maguire and Joseph Baucus contracted with Edison in August 1894 to 'exhibit and sell Kinetoscopes in Mexico, the West Indies, South America and Australia', but as yet there seems scant evidence of where they operated (Spehr 2008: 319).[1]

López also clarified that the 'Omniographo' was a 'modified Lumière apparatus', although the main modification might have been the name used to promote this latest novelty. The fact that what appears to have been the first moving-picture screening in Latin America was quickly followed by shows in Buenos Aires also in July and in Mexico City in August, the latter presented by the Lumière operator Gaston Veyre, strongly suggests that the Rio apparatus was indeed a Cinématographe, even if described otherwise locally in what was a common trope of early showmanship (Trujillo 2005: 48).

Yet establishing what exactly was shown, and by whom, on these historic dates may be to miss the larger point. Similarly, the obligatory mention of Antonio Leal's *Os estranguladores* (*The Stranglers*, 1908) as Brazil's first popular local production may also distract from trying to place these 'firsts' within a much longer and more complex history of visual spectacle, which is truly intermedial, and equally important, which links Brazil with the wider world in what may be termed a recursive relationship, instead of focusing merely on local or national significance. Rather than regarding imported or indigenous projected film as a beginning, I argue that the chronological beginning of Brazil's film history needs to be re-placed in the shifting ensemble of entertainment media, certainly animated by novelty, while also preserving many pre-existing cultural forms. So where should this expanded history begin?

Another aspect of the problem caused by 'firstness' is the search for a single line of succession that would lead up to the privileged moment of film projection. A model for this approach, which relates to Latin America, would be John Fullerton's superb *Picturing Mexico: From the Camera Lucida to Film* (2014), which is largely devoted to surveying the history of pictorial media in play before the arrival of film.

We can, in fact, distinguish at least three traditions within post-Enlightenment visual media, all of which helped to create the eventual apparatus of cinema. One of these dates from the last decade of the eighteenth century, when Robert Barker's cylindrical Panorama buildings established a new scale of immersive visual spectacle in Edinburgh and London (Comment 1999: 7–19), soon emulated in other major cities.[2] But as Erkki Huhtamo, the pioneer media archaeologist, has argued, there is a parallel history of 'peep' media, going even further back, into the seventeenth century, which started with 'view-boxes', the travelling showman's peepshow,[3] and continued into the nineteenth century with the creation of the hand-held Stereoscope – the century's most commercially successful optical novelty (Huhtamo 2012: 3, 24–7). And underpinning, or accompanying, these there was the evolution of the magic lantern, now usually dated from the late seventeenth century, when the Dutch scientist Christiaan Huygens first established its principles. While this remained essentially a domestic instrument for the next century and a half, advances in illumination technology made it capable of entertaining ever larger audiences as the nineteenth century progressed.

What panoramic, 'peep' and projection media all offered was degrees of 'immersion' in a visual representation, which also implied a form of virtual travel – the 'you are there' effect of a panorama or a stereograph. The relationship between the growth of rail travel, with its moving window on the world, and the popularity of these media has been often noted, and indeed was already recognised during the era (see Schivelbusch 1986: 165–6; Christie 1994: 15–19).[4] And the window analogy has returned with modern touch screens, as Nanna Verhoeff discusses in her *Mobile Screens* (2012: 149–66). In the 1850s, stereoscopy brought the new technology of photography into play, so that with a library of stereographs, or indeed the means to make one's own, the armchair viewer became potentially a world traveller.

Where do Brazil, and more generally Latin America, stand in relation to these 'new media'? Inevitably, long-established cultural traditions would first shape their repertoire, with the sites of classical antiquity and of biblical Palestine looming large. But to understand the notably restricted development of visual media within late colonial Latin America, some wider grasp of the economic and political history is required. During the eighteenth century, when both gold and diamond extraction in Brazil peaked, there was every reason why Portugal should wish to discourage foreign knowledge of a major source of its wealth.[5] In the exhibition at the Olavo Setúbal gallery of Instituto Itaú Cultural in São Paulo, a section entitled 'O Brasil Secreto' (Secret Brazil) displays a range of Brazilian images from the seventeenth and eighteenth centuries that testify eloquently to the imperial prohibition on revealing the country to the outside world. Only one panoramic view of Rio de Janeiro is known to have been produced in the eighteenth century; and another was 'hidden' by being painted on the edge of a book's pages, so that it only becomes visible when the pages are fanned.[6]

Yet the former Spanish and Portuguese empires make a surprisingly early appearance after Brazil won its independence from Portugal in 1822. Indeed, it was almost certainly this dramatic development that led to 'The city of Rio de Janeiro' appearing at the Panorama in London in 1827–8, painted by the Panorama's new proprietor, Robert Burford, from his own drawings made in 1823 (Figures 1.1 and 1.2).[7] In a similar spirit, William Bullock, proprietor of London's other great exhibition site, the Egyptian Hall, visited Mexico soon after it had won independence from Spain and staged two landmark exhibitions, 'Ancient Mexico' and 'Modern Mexico' (Figure 1.3).

After the expeditions of John Lloyd Stephens and Frederick Catherwood into Mexico in 1839–41, Mesoamerican culture became a new source of exotic spectacle for North Americans and Europeans (Bueno 2018). The

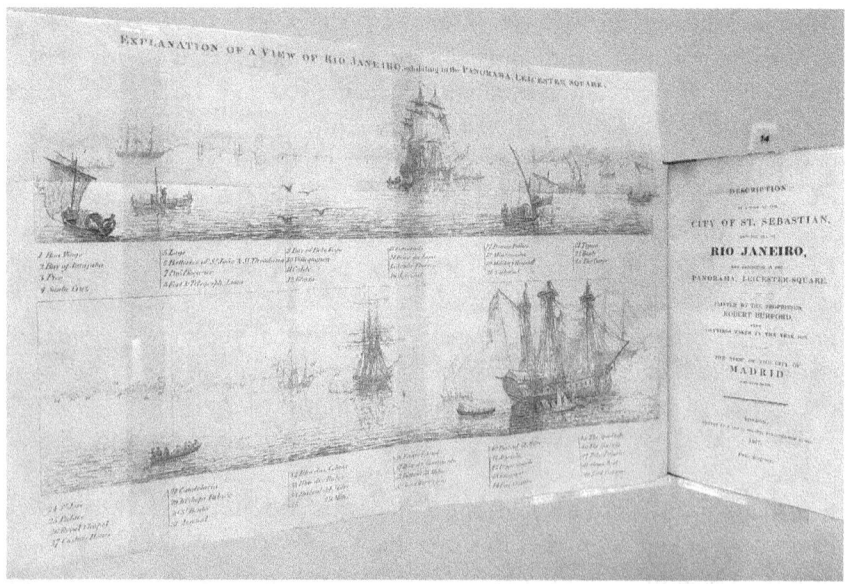

Figure 1.1 Booklet accompanying Burford's large-scale Panorama of the Bay of Rio Janeiro, exhibited at the London Panorama in 1827–8.

Visual Spectacle before Cinema in Brazil 21

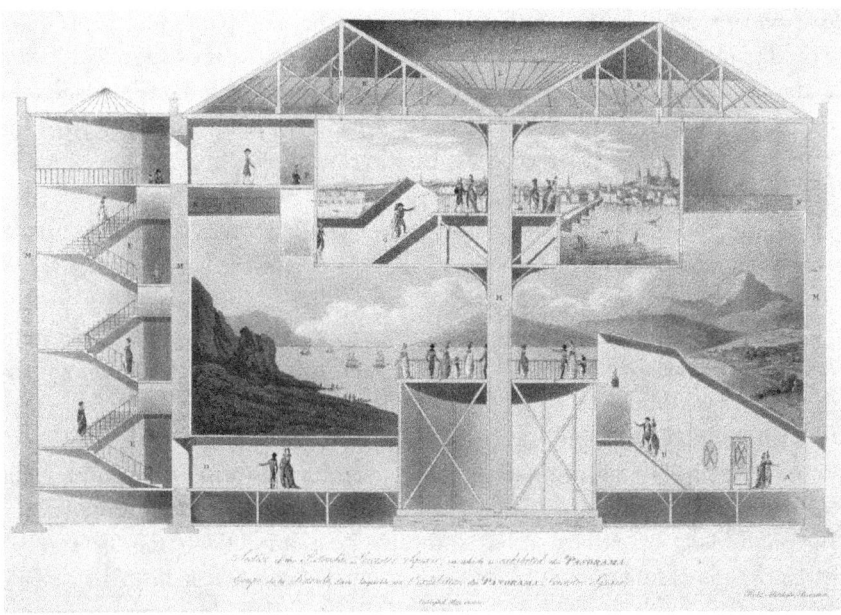

Figure 1.2 Panorama Building in Leicester Square, London. Aquatint published in 1801, showing the scale of this display, where Rio de Janeiro was later exhibited.

Figure 1.3 Lithograph by Agostino Aglio of the 'Modern Mexico' exhibition held at London's Egyptian Hall in 1824, which displayed objects collected by William Bullock and his son on their visit in 1821.

Austrian painter Hubert Sattler, himself the son of a panorama proprietor, would paint the Orizaba Mayan Temple in 1856, giving it exotic allure.[8] And within Brazil, during the 1850s, the German painter Friedrich Hagedorn would produce an extraordinary range of topographic images, many in the 'panoramic' style.[9] His panoramas, of Rio and Recife in particular, quickly became staples of the emerging iconography of Brazil, and would represent the nation in both domestic and international exhibitions. After their appearance as cheap lithographic prints, they would be replicated in other media and formats, some no doubt becoming lantern slides.

By the mid-century, moving panoramas had become a new craze, representing the process of travel itself through the mechanical movement of their scrolls. Huhtamo (2013: 180) reproduces a poster that offered a 'trip' to California, Mexico and the Isthmus in 1851. Spectacular scale could also be combined with movement, as it was in John Banvard's panoramas. His 'Grand Moving Painting of the Mississippi and Missouri Rivers', shown at the Egyptian Hall, was advertised as a 'three-mile picture' depicting 1,200 miles of landscape (Huhtamo 2013: 186). But equally important in this evolving galaxy of new media were the portable devices that developed alongside immersive displays: Polyoramas (a miniature table-top form of the Diorama), stereoscopes as already noted and, at the end of the century, picture postcards and illustrated ephemera, such as cigarette cards. Initially, gathering evidence of these often-fragile images was the province of enthusiasts and collectors, although they are increasingly being catalogued and displayed online by research institutions.[10] However, they have largely remained outside the reckoning of mainstream media history, so there is undoubtedly much work still to be done on the repertoire of the often overlooked ephemeral media, to trace how they interacted, and how their quantity and repetition built up a 'density' in the visual culture of the later nineteenth century.

STEREOGRAPHY

Among these mid-nineteenth-century media, stereoscopy probably remains the least fully appreciated, despite the considerable number of individual stereograph cards in existence. The discovery of the principle of stereopsis by Charles Wheatstone in 1838 coincided with the emergence of photography in the following decade. And the combination of these led to David Brewster's Stereoscope, launched at the Great Exhibition in London in 1851, followed by Oliver Wendell Holmes's simpler and cheaper device in 1861. The stereoscope in its various consumer forms quickly became a worldwide novelty, with companies such as Underwood and Underwood in London and Keystone in Pennsylvania developing massive catalogues of views. Although

Figure 1.4 Photographer Revert Henrique Klumb introduced stereography to Brazil during the 1850s. He produced this popular stereograph of the Emperor Pedro II.

stereoscopes would eventually become accessible to a mass audience, and bring photography into general circulation, many of the early enthusiasts were aristocrats and rulers. Queen Victoria and Prince Albert were keen collectors, as were many of their fellow-monarchs. And in Brazil, the Emperor Pedro II followed suit, commissioning many stereoscopic subjects from the Rio photographer Revert Henrique Klumb (Figure 1.4).

Thanks to Maria Cristina Miranda da Silva's (2016) systematic study of stereograph collections in Rio de Janeiro, it is possible to reach a good overall understanding of the uses and significance of the format in Brazil. Da Silva divides the approximately 700 examples she studied into two categories: those produced by Brazilian photographers for 'internal' commissions, and those taken by foreign photographers for international circulation. A surprising proportion of the 405 indigenous subjects were, in fact, commissioned by the Emperor and his court circle, confirming that stereoscopy began as something of an aristocratic hobby in many countries, which then reached an increasing and probably largely middle-class market.

Klumb produced hundreds of views of the major public monuments and public parks of the time, many ordered by the Emperor Pedro II and largely in the form of stereographs (Figure 1.5).

> [He] presented stereoscopic photographs to the general public for the first time in 1860, at one of the General Fine Arts Exhibitions of the Imperial Academy in the Exhibition of Industry Artefacts and Fine Arts Application section. By the National Exhibition of 1866, the exhibition of stereographs was earning a status of its own. In this exhibition, photographs [were] divided into 'panoramas', 'various panoramas for albums', 'stereoscopes', 'albums' and 'pictures'. In the 'stereoscopes' subclass up to 70 views were announced, several of Rio de Janeiro, Tijuca, Serra dos Órgãos, Teresópolis, Public Garden, Botanical Garden, etc. (Da Silva 2016: 61)

Brazil had become 'exotic' for Europeans and North Americans – Offenbach's operetta *La Vie parisienne* (1866) featured a Brazilian millionaire visiting

Figure 1.5 Part of a stereoscopic view of Porto Alegre by Klumb, probably shown in the National Exhibition of 1866 among his landscape studies.

Paris – and was clearly attracting photographers from the major stereograph publishers, with 313 foreign examples found by Da Silva.

But it was also serving the interests of Brazilian photographers and publishers, who, as Da Silva notes, 'helped in building the image of a "Modern Brazil", recreating its urban spaces and, above all, bringing the observer into a modernity built by the gaze' (Da Silva 2016: 66). Investigating the work of Klumb more closely, she quotes another scholar, Annateresa Fabris:

> In the 'frozen scenes of cosmopolitanism' Brazil can look like any other 'modern' nation, however, as demonstrated by Fabris (1991: 45), the equivalence is only illusory, 'one builds a Brazil that is not Brazil; is a vision of Brazil through bourgeois eyes where the particular becomes exotic and is catalogued as a curiosity'.

In fact, Klumb's range of subjects in the 1860s included a number of sailors, city workers, slaves washing clothes in a Rio public fountain and washerwomen in Rio's Tijuca Forest – a locale that will become significant again in early Brazilian filmmaking. As the stereograph repertoire expanded everywhere during the century, it becomes difficult to characterise them ideologically – unless all the new media are considered, at least in their novelty phase, to be intrinsically 'bourgeois'.

To some extent this would be accurate, since these images were easily reproduced and transmitted. Equipped with a portable stereoscope, the armchair viewer could 'travel' widely, experiencing journeys and perspectives that would have been arduous in reality. As stereograph catalogues expanded dramatically, they took on an encyclopaedic scope, covering the world and its wonders, industries, exotic peoples and so on. The major publishers of stereographs would claim that their 'tours' were actually better than going to faraway places – safer, and with access to key sites guaranteed. And they developed a narrative dimension, with posed 'life-model' scenes – which paralleled those common in lantern-slide narratives. So with these two media converging on narrative by the 1890s, the scene is set for the appearance of 'animated photography', or film, building upon prior mediated 'worlds'.

Magic Lanterns

It might be thought that one field in which lantern projection of images may have flourished in colonial Brazil would be their use by missionaries. Indeed, the origin of the magic lantern was traditionally assigned to the Jesuit 'new media' pioneer Athanasius Kircher in 1671, although it is now believed that Huygens preceded Kircher. The Jesuits were noted for their early use of elaborate forms of theatre and a variety of visual media, but the fact that the order was suppressed in Portugal and its empire in 1759 effectively predated any use of lanterns by the Jesuits in their extensive network of mission settlements or *reducciones*, straddling the borders of present-day Brazil, Argentina and Paraguay.[11]

However, other Christian churches were active after Brazilian independence, notably the Methodist Episcopal church of the United States, which first sent missionaries in 1835. While no information is available about techniques used at this time, there is some residual evidence that the second initiative by Southern Methodists in 1867, after the end of the American Civil War, probably made use of lanterns in its evangelism. Their initial target was Confederate expatriates who had emigrated to Brazil, but by 1880 the Brazilian Methodist church had recruited Brazilian members and ministers. A small collection of surviving slides from c.1920 shows a church in Poços de Caldas, Minas Gerais, and suggests that lanterns were already in regular use (Figure 1.6).[12]

Information about actual missionary practice using the lantern in Brazil seems to be unavailable, but an account by Alejandro Martínez (2010) of work with the Paraguayan Chaco Indians in the 1890s provides an interesting insight into what must have been common experience. Martínez reports

Figure 1.6 Church at Poços de Caldas, Minas Gerais, from a set of lantern slides archived by the American Southern Methodist Episcopal Mission.

that British Anglican missionaries of the South American Missionary Society found the use of lantern images greatly increased their impact on the Enxet Indians, once they had overcome the initial anxiety caused by the projected images. The *Missionary Bulletin* reported:

> It was at this time [1895] that [Wilfrid] Grubb took out a lantern and slides. It was a great event, and marked a new stage in teaching. Hitherto instruction had been given by means of pictures shown to little groups of people. Short informal religious services had been held in the house or near the village. Now came the novelty of the lantern; the young folks were curious and expectant, while the older people were dubious and fearful. On the first occasion the sheet was nicely stretched, the lantern in position, and the audience squatting on the ground in front waiting for something to happen. When the first picture appeared on the screen, they were startled and promptly covered their faces to ward off the impending calamity, for as they put it, 'They were afraid of the little devil that lived in the black box and jumped out to the white blanket'. (Martínez 2010)

Once over their initial fear, the Enxet became attentive and practised spectators. Indeed, the need for good pictures to cater for critical indigenous audiences was soon noted:

> The Indians are most critical, and really good pictures are a necessity. Accustomed as the Indians are to observe minute words [sic] and details of their surroundings, they criticise every picture in a way that an English audience would not. Might I advise that, if possible, each set of pictures be by the same artist? If they see Adam and Eve with fair hair in one picture and dark in the next, they wonder what caused it. They are not acquainted with hairdressers' concoctions. We have two pictures of St. Peter, wherein the details differ, and Mr. Grubb was once explaining these, and the Indians took great objection to it. Such fancy pictures as Christ rising from the dead with a banner are entirely misleading and objectionable. (Martínez 2010)

What is particularly interesting about this account is that it challenges some conventional assumptions about 'natives' being astonished by superior technology. Certainly, these Paraguayans were impressed and attracted, but they quickly became critical viewers – and in this they were probably not very different from the audiences for missionary and temperance lantern shows in Europe at the same period (Vogh-Bienek and Crangle 2014).

However, evangelism was not the only activity that depended on lantern projection. The later decades of the century saw the rise of travel lectures as a popular new genre of urban entertainment. The American John L. Stoddard was the acknowledged star of this world, followed after his retirement in 1897 by Burton Holmes, who would add film to the hand-coloured slides that were the travel lecturers' staple, and coin the term 'travelogue' for his performances. In a long career, Holmes took over 30,000 photographs and produced 500,000 feet of film. There is no record of Holmes visiting Latin America until 1911, although his 1912 lectures focused on 'Buenos Aires, the American Paris', 'Over the Andes' and 'Brazil', which he revisited several times. Typical of his later coverage of Latin America is a film of the spectacular Iguaçu Falls on the border between Brazil and Argentina (*Cataracts of Iguassu*, by Burton Holmes).[13]

During the last quarter of the century, the 'optical lantern', as it was now commonly known (or 'stereopticon' in the United States), was increasingly being used in popular entertainment in theatres around the world. This was largely because the brightness and size of the projected image had greatly increased, due to the use of new forms of illumination. In place of oil lamps, lanterns were now powered by oxyacetylene illumination, or by limelight, which made their images visible to larger theatre-scale audiences. Two of Brazil's most celebrated cultural monuments from this period are the Teatro da Paz in Belém (1874) and the Teatro Amazonas in Manaus (1884), the latter made famous by its appearance in Werner Herzog's *Fitzcarraldo* (1984). But while these are understandably famous for their lavish, European-style architecture and décor, recreated in the midst of the Amazonian forest during the height of the country's rubber industry boom, little is recorded about their actual early presentations.

From what is known about similar theatres elsewhere, it is likely that this included the use of lantern projection, either as a 'linking' device, or as an entertainment in its own right. For concrete evidence of this, we must be grateful for the detailed study that Alice Dubina Trusz (2010) made of the Teatro São Pedro, a comparable grand theatre dating from 1858, in the state capital of Rio Grande do Sul, Porto Alegre (Figure 1.7). What first attracted Trusz to studying the programme of this theatre was its record of showing films from the early date of November 1896. But as she discovered, it was necessary to extend her research back as far as 1861, to take account of the history of projected entertainment at the São Pedro. As she writes, 'cinema did not appear as an accomplished spectacle genre, and neither was projection a new practice' (Trusz 2010: 29)

What Trusz discovered was an already well-established tradition of projection-based formats, within which moving pictures were introduced as an additional novelty from 1896 onwards. This, of course, is exactly what happened everywhere, from the capital cities of Europe and North America to all the smaller cities and towns where moving pictures made their first appearance. In fact, the Lumières' celebrated opening run at a café in Paris from December 1895, consisting entirely of their moving 'views', was very much the exception. In London, New York and also Paris, moving pictures

Figure 1.7 Teatro São Pedro in 1875, photographed by Luigi Terragano.

would form only one item in a variety programme for at least five years; and would only gradually and erratically become a self-sufficient offer around 1907–8, which Trusz's research finds was also the pattern at the São Pedro. In the case of Porto Alegre, she traces how 'a discontinuous and erratic' process led by itinerant exhibitors gradually established cinema as 'a new spectacular genre' (Trusz 2010: 116)

What this valuable detailed longitudinal study of one venue reveals is not only a much longer tradition of projection, but also a pattern of *hybridity* and a recurrent emphasis on novelty across the nearly fifty years surveyed, from 1861 to 1908. The titles alone of the pre-cinema period shows imply enhanced versions of established attractions – a *Poliorama fantasmagórico* presented by a magician in 1863; then a *Grande poliorama elétrico* in 1882; and finally a *Poliorama universal* in 1896. It is difficult to know what form these variations on the 'poliorama' might have taken. The term was used in French and English, as 'polyorama', between the 1820s and 1850s to describe a small, portable version of Daguerre's Diorama, which reflects light on to translucent printed cards to create a kind of optical immersion for the viewer (Huhtamo 2006). But in Porto Alegre, it was apparently a stage-scale projected spectacle, and a genre capable of being updated by addition of the promise of 'electricity'. In the post-1896 period, a similar pattern emerges. In 1897, Faure Nicolay presents the 'Sylphorama', apparently a bifunctional projector – meaning presumably that it projected slides, as well as film – placed among the audience and lit by electricity (Trusz 2010: 116). In fact, almost all early film projectors were equipped to show both slides and film, so this in itself would not have been unusual. But early projection was not electrically powered, so the reference here would have been to electricity as an attraction in itself – which it often was in the decade spanning the turn of the century (Marvin

1988: 9, 161). And the Sylphorama was being offered as an accompaniment to a magic performance.

From 1897 onwards, animated pictures, under whichever of their many trade or invented names, are most often offered in conjunction with electricity and some form of recorded sound (Figure 1.8). Given that Edison had originally announced his development of moving pictures as 'doing for the eye what the phonograph did for the ear', this is perhaps not surprising. The fact that the period before the late 1920s is generally termed 'silent' today refers only to the arrival of 'sound on film' marking a new chapter in cinema history. But early film historians have long known that film shows throughout the 'silent' era were frequently – perhaps almost invariably – punctuated by forms of synchronised image and sound. The degree of synchronisation, between disc or cylinder and film, may have been approximate; but this was commonplace and apparently welcomed.

Toward Cinema

Trusz's chronology of the São Pedro programmes covers the crucial years when a recognisably modern 'cinema' was taking shape around the world. What it reveals is the gradual appearance of organisations that would tour standardised programmes around a number of venues. One of these, the Candburg company, had 'established a good reputation' for its programmes shown in Buenos Aires, Rio de Janeiro and Santos (Trusz 2010: 275). Among the novelties Candburg offered in Porto Alegre were programmes of synchronised musical performances by such notable French stars as Yvette Guilbert and Mercadier, special children's matinées and programmes of 'comic, dramatic, satirical and fantastic films', which 'attracted large numbers' and were received with 'generous applause' (277). Offering a variety of short items within the programme would remain important, until the arrival of longer films around 1911–12 established the typical 'feature' as a standard attraction.

But this pattern was not a smooth progression in Porto Alegre, any more than it would have been in the many other theatres showing film throughout Brazil. At the end of 1906, for instance, the São Pedro showed *The Shipwreck of the SS Sírio*, portraying the recent loss of an Italian steamer that had sunk off the Spanish coast in August, drowning at least 150 Italian and Spanish emigrants bound for Argentina. Films about topical events, especially with local significance, were already entering the programme. So too were perennial attractions, such as a multipart *Life and Passion of Our Lord Jesus Christ*, shown in the following week of November of that year. Advertised as consisting of thirty parts, this could have been Alice Guy-Blaché's new *La Vie du Christ* (Gaumont), which ran for over thirty minutes (Figure 1.9); or possibly a

Figure 1.8 A 1901 programme of films shown daily at the Teatro São Pedro on the 'Grand-Prix marvellous cinematograph' by Henrique Sastro. Films seem to have been mainly from the Lumière brothers, with *Guilherme Tell* and *Morte de Chocolat* featuring two famous clowns filmed at a Paris circus in 1897.

Figure 1.9 Alice Guy's 1905 *Life of Christ* (Gaumont) was a big Christmas success at the Teatro São Pedro in Porto Alegre.

revival of Zecca's 1904 *La Vie et la passion de Jésus-Christ* for Pathé; or quite possibly a composite of the various passion-films that were circulating at this time. At any rate, its appeal to a religious and predominantly female audience was noted.

Many of these special attractions were effectively 'remediations' of proven attractions in earlier media. The subjects of the long films that gave cinema new status and appeal between 1910 and 1914 had already been represented in novels, plays, operas and paintings. So when *The Last Days of Pompeii* (with two rival Italian versions in 1913) and *Ben-Hur* (first filmed in 1907), and in a different genre the crime thriller *Fantômas* (Louis Feuillade, 1913), appeared on screen, they were effectively novel, enhanced versions of familiar texts – in short, remediation supplies the dynamic of the hectic intertextuality that marked cinema's emergence as a new social and cultural institution. And the same logic applied to traditional, venerable subjects, such as the biblical passion story, which had provided the earliest impulse to link series of short films into a narrative whole (Christie 1994: 121–3).

So we reach the moment when locally made dramas first appear on Brazilian screens, as recorded in the traditional production-oriented histories

Figure 1.10 *Os estranguladores* (*The Stranglers*, 1908) reconstructed a notorious recent crime in Rio de Janeiro, inaugurating a series of 'true crime' dramas that launched early Brazilian cinema into an international genre.

of Brazilian cinema. But as Rielle Navitski (2017) has shown, discussing the success of such films as *Os estranguladores* (*The Stranglers*, Antonio Leal, 1908) (Figure 1.10) and *Um drama na Tijuca* (*A Drama in Tijuca*, Antonio Leal, 1909), these drew heavily on their audience's familiarity with the actual locations, portraying them in a newly glamorised mode of remediation. The former, she observes, showed 'the space of the capital as ambivalent emblem of a national modernity', giving 'the precise locations where the events of the case unfolded, as reported by local newspapers' (2017: 126). And the latter exploited the image of Tijuca, Rio's rainforest enclave, as 'an elite haunt with picturesque qualities' (159). The film promised its viewers a 'real and characteristic scene of the intimate life of Rio's finest society, with tableaux of astonishing artistic effect, some taken on the natural sites of that fantastic mountain, full of beauty and a witness to innumerable amorous adventures' (159).

Rather than foundational novelties, it might be argued that these films appeared as precocious local examples of a worldwide process by which the established form of the literary 'urban mystery' was remediated in filmic form. In the successful Danish company Nordisk's thrillers, filmed around Copenhagen, and in Gaumont's screen versions of *Fantômas*, a similar process was at work, recalling that an important aspect of the appeal of stereographic representation, as distinct from the panoramic era, was the sense of *actuality*, as much as the spectacular. The developing new genres of film, notably the urban melodrama, would effectively remobilise this sense of a shared everyday reality, as a background to narratives that drew upon both true-life reportage and sensational crime fiction. What was particular to Brazil's 'belle époque' was the role of cinema in confirming a sense of its cities becoming part of international modernity – a sense that had been fostered by earlier new visual media over the previous century, with Brazil increasingly advertised to the wider world.[14]

Media archaeology asks us to set aside judgements about media improvement and 'progress', paying due attention to transient and apparently 'failed' devices. The digital media revolution that we are living through intensively today offers us not only new media affordances, but also the resurrection of many media of past centuries that can be accessed and explored as never before, especially through their documentation in searchable digitised records. A good example of the fruits of such an archaeological approach would be to challenge the assumption that the arrival of the Cinématographe in Brazil in mid-1896 was inevitably seen as superseding the Kinetoscope experience (see Johnson and Stam 1987: 21). Certainly, the scale of the projected image was impressive, and communal viewing created a different experience from the Kinetoscope's individual spectators – although one that would have been familiar from Magic Lantern shows. But accounts of the earlier device, as reported in 1894, conveyed a closer attention to what was being shown, how it worked and a sense of 'wonder':

> This is Edison's latest invention, and like all the creations of this learned and prolific inventor, it is a wonder. We saw a cockfight with all its thrills, the spectators' cheers and enthusiastic gestures. Then we saw a serpentine dance, correctly done, and finally a curious fight in a tavern ... The kinetoscope consists of a film with 150 images rotating one thousand times a second ... This film ... exposed at extraordinary speed to capture all the movements to be represented, is set in motion by a 20 volt engine.[15]

The equivalent first reports on Cinématographe projections in 1896 dwelt on the novelty of electric light in the room, before this was extinguished, and the number of chairs, but made no comment on the subjects shown. Johnson claims, as others have implied, that the Omniographo of 1896 had 'a much greater impact' than the Kinetoscope, on the grounds that it was seen by many rather than by 'only one person at a time'. But did it? This is surely an example of the 'medium imperialism' of film and its extensive subsequent theorisation as obstacles to a truer understanding of the history of mediation, and the part it has played in spectators' lives. Cinema of the 1960s and 1970s created a sense of cultural permanence that led to an aesthetic of cinema which was ultimately solipsistic and ahistorical. As we search for more about what came before, and live through what has come after, we should be increasingly alert to the intrinsic hybridity and relative transitoriness of all media regimes. Remediation and intermediality are two aspects of the same process at work, driven by the dynamics of invention, novelty and profit-seeking investment.

In a book about the role of drawing for the Soviet filmmaker and theorist Sergei Eisenstein, the Russian scholar Naum Kleiman invoked a phrase of Eisenstein's:

> when he was trying to understand what the cinema resembled, he looked not for what was "specific to it" but for its "genetic code" – for the way the general laws of the perception of the world in terms of images came through in it. (Kleiman 2017: 21)

Rather than search for the 'specificity' of any media form, it is more illuminating to understand what function this serves at a given social and economic moment. Actualities made by Brazilians at the turn of the century, and *Os estranguladores* and *Um drama na Tijuca*, were undoubted attractions in their own time. But they need to be integrated into the much longer, and continuing, history of imaging Brazil.[16]

Notes

1. Very little research has so far focused on the Kinetoscope era regionally or nationally, with Richard Brown and Barry Anthony, *The Kinetoscope: A British History* (2017) a rare exception. Ray Phillips refers to the President of Mexico attending 'the introduction of the Kinetoscope on 17 January 1895', without any source (Phillips 1997: 71). See also Chapter 1 of my *Robert Paul and the Origins of British Cinema* (2019: 7–33).
2. Apparently Robert Barker, inventor of the Panorama, paid an artist the substantial sum of 70 guineas in 1808 for a view he had drawn of Rio. But this was not featured as a Panorama subject until 1828 (Altick 1978: 421).
3. On peepshows, see Peepshows and Optical Toys, Marlborough Gallery sale catalogue. See also: *Perspective Views Peepshow Box*, Bill Douglas Centre, Exeter University.
4. See also the television series *The Last Machine* (writer and co-producer Ian Christie; director Richard Curson-Smith; BBC/BFI, Illuminations TV, 1994), episode

1, available at <https://www.youtube.com/watch?v=1ri0z8fYRvM&t=166s> (last accessed 28 June 2020).
5. Nearly all copies of the book by Antonil, *Cultura e opulência do Brasil, por suas drogas e minas* (Culture and Opulence of Brazil, from its Drugs and Mines), published in 1711, were destroyed by the Portuguese authorities. The first book printed in Brazil, *Relação da entrada que fez o excellentíssimo, e reverendíssimo senhor D. Fr. Antonio do Desterro Malheyro Bispo do Rio de Janeiro [. . .]* (*Notes of the Bishop's Arrival in Rio de Janeiro*) (1747), was also banned, and the prohibition against all publishing was maintained until 1808. Information from displays in the Itaú Cultural, Olavo Setúbal Space, Module 3, 'O Brasil Secreto' (Secret Brazil).
6. The technique of 'fore-edge' painting dates back to medieval times, but has been revived at times when secrecy, or esoteric conspiracy, is required. On its wider history, see the catalogue *On the Edge: The Hidden Art of Fore-edge Book Painting* (2013).
7. See Costeloe (2006: 275–309). Also illustrations in the London Metropolitan Archives collection.
8. Sattler's *Orizaba* is reproduced in colour in Hyde 1989: 107.
9. Friedrich Hagedorn (1814–89) lived and worked in Brazil for twenty years. In 1854, he had an atelier in Rio de Janeiro, advertised in the *Almanak Laemmert* (Laemmert Almanac). His great panorama of the city, viewed from Morro da Conceição, was published in lithographic form. He later travelled through the cities of Teresópolis, Petrópolis and Niterói in the state of Rio de Janeiro, as well as the provinces of Minas Gerais, Bahia and Pernambuco, representing their landscapes mainly in watercolour. His panorama of Recife, engraved from three coloured lithographs, was published in 1855, showing how this originally large exhibition form had evolved to become a popular printed graphic format. See <https://en.wikipedia.org/wiki/File:Frederick_Hagedorn_-_Panorama_do_recife_-_1855.jpg> (last accessed 10 December 2021).
10. See, for instance, the stereograph collections of the New York Public Library. Also the NYPL Brazil image collection.
11. See, for instance, the UNESCO site on the Jesuit missions to the Guaranis.
12. See slides held in Perkins Library collections, Southern Methodist University, Dallas, Texas.
13. The film can be found at <http://www.travelfilmarchive.com/item.php?id=11767&filmmaker_id=3&startrow=0&keywords=Burton+Holmes> (last accessed 22 June 2020).
14. After Offenbach's operetta, *La Vie parisienne*, French fascination with other aspects of Brazil was confirmed by Jules Verne's 1881 novel *Eight Hundred Leagues on the Amazon* (*Huit cents lieues sur l'Amazone*). See also the discussion of transatlantic fashion influences in the chapter 'Fashion, Cultural Transfers and the History of the Book', by Ana Claudia Suriani da Silva (2015: 139–65).
15. *Jornal do Brasil*, 9 December 1894, quoted in Süssekind and Britto (1997: 23).
16. An important contribution to clarifying the complexity of showmanship in Brazil in the mid-1890s has been the work of José Inácio de Melo Souza, a

former researcher at the Cinemateca Brasileira. Souza's valuable essay 'Do kinetoscope ao kinetoscópio: variações sobre o mesmo tema' ('From the kinetoscope to the kinetoscópio: variations on the same theme') (pub. 2013 at http://mnemocine.tempsite.ws/index.php?start=90) is now included in his collection *Salvados digitais* (2020).

REFERENCES

Altick, Robert (1978), *The Shows of London*. Cambridge, MA: Harvard University Press.
Bolter, Jay David and Richard Grusin (2000), *Remediation: Understanding New Media*. Cambridge, MA: MIT Press.
Brazil image collection, New York Public Library, available at <https://digitalcollections.nypl.org/collections/voyage-pittoresque-et-historique-au-brsil-ou-sjour-dun-artiste-franais-au-brsil#/?tab=about&scroll=28> (last accessed 24 June 2020).
Brown, Richard and Barry Anthony (2017), *The Kinetoscope: A British History*. Eastleigh: Libbey.
Bueno, Isabel (2018), 'Machetes and Sketchbooks Introduced the Maya to the World', *National Geographic History Magazine*, available at <https://www.nationalgeographic.com/archaeology-and-history/magazine/2018/09-10/history-maya-archaeology-stephens-catherwood/> (last accessed 20 June 2020).
Burton Holmes Travel Film Archive, available at <http://www.travelfilmarchive.com/item.php?id=11767&filmmaker_id=3&startrow=0&keywords=Burton+Holmes> (last accessed 23 June 2020).
Christie, Ian (1994), *The Last Machine: Early Cinema and the Birth of the Modern World*. London: British Film Institute/BBC Education.
Christie, Ian (2019), *Robert Paul and the Origins of British Cinema*. Chicago: University of Chicago Press, pp. 50–6.
Comment, Bernard (1999), *The Panorama*. London: Reaktion.
Costeloe, Michael (2006), 'William Bullock and the Mexican Connection', *Mexican Studies/Estudios Mexicanos*, 22:2, Summer, pp. 275–309.
da Silva, Ana Claudia Suriani (2015), *The Cultural Revolution of the Nineteenth Century: Theatre, the Book-Trade and Reading in the Transatlantic World*. London: Bloomsbury Academic.
da Silva, Maria Cristina Miranda (2016), 'Stereoscopy in Nineteenth-century Brazil: The Case of Rio de Janeiro', *International Journal of Film and Media Arts*, 1:2, available at <https://revistas.ulusofona.pt/index.php/ijfma/article/view/5711> (last accessed 28 June 2020).
Fabris, Annateresa (1991), 'O circuito social da fotografia: estudo de caso – II', in Annateresa Fabris (ed.), *Fotografia: usos e funções no século XIX*. São Paulo: EDUSP, pp. 59–82.
Fullerton, John (2014), *Picturing Mexico: From the Camera Lucida to Film*. New Barnet: John Libbey.
Huhtamo, Erkki (2006), 'The Pleasures of the Peephole: An Archaeological Exploration of Peep Media', in Eric Kluitenberg (ed.), *The Book of Imaginary Media: Excavating the Dream of the Ultimate Communication Medium*. Rotterdam: NAi Publishers, pp. 74–155.
Huhtamo, Erkki (2012), 'Toward a History of Peep Practice', in André Gaudreault, Nicolas Dulac and Santiago Hidalgo (eds), *A Companion to Early Cinema*. Hoboken, NJ: Wiley, pp. 32–51.
Huhtamo, Erkki (2013), *Illusions in Motion: Media Archaeology of the Moving Panorama and Related Spectacles*. Cambridge, MA: MIT Press.

Huhtamo, Erkki and Jussi Parikka (eds) (2011), *Media Archaeology: Approaches, Applications, and Implications*. Berkeley, Los Angeles and London: University of California Press.

Huhtamo, Erkki and Jussi Parikka (2012) 'Toward a History of Peep Practice', in André Gaudreault, Nicolas Dulac and Santiago Hidalgo (eds), *A Companion to Early Cinema*. Hoboken: Wiley, pp. 32–51.

Hyde, Ralph (1989), *Panoramania!*, Catalogue of the exhibition at Barbican Art Gallery, London.

Johnson, Randal and Robert Stam (eds) (1995), *Brazilian Cinema*. New York: Columbia University Press.

Kleiman, Naum, with an introduction by Ian Christie (2017), *Eisenstein: The Graphic Work*. London: Thames & Hudson.

London Metropolitan Archives collection, available at <https://collage.cityoflondon.gov.uk/view-item?i=323083&WINID=1549554621388> (last accessed 24 June 2020).

López, Ana (2005), 'Brazil', in Richard Abel (ed.), *Encyclopedia of Early Cinema*. Abingdon: Routledge.

Martínez, Alejandro (2010), 'Evangelization, Visual Technologies, and Indigenous Responses: The South American Missionary Society in the Paraguayan Chaco', *International Bulletin of Missionary Research*, 34:2, pp. 83ff, available at <https://journals.sagepub.com/doi/abs/10.1177/239693931003400205> (last accessed 23 June 2020).

Marvin, Caroline (1988), *When Old Technologies Were New: Thinking About Electric Communication in the Late Nineteenth Century*. New York: Oxford University Press.

Mesguich, Felix (1933), *Tours de manivelle*. Paris: Grasset.

Navitski, Rielle (2017), *Public Spectacles of Violence: Sensational Cinema and Journalism in Early Twentieth-Century Mexico and Brazil*. Durham, NC: Duke University Press.

Newman, Kathleen (2005), 'Argentina', in Richard Abel (ed.), *Encyclopedia of Early Cinema*. Abingdon: Routledge.

On the Edge: The Hidden Art of Fore-edge Book Painting (2013), Boston Public Library, available at <https://publicdomainreview.org/collection/fore-edge-book-paintings-from-the-boston-public-library> (last accessed 23 June 2020).

Otavo Setúbal Collection, Instituto Itaú Cultural, São Paulo, Brazil (visited 2016).

Peepshows and Optical Toys, Marlborough Gallery sale catalogue of Peepshows, available at <http://www.marlboroughbooks.com/catalogues/pdfs/MRB_Catalogue_219.pdf> (last accessed 14 June 2020).

Perkins Library collections, Southern Methodist University, Dallas, Texas, available at <https://www.smu.edu/Bridwell/SpecialCollectionsandArchives/Exhibitions/VirtualAndReal/MECS> (last accessed 24 June 2020).

Perspective Views Peepshow Box. Bill Douglas Centre, Exeter University, available at <http://www.bdcmuseum.org.uk/explore/item/69027/> (last accessed 26 June 2020).

Phillips, Ray (1997), *Edison's Kinetoscope and its Films: A History to 1896*. Trowbridge: Flicks Books.

Rajewsky, Irina (2005), 'Intermediality, Intertextuality, Remediation: A Literary Perspective'. *Intermédialités*, 6, Autumn, pp. 43–64, available at <http://cri.histart.umontreal.ca/cri/fr/intermedialites/p6/pdfs/p6_rajewsky_text.pdf> (last accessed 23 June 2020).

Rajewsky, Irina (2011), 'Intermediality, Intertextuality, Remediation: A Literary Perspective', *Intermédialités*, available at <http://cri.histart.umontreal.ca/cri/fr/intermedialites/p6/pdfs/p6_rajewsky_text.pdf> (last accessed 23 June 2020).

Schivelbusch, Wolfgang (1986), *The Railway Journey: The Industrialisation of Time and Space in the 19th Century*. Berkeley, Los Angeles and London: University of California Press.

Souza, José Inácio de Melo (2020), *Salvados digitais*. São Paulo: Gráfica Bartira.

Spehr, Paul (2008), *The Man Who Made Movies: W. K. L. Dickson*. New Barnet: John Libbey.
Stereograph collections, New York Public Library, available at <https://digitalcollections.nypl.org/collections/robert-n-dennis-collection-of-stereoscopic-views#/?tab=navigation> (last accessed 24 June 2020).
Süssekind, Flora and Paulo Henriques Britto (1997), *Cinematograph of Words: Literature, Technique and Modernization in Brazil*. Stanford: Stanford University Press.
Trujillo, Gabriella (2015), 'Le Brésil et la construction problématique d'un cinéma national (1896–1954)', *1895*, 77, pp. 48–67.
Trusz, Alice Dubina (2010), *Entre lanternas mágicas e cinematógrafos, 1861–1908*. São Paulo: Terceiro Nome.
UNESCO overview of the Jesuit missions to the Guaranis, available at <https://whc.unesco.org/en/list/275> (last accessed 21 June 2020).
Verhoeff, Nanna (2012), *Mobile Screens: The Visual Regime of Navigation*. Amsterdam: Amsterdam University Press.
Vogh-Bienek, Ludwig and Richard Crangle (eds) (2014), *Screen Culture and the Social Question 1880–1914*. New Barnet: Kintop/Libbey.

CHAPTER 2

Intermedial Landscapes in the Work of Cao Guimarães
Alison Butler

In 2009, the Brazilian artist Cao Guimarães made a series of seven photographs entitled *Paisagens reais – homenagem a Guignard* (*Real Landscapes – Homage to Guignard*). These depict banks of clouds in delicate crepuscular hues, with just the tops of tower blocks and the spires of churches poking through. Guimarães describes how he took the photographs from his home, high in the hills of Belo Horizonte, Minas Gerais, on a morning when 'the city woke up suspended in clouds'.[1] The title refers to a series of paintings entitled *Imaginary Landscapes* by Alberto da Veiga Guignard, an artist based in Minas Gerais. The photographs do indeed resemble these paintings, in which churches and other buildings are depicted rising from the clouds, as if floating in the air. A similar view appears in several shots of the experimental documentary film *Acidente* (*Accident*, Cao Guimarães and Pablo Lobato, 2006), but with trees and hilltops instead of buildings showing through layers of cloud (filmed in a town named Descoberto, which, ironically, means 'uncovered'). As an artist working with reproductive media, Guimarães simultaneously inserts his cinematic and photographic work into art history and draws art history into photography and cinema. Through the indexical basis of these arts, he brings Guignard's imaginary landscapes back down to earth in real locations like those that inspired the painter. In an illuminating article on the 'aesthetic relation' in his work, Picado and Lins (2017: 285) note that, along with an acute eye for the real, the artist also brings to bear 'a look formed by the experience of works of art, which makes him perceive a vision in the chance appearance of a cloudy morning' (my translation).

Guimarães exemplifies the intermedial practice of the contemporary artist filmmaker, moving fluently between media forms and artistic conventions as well as between the institutions of fine art and cinema. After studying philosophy and photography, he began his career as a photographer, but quickly branched out into film and video. He has directed or co-directed nine feature films, mostly documentaries. His videos have been shown as installations in art galleries, including a recent exhibition – titled *Locus* – with Apichatpong

Weerasethakul at the EYE Filmmuseum in Amsterdam (16 September to 3 December 2017). Working in several media, Guimarães has produced a body of work that crosses boundaries between them, but beyond this he has developed artistic strategies in relation to the formal qualities and traditions of the visual arts, and has brought these to bear intermedially on his work in the medium of film. As Consuelo Lins (2007) explains, he invents 'narratives, devices and new perceptions of the real, thereby suggesting that cinema has a lot to gain from what is "exterior" to it'. Landscape and location are prominent concerns in his work, particularly in their relation to questions of daily life. In fact, it might be more accurate to characterise his interest in place as an interest in habitats, and the inventiveness with which humans and other living creatures accommodate themselves, wherever they happen to be. This interest exists, in his work, in tension with a pictorial conception of landscape as that which tends to erase or obscure the signs of habitation, just as the clouds in his *Real Landscapes* conceal the life of the city below. In this chapter I will argue that two modes of landscape representation operate intermedially in Guimarães's films: a painterly/cinematic mode which corresponds to the view from a distance, and a photographic/videographic mode that relates to embodied perception and intimate space. The tension between these two modes is used to articulate fundamental ethical and ecological concerns about the habitability of the world on which human activities have made such an impact.

That landscape should function as an intermedial bridge in this way is not surprising. As W. J. T. Mitchell (2002: 2) points out, the study of landscape has moved beyond 'fixed genres (sublime, beautiful, picturesque, pastoral), fixed media (literature, painting, photography), or fixed places treated as objects for visual contemplation or interpretation'; instead 'landscape *circulates* as a medium of exchange, a site of visual appropriation, a focus for the formation of identity' (emphasis in original). Mitchell describes landscape, on more than one occasion, as a medium in itself. The study of landscape, across a number of disciplines, has been structured by the opposition between a naturalistic view of the landscape as a given backdrop to human activities, and an understanding of landscape as a cultural construction, shaped by the formation of the observer. In recent years, this has been succeeded by an opposition between proximity and distance, understood as a tension between the Cartesian perspective inherent in both naturalistic and constructionist interpretations, and a phenomenological perspective based on the experience of landscape as inhabited place. As anthropologist Tim Ingold explains, two contrasting views may be taken of landscape, as 'a cultural image, a pictorial way of representing or symbolising surroundings' (Daniels and Cosgrove 1988: 1, cited in Ingold 1993: 154), or as 'the world as it is known to those who dwell therein, who inhabit its places and journey along the paths connecting them' (Ingold 1993: 156). These somewhat simplistic binaries – detachment/ involvement, distance/proximity – are complicated by the transformative effects of modernity on landscape painting. The idea that landscape is the product of detached observation aligns it with other modes of representation and technologies of vision, including mapping and telescopy, that are paradigmatic of scientific rationality and imperialist expansion. However, in modern landscape painting, the distant viewpoint is no guarantee of fixity, objectivity or even clarity, as can be seen from the debates around Cézanne's work and its relationship to modernity. As Jonathan Crary (1999) has argued, the decline of certainty in modern landscape painting registers the epistemological changes of the times, including the questioning of certainty in scientific thought.

In a Brazilian context, the history of landscape representation is intertwined with the history of colonialism and the politics of popular resistance. European painting and illustration arrived in Brazil with the colonists and served an important purpose for them: the Dutch artist Frans Post, considered the first European artist to paint the landscape of the Americas, was brought to Brazil in 1636 at the behest of Johan Maurits, the governor of the Dutch colony, in order to document its flora and fauna. Blending the exotic and the pastoral, Post's paintings inscribed colonial perspectives in Brazilian landscape painting at its very inception. Imported European traditions such as Romanticism and Impressionism continued to shape Brazilian landscape representation until the emergence of Brazilian modernism and its embrace of indigenous culture in the twentieth century. Photography played a significant part in this recoding of landscape images, as can be seen from Esther Gabara's (2008: 70) account of the landscape photography of Mário de Andrade. In Brazilian cinema, rural landscape – particularly that of the northeast – the *sertão* – has tended to symbolise the national past, either as a remote myth, in the classical period, or as a space of socio-political struggle in the films of the 1960s, such as *Vidas secas* (*Barren Lives*, Nelson Pereira dos Santos, 1963), *Os fuzis* (*The Guns*, Ruy Guerra, 1963) and *Deus e o diabo no terra do sol* (*Black God, White Devil*, Glauber Rocha, 1964). In recent years, scholarship on contemporary Brazilian cinema has identified a shift in the ways that landscape signifies in films. With the revival of the film industry in the 1990s, the *sertão* reappeared in films such as *Sertão das memórias* (*Landscapes of Memory*, José Araújo, 1997), *Baile perfumado* (*Perfumed Ball*, Paulo Caldas and Lírio Ferreira, 1997) and *Central do Brasil* (*Central Station*, Walter Salles, 1998), but instead of a space of irreconcilable contradictions, it had become, in the words of one scholar, 'a stage for cathartic reconciliation or existential redemption' (Oricchio 2003: 156). Isis Sadek has described the representation of space and place in films of the Retomada (the 1990s cinematic revival) as constructing 'intimate spatialities' that move away from the national imaginary of Cinema Novo (Sadek 2010), and Kleber Mendonça Filho (2010) has written of the 'intimate and personal terrain' ('terreno intimista e pessoal') of *Viajo porque preciso, volto porque te amo* (*I Travel Because I Have to, I Come Back Because I Love You*, Marcelo Gomes and Karim Aïnouz, 2009), a key film in this tendency.

'Intimate spatiality' is a hallmark of Guimarães's ongoing photographic series *Gambiarras* (2000–), in which he documents found instances of people's ingenuity in mending and making do, fixing broken things with whatever is to hand and repurposing old things to meet current needs. *Gambiarra* is a popular term that translates into English as 'bodge' or 'kludge'. The photographs document makeshift solutions to everyday problems, ways that people improvise when they cannot afford or cannot find replacements or repairs for things that break or do not work as they might. These are life hacks for ordinary people: an upturned crate used as a table for beer glasses; a window wedged open by a plastic pop bottle; another held open by a chopping board; half a lime used as an ash tray; a lightshade made from a CD; broken spectacles mended with wire; a potato with a cocktail stick in it used to spike a pile of receipts. The photographs rarely depict people, instead showing the *gambiarras* as they would be seen by their makers, close up and often in shallow focus, which creates a haptic effect, making them stand out from their surroundings as if the viewer could almost touch them. The photographs depict location from the point of view of its inhabitants, who adapt it to their needs. The evident poverty of the *gambiarras* and their settings is not aestheticised in a conventional sense, but their ingenuity is admired in a way that constitutes an alternative aesthetic, based in the indefatigable creativity of human beings. In an essay on the *Gambiarras* photo series, Rodrigo Moura (2006) writes:

> Once rescued from the effacement to which they are doomed, Cao Guimarães's *gambiarras* come forth not only as the solution offered in view of scanty resources, but also as denial of pre-fabricated, massified, and conforming industrial solutions. Usage and creation become one, they go against the grain, in an 'opposition', as Lagnado has defined them, d'après Hélio Oiticica. In his photographs, Guimarães deals with the desire to transform everyday life, not as something utopian, but as a means to create a proof that attests to this transformation taking place, on a daily basis, all over the world.

An aesthetic of the *gambiarra* would be closely affiliated to the aesthetics of garbage, which, as Robert Stam has argued, are quintessentially heterotopic and hybrid; like garbage, *gambiarras* are constitutively mixed (Stam 1998).

In his video art, Guimarães stages or discovers miniature landscapes and small-scale spaces of inhabitation. As a medium, video is predisposed to use in domestic and everyday settings and for personal self-expression; it comes with a kind of artistic licence to engage with the intimate and the ephemeral, to find meaning in the fleeting and inconsequential moment. Guimarães puts this to use in small-scale works that focus on micro-events. Several of his short videos highlight different aspects of this miniaturism. In *Quarta-feira de cinzas/Epilogue* (*Ash Wednesday/Epilogue*, with Rivane Neuenschwander, 2006) ants stage their own celebration after the carnival, or clear up after the humans. In the video, which is shot at ground level in extreme close-up, coloured sequins are seen glinting in the light as they move around on the soil, carried by ants taking them back to their nest (unknown to the viewer, the artists smeared the sequins with pork fat and honey to attract the insects). A quietly percussive soundtrack suggests ant music to accompany the performance. In *The Tenant* (with Rivane Neuenschwander, 2010), the protagonist is a soap bubble floating around an apartment that is being refurbished, as if it is thinking of moving in. The bubble moves quickly and seemingly deliberately over a series of different surfaces, foregrounding texture as a source of interest. Its movements appear intentional, so that when it lingers by newspaper pages left by the decorators, it seems to be reading. The soundtrack consists of uncanny noises of human habitation, evoking the past or future tenants of the apartment. Taking an insect or an inanimate object as the main character, these videos scale down spaces inhabited by humans, to make miniature landscapes for tiny visitors. One critic has described this tendency in Guimarães's work as 'a perceptive phenomenology where that which is molecular always prevails' (Montejo Navas 2013: 60).

Other videos, such as *Sin peso* (*Weightless*, 2007), view events from a human point of view, but give only partial glimpses of a world which is scaled to embodied perception. *Sin peso* begins with what appears to be an abstract image: the screen striped with bands of brilliant colour. The second and third shots are overhead views of the legs of a child who is seated on a step, with a carrier bag full of rolls of coloured fabric between her knees. This is followed by a series of shots showing the reverse field, as if from the child's position, looking upwards at brightly coloured fabrics with light pouring through, which are gradually revealed through wider shots as canopies. Finally, we are shown more of the setting, a street market in Mexico. Here, rather than showing the lifeworld of a very small being, Guimarães reduces the wider world to a smaller scale by showing momentary and partial views, framed as the reverie of a child. Marcos Moraes (2006) terms this way of seeing 'sensitive landscape'. The emphasis on colour for its own sake evokes abstract painting and abstract animation, without making an explicit reference to art. In other videos, however, 'sensitive landscape' is clearly linked to the aesthetic. *Sculpting* (2009) is a short video showing the mooring chains of a boat attached to a post in a Venice canal, rising and falling with the waves. The chain is covered in thick plastic rings that serve as buffers to prevent damage, and these give its moving form a fascinating, voluptuous appearance, like a kinetic sculpture. The setting – just glimpsed in the background of the tightly framed shot – adds to the suggestion of an artistic project, as it seems likely that the video was made when the artist was visiting the city for the Biennale. The video *Drawing* (2011) shows an overhead view of some decorative paving, patterned with grooves in a geometric design. Water is poured on to this surface, and moves quickly through the grooves, outlining them in a darker shade, then spreads and gradually darkens the whole surface. The titles of these two short videos announce their self-conscious engagement in the construction of an artistic landscape, which they do intermedially, by invoking artforms other than video. In his short videos, Guimarães blurs the boundaries between artforms and refuses the distinction between art and daily life, suggesting that art can be found anywhere in the built environment. While not overtly political, this work is permeated by an attitude of modest improvisation and thrifty creativity that has ethical and ecological implications.

These implications are taken up in the film *O fim do sem fim* (*End of the Endless*, with Beto Magalhães and Lucas Bambozzi, 2001), which documents trades and professions on the verge of extinction, and their practitioners, steadfastly resisting technological and cultural change. Shot in 1999, the film has a millennial feel, as the interviewees, most of whom are old, talk about the future both in social and in spiritual terms. They include a bell-ringer, a shoeshine, a lift operator and a lighthouse keeper, but also, with a reflexive nod to film and photography, a cinema usher and a street photographer who develops and prints pictures at the side of the road. More esoteric trades, including a prophet and a *benshi* (Japanese silent film narrator), contribute to the film's thesis that there is poetry in obsolescence.

The filmmakers reflect on extinction and preservation in their own trade by shooting on the near-obsolete gauges of Super-8 and 16mm, favoured by amateur and low-budget filmmakers, as well as digital video. Landscape is shown mainly in lyrical montages shot on grainy, handheld Super-8, often using superimposition, creating intimate, haptic spaces rather than wide vistas. Laura Marks (2000: 162) defines haptic visuality in terms of proximity:

> Haptic visuality is distinguished from optical visuality, which sees things from enough distance to perceive them as distinct forms in deep space: in other words how we normally conceive of vision. Optical visuality depends on a separation between the viewing subject and the object. Haptic looking tends to move over the surface of its object rather than to plunge into illusionistic depth, not to distinguish form as much as to discern texture. It is more inclined to move than to focus, more inclined to graze than to gaze.

The Super-8 footage seems tactile and close to the body, with its grainy texture, short focal length and handheld camerawork. *O fim do sem fim* draws on these aesthetic qualities to depict landscape from a subjective, embodied point of view as a piecemeal way of making sense of the world.

In his feature films, Guimarães often works on a larger scale, depicting landscape in a more spectacular manner, but this does not render it with more clarity or coherence – it is not mapped or allegorised. If anything, it becomes harder to see and understand. The very idea of landscape seems to invite self-conscious stylisation, based on the striking composition of a single, static frame, like a painting. The inclusion of a figure in the landscape can provide a way into it, and this is the strategy Guimarães deploys in *Andarilho* (*Drifter*, 2007), a documentary portrait of three men of the road. *Andarilho* was filmed on and around highways BR-251, BR-135 and BR-122 in the northeast of Minas Gerais. The emphasis on roads communicates the film's theme – the lives of those who pass through places, rather than dwelling in them – but despite its emphasis on travel, the film is concerned with the lifeworlds of its transitory subjects. There are two distinct spatial systems in the film, conveying the tension between the experience of place and the idea of landscape: sequences showing the three men speaking to an unseen interviewer or performing daily tasks by the side of the road or nearby are filmed in long or medium shot; scenic views, almost invariably centred on roads, are filmed mostly in extreme long shot, with a static camera, often using quite long takes.

The scenic views, like many landscape paintings, border on abstraction. The second sequence in the film consists of a long travelling shot moving down the highway in the dark, in which the sharp, bright road markings are almost all that can be seen. The composition evokes cinematic precedents including *Kiss Me Deadly* (Robert Aldrich, 1955) and *Lost Highway* (David Lynch, 1997). In other shots, heat haze and mirage are used to considerable effect, dissolving the road into an atmospheric blur or producing inverted reflections of people and vehicles, reminiscent of Bill Viola's painterly landscape video, *Chott El-Djerid* (1979). Shallow focus, distance and darkness are also used to simplify and abstract the image. The film closes with a shot of a straight mud track beside the winding highway, viewed from a raised and distant vantage point. It is hard to tell if a meaningful comparison between the two types of road is being suggested, or if it is simply an arresting visual image. The striking thing about these landscapes is how hard they are to read: either the image is ambiguous or in some way obscured, or, when we can see clearly, we are unsure what we are looking at and why. Roads dominate the film, but their importance is compositional rather than narrative – no information is given about where they lead, and the three men do not indicate that they are travelling towards particular destinations. The reddish soil by the sides of the road serves as a constant reminder of the rich mineral deposits in the region and the dominance of the extractive industries from which the state takes its name (Minas Gerais means 'general mines'). The massive trucks passing by at high speed point to the industrial forces that have shaped the landscape around the road, as, over the years, mining companies have moved into and out of the area, leaving in their wake abandoned mines and buildings, spoiled land, and new vegetation as nature returns. Although it is tempting to regard the landscape images in the film as overly stylised, it makes sense, given the location, to understand their strangeness as expressionistic renderings of the incoherence of the place itself.

In the sequences that document the ways that the three men live by the roadside, their surroundings are represented from their point of view, as spaces which can accommodate them to a greater or lesser extent. They explore and adapt features of the landscape, using a walking stick made from a tree branch or bathing in the washroom of a derelict petrol station. The space they inhabit could be described using Ingold's term, as a 'taskscape':

> Just as the landscape is an array of related features, so – by analogy – the taskscape is an array of related activities. [. . .] In short, the taskscape is to labour what the landscape is to land, and indeed what an ensemble of use-values is to value in general. (Ingold 1993: 158)

One of them dries his laundry on the ground in the sunshine, then swiftly and expertly packs it up into a roll that he carries on his back. Another pulls a cart from which he unpacks a shelter and even a small grill and a cooking pot. In one of the most interesting sequences a man climbs on a group of abandoned structures that resemble modernist sculpture or urban landscaping, adapting these ruins to make a habitable space for himself. In such sequences, Guimarães establishes the theme of the relationships between individuals and their immediate surroundings, familiar from his photography and video, and in fact some of the sequences could work as self-contained experimental videos. It is significant that the cinematography in these scenes adopts a smaller scale, as in Guimarães's 'sensitive landscapes'. One suspenseful scene, reminiscent of *Quarta-feira de cinzas*, uses extreme close-ups to show a grasshopper perilously crossing the road while trucks roar past, drawing attention to its precarious existence and also offering a metaphor for the drifters' circumstances.

The sequences depicting the men's everyday survival, like the *Gambiarras* photographs, show the ingenuity and practicality with which they inhabit the environment. The landscape views, which have a distinctly painterly or self-consciously cinematic aesthetic, situate them in a wider context in which they appear alienated and powerless. When the most resourceful of the drifters produces a tattered map and points to the road he has travelled, instead of locating him, the gesture makes him seem lost in a space that cannot be symbolised cartographically. Through an intermedial approach, Guimarães invokes two distinct ways of regarding landscape and place, using the tension between them to describe the situation of people for whom the world has no place, but who inhabit it nonetheless. The Messianic discourse of one of the men, who seems mentally disturbed, also frames the inhospitable landscape in a longer temporal perspective, pointing to questions about the future of the environment.

The theme of solitary survival in an inhospitable place is transposed to a very different milieu in Guimarães's first fiction feature, *O homem das multidões* (*Man of the Crowd*, with Marcelo Gomes, 2013), which is set in the mediatised landscape of the contemporary city. The film deals with a tenuous relationship between two alienated city-dwellers, who are represented in much the same way as the drifters, as figures isolated against a background that is often out of focus or abstracted in some way. Juvenal (Paulo André) is a train driver for the metro in Belo Horizonte and Margô (Sílvia Lourenço) is a train traffic controller. The two characters develop a tenuous friendship which seems like a possible romance, until Margô asks Juvenal to be a witness at her wedding to a man she met on the internet. The suggestion of a relationship resurfaces at the end of the film, when the marriage seems to have failed, although the passivity and singularity of both characters render it improbable. The film is inspired by a short story by Edgar Allan Poe, in which a man spends a night following a sinister looking stranger who wanders aimlessly through the busy streets of London, always alone in the crowd. In the film, Juvenal, the older of the two characters, is the man of the crowd, leading a solitary existence in close proximity to strangers; Margô is an updated version of him, equally lonely but connected to the world via electronic devices. The film's mise-en-scène associates Juvenal with windows, which enable him to observe the world from behind a barrier, but which also sometimes fill the screen with reflections, multiplying the crowd and confusing the image; Margô is associated with screens, which she uses at work, where she sits facing a bank of CCTV monitors, and in her leisure time, which seems to revolve almost entirely around screen-based activities, including feeding a virtual pet fish. The paradigmatic encounter between the two characters occurs when Juvenal, standing on a metro platform, looks up at the CCTV camera, and Margô, in the CCTV control room, zooms in to look back at him. This mediated meeting of their gazes encapsulates the just-missed quality of all of their encounters, and points towards a more general social malaise in a world of proliferating screens. Like its characters, the film privileges personal space over shared space and phenomenological perception over understanding, while gesturing towards a bigger picture that is symptomatically incoherent or illegible.

The film's landscape is, to a considerable extent, constituted by the frames and surfaces of windows and screens, pressing home the point that media technology has completely pervaded the environment. It has an unusual 1:1 aspect ratio that resembles an old Polaroid photograph or an Instagram post. Instead of cutting, the camera sometimes pans from side to side, following the characters like a surveillance camera. In this instance, the film is not informed by intermediality but actually formed by it: its world, which once again is visually disorienting, is composed to a large extent of other media, or seems to be, even when it is not. In one scene, when Margô walks past a series of windows in a restaurant, these momentarily appear like the screens that she faces every day in her job. The next scene begins with what looks like a close-up of her face, but turns out to be the screen of a computer running an application that shows users what they would look like with different haircuts. The prevalence of reflections and simulations in the mise-en-scène suggests a principle of connection other than authentic attachment: likeness. When Juvenal attends Margô's wedding, he gravitates towards her father, to whom he bears a striking likeness, although he is much younger. The idea of the double may have been suggested by Poe's story, in which there seems a distinct possibility that the protagonist, like a Borges character, is following an older version of himself. It generates an uncanny atmosphere despite the film's ostensibly naturalistic aesthetic, and points to the replacement of social bonds by logics of similitude and simulation. Despite its tentatively hopeful ending, the film is Guimarães's least optimistic representation of landscape, as its characters seem incapable of making a positive impact on their surroundings.

Surveying contemporary Latin American cinema, Jens Andermann posits the notion of an 'exhausted landscape', which at first glance might seem to be drained of political signification, but which gestures towards the historical conditions of a crisis in representation. Although it is not referenced directly, the notion of exhausted landscape surely comes from W. J. T. Mitchell, who describes landscape as 'an exhausted medium, no longer viable as a mode of artistic expression' (Mitchell 2002: 5). Andermann uses the term to explain

> the demise of landscape as a potential catalyst for an ethical and epistemological unsettling that might propel a 'change of view' (as in the cinematic ruralisms of the 1960s and 1970s, where coming face-to-face with rural otherness was expected to trigger an emergent revolutionary consciousness). (Andermann 2014: 59)

He analyses a group of films that attempt to reclaim the landscape image by undertaking a cognitive mapping of its conditions of emergence, with 'an archival self-consciousness' that simultaneously calls on and distances itself from images of landscape in modern film history. This is essentially a reflexive and intertextual strategy, positioning current films in an ironic relationship to their predecessors. Cao Guimarães responds to this same condition of historical exhaustion, but his approach is somewhat different. Rather than producing an intertextual cognitive mapping of the landscape image, he reconstructs it, intermedially, reaching outside of film history for inspiration. Drawing on the intimist potential of documentary photography and artists' video, forms which blur the distinction between the amateur and the professional, the personal and the public, he uses intermediality to articulate shifts in perspective and perception that favour spatial proximity, sensory engagement and smallness of scale. While this approach may be less radical than the allegorical landscapes of the 1960s and 1970s, its politics may be better suited to our times and to the question of whether and how human beings can continue to inhabit the landscapes that they have created.

Note

1. The quotation comes from an interview with the artist, in a video on the Galeria Nara Roesler website, available at <https://nararoesler.art/en/video/8/> (last accessed 20 January 2019).

References

Andermann, Jens (2014), 'Exhausted Landscapes: Reframing the Rural in Recent Argentine and Brazilian Films', *Cinema Journal*, 53:2, pp. 50–70.

Crary, Jonathan (1999), *Suspensions of Perception: Attention, Spectacle and Modern Culture*. Cambridge, MA: MIT Press.

Daniels, Stephen and Denis Cosgrove (eds) (1988), *The Iconography of Landscape*. Cambridge: Cambridge University Press.

Gabara, Esther (2008), *Errant Modernism: The Ethos of Photography in Mexico and Brazil*. Durham, NC, and London: Duke University Press.

Ingold, Tim (1993), 'The Temporality of the Landscape', *World Archaeology*, 25:2, pp. 152–74.

Lins, Consuelo (2007), 'Time and Device in Cao Guimarães' Films', Galeria Nara Roesler website, available at <http://www.caoguimaraes.com/wordpress/wp-content/uploads/2015/02/TimeandDevice_Consuelo.pdf> (last accessed 20 January 2019). Originally published as 'Tempo e dispositivo no documentário de Cao Guimarães', *Devires*, 4, pp. 118–27.

Marks, Laura U. (2000), *The Skin of the Film: Intercultural Cinema, Embodiment and the Senses*. Durham, NC, and London: Duke University Press.

Mendonça Filho, Kleber (2009), '*Viajo Porque Preciso, Volto Porque te Amo*', *CinemaScópio*, available at <http://cinemascopiocannes.blogspot.co.uk/2009/09/viajo-porque-preciso-volto-porque-te.html> (last accessed 20 January 2019).

Mitchell, W. J. T. (ed.) (2002), *Landscape and Power*, 2nd edn. Chicago: University of Chicago Press.

Montejo Navas, Adolfo (2013), 'Poetica molecular/Molecular Poesy', *Lápiz Revista Internacional de Arte*, pp. 54–75.

Moraes, Marcos (2006), 'Sensitive Landscape', Associação Cultural Videobrasil, available at <http://site.videobrasil.org.br/en/acervo/artistas/textos/99257> (last accessed 20 January 2019).

Moura, Rodrigo (2006), 'Photographing on the Leg', Galeria Nara Roesler website, available at <http://www.caoguimaraes.com/wordpress/wp-content/uploads/2015/02/article_04.pdf> (last accessed 20 January 2019).

Oricchio, Luiz Zanin (2003), 'The *Sertão* in the Brazilian Imaginary at the End of the Millennium', in L. Nagib (ed.), *New Brazilian Cinema*. London and New York: I. B. Tauris, pp. 139–56.

Picado, Benjamim and Consuelo Lins (2017), 'Dimensões da relação estética na obra fotográfica de Cao Guimarães', *Significação*, 44:47, pp. 278–97.

Sadek, Isis (2010), 'A Sertão of Migrants, Flight and Affect: Genealogies of Place and Image in Cinema Novo and Contemporary Brazilian Cinema', *Studies in Hispanic Cinemas*, 7:1, pp. 59–72.

Stam, Robert (1998), 'Hybridity and the Aesthetics of Garbage: The Case of Brazilian Cinema', in *Estudios Interdisciplinarios de América Latina y el Caribe*, 9:1, available at <http://www7.tau.ac.il/ojs/index.php/eial/article/view/1091> (last accessed 20 January 2019).

CHAPTER 3

'The most innocent film of the year': Comic Books, Sex and Cinema Marginal
Stefan Solomon

> It is very difficult to disassociate cinema from comics [. . .] Our background was basically cinema and comics. (Carneiro 2009)[1]
> João Callegaro

While connections between cinema and comics suggest themselves readily to viewer and reader alike, it is difficult to draw conclusive, generalised links between their forms. One may point intuitively to a family resemblance that suggests the obvious influence of the older drawn medium on the newer practice of capturing moving images, especially at the dawn of cinema, but the comparison is not so easily established. On the one hand, filmmakers of the silent era appear to have honed their craft without obvious assistance from the *fin de siècle* comic strip's formal arrangements of panels and gutters, images and text. On the other hand, the comic strip might have anticipated several of the formal narrative solutions that cinema would later adopt, thereby demonstrating its influence. Whatever the case, it is not possible to make such broad statements with any confidence.

It may be too strong a claim to suggest that comics played midwife at the birth of cinema; yet there is little doubt that the older medium would make its presence truly felt in filmmaking in the second half of the twentieth century, most obviously in the graduation of comic narratives to the screen. 'Comic-book movies were scarcely a genre in the studio era', as David Bordwell has observed, 'but they became a central one with the arrival of the blockbuster' (Bordwell 2006: 54). Many adaptations of comic-book titles certainly followed in the wake of *Superman: The Movie* (Richard Donner, 1978), but just prior to the era of big-budget productions in the United States, comics had already worked themselves into cinema across the globe in a variety of subtle and inventive ways. Comics were used as both a wry prop and an important part of the narrative in *Artists and Models* (1955), Frank Tashlin's deceptively funny exploration of American pop culture at mid-century. The panels of comic strips played an increasingly prominent part in Jean-Luc Godard's mises-en-scène for a stretch of his career extending from *Pierrot le fou* (1965) to *Tout va bien* (1972) (Morton 2009). And in *Ninja bugei-chō* (*Band of Ninja*, 1967), Nagisa Oshima's adaptation of the manga epic by Sanpei Shirato, static drawings are put into 'motion' by way of strategic movements of the camera across the page. These are but a few examples, and a fuller genealogy of postwar cinema and comics would also necessarily include Alain Resnais's lifelong interest in the medium: *The Inmates* and *The Monster Maker*, his two famous unrealised collaborations scripted by Marvel Comics' Stan Lee in the early 1970s; *L'An 01* (1973), the adaptation of Gébé's eponymous *Charlie Hebdo* comic strip by Resnais, Jacques Doillon and Jean Rouch; and *I Want to Go Home* (Resnais, 1989), a combination of live action and animation about – and written by – the American cartoonist Jules Feiffer (Patton and Shurts 1972; Durham 1998).

Such are the incursions of the world of comic books into the various cinematic new waves that swept across the globe from mid-century onwards, with the medium inveigling itself on to the screen by way of adaptation, aesthetic appropriation, or its metonymic connotations of mass culture and kitsch more broadly. And this was not a uniform phenomenon by any means: the above sample includes national variants – *manga* for Oshima, *bande dessinée* for Resnais and co. – and genuine transnational possibilities, as well as signs of the tentacular hegemony of those American superhero comics that comprised the so-called 'Golden' and 'Silver' ages of the form from the 1940s through to the 1970s: *Superman*, *Batman*, *Wonder Woman*, *The X-Men*, *The Amazing Spider-Man* and so on.

In Brazil, comic books would form an almost ubiquitous element in those films gathered together under the umbrella term Cinema Marginal. The particular manifestations of comics within Brazilian underground cinema of the late 1960s and 1970s suggest some of the same associations between the two media that emerged in other national cinemas during these decades. However, while Cinema Marginal's affinity with comic books is evidently part of its wider reaction against national cultures – especially as represented by its precursor, Cinema Novo – it is also worth attending to the specificities of comics in Brazilian films. Indeed, focusing on the precise details of comic art and its intermedial relationship with cinema provides a means of recalibrating our understanding of Brazilian – and global – film history.

This chapter will offer a survey of the connections between comics and Cinema Marginal before turning its attention to a case study that draws out some of the most interesting aspects of that relationship: Carlos Zéfiro's *catecismos*, the pornographic comics that circulated in Brazil from the mid-1950s until the early 1970s. Following a brief consideration of the history of Brazilian pornographic cinema, the *catecismos* will be analysed as a non-cinematic form of pornography that was capable of showing explicit sex before the cinema could, and which, in so doing, complicates the conventional historical evolution of national on-screen erotica from the *pornochanchadas* to hardcore films in the 1980s. Finally, this chapter will examine an earlier fictionalised representation of Zéfiro's work as depicted in João Callegaro's Cinema Marginal film *O pornógrafo* (*The Pornographer*, 1970). Here, we can see how the aesthetics of comics more broadly might offer a reinterpretation of the final sequence from Orson Welles's *The Lady from Shanghai* (1947), a paradigmatic moment that stands at the crossroads of the 'classical' and the 'modern' in traditional evolutionary models of film history.

COMIC BOOKS AND CINEMA MARGINAL

The history of comics in Brazil is a long and detailed one, and this chapter is far too brief to do justice to its complex twists and turns. However, it is worth pointing out at least some of the basic contours of the national comics history here, since this history also resonates with the trajectory of Brazilian cinema – and especially Cinema Marginal – in some respects. Just as Brazil's film industry would begin by importing American and European films in the silent era, would later attempt to emulate the success of Hollywood's studios with its own Vera Cruz and Atlântida Cinematográfica, and then would alternately repel and cannibalise the promises of foreign film production, so too would the nation's comics find their own way after long periods in thrall to United States models.

As Waldomiro Vergueiro has articulated it, Brazilian comics developed from the very beginning in dialectical relation to US comics, with foreign production enabling the access of many to comics, but also signifying 'barriers for the establishment of local comics' (Vergueiro 2009: 158). From the early transformation of the American character Buster Brown into the Brazilian boy Chiquinho, to the later syndication in Portuguese of titles like *The Phantom*, there was always a parasitical element in play ensuring the continued development of comics in the South American nation. Alongside this near unilateral relationship, however, were the appearance of imitations of famous American superheroes in a Brazilian vein and, more importantly, the development in Brazil of original narratives based on existing US comics that had been discontinued in the north because of a poor readership or for reasons of censorship. With the establishment of the United States Comics Code in 1954 putting a premature end to titles like EC Comics' *Tales from the Crypt* (1950–5), Brazil managed to capitalise on a space in the market, producing many local horror comics without restrictions on content (de Sá 2010: 181–7).

Cinema would also stand to benefit from this rise in local production. One of the most thoroughgoing interactions between cinema and horror comics can be discovered in the work of José Mojica Marins. His character, Zé do Caixão (Coffin Joe), would later find success away from the screen, becoming a multimedia entity thanks to the work of the prolific pulp writer Rubens Francisco Lucchetti (de Sá 2010: 197–204). Working in the opposite direction, Lucchetti (along with renowned artist Júlio Shimamoto) would go on to rework 'The Living Mummy' storyline from Marvel Comics' *Supernatural Thrillers* series (1972–5) into the six original issues of *A múmia viva* produced from 1977 to 1978; this would go on to inspire (indirectly) the script Lucchetti wrote for Ivan Cardoso's *O segredo da múmia* (*The Secret of the Mummy*, 1982).[2]

These are perhaps two of the most noteworthy exchanges between horror comics and Brazilian cinema that emerged from the late 1960s onwards, but a survey of the works associated with Cinema Marginal reveals further instances.[3] In part a reaction formation against Cinema Novo, Cinema Marginal negotiated the forces of cultural imperialism from the northern hemisphere, embracing all that was kitsch and bad taste from Hollywood, and reconstituting it to create a genuinely unique set of films that resisted simple classification. In line with their voracious appetite for foreign cultural products, many Cinema Marginal films abound with images and citations of American comic books, each of which serves a different function dependent on its appearance in the given film. The varied effects of comic books in Cinema Marginal films – both at the level of content and at the level of form – attest to the perennial tensions between cultural imperialism and local production, with the predominant appearances of American titles also supplemented by Brazilian appropriations of foreign comic aesthetics, and on rare occasions by original works from Brazil. Often, the incorporation of comics in such films also raises questions about the circulation of mass culture to Brazil from the United States, but also from Europe.

A case in point is Júlio Bressane's *Cara a cara* (*Face to Face*, 1967), a film that, in some ways, represents the transition from Cinema Novo to Cinema Marginal, and for which one of the momentary gestures away from the national culture involves the surprising sight of a comic strip in the mise-en-scène. In the scene in question, Luciana (Helena Ignez), the daughter of a corrupt politician who leads a life of luxury, is trying on a dress in a boutique. Here, she admires the wallpaper of the store's changing room, which has been repurposed from Jean-Claude Forest's comic *Barbarella*, smiling at a number of decontextualised frames from the original narrative (Figure 3.1).[4] The panels from the comic have been appropriated here as wallpaper, and out of sequential order, only one year after their publication. This is a title whose protagonist and publication history might in part offer an allegory of

Comic Books, Sex and Cinema Marginal 55

Figure 3.1 While trying on a dress, Luciana (Helena Ignez) is amused by a panel from Jean-Claude Forest's *Barbarella* (1962–4) in *Cara a Cara* (1967).

Luciana's own life: sexually liberated, enjoying her leisure time, a representative of a new generation of women (indeed, in the following scene Luciana's friend shows off a dress she bought coincidentally in imitation of Jane Fonda, who would not appear in Roger Vadim's adaptation of Forest's comic until a year later). Although it is not clear if she has made a connection between herself and the comics on the wall, the images and some of the scenarios can still provide instant amusement for Luciana.

Where this fleeting, chance encounter with the comic strip suggests the rapid recycling and adaptability of such images – from translated, readable literature one year to makeshift wallpaper the next – we also see the emergence of the exact same frame from *Barbarella* (albeit here in its Portuguese translation) in Rogério Sganzerla's short documentary made two years later, *HQ: História em Quadrinhos* (*Comics*, 1969).[5] *HQ* presents a ten-minute historical survey of comic art, focusing on works mostly from the United States, but also gesturing towards an international history of the form, especially as concerns Brazil. One of its many images is that frame lifted from *Barbarella* – by way of *Cara a Cara* – and its appearance, while surprising, makes sense, considering that Bressane and Sganzerla worked closely on their Belair Filmes project for several months in 1970, and went into exile together that same year. But the film also depicts comics from their very beginnings, including panels from – among others – *The Yellow Kid* (1895–8), *Dick Tracy* (1931–present), *Flash Gordon* (1934–2003) and *Terry and the Pirates* (1934–73), ending with images from Marshall McLuhan and Quentin Fiore's 1967 cult classic, *The Medium is the Massage*, a collage of photographs and text that incorporates comic book onomatopoeia (McLuhan and Fiore 1967).

Sganzerla was assisted on this short by Álvaro de Moya, a journalist and cartoonist who was one of the organisers of the First International Comics Exhibition in São Paulo in 1951 (the same year as the city's first Biennial).[6]

That exhibition had been motivated by a desire to prove that comics had attained the status of art, and while there was a case made for the autonomy of the comic book, there were also efforts to draw on the support of other forms of cultural expression, like literature and cinema; in the case of the latter, Will Eisner's famous comic strip *The Spirit* (1940–52) was submitted as a work that shared with its contemporary, *Citizen Kane* (Orson Welles, 1941), a certain 'expressionistic technique of lighting, framing and sound'.[7] Comics in Brazil were thus considered alongside other narrative and pictorial art forms. Just as in São Paulo in 1951 they had benefited from their association with those forms, comics were now able to return the favour, lending aspects of visual structure, narrative organisation and methods of characterisation to works of Cinema Marginal.

While notably informing the work of artists like Antonio Dias, Raymundo Colares, Anna Maria Maiolino and Antonio Manuel in the mid- to late 1960s, for example, structural elements of comics – which equally intersected with Soviet constructivism and the rectangular compositions of the De Stijl artists – also announced themselves in the poster art and title credits of films like *Adultério à brasileira* (*Adultery Brazilian Style*, Pedro Carlos Rovai, 1969), *Os monstros de Babaloo* (*The Babaloo Monsters*, Elyseu Visconti, 1970), *O Capitão Bandeira contra o Dr. Moura Brasil* (Antonio Calmon, 1971) and *Prata Palomares* (André Faria, 1971) (da Silva 2008). In another dimension entirely, comics would also inspire various characters and scenes, such as the live-action parodies of Batman and Hal Foster's Tarzan in *Meteorango Kid: o herói intergalático* (André Luiz Oliveira, 1970).[8]

Finally, in the same year that he made *HQ*, Rogério Sganzerla's fascination with comics was also in evidence in *A mulher de todos* (*Everyone's Woman*, 1969), a film in which the villainous Doktor Plirtz is not only a silver-mining magnate, but also owns a radio station and a comic-book trust. Plirtz, who is known as a 'collector of people' as well as of comics, is introduced next to a copy of *Cavaleiro negro* (a Portuguese translation of Marvel's *Black Knight*), and later shares the frame with an employee who is reading the *Tales of Suspense* series split between stories of Iron Man and Captain America. Late in the film, in a scene that clearly rehearses the film's anthropophagic digestion of foreign cultural objects, Plirtz is seen voraciously eating an issue of *Batman*, then rising out of the ocean with a copy of *Superman*.

From the brief sketch above, it is possible to trace some of the historical transactions between the two media in Brazil, and to have a sense of the stakes in both the 1960s and the 1970s. In the following section, I will explore a case study that points up the differences between each medium, especially with respect to the possibilities of visual representation in both cinema and comics. As a particular form of comic art that was native to Brazil,

Carlos Zéfiro's pornographic *catecismos* stand at the crux of these issues, and their intermedial connections to the national cinema derive both from their graphic sexual content and from their particular formal properties as comics. Before considering these connections, it will be necessary to offer a very brief overview of sex on screen in Brazil in that historical moment.

BRAZILIAN PORNOGRAPHY AND THE *CATECISMOS*

In Brazilian cinema, the increasingly explicit nature of pornography during the years of the dictatorship (1964–85) seems clear: such a trajectory runs from the first female full-frontal nudity shot – Norma Bengell's horribly humiliating exposure on the beach in *Os cafajestes* (*The Unscrupulous Ones*, Ruy Guerra, 1962) – to depictions of unclothed escorts – Odete Lara and Bengell again in *Noite vazia* (*Men and Women*, Walter Hugo Khouri, 1964) – to the more casual deployments of nudity in Cinema Marginal and in the *pornochanchadas*, the softcore sex comedies that descended from the *chanchadas*, the musical comedies that had flourished until the 1950s. These films, which mixed eroticism with conservative morality, rose to prominence because of 'the introduction of compulsory screen quotas' (Dennison 2009: 232) in Brazil, and were 'hypocritically tolerated and even encouraged' (Johnson and Stam 1995: 405) by the censors in what became tantamount to the repressive desublimation of sex under the military dictatorship. Such an evolution would reach its logical endpoint with the realisation of what Melissa Schindler (channelling Jean-Claude Bernardet) contends was 'the pornochanchada's only revolutionary promise', which 'lay in its potential to say something graphic about sex'; indeed, sexual suggestiveness became fully explicit in the hardcore films of the 1980s (Schindler 2014: 326). At this 'penultimate' stage, the anthology film *A noite das taras* (*The Night of Perversions*, 1980) was able to show more explicit (although still simulated) sex scenes, while Ody Fraga's *Fome de sexo* (*Sex Hunger*, 1981) depicted real penetrative sex without the money shot, offering a kind of 'contained' version of pornography (Ramos 1987: 439). From here, Brazil's entry into the hardcore film market became something of an inevitability, even accounting for 'almost three-quarters of film production' in the country by 1985 (Shaw and Dennison 2007: 99).

To a degree, this linear historical narrative of Brazilian cinema's creeping pornification under the military dictatorship is more or less accurate when confined to the cinema as a discrete entity. And yet a cursory reading of the parallel history of another pornographic form – comics – reveals a more intricate picture. During the 1950s and 1960s, a public servant named Alcides Aguiar Caminha – operating under the pseudonym Carlos Zéfiro – produced hundreds of erotic minicomics depicting crudely drawn casual sexual encounters between anonymous men and women (and sometimes between men).⁹ These comics, which were distributed clandestinely, came to be known ironically as the *catecismos* (catechisms) – in part inspired by the so-called *Tijuana Bibles* of the US, which also circulated outside of any official market – were hand drawn by Zéfiro, and copied on inexpensive vegetable paper for mass distribution. Each *catecismo* (like its Catholic counterpart) was one-quarter of letter page size – so that they could be easily hidden from view – and featured 24 or 32 separate panels, with each occupying a single page (except in very rare instances of experimentation) (Nazareth 2017: 35).

According to different sources, Zéfiro may have produced anywhere between 300 and 900 *catecismos* over his career (Nazareth 2017: 34–5). Although he would sometimes recycle materials from elsewhere – from *fotonovelas* and from comic strips and supplements in the Brazilian daily newspapers (37–40) – and would even reuse some of his own figures, the potential monotony of the narrative form was belied by the general atmosphere of discovery or of a 'first time' in each separate text (Barros 1987: 26). Innovation and transgression were coupled with tradition and repetition: as Vergueiro has summarised the genre, the *catecismos* appealed to their ('hypothetically male') readers by combining graphic images of trysts – replete with copious amounts of male and female nudity and close-ups of genital contact – with a certain respect for 'Brazilian family values', such as gentlemanly conduct, seduction as opposed to violence or force, and an observance of the incest taboo (Vergueiro 2009: 163).¹⁰

The stories, often adopting a first-person narrative perspective, would customarily follow a man who 'meets a woman, flirts with her during the first eight to ten pages of the story, takes her to an appropriate place, and has sex with her in a variety of manners' (Vergueiro 2001: 74). For this reason, Zéfiro's comics would also come to be known as *revistinhas de sacanagem* – literally, 'little pornographic magazines', but perhaps more accurately, given their structure, *sacanagem* here might refer to non-traditional sexual acts, often conducted in a sequence. As one commentator points out, 'sacanagem starts with oral sex, goes on to anal sex, and all the ways and proportions and positions that you can find to satisfy your sexual fantasies' (Linger 1992: 141). More particularly as regards the *catecismos*, which begin with scenes of flirtation and seduction before moving to the iterations of different sex positions, the sequential movements of *sacanagem* that unfold over the comic's panels ultimately offer the promise of revealing all by the end.

As many scholars have asserted, comics and cinema share a great deal in terms of their modes of expression, with both mediums articulating their narratives in a sequential series of framed images. While there is no simple equivalence between the cinematic shot (or the photogram) and the panel of a comic strip, the visual similarities between comic books and film storyboards have also given credence to the idea of a certain degree of continuity between the two. In spite of the technical spatio-temporal divergences between comics and cinema – the succession of images in the former distinguishing itself from the 'system of co-presence' (Beaty 2011: 108) in the latter – the reciprocity of these mediums as regards their shared sense of a particular visual syntax (including certain ideas governing framing, angles and lighting) continues to inform a widespread perception of commonality (see also Rowe 2016).

Whatever the precise chains of influence, it is difficult to read the *catecismos* – like many comics before them – without one eye on the grammar of cinema, given their regular sequences of establishing shots, two-shots and close-ups. Yet more specifically, as suggested by the increasingly explicit sequential operations of *sacanagem*, Zéfiro's comics also mimic – and may have been the inspiration for – the progressively more revealing motions of pornography on screen: just as pornographic cinema, in its 'quest for greater knowledge of the truth of pleasure', moves through different stages of representation – in Linda Williams's taxonomy the 'genital show', the 'genital event' and the 'money shot' – so too do the *catecismos* unveil their erotic encounters in a series of intensifying panel images (Williams 1989: 181–2).[11]

While the *pornochanchadas* of the 1970s may have developed for the screen the same kinds of scenarios offered up by Zéfiro, and would follow a similar process of sexual exposure up to a point, they could never hope to approximate the level of graphic content of the *catecismos*. As such, the signal intermedial achievement of Zéfiro's works as regards their pornographic content is to point up the limits of the visible in cinema, the medium apparently far better equipped to realise his narratives on mimetic grounds: what is offered by the *catecismos* as comic books is nothing less than Brazilian cinematic pornography *avant la lettre*. With this claim in mind, it will be worth briefly observing how they continued to influence the national cinema even after restrictions had been lifted on the depictions of explicit sex.

In the mid-1980s, a decade in which the Brazilian market was flooded with explicit porn cinema, Zéfiro's works were used as source texts for a hardcore film, *Os anos dourados da sacanagem* (*The Golden Years of Pornography*, Paulo Antonione, 1986). After the opening credits – which feature images from the *catecismos*, and which confirm that the film is 'based on the work of Carlos Zéfiro' – we see a young boy at home, left to watch cartoons as his mother leaves for a night out. As soon as she exits the house, however, the boy begins watching a pornographic video.[12] Suddenly, the boy's grandfather arrives home, catching his grandson watching the film. He takes a *Biblia sagrada* (Holy Bible) from the cabinet, with the seeming intention of lecturing

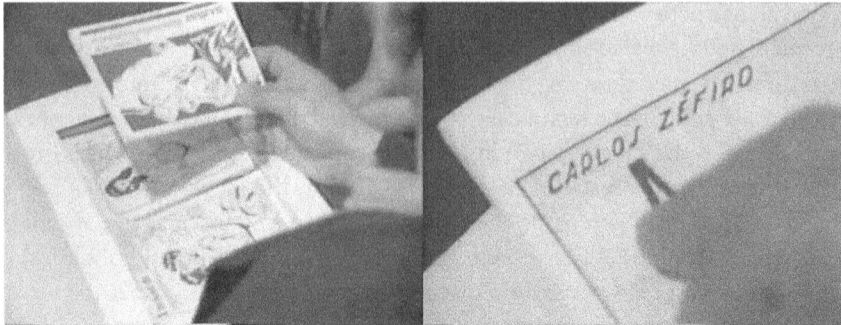

Figure 3.2 A sample of Carlos Zéfiro's *catecismos* concealed inside a bible in *Os anos dourados da sacanagem* (1986).

the boy, but opens the book to reveal that its hollowed-out pages contain nothing less than copies of Zéfiro's *catecismos* (Figure 3.2).

There is nothing new in the boy's pornographic explorations, his grandfather assures him: the live-action porn seen on his VHS tape was antedated three decades earlier by comics whose narratives and framing had much in common with their new media descendants. The film's ensuing episodes all derive from the Zéfiro materials, but result in a supreme irony. Instead of returning to his pornographic movie, the boy now reads the *catecismos* and imagines, in his mind's eye, the hand-drawn figures on the page not as cartoons but as living people engaged in real sex acts: sex acts which are then shown to viewers of *Os anos dourados da sacanagem*. Ultimately, then, while the boy substitutes the 'cold' medium for the 'hot', the alluring sketches of the *catecismos* for his videotape and its moving images of real sex, the viewers of Antonione's film are never denied the scopic pleasures of such scenes.[13]

In this instance, Zéfiro's comics would appear to have been completely superannuated by the newfound explicit possibilities of hardcore pornography. And yet the film seems to defer to its forebear by incorporating the comics wholesale in its narrative structure, thus generating the following historical paradox: the older illustrated form is here both thoroughly ahead of its time and inescapably juvenile in appearance, while the new pornographic media are more technically sophisticated and yet – especially in this case, as they seek to adapt the *catecismos* – are completely derivative in narrative and formal terms. Here, the intermedial tensions between comics and cinema, as triangulated by pornography, suggest that graphic representations of sex in Brazilian culture did not emerge along a linear trajectory, but are the result of complex historical exchanges between different artistic and media forms that transpired over the course of many years.

O PORNÓGRAFO

As the filmmaker João Callegaro once observed in an interview, the formerly illicit nature of the *catecismos* was inevitably appropriated in the 1970s as 'the bourgeoisie took over everything', and nudity became acceptable in magazines like *Saúde* and *Ele Ela*, both established by the publishing house Abril. According to Callegaro, while Zéfiro stopped producing new *catecismos* in this decade, his work had nevertheless laid the foundations for the cinema of the Boca do Lixo,[14] and of all of the *pornochanchadas* that – unlike their comic book predecessors – could be released in broad daylight: 'If you think about it, the *catecismos* were the origin of porn in Boca – the softcore porn it had first, the *pornochanchada*, had a lot to do with Zéfiro, because everyone read him.'[15] Before the possibility of photographic and cinematic nudity, sex had to be illustrated and read, and in this regard Zéfiro's work was key.

But aside from their skewering of traditional historiographies of Brazilian audiovisual pornography in terms of their content, the *catecismos* as comic books also exerted a formal influence on cinema. There was a brief suggestion of this in a piece published in the pressbook for the omnibus film *As libertinas* (João Callegaro, Antônio Lima, Carlos Reichenbach, 1968), in which Callegaro announces the arrival of the *Cinema cafajeste*. This cinema, as the author points out, adopts, among other things, 'the aesthetics of the *teatro de revista*, the barbershop conversations, and the pornographic magazines', as well as 'the language of the *Notícias Populares*, of *Luta Democrática*, and of 'the "specialised" magazines (in other words: Carlos Zéfiro)' (Callegaro 1968).[16] The influence of the author of the *catecismos* would be even more palpable in Callegaro's single feature film, *O pornógrafo*, which stages a speculative vision of Zéfiro's reach in the world of magazines, showing images of the comics themselves, but also offering a more technical intermedial connection between cinema and the *catecismos*.[17]

O pornógrafo is centred on Miguel Metralha, a lowly writer who is fired from his position at a gastronomic magazine (*Comer Mais*), but then manages to find employment at a pornographic publication, and soon takes over after his boss dies of a heart attack. In league with his colleague (who bears the homophobic homonym Peter Aster), Miguel improves his company's fortunes by way of tapping into the new market of *entendidos* – a slang term denoting a middle-class gay identity that arose in the late 1960s (Green 1999: 191–2) – offering the innovation of gay content so as to keep pace with the American competition. However, these changes are deemed an affront to public morality by Madame Rosalia, the owner of the magazine; in an increasingly bizarre plot, both Miguel and Madame Rosalia hire the same assassin to eliminate their respective rival, and each is left dead by the end. A delirious mixture of Welles, Godard and film noir, and inspired by the title of Shohei Imamura's *Erogotoshitachi* (*The Pornographers*, 1966), *O pornógrafo* features insert shots from studio films like *The Public Enemy* (William A. Wellman, 1931) and *Little Caesar* (Mervyn LeRoy, 1931), which emerge throughout so as to ground Miguel's existence in his consumption of popular images and the identification with certain character types: indeed, Stênio Garcia in the lead role models his appearance quite explicitly on Marlon Brando's in *The Wild One* (László Benedek, 1953).

Aside from its Hollywood reference points, Callegaro's interest in comic books is foregrounded in the film's poster, designed by the painter Mixel Gantus: a parody of *MAD* magazine's Alfred E. Neuman, here blended with the film's protagonist, Miguel, exclaiming that this is 'the most innocent film of the year', the equivalent of the magazine's original catchphrase of indifference: 'what, me worry?'[18] The film's more sustained reference to comics, however, is to the *catecismos*. Miguel reads Zéfiro's work, but makes the complaint to a friend that the stories are always the same, and that there is little imagination involved. He suggests that it is possible to offer more interesting developments in each of the stories (one of which has a queer narrative angle), instead of repeating the same formula, and so creates his own comic in Zéfiro's style, which proves a success when he gives copies to his friends.

Again, as with the appearance of the *Barbarella* panels in *Cara a cara*, the images from Zéfiro's comics here are afforded very little screen time, so that while the pornographic nature of the images is clear, it is almost impossible to read the speech bubbles and captions. The editing of the scenes featuring the comics almost appears to echo the same kind of furtiveness with which Zéfiro's works were originally consumed by readers, printed as they were at a size small enough to be enveloped by larger books, thus hiding their lewd contents (as is evident in *Os anos douradas da sacanagem*, and in the first sight of Zéfiro's work in Callegaro's film, where one of the *catecismos* is encased in the respectable popular magazine *Fatos e Fotos*).[19]

Given the film's own hesitation to disclose the contents of the *catecismos* fully on screen, it is not entirely surprising that, although *O pornógrafo* draws inspiration from Zéfiro's contributions to comic art and to liberated sexual representation, the final imprint of comics on the film is not a connection with pornography at all, but a deceptively clever mediation of the closing sequence of Orson Welles's *The Lady from Shanghai*. In that earlier film, the sequence in question is the famous shootout that takes place in the Magic Mirror Maze, between Welles's trusting naïf, Michael O'Hara, Rita Hayworth's *femme fatale*, Elsa Bannister, and her husband, played by Everett Sloane. The venue in which this climactic showdown takes place is the objective correlative to

Figure 3.3 Elsa Bannister (Rita Hayworth) attempts to explain her actions in the funhouse hall of mirrors in *The Lady from Shanghai* (1947).

Elsa's duplicitous character, an infinite play of reflective surfaces designed to attract and confuse the sincere Michael (Figure 3.3).

But this incredible mise-en-abyme – an intensified version of the deep-focus mirror images seen in *Citizen Kane* – also suggested to major voices in film philosophy a laying bare of the cinematic apparatus itself. For Gilles Deleuze (1989: 70), the scene represented 'a perfect crystal image' in which the actuality of the characters was absorbed by the virtuality of their proliferating mirror images, such that 'the character is no more than one virtuality among others.'[20] For Alain Badiou (2013: 58), meanwhile, it formed nothing less than the hinge separating classical from modern: against the 'transparent propaganda' of the former, here Welles constructed a scene in which 'the way the image was organized could be perceived'. In each of these readings, the singular quality of the scene lies in its novelty of making visible what was customarily hidden from sight in classical filmmaking, advancing cinema into new territory.

Callegaro's version of the scene offers a more modest and lighthearted vision. He too accentuates the medial self-awareness that was present in Welles's film; however, by incorporating the unique formal peculiarities of the comic book, he also raises a question about the provenance of such a defamiliarising gesture in cinema alone. He transposes Welles's funhouse to the Boca do Lixo area, and while the scene is clearly intended as a parody of its forebear, here the mirrors also allegorise the tissue of allusions that has spread itself throughout the film, one in which even Zéfiro's work is appropriated. *O pornógrafo* closes with Miguel's death at the hands of an assassin, which initially is foreshadowed in a fine passage of cross-cutting between Callegaro's footage and images from the final sequence from *Angels with Dirty Faces* (Michael Curtiz, 1938) in which James Cagney's proud gangster is escorted to his fate in the electric chair.

But the scene fittingly ends with a tribute to comic books: in an unprecedented move, the screen splits into four equal frames, with two of the squares playing images from earlier in the film, the third showing the death we have just witnessed, and the last depicting the narrative present as the killer leaves the carnival. It is possible here to view all four scenes at once, or at least to shift focus between each of the four as they take place. Taking its lead both from Welles's hall of mirrors and from the comic-book form, the scene reproduces multiples of the same character from different angles, and then of the same character at different points in the narrative. What we have is not exactly akin to the simultaneous panels of a comic book, as each of the four scenes plays out and then freezes in turn, with the word 'Fim' ('End') emerging to signal the closure of each one (Figure 3.4).

The quadruple split-screen effect of *O pornógrafo* at first blush seems to pay superficial homage to Welles, a final tongue-in-cheek gag in a film that does not take itself very seriously. And yet there is more to be said about this strategy, considering that its combination with the citation of *The Lady from Shanghai* amounted to what Jairo Ferreira (2016: 104) would call a 'perfect remake' of the sequence. On the one hand, Callegaro makes even more obvious the defamiliarisation effect of Welles's film for his own viewers by openly referencing the mirror sequence – and so reminding us of the pastiche tendencies of *O pornógrafo* – and then by converting the creative elegance of Welles's multiple reflective surfaces in the mise-en-scène – with their confusions of actual and virtual, reality and construction – into the far more jarring formal division of the film frame. On the other hand, this shift to a split screen is specifically motivated by the subject matter of Callegaro's film – comic books – such that the structure of the comics page triangulates the relationship between *O pornógrafo* and *The Lady from Shanghai*.

Although initially drawn to the single-page panels of the *catecismos*, the citation of Welles prompts Callegaro to consider a more unique formal property of the comic book as the foundation for his split-screen finale: the layout of a sequential narrative in which temporally distinct segments

Figure 3.4 The life and death of Miguel Metralha (Stênio Garcia) depicted across four comic-book panels in the final sequence of *O pornógrafo* (1970).

can be viewed simultaneously. Here, in the film's presentation of a temporally fragmented multiframe, the end credits shot mimics that formal effect of comics that distributes different chronological moments of a narrative across the page as separate panels, determining that – as Scott McCloud (1993: 100) has famously argued – 'time and space are one and the same'.

The Lady from Shanghai might suggest an innovative modernising of standard modes of cinematic vision, replacing the edits of cross-cutting by delegating them to the reflective surfaces of the mise-en-scène. But in its intermedial gesture away from cinema itself, *O pornógrafo* submits that comic art already has a stake in such a manoeuvre, presupposing the refracted images of Welles's film as the normative layout of the comic strip. While for Deleuze and Badiou the Wellesian hall of mirrors is supposed to have revealed to its spectators something obscured from view in classical cinema (that is, the mechanisms of production themselves), then comics had long habituated their readers to something similar in their repeated arrangement of multiple images on the same page.

In their representations on the screen, Carlos Zéfiro's *catecismos* suggest an intermedial tension between cinema and comics, at the levels of both content and form. Historically, the drawn pornographic content of Zéfiro's work precedes the visibility of real sex in Brazilian cinema, offering a different perspective on the traditional perception of increasingly explicit depictions of sex in the nation from the *pornochanchadas* to hardcore films. In João Callegaro's *O pornógrafo*, the *catecismos* are at the centre of the narrative, but are also formally folded into the film's final shot, which reimagines a key sequence of modern film history in kinship with a technique customarily associated with comics. By exploring the intermedial connections between a very particular phenomenon in Brazilian comics, and its reverberations in both pornographic cinema and film history more generally, it is possible to reconceive of the different historical trajectories of Brazilian cinema, erotic cinema and modern cinema itself.

Notes

1. 'É muito difícil dissociar o cinema dos quadrinhos [. . .] A nossa formação foi basicamente de cinema e quadrinhos' (translation by the author).
2. Alongside the Argentine artist Rodolfo Zalla, Lucchetti would also go on to write an adaptation of the film as a comic of the same name (also released in 1982). Cardoso mentions that this crossover represented a rarity in Brazilian film history, an honour he shared only with Mojica (Remier 2008: 286).
3. The mutually beneficial exchanges between cinema and comics in Brazil, often leveraged so as to capitalise on the popularity of a particular character, had begun even earlier: in the 1950s, the comic book adaptations *Oscarito e Grande Otelo* and *Mazzaropi* had carried the eponymous screen comedians to fame in another medium.
4. While the comic was originally published and collected in France from 1962 to 1964, the edition on display here is the English translation, published in the US in *Evergreen Review* from 1965 to 1966.
5. The film was screened in Brazilian cinemas in tandem with Pier Paolo Pasolini's *Teorema* (1968) (de Moya 2010: 53).
6. De Moya would later go on to make the hardcore film *A b . . . profunda* (*Deep Ass*, 1984), a parody of the classic *Deep Throat* (Gerard Damiano, 1972), under the pseudonym Geraldo Dominó (Schindler 2014).
7. '[*The Spirit*] era, curiosamente, similar ao *Citizen Kane*, de Orson Welles em técnica expressionista da luz, enquadrações e do som' (de Moya 1977: 68) (translation by the author).
8. In this vein we could also include the later *Superman* parody *SuperOutro* (1989), directed by Edgard Navarro, a figure first associated with the nationwide Super-8 movement of the 1970s.
9. Zéfiro was by no means the only author of *catecismos*, but was so well known that his name became synonymous with the genre. Zéfiro's true identity was

revealed in 1991, when he outed himself in an interview with Brazilian *Playboy* (Kfouri 1991). In the mid-1950s, Zéfiro (credited as Caminha) would contribute to the compositions of samba songs for Nelson Cavaquinho, including 'Notícia' (1955), 'Capital do samba' (1957) and 'A flor e o espinho' (1957) (Nazareth 2017: 74).

10. This is a paradox, too, that framed the critical re-evaluation of Zéfiro's legacy in the 1980s, when his work was no longer considered particularly risqué. In her important reading of this period, Erika Cardoso (2013) points out that the artist's reputation contained certain tensions that came to light during the decade: for the critics evaluating Zéfiro's work, the *catecismos* managed to encompass at once a conservative, retrograde attitude towards sex and gender relations, a modicum of progress as concerns male (not female) homosexuality, and the evocation of a time of innocence and naïvety concerning sexual representation and knowledge.

11. In an essay on Japanese pornographic comics for women readers, Deborah Shamoon (2004) has considered what Williams calls an aesthetic of 'maximum visibility' in relation to drawn pornography, which, in her case study, can achieve what is not visible even in hardcore cinema.

12. It is important to note that while the child actor himself might not technically have viewed the sex acts depicted in the film, the fact remains that this is a pornographic film featuring a child.

13. The short film *A desforra da titia* (*Auntie's Revenge*, Eduardo Quirino and Reinaldo Pinheiro, 1995) offers a live action reimagining of scenes from the *catecismos*, but since it is not a pornographic film, it substitutes images from Zéfiro's work in place of actual sex. Available at <http://portacurtas.org.br/filme/?name=a_desforra_da_titia> (last accessed 1 July 2020).

14. 'Boca do Lixo' or 'Mouth of Garbage' refers to an area of central São Paulo that lent its name to a cycle of films made in this part of the city during the dictatorship. Including *A Margem* (Ozualdo Candeias, 1967) and *O Bandido da Luz Vermelha* (Rogério Sganzerla, 1968), they focused on the denigrated members of society and were often erotic or violent in nature.

15. 'Se pensar bem, Os Catecismos foram a origem do pornô da Boca – o pornô softcore que teve no início, a pornochanchada, teve muito a ver com o Zéfiro, porque todo mundo lia' (Carneiro 2009) (translated by the author). Melissa Schindler (2014: 326) has similarly pointed out that *pornochanchadas* were not – as José Carlos Avellar has argued – 'born' with the advent of censorship in 1969, but have a much deeper history, employing 'decades-old narrative and cinematic tropes, such as those used by Brazilian and Italian *chanchadas*, musicals, stock characters, and parody'.

16. The reference to Zéfiro is not included in the version of this text cited in Ferreira (2016: 101).

17. A disclaimer in the opening credits assures viewers that 'any resemblance to persons living or dead, real or imagined, is purely coincidental, for which we are not responsible' ('Qualquer semelhança com pessoas vivas ou mortas, reais ou

imaginárias é mera coincidência, pela qual não nos responsabilizamos') (translation by the author).
18. *MAD* magazine was created in the United States in 1952, and a Brazilian version began publication in 1974. Copies of the English-language edition can be spotted on a newsstand in Sganzerla's short *Documentário* (1966).
19. In slight contrast to the brief displays of nudity in *O pornógrafo*, 'Ana' – Callegaro's contribution to *As Libertinas* – features a three-minute-long take of a striptease. As Reichenbach points out, this was in homage to the Brazilian film *Superbeldades* (Konstantin Tkaczenko, 1964), which, surprisingly for the period, was shot in Eastmancolor and comprises ten unique sequences of different full-frontal stripteases (Lyra 2007: 81–2).
20. As Seung-hoon Jeong (2012: 216) has demonstrated, in Deleuze's reading the mirrors – which resemble 'quasi-filmstrips' – create a 'total indiscernibility between the actual villain and his virtual doubles', and that by condensing a shot and its reverse shot in the same image, have the effect of 'continuously deranging the classical suture system'.

REFERENCES

Badiou, Alain (2013), 'Reference Points for Cinema's Second Modernity', in *Cinema*, texts selected and introduced by Antoine de Baecque, trans. Susan Spitzer. Cambridge and Malden, MA: Polity Press, pp. 58–63.
Barros, Octacílio D'Assunção (1987), *O quadrinho erótico de Carlos Zéfiro*. Rio de Janeiro: Record.
Beaty, Bart (2011), 'Introduction', *Cinema Journal*, 50:3, Spring, pp. 106–10.
Bordwell, David (2006), *The Way Hollywood Tells it: Story and Style in Modern Movies*. Berkeley and Los Angeles: University of California Press.
Callegaro, João (1968), 'Nasce o cinema cafajeste', in Pressbook for *As Libertinas* (1968). Available in the MAM-Rio de Janeiro collection.
Cardoso, Erika (2013), 'O pornógrafo ingênuo: Carlos Zéfiro entre a história e a memória', in *XXVII Simpósio Nacional de História*. Natal, RN: Anais Electrônicos, pp. 1–13, available at <https://anpuh.org.br/uploads/anais-simposios/pdf/2019-01/1548874917_0646b6b5c8451390998b1a574db951a7.pdf> (last accessed 1 July 2020).
Carneiro, Gabriel (2009), 'Entrevista com João Callegaro Parte 3: *Boca do Lixo* e *O Pornógrafo*', Dossiê João Callegaro, *Revista Zingu!*, 35, September, available at <http://revistazingu.blogspot.com/2009/09/djc-entrevista-3.html> (last accessed 1 July 2020).
da Silva, Simone Albertino (2008), *O design de cartazes no cinema marginal e na pornochanchada*. MSc thesis, Pontifícia Universidade Católica do Rio de Janeiro, available at <https://www.maxwell.vrac.puc-rio.br/colecao.php?strSecao=resultado&nrSeq=12359@1> (last accessed 1 July 2020).
de Moya, Álvaro (1977), *Shazam!* São Paulo: Perspectiva.
de Moya, Álvaro (2010), 'The Eighth Global Art or I Can Smell the Aroma of Curry', in Joel Pizzini (ed.), *Ocupação Sganzerla*. São Paulo: Instituto Itaú Cultural, pp. 48–53.
de Sá, Daniel Serravalle (2010), *Brazilian Horror: Zé do Caixão in the Multimedia Work of José*

Mojica Marins. PhD thesis, University of Manchester, available at <https://ethos.bl.uk/OrderDetails.do?uin=uk.bl.ethos.525674> (last accessed 1 July 2020).

Deleuze, Gilles (1989), *Cinema 2: The Time-Image*, trans. Hugh Tomlinson and Robert Galeta. Minneapolis: University of Minnesota Press.

Dennison, Stephanie (2009), 'Sex and the Generals: Reading Brazilian Pornochanchada as Sexploitation', in Victoria Ruétalo and Dolores Tierney (eds), *Latsploitation, Exploitation Cinemas, and Latin America*. New York and London: Routledge, pp. 230–44.

Durham, Carolyn A. (1998), *Double Takes: Culture and Gender in French Films and Their American Remakes*. Lebanon, NH: University of New England Press.

Ferreira, Jairo (2016), *Cinema de Invenção*, 3rd edn. Rio de Janeiro: Beco do Azougue.

Green, James N. (1999), *Beyond Carnival: Male Homosexuality in Twentieth-Century Brazil*. Chicago, IL, and London: University of Chicago Press.

Jeong, Seung-hoon (2012), 'The Surface of the Object: Quasi-Interfaces and Immanent Virtuality', in David Martin-Jones and William Brown (eds), *Deleuze and Film*. Edinburgh: Edinburgh University Press, pp. 210–26.

Johnson, Randal and Robert Stam (1995), *Brazilian Cinema*, expanded edn. New York: Columbia University Press.

Kfouri, Juca (1991), 'O fim de 30 anos de mistério', *Playboy*, 17:196, November, pp. 94–6, 159.

Linger, Daniel Touro (1992), *Dangerous Encounters: Meanings of Violence in a Brazilian City*. Stanford, CA: Stanford University Press.

Lyra, Marcelo (2007), *Carlos Reichenbach: o cinema como razão de viver*, 2nd edn. São Paulo: Imprensa Oficial.

McCloud, Scott (1993), *Understanding Comics: The Invisible Art*. New York: HarperCollins.

McLuhan, Marshall and Quentin Fiore (1967), *The Medium is the Massage: An Inventory of Effects*. Harmondsworth: Penguin.

Morton, Drew (2009), 'Godard's Comic Strip Mise-en-Scène', *Senses of Cinema*, 53, December, available at <http://sensesofcinema.com/2009/feature-articles/godards-comic-strip-mise-en-scene/> (last accessed 1 July 2020).

Nazareth, Rafael Santos Degenring Fernandes (2017), *Zéfiro ontem e hoje – narrativa, autoria e ressignificação dos catecismos de Carlos Zéfiro*. MA thesis, Pontifícia Universidade Católica do Rio de Janeiro.

Patton, Phil and Sharon Shurts (1972), 'Alain Resnais: From Marienbad to the Bronx', *The Harvard Crimson*, 14 April, available at <https://www.thecrimson.com/article/1972/4/14/alain-resnais-from-marienbad-to-the/> (last accessed 1 July 2020).

Ramos, José Maria Ortiz (1987), 'O cinema brasileiro contemporâneo', in Fernão Ramos (ed.), *História do cinema brasileiro*. São Paulo: Art Editora, pp. 399–454.

Remier (2008), *Ivan Cardoso: o mestre do terrir*. São Paulo: Imprensa Oficial.

Rowe, Christopher (2016), 'Dynamic Drawings and Dilated Time: Framing in Comics and Film', *Journal of Graphic Novels and Comics*, 7:4, pp. 348–68.

Schindler, Melissa (2014), 'Butts, *Bundas*, Bottoms, Ends: Tracing the Legacy of the Pornochanchada in *A b . . . profunda*', in Tim Dean, Steven Ruszczycky and David Squires (eds), *Porn Archives*. Durham, NC: Duke University Press, pp. 317–37.

Shamoon, Deborah (2004), 'Office Sluts and Rebel Flowers: The Pleasures of Japanese Pornographic Comics for Women', in Linda Williams (ed.), *Porn Studies*. Durham, NC, and London: Duke University Press, pp. 77–103.

Shaw, Lisa and Stephanie Dennison (2007), *Brazilian National Cinema*. London and New York: Routledge.
Vergueiro, Waldomiro (2001), 'Brazilian Pornographic Comics: A View on the Eroticism of a Latin American Culture in the Work of Artist Carlos Zéfiro', *International Journal of Comic Art*, 3:2, Fall, pp. 70–8.
Vergueiro, Waldomiro (2009), 'Brazilian Comics: Origin, Development, and Future Trends', in Héctor Fernández L'Hoeste and Juan Poblete (eds), *Redrawing the Nation: National Identity in Latin/o American Comics*. New York: Palgrave Macmillan, pp. 151–70.
Williams, Linda (1989), *Hard Core: Power, Pleasure, and the 'Frenzy of the Visible'*. Berkeley and Los Angeles: University of California Press.

CHAPTER 4

Photographs of the Invisible: Intermedial Figurations of Social Exclusion in Babás *and* Aquarius
Tiago de Luca

In her illuminating *Death 24× a Second: Stillness and the Moving Image* (2006), Laura Mulvey ruminates on the ties between the academic practice of textual analysis and the flexible spectatorial modes now identified with domestic viewing. For Mulvey, the ability of viewers to pause, rewind and slow down images replicates textual analysis's dissecting and inspecting eye. Following Raymond Bellour (2011), for whom the appearance of photographs in films gives rise to a 'pensive spectator' who reflects on cinema's constitutive stillness as embodied in the photogram, Mulvey envisions an updated version of this spectatorship in relation to the viewer's capacity actually to pause a moving image and change it into a freeze frame. In addition to constituting a new mode of cinephilic engagement, this freezing, for Mulvey, can serve a historiographic function. She writes: 'delaying the image, extracting it from its narrative surroundings, also allows it to return to its context and to contribute something extra and unexpected, a deferred meaning, to the story's narration' (Mulvey 2006: 151).

To prove this point, Mulvey analyses the opening of Douglas Sirk's *Imitation of Life* (1959), which foreshadows its racial thematics by showing its main character, the blonde Lora (Lana Turner), looking for her daughter on a crowded beach and brushing past her soon-to-be maid, the black Annie (Juanita Moore). Only by pausing this sequence, Mulvey maintains, can one notice 'that black extras both foreshadow and accompany [Lora's] first appearance', since the 'extras are not only on the screen so fleetingly that it would be difficult, if not impossible, to register their presence at 24 frames a second, but they are also placed at the edge of the frame' (156). For Mulvey, the recovery of these extras standing on the margins add *textual* weight to the film, in the sense that 'the fleeting presence of the extras relates to Annie's invisibility as the worker on whom Lora's visibility depends' (157). But it also endows the film with a renewed *contextual* significance, insofar as these black extras can be seen as 'standing in for and conjuring up the mass of "coloured people" rendered invisible by racism and oppression, very particularly by Hollywood's culture and representation' (158).

Inspired by, or in the wake of, Mulvey's seminal book, a number of publications followed suit, including *Still Moving: Between Cinema and Photography* (Beckman and Ma 2008); *Photography and Cinema* (Campany 2008); *Between Stillness and Motion: Film, Photography, Algorithms* (Røssaak 2011); *Between Still and Moving Images: Photography and the Cinema in the 20th Century* (Guido and Lugon 2012) and *The Still Point of the Turning World: Between Photography and Film* (Campany and Naudts 2017). As these quasi-identical titles demonstrate, the bulk of this scholarship is interested in complicating usual attributions of photographic 'stillness' and cinematic 'movement', which have been blurred and reconfigured by digital technology and media. Granted, not all of these studies define themselves in relation to 'intermediality' as a clearly outlined method and field whose scholarly consolidation coincides with their own appearance (Elleström 2010; Pethő 2011; Nagib and Jerslev 2014). Yet, as the ubiquity of the preposition 'between' in their titles attests, they are part and parcel of the same impetus to revitalise the study of film by locating it at the interstices of other media – in this case, photography – and thus in line with Ágnes Pethő's (2011: 1) contention that intermedial theorising must be focused on 'relationships, rather than structures, on something that "happens" in-between media rather than simply exists within a given signification'.

This chapter specifically takes Mulvey's pausing gesture as its methodological inspiration. It will consider the ways in which the use of photography can function as an in-between device to provoke reflection on that which is only partially visible, or almost invisible, at the edge of the frame, and on how this marginal visibility acts as the visualisation of wider, structural and social, forces of marginalisation. To explore this, my focus will be on two films: the short audiovisual essay *Babás* (*Nannies*, Consuelo Lins, 2010) and the fiction film *Aquarius* (Kleber Mendonça Filho, 2016). While vastly different in themselves, these films are nonetheless part of a prolific recent trend in Brazilian cinema interested in exploring domestic socio-economic relations in today's Brazil, often in relation to its slave-holding past and via the figure of the maid. Examples include *Trabalhar cansa* (*Hard Labour*, Juliana Rojas and Marco Dutra, 2011), *Doméstica* (*Housemaids*, Gabriel Mascaro, 2012), *O som ao redor* (*Neighbouring Sounds*, 2012), *Que horas ela volta?* (*The Second Mother*, 2014) and *Casa grande* (Filipe Furtado, 2014), among many others.

I have argued elsewhere (de Luca 2017), while focusing on the last two titles, that a discernible aesthetic strategy of this trend is the application of André Bazin's cherished depth of field technique (see Bazin 1997; 2005). In such films, the dynamic between the foreground and the background of the image is activated as a way to visualise and demarcate a segregational space that mirrors the invisible social boundaries regulating the home. The interaction between foreground and background is also key to an understanding of *Babás* and *Aquarius*. Yet here I want to cast light on the fact that this interaction is set in motion via the films' recourse to real or imagined photographs; hence the necessity of an intermedial approach to grasp their aesthetic mechanisms fully. By replicating or resonating with Mulvey's pausing gesture in relation to still and moving images depicting black maids at the edges of the frame, these two films, I wish to argue, encourage a spectatorial attitude endowed with the potential for textual analysis. In them, photographs are not merely diegetic props or indexical documents certifying the past, although they do serve these functions, too. Above all, photography is used as a means – a medium – through which to retrain and refine the spectator's visual acuity when it comes to elements such as posing, focus, framing and cropping, and in relation to how these elements can both conceal and reveal historical processes and structures of power.

The specific intertwining between photography and cinema activated by the two films under discussion here differ considerably. Whereas *Babás* adheres to the codes of portrait photography as a corrective to accidental recording, *Aquarius* shows that cinema can function as a form of visual reparation of photography's exclusionary framing and fixed attributes, even if, in the end, both films equally necessitate the arrested gaze of photography in order to draw the viewer's attention to the particularities and processes of imaging the world. This is not only because the details flooding the screen may sometimes be too fleeting or plentiful for one to notice them. The cropped edges of the image are more pronounced in photography because of their fixity – a fixity that, in the cinema, can easily and variously come unstuck by on-screen movement, off-screen sound and camera movement, all of which dissolve the boundaries of the frame as the limit of the visible.

No one has described photography's intransigent borders more cogently than Stanley Cavell (1979: 24), when he notes that

> objects in photographs that run past the edge do not feel cut; they are aimed at, shot, stopped live. When a photograph is cropped, the rest of the world is cut out. The implied presence of the rest of the world, and its explicit rejection, are as essential in the experience of a photograph as what it explicitly presents.

Writing in 1979, Cavell did not have in mind the avalanche of digital photographs of anything and everything we currently store on our phones and laptops, but the material photographs, usually printed on gelatine-coated papers, that one used to collect and arrange in family albums not so long ago. This is an important detail since the cropping in these printed pictures is arguably even more visible than in their digital counterparts: whether we encounter these pictures laid out next to each other in album pages or handle them one by one, the edges of such objects are a physically verifiable, tactile phenomenon. As a result, as both *Babás* and *Aquarius* illustrate, the specific rapport with history enacted by photography's automatic forming of 'an image of the world' (Cavell 1979: 20) is doubled when it comes to analogue photographs, whose tangible existence as tactile things in the world has itself become a thing of the past, the stuff of history.

Babás

Released in 2010, the short film *Babás*, by Consuelo Lins, is often classed as a documentary. It seems to me, however, that the film is more appropriately situated within the remit of the essayistic form. This is, first, because of the 'personal I' and subjective inclinations of the 'essay film' through cinema history (see Rascaroli 2009), which, as Timothy Corrigan (2008) has further shown, often showcases photographs in its textual constitution. Although the film is in fact narrated by Lins's friend and the film's producer, Flávia Castro (Souto 2020: 75), this first-person narration literally vocalises Lins's reflections on her bonds with the nannies she has encountered through her life, from the one who looked after her when she was a child to the legion of nannies she has employed to take care of her son. Tempered by nostalgia, melancholia and guilt, the film enfolds the social on to the personal, with structural exploitation and historical marginalisation filtered through Lins's own experiences. Second, *Babás* calls to mind the recent 'audiovisual' incarnation of the essay form, which has transformed the scholarly textual analysis, previously dependent upon the written word, into a videographic mode and practice. Weaving together colonial photographs, silent films and contemporary homemade videos and photographs, including Lins's own, *Babás* is as much a personal meditation as it is a reflection on the recorded image in relation to social regimes of visibility. A film scholar herself, Lins inspects, magnifies, zooms in on, compares and pauses over these images with a sharp analytical eye eager to uncover their hidden secrets, especially when one looks closely at unintended elements. More to the point, as I hope to show, *Babás* is suspicious of the cinematic medium because of the fugitive quality of its images, recruiting photography, and more specifically portrait photography, due to the intentionality of its gaze.

Babás begins with a yellowed photograph, taken in the Recife of 1860 by João Ferreira Villela, depicting a small white boy, Augusto Gomes Leal, with his 'wet nurse', the black slave Mônica. Taken in a studio against a neutral background, the photograph recalls the nineteenth-century carte de visite and bears the mark of its restrictive technical limitations, which required subjects to sit immobile in front of the camera for a long time so as to prevent blurs. Initially focused on Mônica's face, which takes up the screen, the camera unhurriedly retreats to reveal the little boy clinging to her on the left-hand side of the image. Then, as the narrator starts describing the image – the boy's leaning on her arm, her stern expression – the camera hovers over these details in a caressing, tactile gaze that recalls Laura Marks's (2000: 162) concept of haptic visuality, according to which 'the eyes themselves function like organs of touch'.

The reality of slavery and the possible affectionate relationship between the little boy and his 'slave mammy', exploitation and intimacy, cannot be so easily extricated from each other. Paraphrasing the historian Luiz Felipe de Alencastro, the voiceover notes: 'Almost all of Brazil fits into this picture.' Yet if this picture condenses Brazil's socio-historical contradictions, and while it was not entirely uncommon for aristocratic families in colonial Brazil to have pictures of slaves posing for the camera with the children they looked after, this picture is also, as the narrator notes, a relative anomaly in a wider historical context. Tracing a direct line between Brazil's slave-holding past and the country's staggering reliance on domestic servants – Brazil has the highest number of maids in the world, mostly black-descendant women (see Gallas 2016; Dorcadie 2018) – the voiceover comments that 'it's rare to find images of nannies and maids in public or private archives in Brazil. When they do appear, they do so often by chance, in family scenes involving children.'

To illustrate this point, *Babás* goes on to combine Brazilian films from the silent era in which black maids and nannies are placed at the edge of the frame, often tending to the white children, in turn centralised and in the foreground. In one of these, *Uma aula de Charleston* (*Charleston's Class*, 1920), a black nanny, sitting on the floor on the right-hand side of the frame and with her body partially cut off, claps along as a little girl, Marieta, dances merrily at the centre (Figure 4.1). This image, the narrator remarks, bears an uncanny resemblance to a homemade video of Lins's own son dancing to a salacious Brazilian song, 'Dança da Bundinha' (Little Ass Dance), where we similarly see his nanny on the left truncated by the frame. In another family recording, titled *O baptisado de Paulo* (*Paulo's Baptism*, 1913), the camera slowly pans from right to left: while the family members are all lined up horizontally in the foreground, a well-dressed black nanny holding a baby, alone, can be seen, in passing, just behind these people, at which point *Babás* pauses the image. Previously only a background figure captured fleetingly by the pan, the maid suddenly becomes centralised and still, with her eyes, now staring intently into the camera, forcefully soliciting the viewer's attention (Figure 4.2).

Figure 4.1 A silent film in *Babás* reveals the mutilation effected by the framing, as the nanny is partially cut off.

Figure 4.2   By pausing an early film, *Babás* centralises and makes visible a black nanny in the background.

By stopping this silent film, *Babás* recalls Mulvey's pausing gesture: only by halting the film's flow and turning it into a freeze frame can one really *see* the black nanny behind the family members. This idea is reinforced immediately after, as the film goes on to show a few more pictures from the colonial era of elegantly dressed black slaves posing with white children, leading the narrator to speculate on possible reasons for their existence, given their rarity: perhaps the bosses wanted to keep a visual document of these women as a memory token; perhaps they wanted to show a less cruel image of Brazil's slavery just before abolition; or perhaps they simply needed these women to keep the children still in front of the camera. Whatever the case, one of *Babás*'s aims is to show that these nineteenth-century pictures, with the women in the foreground, are scarce, sitting in contrast with the fugitive appearance of maids in early films all the way down to contemporary homemade videos.

Although not stated by the narrator, one reason behind these different modes of visual inscription lies in issues of medium specificity. As Mary Ann Doane (2002) has shown, during its infancy, cinema was especially valorised because of its ability to capture real-world contingency: unexpected moments and unprogrammed occurrences emanating from the messiness of reality. Not only is this dynamic and disorderly wealth of details significantly reduced when it comes to photography's frozen gaze; photography also had to await the introduction of snapshot cameras in the late nineteenth century in order to capture reality more fortuitously. Up until that point, as noted, subjects had to pose in studios to the deliberate gaze of the camera, with no interference of extraneous elements. Lins is aware that intentionality, which visually translates in these colonial pictures into centrality, is not synonymous with agency, as evinced by the narrator's aforementioned speculations. Yet the idea is that this composition at least does justice to these women's centrality in the lives of the children with whom they are seen in these photographs and, more broadly, in Brazil's social structure. Here, at least, they are visible.

Babás's main goal is to counter an accidental gaze with portrait photography's purposive stare. Thus, when recording her own former nannies – Vera Lúcia, Denise, Vera, Creuza, Andrea – in a leafy square in Rio de Janeiro, Lins arranges them together in a horizontal line. They all stand, motionless, staring into the camera as if posing for a portrait, while a stop trick turns the top of their outfits into white T-shirts, in a reference to the prevalence of this colour, with its connotations of cleanliness and asepticism, in maids' uniforms in Brazil. Shortly after, while we briefly hear some of these subjects on the soundtrack reflecting on their lives and hardships, the film intersperses close-up shots of their faces staring into the camera, recalling the widespread understanding of this technique as breaking the narrative flow via moments of 'stilled contemplation' (Campany 2008: 46). Then, as *Babás* moves on to interview other nannies, unrelated to Lins, these are also introduced posing outside their houses and intercut with facial close-ups. And as if to drive the point home that the inspiration for this posing and framing lies in portrait photography, *Babás* sets off a mise-en-abyme by having some of these women carrying their own private portraits – of their own relatives, of their younger selves holding the babies they looked after, of their own children in graduation gowns. In all of these cases, the film subscribes to Roland Barthes's (1997: 67–8) precept that to look longer than expected . . . disturbs established orders of every kind, to the extent that the time of the look is controlled by society; hence the scandalous nature of certain photographs and certain films, not the most indecent or the most combative, but just the most 'posed'.

There is a notable effort in the film to gather still photographs in which nannies are not at the edge of the frame but posing with the children and babies they have nurtured. These family photographs punctuate the entire film, sometimes in horizontal arrangements. Their links with the ones from Brazil's slave-owning past then gain visual concreteness at the film's end, which shows a digitally composed mosaic displaying all the photographs featured throughout (Figure 4.3). As at the opening of *Babás*, the camera recedes with deliberate motion, though we no longer see only the picture of Mônica with little Augusto, but this picture among a multitude of old and new photographs. As Gustavo Procopio Furtado (2019: 51) rightly points out: 'By inverting the familial image's foreground and background as well as its margins and center, [this imagined mosaic] invites us to imagine alternate archives of private life that would put on display a matter of public concern.'[1] I would add that crucial to this inverting process is the film's use of photography as an intermedial device. The placement of Mônica's photograph in a sea of pictures – a bigger picture – confirms the film's intention to provide a corrective to its historical singularity as derived from its relative rarity: replacing the residual, marginal appearance of maids in moving images with their centralised visibility in posed images, these pictures aim to make visible the importance of these women in Brazil's familial and social relations within a historical genealogy whose inaugural, violent scene is slavery.

Babás's reference to slavery is proof that the film is aware of the structural violence underpinning Brazil's deep-rooted reliance on this domestic workforce, and indeed, one of the merits of the film is to sketch this genealogy, via photography, in unequivocal terms. But it is also true that the film is less interested in conducting a social investigation than in exploring – often in an emotional (though never sentimental) register – the indisputable fact that, despite this violence, affective ties are forged between these women and the children for whom they care. In doing so, *Babás* invites trouble. A common criticism levelled at the film is that it perpetuates a colonial, or at least an employer's, gaze precisely as it attempts to deconstruct it. Rachel Randall (2018: 287), for example, notes that the 'expression and exploration of emotional attachment in *Babás* somewhat obfuscates an interrogation of abusive labour relationships'. Mariana Souto (2020: 75) strikes a similar chord by arguing that 'in [Lins's] reflections, there is hardly a search for the actual causes of [these women's] invisibility'.[2]

Figure 4.3 A digitally composed mosaic of portraits at the end of *Babás* materialises the film's quest to become photography.

I am, in principle, sympathetic to these criticisms and agree that the risk of romanticisation is one that sometimes lurks beneath the film. Yet I also think it is important that we unpack some of the governing assumptions underpinning this critique. By largely focusing on questions of (mis) representation and presupposing an approach that would be 'proper' to the subjects and subject matter depicted, these criticisms resonate with what Jacques Rancière defines as the representational regime and its corresponding mode of critical decoding. This, according to Rancière (2010: 143), expects a certain didacticism from 'critical art', 'whose purported task is to produce forms of political awareness and mobilization', while issuing 'rules of appropriateness between a particular subject and a particular form' (2009: 118). For Rancière, however, critical art, which must introduce 'dissensus', 'is not so much a type of art that reveals the forms and contradictions of domination as it is an art that questions its own limits and powers, that refuses to anticipate its own effects' (2010: 149). This it does by reframing what he terms the commonsensical 'partition of the sensible': that is, 'specific distributions of space and time, of the visible and the invisible', by changing 'the frames, speeds and scales according to which we perceive the visible' (Rancière 2010: 141). Dissensus, in this context, means reshuffling dominant regimes of visibility – which dictates what gets to be framed, and what remains off frame – by creating 'a new scenery of the visible' and 'new forms of perception of the given' (141). It means making a film in the awareness that 'a film remains a film', one that can 'rework the frame of our perceptions and the dynamism of our affects' but one that cannot avoid 'the aesthetic cut that separates consequences from intentions' (Rancière 2011: 82).

Rancière's reflections, I believe, can be productively invoked here, since *Babás* is concerned with the very issue of social regimes of (in)visibility, and more specifically with how the partitioning of the visible can be both reinforced and undone by image-making technologies. To put it differently, here is the case of a film quite literally intent on reworking 'the frame of our perceptions' by activating the viewer's peripheral vision and drawing attention to the way in which the frame of the image directly participates in the dominant distribution of the sensible. At the same time, *Babás*'s acknowledgement of its own insufficiency when it comes to its limits and powers is not only the result of Lins's qualifying of her gaze as emanating from her own social experience and the fact that this is 'only a film', and a short one at that. It is also the result of its recognition that film itself as a medium is complicit with processes of marginalisation and therefore insufficient on its own terms to grapple with processes of such complexity and magnitude, hence its recruiting of photography for the purposes of reframing.

To be sure, Rancière does not exactly explore intermediality as conducive to this reframing, even if he does mention that '[d]oing art means displacing art's borders, just as doing politics means displacing the borders of what is acknowledged as *the* political' (2011: 149, emphasis in original). Indeed, as Lúcia Nagib (2014: 31) has noted, intermediality can be productively aligned with 'dissensus', given that 'the recourse to different media within a film immediately suspends the pedagogical character of representational narratives by introducing a dilemma', thus 'evidencing a moment of crisis of the medium which requires another for its completion' (37). I would add that the incorporation of other lens-based media, and especially photography, within a given film, enacts an incision in the way cinema, as a recording technology, 'sees' the world by opening up alternative modes of modulating it and visualising it within the film's visual structure and textual constitution, thus making us see both mediums, and their rendering of the world both within and outside the frame, in a new light.

In this sense, *Babás*'s potentiality is not so much located in its representational dimension than in the intermedial relations it engenders between photography and cinema as a way to 'make the invisible visible or to question the self-evidence of the visible' (Rancière 2010: 141). It is through the entwining of photography and film that *Babás* recalibrates our perception of structural marginalisation as alternately concealed and unveiled by regimes of visuality whose particularities are themselves dependent upon medium specificity. Whether we think of photographs taking up the screen or arranged next to each other, the pausing of moving images or the intermedial borrowing of elements identified with the portrait genre, photography in *Babás* is not a technical flourish or an ornament in the service of a pedagogical message. To paraphrase Marshall McLuhan (1964), *photography* is the message here.[3] Another way of putting this would be to say that the film's driving idea is that cinema must be stilled, its gaze stretched in time so as to allow pause for thought and a more deliberate and directive gaze; in short, *Babás* proposes, cinema must become photography.

AQUARIUS

Released in 2016, *Aquarius* is the second feature film by Kleber Mendonça Filho, who is no stranger to incorporating photographs into his films. The follow-up to *O som ao redor* (*Neighbouring Sounds*, 2012), *Aquarius* begins, like that film, with a slideshow montage of black-and-white photographs to the sound of Taiguara's 1968 song 'Hoje' (Today). Selected from archives at the Joaquim Nabuco Foundation, in Recife, these real photographs, in both films, do not bear any straightforward relationship to the plot diegesis or the characters, although they do situate the narrative themes in a wider geographical frame and deeper historical context. In *O som ao redor*, pictures showing Recife's colonial manor houses and sugar cane plantations gain in significance as the film unfolds and the viewer becomes aware of the links between contemporary property speculation and colonial land possession. These links find diegetic incarnation in the character of Seu Francisco (W. J. Solha), a former sugar baron who owns most properties lining the street on which the film's multinarrative plot focuses, with an emphasis on the relationship between bosses and domestic servants.

Property speculation and class struggle are also at the heart of *Aquarius*, though the focus here is on one single character. The film depicts the escalating animosity between a widow, Clara (Sônia Braga), and a property development company eager to demolish the three-storey beach-front building (the titular Aquarius), of which she is the last tenant, in order to erect a luxury tower block in its place. These architectural monstrosities are now the norm on the coast of Recife's affluent quarters, as seen in many panoramic shots throughout *Aquarius* (filmed in widescreen), which sit in contrast with the opening pictures, taken by famous Pernambuco-born photographer Alcir Lacerda. As Mendonça Filho has explained, these photographs, many of which are aerial views, were chosen due to the fact they depict precisely the coastal area in Recife where the film is set.[4] Showing wide, empty avenues with practically no cars and coastlines sparsely dotted with a few buildings here and there, they provide the indexical certification of a bygone era when Recife's beaches had not yet been corrupted by heavy traffic and phallic buildings.

I will return to this opening at the end of this chapter. Let us note for now that *Aquarius*'s recourse to photography is not reduced to its extratextual opening but extends to the use of printed and digital photographs within its textual mesh. As my following analysis will show, more than mere diegetic props, these photographs are crucial for an understanding of Clara's past and present relationships with domestic maids, an important subplot in the film that provides insight into wider socio-historical issues in Brazil. A former music journalist, Clara is *Aquarius*'s heroine: a progressive woman who has had her share of pain in life (including a mastectomy) and with whom the spectator is meant to identify. Yet the film also paints Clara as a complex character whose own contradictions mirror Brazil's own, especially when it comes to her overreliance on her loyal housemaid Ladjane (Zoraide Coleto). On the one hand, the film gives us no reason to suspect that Clara's affection for Ladjane is anything but genuinely nurtured and felt. On the other hand, there is reason to believe that Clara is not simply oblivious to the fact that she benefits from structural exploitation, but in fact conveniently chooses to turn a blind eye to these structures. These contradictions are made especially visible in two scenes, both of which make recourse to photography as a way to retrain and expand the spectator's perception of class relations in Brazil within a wider frame of visuality and historical reference.

The first scene depicts Clara's visit to Ladjane's modest house on the occasion of her birthday, where a number of people congregate on a makeshift terrace overlooking Recife's affluent neighbourhoods, where Clara herself lives. Clara brings along her nephew, Tomás (Pedro Queiroz), and his girlfriend, Julia (Julia Bernat), and upon arrival runs into her friend Letícia (Arly Arnaud), who, as it turns out, employs Ladjane's sister, Lara, as her housemaid. Judging from this scene, the relationship between bosses and servants is one governed by warmth and conviviality, ostensibly unconstrained by class barriers: they chat in friendly tones, make jokes and, of course, take a photograph to register the moment, with the four of them posing, smiling, for Tomás and Julia, who snap the pictures on their phones (Figure 4.4).

A later scene, however, complicates these seemingly straightforward affective ties and the apparent corroboration of such ties via photography. It takes place in another informal gathering, now in Clara's flat, and in the presence of her brother and his extended family. Ladjane is also in the flat but not as a party guest: confined to the kitchen, she is busy preparing food. Drinking wine and going through old family albums, they study old photographs in leisurely fashion and reminisce about the past. Meanwhile, Clara's other nephew, Felipe (Bernardo Sampaio), rephotographs pictures

Figure 4.4 Clara (far left) poses for a snap with her maid Ladjane (beside her) at the latter's birthday party, in *Aquarius*.

of himself as a child on his phone. The transition from analogue to digital media is, in fact, an underlying theme of the film. For example, Clara is reluctant to use MP3 formats and is emotionally attached to her old vinyl albums. When being interviewed for a newspaper in a previous scene, and holding John Lennon and Yoko Ono's 1980 record *Double Fantasy*, Clara mulls over the fact that she found inside the album, which she purchased at a second-hand shop, an article on John Lennon's 'plans for the future' that had been published a few weeks just before his assassination: 'this record I'm holding in my hands', she concludes, 'becomes a special object'; it's like 'a message in a bottle'.

Clara's relationship with old photographs, which she caresses in the albums and scrutinises with her brother and sister-in-law, Antonio (Buda Lira) and Fátima (Paula de Renor), seems to attend to a similar logic whereby they accrue added memory value and become 'special objects' one can touch and feel. Just as importantly, *Aquarius* suggests, these relics of the past retain unexpected messages waiting for retrieval. Looking through a number of pictures of her two sons and her daughter, Clara becomes transfixed not by her own offspring but by the fact they are always accompanied by a black, uniformed maid whose face we cannot see, whether this is because she is out of focus in the background or because she is mutilated by the framing, her body reduced to mere limbs trying to hold the children (Figures 4.5 and 4.6). As Stephanie Dennison (2018: 334) notes, insofar as the maid is reduced to a face whose features we cannot make out or else to bodily parts, she becomes reduced to an 'embodiment of blackness . . . that is perceived as threatening and dangerous'. This is an important point insofar as the maid's fuzzy appearance in one photograph seems to be the result of the racial bias historically built into photography, which, as is well known, had fair skin tones as the parameter for colour film toning. And it gains further in significance when one considers that this scene is intercut with shots of Felipe using an app to whiten his own skin colour in the rephotographed pictures of himself on his phone.[5]

Despite (or rather, because of) her interrupted visibility, like a Barthesian punctum, the maid pierces Clara, who mutters that 'it turns out that she was a bitch who stole our jewellery', to which Fátima replies, absentmindedly: 'well, it's inevitable, isn't it? We exploit them, they steal our jewellery'. Although brief, this remark seems to spark a realisation on the part of Clara, who agrees – 'you're right' – and becomes obsessed with remembering the maid's name. Then, as Clara gets up to fetch more albums and disappears into her room, the camera frames its door from a distance with Fátima in focus in the foreground, and the maid, as though emerging from the past, suddenly crosses the frame in the background and enters into an adjacent

Figures 4.5 and 4.6 A faceless maid, accidentally captured in family photographs, functions as a Barthesian punctum, in *Aquarius*.

room. At this point the scene pulls its focus just in time for the viewer to get a glimpse of the maid, followed by a short-distance, sharply focused shot that partly repeats the same action, as if to make sure the viewer will not fail to notice the occurrence this time (Figures 4.7 and 4.8). Clara then emerges from her room, muttering to herself: 'Juvenita, she was called Juvenita.'

Raymond Bellour (2011: 119) has argued that the presence of photographs in films 'gives rise to a very particular trouble. Without ceasing to advance its own rhythm, the film seems to freeze, to suspend itself,' which has 'the effect of uncoupling the spectator from the image' (122). In *Aquarius*, there is a doubling of this process, since, for a moment, the photographs of Juvenita seem to uncouple from the image not only the spectator but the very laws governing the plausibility of the film's world. Although lasting on screen for barely 3 seconds, the supernatural inclusion of Juvenita in this contemporary

Figures 4.7 and 4.8 A focus pull enables *Aquarius* to bring the maid Juvenita into visibility.

family scene suddenly plunges the objectivity of the diegesis into uncertain waters, prompting the viewer to question their perception of the onscreen reality. When watched under domestic conditions, this fleeting occurrence, we can perhaps speculate, may even induce Bellour's 'pensive spectator' to mutate into Mulvey's one, compelled to rewind and pause the scene so as to certify what their eyes have just seen. To go even further, although *Aquarius* never stills its moving images, its focus pulling and replication of the same incident from a closer perspective can be seen as the aesthetic equivalent of a pause in the film's flow, itself triggered by the stillness of the photographs and their cropped framing. Juvenita's passing appearance, at first unfocused, in the background, rehashes exactly the aesthetic logic in place in the photographs adorning the family albums. This mise-en-abyme is then reinforced when Ladjane enters the living room to show the picture of her deceased son, who died in a car crash, the culprits not yet found due to police negligence. Tellingly, she is no longer centralised and properly framed, as in the picture she posed for with Clara at her own party, but is now herself cropped, a faceless figure with only the lower part of her body visible on screen.

Dennison has noted that the truncating of Juvenita in the family photographs, and the film's replication of this gesture when framing Ladjane, recall contemporary Latin American projects whose aim is to shed visibility on maids and nannies often rendered invisible in contemporary family photographs. She cites the work of the Peruvian photographer Daniela Ortiz, who selected ninety-seven photographs from Facebook 'in order to highlight the common practice of erasing, editing out, blurring and truncating the presence of maids in middle-class homes in Peru' (Dennison 2018: 334). These real photographs in Ortiz's project and the fictional ones in *Aquarius* remind us that, like moving images, photography can also cut off, mutilate and fragment in line with segregational regimes of visibility – perhaps more so than ever, given the rapidity and ease with which one can take a photograph and manipulate it these days.

One could argue, in this context, that *Aquarius* does not convey the same belief in photography as the purveyor of a more reliable look in the same way that *Babás* does. It may even be said that *Aquarius*, while harnessing the photographs of Juvenita as a means to enhance the viewer's perceptiveness, performs a compensatory gesture by positing cinema as a medium that can sometimes repair the erasure enacted by photography. Indeed, when Juvenita unexpectedly appears on screen, the film's reframing of her is achieved through specifically cinematic means. Whereas her blurry, fragmented self is condemned forever to this frozen state in the photographs, thanks to the film medium *Aquarius* is able to redress this, however momentarily, through a focus pull and while she is still on screen. The same is true of the following shot of Juvenita, which can only provide a closer look at her presence thanks to editing.

This idea gains further significance when we consider the second time Juvenita appears on screen towards the end of the film. This time, her spectral presence is attributed to Clara's dream (or nightmare), as confirmed by a shot of Clara waking right afterward. Juvenita is initially visible in Clara's kitchen in a static long shot taken from the living room. It is nighttime and all lights are out. The open kitchen door, centralised but in the background of the frame, functions as a frame-within-frame composition. Juvenita crosses the kitchen and stops at the counter on the left-hand side, with the kitchen door cutting off her body and recalling the old photographs of herself, an aspect reinforced by her momentary stillness and the stationary quality of the shot. Then, as she leaves the kitchen and walks to Clara's room, the scene cuts to a shot of her walking directly towards the camera, facing the viewer until her face takes up the entire screen. In some ways, this shot could be seen as analogous to *Babás*'s strategy of having nannies and maids posing for the camera as a way to redress their former invisibility: Juvenita is no longer a marginal, faceless, fortuitously captured detail, but a commanding presence confronting the viewer head on.

Significantly, however, not only is Juvenita in constant movement but the film frames her through a variation of the 'dolly zoom' shot pioneered in Hitchcock's *Vertigo* (1958), achieved through zooming the camera lenses and physically moving the camera simultaneously but in opposing directions. As intended by Hitchcock, the disturbing effect of this technique is to undermine visual perception. Depending on the direction of the zoom lenses and the camera movement, the background and the foreground appear to be either stretching further apart from each other or, as in the case of *Aquarius*, collapsing on to themselves. This does not just have the effect of heightening the unreality of the scene. By simultaneously compressing the background and the foreground while Juvenita remains entirely in focus, placidly staring into the camera, the film is able to erode the apportioning of the visible that had firmly assigned her to a specific place in the image and pushed her into the background. Not only is Juvenita granted visibility, then, but she is formulated as a specifically cinematic visibility that engenders a dissolution of previously fixed visual structures and spatial boundaries.

This is confirmed immediately after. Now in Clara's room and rummaging through a jewellery box, Juvenita is in the foreground in the image, her face in profile, while Clara, in the background, lies on her bed, looking apprehensive (Figure 4.9). Here, too, a sense of unreality and distortion prevails, though no longer achieved via the dolly zoom technique but through the use of a split dioptre lens, a curved mirror that allows a shot to have two planes of focus

Figure 4.9 Now in the foreground of the image, Juvenita haunts an enfeebled Clara, in *Aquarius*.

without respecting the actual depth separating these planes, with the resulting image displaying distortions in scale. And here, too, the image exudes a cinematic quality, given the canonisation of this technique through film history in conjunction with the widescreen format, as seen, for example, in Sergio Leone's westerns and Brian de Palma's thrillers.[6] The distance between the two women appears stretched, while there is a discrepancy between the gargantuan size of Juvenita's face in the foreground on the left-hand side of the frame and the diminutive size of Clara's whole body on the right in the background. Whereas before she had been relegated to the edges of the frame or reduced to a featureless face, here Juvenita becomes the frame's imposing presence, returning from the past to dwarf and haunt Clara, whose own cancer, the film further suggests by showing her left breast bleeding, mirrors Brazil's open scars resulting from its abysmal (and ongoing) social and racial inequalities.

The two scenes in which Juvenita appears in *Aquarius* are therefore emblematic in terms of how they expand the viewer's perception concerning technical aspects such as framing, cropping, posing, focus and zoom, all in relation to the spatial dynamics between background and foreground. This renewed perception is first unleashed by the presence of Juvenita's photographs, which, like a shock wave, command a response on the part of the film to redress her invisibility via film-specific means. *Aquarius* thus replies to *Babás* by suggesting that cinema may have something to give to photography when it comes to compensating for the marginal visibility of the socially excluded. This is not to say that the film privileges one medium over the other, but that it needs both to recast the viewer's peripheral vision and to redirect our attention towards the edges of the frame.

In this sense, *Aquarius* anticipates in its textual constitution not only Bellour's but also Mulvey's 'pensive spectator', one who, we can perhaps wonder, may be compelled to revisit scenes after the photographic and cinematic appearances of Juvenita, then to come across other occurrences in the film where maids and servants are only subliminally visible. This spectator may notice that in a scene located in a bookshop (presumably Fátima's), set in the present day of the diegesis, a fleeting appearance of a yellow uniform, out of focus in the background, is seen passing behind Fátima in a visual composition that directly prefigures the one showing Juvenita during Clara's gathering. Rewinding the film further to the extended prologue showing Clara at a younger age, they may now be able to see, with newfound clarity, that black maids can also be briefly glimpsed during a party at her house in the background (Figures 4.10 and 4.11). They may even be compelled to inspect the opening's series of photographs, which, while still, nonetheless stay on screen for 4 seconds each, thanks to montage as part of a slideshow.

90 Tiago de Luca

Figures 4.10 and 4.11 A profusion of maids in the background finally become prominent in *Aquarius*.

Then, on arresting these arrested images further, the viewer may notice that in the second photograph opening the film, a panoramic view of a beach lined up with straw sunshades and coconut trees, and filled with beach revellers, a dark-skinned woman on the far right, at the edge of the frame, looks into the camera (Figure 4.12). But it is not only her gaze at us that makes her stand out and pierce us like a Barthesian punctum. Sitting upright on the sand, her hands resting on her knees, she is fully dressed, while her posture is different from that of the two women who flank her. Surrounded by babies and children, these two women seem more relaxed while talking to each other, and, as it happens, they are also of a whiter skin tone. One will probably never know who our gazing woman was, whether she was in fact feeling out of place or what her relationship was to these women, but the fact is that her skin colour, her placement at the image's borders and her direct gaze gain in significance in the context of *Aquarius*'s themes of social and racial segregation. In turn, this picture adds a new layer to the film's themes, amplifying them by way of its indexical and historical dimension.

Figure 4.12 A pause on a still photograph, in *Aquarius*'s opening slideshow, suddenly reveals hidden secrets.

Cinema and photography thus feed into one another in an endless loop that renders both mediums symbiotic and co-dependent, and out of which fiction and reality are rendered newly visible.

Notes

1. Curiously, inspired by *Babás*, Furtado goes on to examine a moment from the documentary *Santiago* (João Moreira Salles, 2006) where the hands of a maid, truncated by the edge of the frame, are only just visible next to a pool with people in it. Although he does not reflect on the pausing gesture that allowed him to retrieve this moment out of the film's relentless forward drive, its illustration as a still picture in his book confirms this gesture.
2. Translations mine, unless otherwise indicated.
3. The phrase 'the medium is the message' was famously coined by McLuhan in his seminal *Understanding Media* (1964).
4. Incidentally, Alcir Laceda makes a cameo appearance as a photographer in *O pedido* (*The Request*, 1999) by Recife-born Adelina Pontual. I take this information from the film *Passages* (Lúcia Nagib and Samuel Paiva, 2019), where Mendonça Filho also talks about the use of photographs in his first two feature films.
5. The idea of dark skin tones as threatening to the middle and upper classes reappears later in the film, when Clara is disparaged by the estate agent Diego (Humberto Carrão), who makes the racist assertion that her 'dark-skinned tone' means that she must have come from a family who fought hard to climb up the social ladder.
6. My thanks to Mendonça Filho, who confirmed these influences in a personal email and inadvertently confirmed my hypothesis by calling this shot 'a cinematic image' ('uma imagem de cinema').

References

Barthes, Roland (1997), 'Dear Antonioni . . .', reprinted in Geoffrey Nowell-Smith, *L'avventura*, BFI Film Classics. London: British Film Institute, pp. 63–8.

Bazin, André (1997), 'William Wyler, or the Jansenist of Directing', in André Bazin, *Bazin at Work: Major Essays & Reviews from the Forties & Fifties*, ed. Bert Cardullo, trans. Alain Piette and Bert Cardullo. New York and London: Routledge, pp. 1–22.

Bazin, André (2005), 'The Evolution of the Language of Cinema', in André Bazin, *What is Cinema?*, vol. 1, ed. and trans. Hugh Gray. Berkeley, Los Angeles and London: University of California Press, pp. 23–40.

Beckman, Karen and Jean Ma (eds) (2008), *Still Moving: Between Cinema and Photography*. Durham, NC, and London: Duke University Press.

Bellour, Raymond ([1984] 2011), 'The Pensive Spectator', in David Campany (ed.), *The Cinematic*. London and Cambridge, MA: Whitechapel and MIT Press, pp. 119–23.

Campany, David (2008), *Photography and Cinema*. London: Reaktion.

Campany, David and Joachim Naudts (eds) (2017), *The Still Point of the Turning World: Between Photography and Film*, multilingual edn. Heidelberg: Kehrer.

Cavell, Stanley (1979), *The World Viewed: Reflections on the Ontology of Film*. Cambridge, MA, and London: Harvard University Press.

Corrigan, Timothy (2008), '"The Forgotten Image Between Two Shots": Photos, Photograms and the Essayistic', in Karen Beckman and Jean Ma (eds) (2008), *Still Moving: Between Cinema and Photography*. Durham, NC, and London: Duke University Press, pp. 41–61.

de Luca, Tiago (2017) '"Casa Grande & Senzala": Domestic Space and Class Conflict in *Casa grande* and *Que horas ela volta?*', in Antônio Márcio da Silva and Mariana Cunha (eds), *Space and Subjectivity in Contemporary Brazilian Cinema*. Cham: Palgrave Macmillan, pp. 203–19.

Dennison, Stephanie (2018), 'Intimacy and Cordiality in Kleber Mendonça Filho's *Aquarius*', *Journal of Iberian and Latin American Studies*, 24:3, pp. 329–40.

Doane, Mary Ann (2002), *The Emergence of Cinematic Time: Modernity, Contingency, The Archive*. London: Harvard University Press.

Dorcadie, Mathilde (2018), 'The Precarious Status of Domestic Workers in Brazil', *Equal Times*, available at <https://www.equaltimes.org/the-precarious-status-of-domestic#.YHBwTRNKi8U> (last accessed 9 April 2020).

Elleström, Lars (ed.) (2010), *Media Borders, Multimodality and Intermediality*. Basingstoke: Palgrave Macmillan.

Furtado, Gustavo Procopio (2019), *Documentary Filmmaking in Contemporary Brazil: Cinematic Archives of the Present*. New York: Oxford University Press.

Gallas, Daniel (2016), 'Maid in Brazil: Economy Troubles Push Women Back into Old Jobs', *BBC News* (11 May), available at <https://www.bbc.co.uk/news/business-35705464> (last accessed 3 March 2021).

Guido, Laurent and Oliver Lugon (2012), *Between Still and Moving Images: Photography and the Cinema in the 20th Century*. New Barnet: John Libbey.

McLuhan, Marshall ([1964] 2001), *Understanding Media: The Extensions of Man*. Abingdon: Routledge.

Marks, Laura U. (2000), *The Skin of the Film: Intercultural Cinema, Embodiment and the Senses*. Durham, NC, and London: Duke University Press.

Mulvey, Laura (2006), *Death 24× a Second: Stillness and the Moving Image*. London: Reaktion Books.

Nagib, Lúcia (2014), 'The Politics of Impurity', in Lúcia Nagib and Anne Jerslev (eds), *Impure Cinema: Intermedial and Intercultural Approaches to Film*. London: I. B. Tauris, pp. 21–40.

Nagib, Lúcia and Anne Jerslev (eds) (2014), *Impure Cinema: Intermedial and Intercultural Approaches to Film*. London: I. B. Tauris.

Pethő, Ágnes (2011), *Cinema and Intermediality: The Passion for the In-Between*. Newcastle-Upon-Tyne: Cambridge Scholars Publishing.

Rancière, Jacques (2009) *The Future of the Image*. London and New York: Verso.

Rancière, Jacques (2010), *Dissensus: On Politics and Aesthetics*. London and New York: Continuum.

Rancière, Jacques (2011), *The Emancipated Spectator*. London and New York: Verso.

Randall, Rachel (2018), '"It's Very Difficult to Like and to Love, but Not to Be Respected or Valued": Maids and Nannies in Contemporary Brazilian Documentary', *Journal of Romance Studies* 18:2, pp. 275–99.

Rascaroli, Laura (2009), *The Personal Camera: Subjective Cinema and the Essay Film*. London and New York: Wallflower Press.

Røssaak, Eivind (ed.) (2011), *Between Stillness and Motion: Film, Photography, Algorithms*. Amsterdam: Amsterdam University Press.

Souto, Mariana (2020), 'Relações de classes em documentários brasileiros contemporâneos', *Significação: Revista de Cultural Audiovisual*, 47:53, pp. 70–89.

CHAPTER 5

Exploring the Cinematic Imaginary: Carlos Adriano, André Parente and the Precision of the Vague
Martine Beugnet

Art and technology are strongly intertwined in the theorisation and creative practice of film and media in Brazil today. No doubt such hybridisation can be traced in the continuing curiosity and openness to modernity described by Vilém Flusser in his observations as a long-term resident and cultural chronicler of the country (Medeiros 2015).[1] In turn, in her attempt to define the specificity of the Latin American context, Vivian Schelling (2001: 2) talks of the layering of old and new traditions that combined with elements of European and North American modernities to create 'an experience *sui generis*, with its own dynamic and possibilities'. In Brazil, the legacy of the first modernity has been continuously revisited, notably through the prism of the key European thinkers of the 1970s and 1980s (Marques et al. 2013), and, in the following decades, with reference to emergent media archaeology and intermedial approaches (see Nagib and Solomon 2019). In the resulting bent towards reflexivity in evidence in the conceptualisations and practice of Brazilian scholars and artists, cinema plays a key role – not only as the emblematic modern artform internationally, but as one that was implanted early in the country. To consider the medium from the vantage point of the long history of apparatuses and lens-based images, as the artists discussed in this chapter do, is not to deny its specificity, but to recast it within a continuing web of exchanges between art and science, and between film and other arts. Envisaged in this way, intermediality becomes a historiographic method, a means to explore the traces of the long-lasting heritage of Brazil's cultural modernity, as they surface in the experiments of contemporary filmmakers and artists.

More specifically, in what follows I propose to explore the persistent fusion of art and the machine heralded by protocinematic devices and effected by photography and cinema. When envisioned from an intermedial standpoint, I suggest, this fusion helps to shift the classic discourses (Krauss 2000; Aumont 2010; Bolter and Grusin 1999) opposing medium specificity to remediation and self-differentiation back to the images themselves – the question of their production, actualisation and reception. At stake is the renewed acknowledgement that film's massive contribution to the recent evolution of 'visuality', defined by Whitney Davis (2011: 8) as a historical phenomenon that lies at 'the intersection of vision (and visibility) and culture (and visible culturality)', continues to be born out of the moving image's paradoxical standing at the intersection between photographic precision and visual uncertainty (see Beugnet et al. 2017).

In terms of media, form and apparatus, the works considered in the following are very different. Carlos Adriano's *Remanescências* (*Remainiscences*, 1997) is an experimental film that foregrounds the material appearance and transformation of the analogue film image. André Parente's *Figuras na paisagem* (*Figures in a Landscape*, 2010) is a multimedia installation focusing on the ways in which particular *dispositifs* determine the conditions of our perceiving and imagining in the era of digital technology.[2] However, the works compare in two crucial aspects. On the one hand, in their contrasted ways and at different stages of the process of imaging, they both emphasise gesture in the sense suggested by Giorgio Agamben. Recalling Albert Simonond's (1958: 54–5) notion of 'milieux associés', Agamben (2000: 58) points to the ways in which gesture, rather than opposing technology to the human, serves as both vector and expression of an acclimatisation of the human body and consciousness to mediated environments (and vice versa): 'as the exhibition of a mediality that allows the emergence of a being-in-a-medium of human beings' (see also Montani 2018). On the other hand, and together with their espousal of mediality as a form of 'being-in-a-medium', both works point to the existence of a 'technological imaginary' that manifests itself through media cross-breeding, and in the deployment of a recurrent motif: the image and concept of the *vague*, for at the core of Adriano's and Parente's work is the acknowledgement that the film image's power to trigger the imagination is born out of its fundamentally elusive nature. No matter the quality of definition and resolution, the movement that conditions their appearance as film images makes them infinitely variable, and therefore inherently in-definite, as ungraspable as the waves that constantly modify the surface of the sea. This non-finitude produces a 'dynamics of imagination' (Huppauf and Wulf 2009) equally present in digital and analogue media, yet diversely conditioned by the *dispositifs* that determine the production and reception of images.[3] The subject of the obsessive, systematic reworking of a few photograms of waves in Adriano's work, a common cinematic imaginary also emerges in the form of a complex weaving of literary sources and video footage of the sea in Parente's installation.

THE MEDIALITY OF GESTURE

In French as in Portuguese, the word 'vague' [vag], 'vago/a', has two related meanings: as an adjective, it is synonymous with indeterminate or indistinct; as a noun, it translates as 'wave' (*la vague* in French; *vaga* in Portuguese, though rarely used). Although their etymologies are different, the meaning of the two words overlaps from the start: the adjective comes from the Latin *vagus*, something random, in perpetual motion, something indefinite or indecisive. The noun, on the other hand, has an Indo-European etymology that refers to the ceaseless movement and endless transformation of the sea. Both definitions thus point to the particularity of the wave as Leibniz classically described it: a perceptual object marked by uncertainty. We hear the roar of the sea, made of all the crashing waves, and we identify it as the sound of the sea, Leibniz (1714) wrote, even though we cannot distinguish the sound of each individual wave. We can see it and listen to it as it forms, grows and vanish at the surface of the water, yet a wave can never be isolated or fixed long enough to be perceived accurately and in all its detail. Its rendering can only be impressionistic.[4] As Leibniz ([1714] 1900: 729) concluded, the wave is an epitome of the 'clear and confused': as an observable phenomenon, it defeats our attempts at perceiving it in an entirely precise and complete fashion. Accordingly, Georges Didi-Huberman (2009: 49–50) has remarked that the wave, because it hovers between form and formlessness, and can only ever be grasped elusively, is the favoured stuff of poetic creation.

But to the precursors of the cinema – engineers rather than artists, and who saw in film, first and foremost, a means of augmenting and refining human perception and observation – the wave would likely have been considered, first and foremost, a natural challenge. The first film ever shot in Brazil was probably José Roberto Cunha Salles's 1897 *Ancoradouro de pescadores na Baía de Guanabara* (*Fishing Pier at Guanabara Bay*), of which there survives a brief series of frames (Figure 5.1).[5] It shows waves beating against the pillars of a pier, foamy water rising against the human-made obstacle. The images bear an uncanny resemblance to another film, dated a few years earlier: *La Vague*, hailed as Etienne Jules Marey's first chronophotographic film, was shot in 1891, and similarly depicts the sea crashing against the pillars of a jetty. In Marey's case, the film most likely had little value in itself: as a scientist, he would have seen no point in showing, in the form of moving images, that which we can see with our own eyes.[6] Typically, his objective would have been to elaborate, on the basis of the footage, a graph precisely describing the movement of a wave. Though by no means an established figure like Marey, Cunha Salles also had scientific interests, and it is possible that, like his French counterpart, his primary concerns when shooting these images had less to

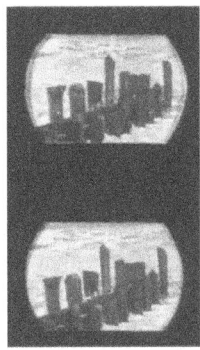

Figure 5.1 Carlos Adriano's *Remanescências* (*Remainiscences*, 1997), based on José Roberto Cunha Salles's *Ancoradouro de pescadores na Baía de Guanabara* (*Fishing Pier at Guanabara Bay*, 1897). Courtesy of the artist.

do with their power of expression than with their capacity to demonstrate the extent of the technical novelty of the new medium. Whatever the case, to choose the sea as subject matter for a film was to immediately confront oneself with the limits of the medium as a scientific tool for the measuring or observation of phenomena. In its ability to record everything photographically, including those details, elusive movements and manifold alterations that escape human perception, film may seem like a perfect method for the capture and analysis of complex phenomena. Yet paradoxically, for the same reasons, film is uniquely suited to account for that which, as Leibniz intuited, eschews precise measuring and clear and distinct perception: the world's infinite complexity and changeability.[7]

Tellingly, today even more than at the time of their recording, what is likely to strike the spectator watching Marey's or Cunha Salles's images is precisely that which lies outside of purely scientific observation: their poignancy as precious glimpses of a long-gone moment; the evocation of nature's unbound force that, in spite of our jaded attitude to images, may give us an inkling of how films affected their first spectators; and, in the wondrous sight of the movement of the water, caught in all its diffuse and simultaneous variations, the renewed sense of the uniqueness of film's record of reality.[8]

In 1994, Carlos Adriano recovered a sequence of eleven of Cunha Salles's photograms. Working in collaboration with Ronald Palatnik, he turned them into an 18-minute experimental film called *Remanescências*.[9] In doing so, Adriano was contributing to a long tradition of experimental filmmakers who use found footage to bring to light and intensify film's aesthetic potentialities, or, in the case of documentary or scientific footage that bears no artistic ambitions, the medium's capacity to generate what André Bazin

(1947: 144–7) once termed 'accidental beauty'. Indeed, Adriano's project presents itself as a knowingly doomed attempt at exhausting the visual variations born out of its base material, an approach that Nicole Brenez (2002: 61) identifies as experimental cinema's 'analytical use' of found footage. Interestingly, Brenez (61) points out that the analytical method bears some similarity to scientific experimentation: in the systematic exploration and manipulation of a particular filmic object that the analytical approach supposes, filmmakers adopt 'the model of the scientific investigation, but are able to override or subvert its rationality'. In the case of *Remanescências*, though Adriano engages in the methodical application of the techniques of direct intervention on the film strip, he does so through a resolutely artisanal process that leaves space for imprecision and chance happenings: the alterations of the images are visibly the result of an alliance between the hand and the machine, of a manual gesture interfering with or prolonging a technological procedure. Hence, in the tradition of artisanal experimental filmmaking, at the cross between what Vilém Flusser (2014: 46) called a 'gesture of making',[10] and the performance of the Agambenian (2000: 56–7) 'mediality of gesture', his work shifts the attention away from the notion of a finished artwork towards that of potentiality – an exploration of the image in becoming.[11]

Using an optical printer allows him to supplement the customary techniques (slowing down the speed, superimposing and splitting frames, applying colour filters, reversing the negative) with more hands-on, frame-by-frame operations, such as inserting objects (such as pieces of a broken mirror) between the camera lens and the filmstrip, as well as manually moving or exposing the filmstrip to peripheral sources of light. At the same time that this technique points to the inherently cinematic nature of its material, it alternately enhances its kinetic qualities (the shock of the still images becoming animated; the heavy flickering that reminds us of the fluctuation of the images passing through the projector), as well as its photographic nature (the single and serialised frame; the alternation of negative and positive). Adriano also pulls the images towards the painterly, in particular where the manipulations emphasise their chemical basis (subjecting the strip to sudden changes of tint and to the effect of the extreme close-up that breaks the figures down into grainy matter).[12]

Remanescências starts with a few frames from a film lead, and in the course of its 18-minute duration, it repeatedly shows a filmstrip passing under the optical printer's lens, often deframing it so as to let its sprocket holes appear. Yet if *Remanescências* thus constantly returns to analogue film as the matrix of its visual experimentations, the use of round-edged frames and of extreme close-ups – filling the frame with a small part of the already grainy image, dissolving the figurative content into its smallest, abstract constituents, stains or blots – is also reminiscent of artistic uses of still photography.[13] Furthermore, the effect of the filters that turn the images into series of bright, colourful variations brings to mind Pop Art experiments and in particular Andy Warhol's series of silk prints. Tinted in deep blue, the credit sequences' much-enlarged detail offers itself as a striking pictorial treatment of the sea that borders on the abstract.

The cinematic principle, however, remains at the core of the film, exemplified by the enduring effect of the medium's 'aesthetic of astonishment' (Gunning 1999). The first 2½ minutes show only still photograms. But when the looped images are at last set in motion, and the content of these few miraculously preserved images suddenly begins to move, with the waves starting to beat against the pillars, the soundtrack becomes silent, as in stunned astonishment.

The complex layering of classic and modern influences that emerges in the images' visual treatment also comes into relief through the soundtrack's mix of Brazilian, European and North American music spanning several centuries. Adriano alternates, and eventually fuses, the sound of the waves with Heinrich Biber's Passaglia for Solo Violin (c.1676), 'Born, Never Asked' by Laurie Anderson (1981) and Antônio Carlos Jobim's 'Samba de uma nota só' (One Note Samba, 1960).[14] Whether in synchronicity or, on the contrary, as a counterpoint to the different tonalities and pace of the film's content and rhythm of montage, the arrangement offers itself as a sequence of musical permutations punctuated by ruptures and repetitions – a sound counterpart to the film's visual study of its object.

Ultimately, and for all its seemingly systematic, methodical process, *Remanescências* revels in the indeterminacy that lies at the heart of photography's encounter with movement. Crucially, through the process of repetition and variation, this quality of non-finitude, which defeats attempts at a precise visual inventory of the content of the image, gives way to an interrogation on the conditions of appearance, or non-appearance, of images. Further than *Remanescências*' assiduous reworking of a handful of photograms, how many more images remain virtual, substituted for those that are actualised, given for us to see?

Such is the question that Laura Marks (2009: 87) addresses as she draws on Leibniz's concept of the fold to describe the process of 'unfolding' through which an image comes to be perceived: 'We may consider the infinite to be constituted of innumerable folds . . . Every perception is an unfolding. To figure out where an image comes from, we need to find out how it arose from the infinite' (see also Marks 2013). In contrast with 'unfolding', 'enfolding' designates the process whereby perceivable matter is filtered. Digital encoding, Marks points out, adds a layer of complexity to the enfolding stage, but, through their modes of selecting and framing, the practices of film and photography are also already a part of the 'enfolding'. For Marks, one of art's functions is to account for the process of enfolding, to make its operation visible or felt.

Remanescências does this in paradigmatic mode, seeking to account for the absent or virtual images through a methodical (and inevitably unfinished) evocation of the infinite variations afforded by a sequence made up of a few photograms. By contrast, Parente's enfolding style could be termed syntagmatic: *Figuras na paisagem* explores the conditions of apparition of the image as determined by the *dispositif*. The process is complicated by the integration of a virtual reality (VR) mode of display as part of the installation; however, 'enfolding' concerns both the conditions of apparition of the image and its mode of reception. Following Marks's terminology, it may still be used to emphasise an awareness of the choices involved in the selection and production of the images included in the VR environment. But enfolding also describes the framelessness of the image, one that effectively enwraps the viewer, producing an immersive regime of perception that arguably overlays the potential awareness of the processes of mediation involved. In *Figuras na paisagem*, these apparently contradictory regimes of imaging and vision are combined and recast as part of a long-lasting technological imaginary.

LOOKING AT OURSELVES LOOKING

A media-archaeology scholar, Parente draws on a long history of intermedial encounters between literature and the moving image, as well as photography, painting and cinema, a web of media interferences that he recasts through contemporary audiovisual technology. Characteristically, his installation evokes two ends of the spectrum in terms of the history of reception: on the one hand, it recalls the traditional *dispositif* of the peep-hole, accessible to a single viewer; on the other, it recreates a version of the painted or photographic panoramas – spectacular, immersive installations that continued to draw crowds even as cinema was starting to establish itself as a mass medium. However, these contrasting modes of spectatorial engagement are revisited through the simultaneous practice and mise-en-scène of immersive technology: the core of the installation is an audiovisual VR system based on a device called Visorama.[15]

Looking through a set of stereoscopic binoculars, a single viewer explores high-resolution 3D panoramic images (Figure 5.2). As with classic VR set-ups combining 360-degree vision with panoramic 3D images, that part of the *dispositif* effectively 'enfolds' the viewer in the environment created by the artist. Placed in the centre of an exhibiting room equipped with a screen,

Figure 5.2 View of André Parente's installation *Figuras na paisagem* (*Figures in a Landscape*, 2010). Courtesy of the artist.

the binoculars are attached to the end of a balancing pole, so as to follow the movements of the viewer's body. The image resulting from the viewer's navigation is projected on to the large 2D screen that adorns one of the gallery walls. The choices made by the person in charge of the binoculars – whatever part of the landscape she chooses to look at or move across – are thus witnessed by the rest of the gallery visitors. Both the viewer, and what she sees, can therefore, in turn, be observed. Similarly, the soundtrack that accompanies the selected images is heard by all present.

The user of the device is given an option: she may choose to navigate the space of a vast library or she can explore a seaside landscape, both punctuated by discreet video presences of the artist reading excerpts of books. The viewer discovers the embedded videos – small windows of moving images inserted within the panoramic still photograph – while surveying the 360-degree views of the library or of the Ipanema beach. By pressing one of the device's buttons, she can then zoom into the video, expanding it to a full screen, while activating the accompanying soundtrack.

Parente's work calls to mind Raymond Bellour's classic notion of *entre-images*, not merely because of the installation's combination of photography, video and VR, but because, in the transition from one to the other, it is the memory of the fourth medium, the cinema, that surfaces. As with *Remanescências*' beginning, *Figuras na paisagem* operates the passage from stillness to movement in a manner reminiscent of early film projections. Tom Gunning (1999) has pointed out that part of the wonder experienced by the first cinema audiences was born out of the medium displaying its own specificity: it was common practice to freeze the initial frame before setting off the spectacular, lifelike effect of figures moving on the screen, so as to delay the moment where the content of the image became animated.[16]

In Parente's installation, the attraction of the moving image manifests itself through a similar contrast between the still panorama and the filmed sequences, but also, paradoxically, through the latter's *arresting* power: to access the video, and immerse herself in it, the viewer in command of the binoculars has to stop her circumnavigation and focus on the content of the animated sequence, giving herself to a flow of images moved by forces outside of her control. Hence *Figuras na paisagem* invites us to reflect on the evolution of reception as triggered by the emergence of competing modes of viewing. Contrary to the ambulatory reception solicited by the 360-degree circular panoramas of old,[17] in the cinema, immersion into movement depends on the immobility of the spectators' bodies. In VR, vision is again connected to bodily motion but this re-embodiment comes at a price: the partial loss of the distance that typically grounds the aesthetic dimension of film as art. Whereas in cinema such an aesthetic experience is steeped in the encounter with another's (the filmmaker's, the director of photography's, the editor's) vision and subjectivity, in VR, the confrontation with the image is partly subsumed into the process of interfacing – less an issue of immersion in the pre-existing image, therefore, than a question of spectatorial investment in partly controlling its transformation (direction, framing, speed).

Relying on Jay David Bolter and Richard Grusin's now classic terminology of remediation, we could say that Parente's installation recasts this question of aesthetic distance as one of 'hypermediacy'. Whereas Marks's unfolding/enfolding concerns the appearance of the images themselves, Bolter and Grusin (1999: 34) focus on forms of remediation (of one medium by another) that include immediacy and hypermediacy: 'if the logic of immediacy leads one either to erase or to render automatic the act of representation, the logic of hypermediacy acknowledges multiple acts of representation and makes them visible'.[18] Here, a group of spectators are given to see doubly mediated images: extracted from the set of photographs and videos created by the artist, the screened images are further re-mediated through one single viewer's vision and choices. Immersion and immediacy (as experienced by the viewer using the binoculars) thus give way to hypermediacy (the audience watching both the images and the user of the device who navigates through them). At the same time, the voiceover, intimate in tone yet heard by all, sustains the sense of distance that establishes itself in the gap between the two modes of reception.[19] Thus, with its superposition of singular interface and collective reception, *Figuras na paisagem* effectively disassembles the framework of the VR effect. Before or after being enfolded *in* the image, we are invited not only to look *at* it, but to look at ourselves looking.

Visually cut off from her immediate surroundings, the 'blind viewer' in charge of the stereoscopic binoculars takes on the slightly monstrous, cyborg-like appearance that characterises all users of VR equipment. Yet arguably more monstrous is the effect of the twofold gaze. One person looks and selects, but her choices are visible to all: the rest of the audience see through her eyes, as it were.[20] Even if the situation is one of co-presence (rather than voyeurism), the strange space thus created between individual observation and collective viewing breeds a feeling of trespassing: for the outer spectators, watching the screened images is a bit like reading someone else's mind.

Furthermore, the stereoscopic binocular viewer or 'experiencer', blinded as she is to her actual environment, remains unaware of the gazes of those members of the audience whose eyes may leave the screen to focus on the experiencer instead. The sense of vulnerability is heightened by the VR user's dance-like performance:[21] the un-self-conscious choreography that the body performs, as he or she moves to look around, engrossed in the exploration of the immersive environment, watched by the rest of the gallery visitors. Yet to describe *Figuras na paisagem* as a mise-en-scène of voyeurism or the power of the simulacra would be to miss the point, for in its complex unfolding of the patterns of technologically mediated vision, Parente's installation offers itself as a performance of 'the media character of corporal movement' (Agamben 2000: 57): the body of the VR user is the tool and filter through which images are communicated to the rest of the audience.

In this sense, Parente's work resonates with Agamben's theorising, but also with Mark Hansen's reassessment of the viewer's engagement in the age of digital media. For Hansen, our relation to images is simultaneously embodied and creative. Contrary to Marks's theory of unfolding/enfolding, Hansen (2004: 2) sees this relation facilitated, rather than hampered, by the advent of the digital: his Bergsonian approach centres on the body functioning 'as a kind of filter that selects, from among the universe of images circulating around it and according to its own embodied capacities, precisely those that are relevant to it'. 'Rather than selecting pre-existent images', he adds, 'the body now operates by filtering information directly and, through this process, creating images' (10).

However, if Parente's work integrates forms of embodied spectatorship that resonate with the premise of Hansen's analysis, it ultimately upholds the anticipatory role and critical intervention of the artist not only in selecting and editing, but in foregrounding the processes (the *dispositif* as well as intermedial interferences) that alternatively enable and prevent us from accessing certain images. There is not one but several embodied, filtering and mediating processes at work in *Figuras na paisagem*. Hence the gestures of the VR user, displayed simultaneously as what Agamben calls a *gesta res* (an object in itself) and as a means to produce a specific series of images, point to the coexistence of different modes of imaging as well as regimes of viewing.

What shows as the VR user moves unpredictably through the 360-degree photographic landscape is not created specifically for the gaze of an audience: the images are made accessible to others through the particular setting designed by the artist, but in such a dispositif, as Hansen stresses, they are selected by and 'relevant to' one specific body (2004: 2): a testimony to the participatory, embodied nature of spectatorship, they also point to its incommunicability. Faintly reminiscent of the phantom rides of old – the swift, erratic pans, the abrupt changes of direction, the sudden stops – the random framing resulting from the VR user's handling of the binoculars is the expression of a self-engrossed, individual experiment. Though included in the aesthetic experience, thanks to the installation's apparatus, these images, resulting from the experiencer's navigation, are essentially devoid of artistic intentionality. In contrast, the looped video sequences, set to the absorbing recitation of the texts chosen by the artist, are designed to be watched – and to do so, as in the old cinematic mode of reception, the VR user has to relinquish her power to interface with the image. In this, *Figuras na paisagem* shares with Adolfo Bioy Casares's book *Morel's Invention* (1940) the melancholy sense of film spectatorship as an experience of separation. Such was also Stanley Cavell's (1979) understanding of the medium: for all its forceful means of triggering identification and its immersive qualities, cinema is a window on to a world in which we cannot partake, on which our presence has no impact. This paradoxical combination of spectatorial engagement and passivity, however, ultimately founds cinema's expressive and affective power.[22]

A Precise Image of Confusion

The fictional account of spectatorship itself, and of the impossibility of a perfectly objective perception, whether as immersion or separation, is at the heart of Italo Calvino's *Mr. Palomar* (1983), one of the texts read as part of the soundtrack to Parente's piece. A distant, fictional cousin to Marey and Cunha Salles, the book's eponymous character is the literary incarnation of the desire to perceive things clearly and distinctly, in complete objectivity. In his (doomed) rejection of all things indefinite and uncertain, Palomar is, as Antonio Costa (2000: 173) observes, 'a small monster'. Like today's VR users, 'he has a body that does not appear to end with a head, but with a strange optico-mechanical or electronic device. A camera, maybe, or a video camera. Or else a telescope, or an optical fibre captor' (173).

Palomar's project to become 'nothing else than the window through which the world looks at the world' (Calvino 1985: 112) recalls André Bazin's (1992) description of the quest for total immersion in 'The Myth of Total Cinema', and seemingly anticipates VR's promises to its users. Yet immersion is, no more than aesthetic experience, a part of Palomar's methods or objectives. Palomar stands on the beach looking at the sea, and he is not interested in the ebb and flow of the waves as an object of beauty; nor does he want to immerse himself in the sensory experience afforded by his surroundings. As in the method of phenomenological reduction, he wants to isolate and observe one single wave so as to perceive its movement accurately, from beginning to end, and to fix it precisely in his mind, thus 'mastering the world's complexity by reducing it to its simplest mechanism' (Calvino 1985: 6). Exercising his vision as if it were as detached and indifferent as the lens of a camera, he tries to analyse the motions of the sea with scientific exactitude. In other words, Mr Palomar wants to construct a *precise* image of the *vague*. A stylistic feat in the vein of what Gérard Genette (1983: 49) once described as the 'rebound effect' (a form of 'reverse' remediation where an older medium such as writing becomes infused with the expressive techniques of a newer medium such as film), Calvino's writing appropriates characteristic cinematic techniques – photographic detail, close-up, change of scale, ellipsis, montage – and though published before the advent of high-definition digital imaging, the text remains a timely reminder of the impossibility to master the perceivable world beyond the threshold of the 'clear and confused'.

In tune with Calvino's literary treatment of visual perception, the videos embedded in *Figuras na paisagem* create a splinter into the panoramic view, lines of flight at the heart of what initially looked like a perfectly enclosed 360-degree virtual world. It does not matter that the videos are shot in high definition and looped: as with Leibniz's perception of the wave, the movement that affects all parts of the image simultaneously and through time can never be grasped entirely and precisely.

Another text chosen by Parente is Rubem Braga's *Homem no mar* (*Man at Sea*, 1953). To listen to it, the user of the binoculars zooms in on a video showing the outline of a swimmer progressing through the waves, far out at sea. In Braga's account, the observer standing on the beach becomes consciously absorbed in the spectacle of the swimmer, deploying a form of superstitious dependability (or said more positively, a heightened sense of responsibility) in the way he keeps his gaze focused on the silhouette throughout its journey. It is as if the description itself constructs the scene, as if the observer's gaze carried the swimmer along – as if, had the observer stopped looking as intently as he did, the swimmer would not have made it safely back to the beach, would have vanished instead into the waves in a moment of the viewer's inattention. Thus the written story, and its immersive multimedia version, combine to form the mise-en-abyme of a process of co-creation, between reader and text, and between art installation and audience, involving a specific mode of spectatorship that strongly contrasts with the usual practice of VR environments: a suspension of all actions save for an attentive, sustained watching.

Like Mr Palomar, who gazes at the sea so intently he starts to feel as unsteady as the waves, or like the observer in Braga's story, with his heightened sense of co-presence, the spectators of *Figuras na paisagem*, whether they look through the device or sit around, partaking in the vision of the immersed viewer who performs the Visorama's blind dance, are made aware of their status as both observers, with a limited point of view that never fully coincides with another, and, simultaneously, a part of that same world observed. As with the realisation of the inherent elusiveness of the field of the visible represented in film, so the sense of a shared field of perception, where one is both subject and object of the gaze, is at once humbling and empowering. In the engrossing pattern of echoes that it establishes between film, video and literature, and past and present media technologies, Parente's work reflects on the coexistence of the observed and observer that makes the latter equally a part of the world's infinite confusion of matter and movements: a *being-in-media* and *being-in-language* coextensive with a being-in-the-world that forms the ethical dimension of gesture, according to Agamben (2000: 55).

'There is no substance, no matter how small, that is not affected by all the others,' Leibniz argued ([1714] 1900: 724). For Laurence Bouquiaux, Leibniz's clear and confused perception, with its basis in what he calls the 'admirable connection of all things', is not only the recognition of the value of sensory perception, but the refutation of the classically distanced Cartesian observer, standing outside that which he observes, endowed with an omniscient, detached point of view. Bouquiaux (2007: 13) stresses that although Leibniz separates the perceiving subject from the perceived object, and talks of perspective and point of view, he 'does not grant man an overlooking position in nature's system'.[23] His theory of perception does not imply that one has 'the possibility to order an object-world that he or she contemplates from the outside'. Rather, Leibniz posits that since both inhabit the same world, all one can do is experience the world from a limited perspective that necessarily includes an element of confusion. In turn, the sense of imprecision and non-finitude that we derive from sensory perception feeds into artistic creation.[24]

Adriano's manual alteration of analogue footage and Parente's reassembling of audiovisual apparatuses into a hybrid *dispositif* both emphasise image, perception and mediality as part of a chain of continually shifting connections and gestures that includes and affects both the observer and the observed. In doing so, their works testify to the persistence of an imaginary – from the beginnings of the cinema to the advent of digital imaging and VR – born out of a particular manifestation of the *vague* that haunts other media and artforms, yet remains, first and foremost, cinematic. Never before the invention of cinema had the elusive complexity and un-finitude of the world we inhabit, so aptly exemplified by the phenomenon and concept of the *vague*, been captured and offered to the gaze with such a precisely rendered confusion of details.

Notes

1. My thanks to André Parente for his precious insights on this topic. Written in 1970, Flusser's *Fenomenologia do brasileiro: em busca de um novo homem* was first published in German in 1994.
2. By *dispositif*, I mean the combination of the technical apparatus (projector, screen, virtual reality headset and so on) and the regimes of vision they may foster (for example, voyeurism).
3. See also the introduction to Beugnet et al. 2017. The connection between the indefinite and imagination is best summed in Da Vinci's classic example of the stained wall in his *Trattato della pittura* (1651).
4. It was for this very reason that Hokusai's *The Great Wave off Kanagawa* (1830/1) fascinated the Impressionist painters.
5. My thanks to João Luiz Vieira, who pointed this out to me. A film reported to have been shot by Afonso Segreto in 1898, titled *Uma vista da Baía de Guanabara* (*View of Guanabara Bay*), also had the sea as its subject.
6. Jacques Malthête (2002: 12) thus points out that 'Not wanting to cultivate the paradox at all costs, one cannot help but stress one notable point that Étienne-Jules Marey (1830–1904) and Georges Méliès (1861–1938) have in common: neither of them saw the interest in reproducing on the screen that which our eyes see in reality. Marey always preferred the analysis of movement to its purely spectacular synthesis, which had little to teach us and was more suited to the fairground shows (. . .).' In a radio interview quoted in Alexis Martinet (ed.), *Le Cinéma et la science*, Lucien Bull (1876–1972), Marey's collaborator from 1896 to 1904, tells Dr Pierre Thévenard that 'film projection did not interest [Marey] in any way' and that 'analysis was the only thing that interested him' (Martinet 1994: 107). My translations.
7. A number of theorists identified this paradox as film's key feature: while Jean Epstein called it cinema's *photogénie*, Siegfried Kracauer talked of film's unmatched capacity to render 'the indeterminate'. See Epstein 1975; Kracauer 1960.
8. Take the well-known account, by journalist Henri De Parville, of the first Lumière films projections, where he marvels at having been able 'to distinguish all the details, the rising swirls of smoke, the waves that come crashing on the beach, the leaves quivering in the wind'. See De Parville 1896. See also my introduction to the volume *Indefinite Visions* (Beugnet 2017: 1–13).

9. My thanks to Carlos Adriano for useful exchanges on his work.
10. Flusser (2014: 46) describes various stages in the gesture of making, including researching of the object, an alteration of the raw material, and finally a presentation that is not, however, a statement of resolution, but one of 'resignation': the 'raw material' always resists completion.
11. These notions are equally crucial to Agamben's thinking, in particular through his revisiting of Aristotle (on potentiality) and Gilles Deleuze's writing (on becoming).
12. Though Adriano uses filters rather than dye, the effect recalls both the tinting of films during the silent period and, as discussed later, Warhol's silk prints.
13. As in the work of Richard Hamilton with extremely enlarged photographs, for example. In this, Adriano's film is also reminiscent of structuralist filmmaking. Speaking of Ken Jacobs's now classic experimental found-footage film, *Tom, Tom, the Piper's Son* (1969), for instance, Kerry Brougher (1996: 83) remarks that Jacobs reduces 'film to its most "primal" elements'.
14. Coincidentally, Jobim is also the composer of the classic Bossa Nova song 'Wave' (1967).
15. To create this work, Parente collaborated with Luiz Velho, a member of the IMPA (the Pure and Applied Mathematics Institute).
16. On freeing the still photographic image from its paralysing spell, see also Agamben 2000: 55.
17. This was different from moving panoramas, which unrolled images before immobile spectators. See Huhtamo 2013. My thanks to Tiago de Luca for reminding me of this point.
18. Bolter and Grusin (1999: 37) mention devices such as the Diorama, the Phenakistoscope and the Stereoscope as early examples of the combination of immediacy and hypermediacy: 'These devices, characterized by multiple images, moving images, or sometimes moving observers, seem to have operated under both these logics at the same time, as they incorporated transparent immediacy *within* hypermediacy.'
19. The sense of a gap, here, recalls Maurice Merleau-Ponty's use of the French word 'écart'. In *The Visible and the Invisible*, he argues (1968: 123) that to perceive consciously is to experience a gap or 'écart': to see, or touch, is to be somehow aware of the experience of being seen and touched: 'between my body looked at and my body looking, my body touched and my body touching, there is overlapping or encroachment, so that we may say that the things pass into us, as well as we into the things'.
20. For a fiction film treatment of a similar idea, see Kathryn Bigelow's *Strange Days* (1995).
21. The expression 'blind dance' was coined by Victa de Carvalho in her description of the installation, available at <http://www.andreparente.net/> (last accessed 25 October 2017).
22. Cinema, Cavell (1979: 41) argues, fosters a sense of presentness imbued with a form of absence making 'displacement appear as our natural condition'. Deleuze

(1985: 218) bypasses the issue of the cinema as an illusory world by reinstating the medium's capacity to rejuvenate 'our belief in the world'.
23. Hence, Bouquiaux (2007: 14) concludes, the world that Leibniz describes ultimately resembles that which twentieth-century phenomenologist Merleau-Ponty describes, one which 'we inhabit' and 'with which we are connected through our bodies'. See also Bouquiaux 1994.
24. Leibniz's disciple and founder of the study of aesthetics, Alexander Gottlieb Baumgarten, argued that art explores and cultivates the *'je ne sais quoi'*: that is, the indefinite part of perception or experience. It is therefore only in the realm of the clear and confused that art can thrive. Artistic intuition and vision thus stem from the incompleteness and constant fluctuation of the perceived, the impossibility of a full and perfect knowledge of the world. See Scholar 2005.

References

Agamben, Giorgio (2000), 'Notes on Gesture', in *Means Without End: Notes on Politics*, trans. Vincenzo Binetti and Cesare Casarino. Minneapolis: University of Minnesota Press, pp. 49–60.

Aumont, Jacques (2010), 'Que reste-t-il du cinéma?', *Trafic*, 79, pp. 95–107.

Bazin, André (1947), 'Le Film scientifique: beauté du hasard', *L'Écran français*, 121, 21 October, pp. 144–7.

Bazin, André ([1962] 1992), 'The Myth of Total Cinema', *What is Cinema?*, vol. 1. trans. Hugh Gray. Berkeley, Los Angeles and London: University of California, pp. 23–7.

Beugnet, Martine, Allan Cameron and Aril Fetveit (eds) (2017), *Indefinite Visions: Cinema and the Attraction of Uncertainty*. Edinburgh: Edinburgh University Press.

Bolter, Jay David and Richard Grusin (1999), *Remediation: Understanding New Media*. Cambridge, MA: MIT Press.

Bouquiaux, Laurence (1994), *L'Harmonie et le chaos: le rationalisme leibnizien et la 'nouvelle science'*. Paris: Editions Peeters.

Bouquiaux, Laurence (2007), 'Dire l'indicible: Leibniz et le partage de l'expérience sensible', unpublished paper (14 pages), available at <web.philo.ulg.ac.be/culturessensibles/wp-content/uploads/sites/34/pdf/Laurence-1.pdf> (last accessed 29 December 2020).

Braga, Rubem (1953), 'Homem no Mar', *Correio da Manhã*, January.

Brenez, Nicole (2002), 'Montage intertextuel et formes contemporaines du remploi dans le cinéma expérimental', *Cinémas: revue d'études cinématographiques / Cinémas: Journal of Film Studies*, 13:1–2, pp. 49–67.

Brougher, Kerry (1996), 'Hall of Mirrors', in Kerry Bourgher (ed.), *Art and Film since 1945: Hall of Mirrors*. Los Angeles: Contemporary Art Museum, pp. 20–138.

Calvino, Italo ([1983] 1985), *Mr. Palomar*, trans. W. Weaver. New York: Harcourt Brace Jovanovich.

Cavell, Stanley (1979), The *World Viewed: Reflections on the Ontology of Film*. Cambridge, MA: Harvard University Press.

Costa, Antonio (2000), '*Palomar*: intermédialité et archéologie de la vision', *Cinémas*, 102:3, pp. 169–84.

Davis, Whitney (2011), *A General Theory of Visual Culture*. Princeton: Princeton University Press.

De Parville, Henri (1896), 'Le Cinématographe', *Les Annales politiques et littéraires*, 26 April.
Deleuze, Gilles (1985), *Cinema 2: L'image temps*. Paris: Éditions de Minuit.
Didi-Huberman, Georges (2009), 'Aesthetic Immanence', in Bernd Huppauf and Christoph Wulf (eds), *Dynamics and Performativity of Imagination: The Image Between the Visible and the Invisible*. London: Routledge, pp. 42–55.
Epstein, Jean (1975), *Ecrits sur le cinéma*, vol. 2. Paris: Cinéma Club/Seghers.
Flusser, Vilem (2014), 'The Gesture of Making', in Vilem Flusser, *Gestures*. Minneapolis: University of Minnesota Press, pp. 32–48.
Genette, Gérard (1983), *Nouveau discours du récit*. Paris: Seuil.
Gunning, Tom (1999), 'An Aesthetic of Astonishment: Early Film and the (In)credulous Spectator', in Leo Braudy and Marshall Cohen (eds), *Film Theory and Criticism*. Oxford: Oxford University Press, pp. 818–42.
Hansen, Mark B. N. (2004), *New Philosophy for New Media*. Cambridge, MA: MIT Press.
Huhtamo, Erkki (2013), *Illusions in Motion: Media Archaeology of the Moving Panorama and Related Spectacles*. Cambridge, MA: MIT Press.
Huppauf, Bernd and Cristoph Wulf (eds) (2009), *Dynamics and Performativity of Imagination: The Image Between the Visible and the Invisible*. London: Routledge.
Kracauer, Siegfried (1960), *Theory of Film: The Redemption of Physical Reality*. Princeton: Princeton University Press.
Krauss, Rosalind (2000), *A Voyage on the North Sea: Art in the Age of the Post-medium Condition*. London: Thames & Hudson.
Leibniz, Gottfried Wilhelm ([1714] 1900), 'Principes de la nature et de la grâce fondés en raison, §13', in Paul Janet and Félix Alcan (eds), *Œuvres philosophiques de Leibniz*, vol. 1. Paris: Félix Alcan, pp. 723–31.
Malthête, Jacques (2002), 'Marey et Méliès', *Bulletin de la Sémia*, 2, p. 12.
Marks, Laura U. (2009), 'Information, Secrets and Enigmas: An Enfolding-Unfolding Aesthetics for Cinema', *Screen*, 50:1, pp. 86–98.
Marks, Laura (2013), 'A Noisy Brush with the Infinite: Noise in Enfolding-Unfolding Aesthetics', in Carol Vernallis, Amy Herzog and John Richardson (eds), *The Oxford Handbook of Sound and Image in Digital Media*. New York: Oxford University Press, pp. 201–15.
Marques, Luiz, Roberto Conduru, Claudia Mattos and Mônica Zielinsky (2013), 'Existe-t-il un art brésilien?', *Perspective: actualité en histoire de l'art*, 2, pp. 251–68.
Martinet, Alexis (ed.) (1994), *Le Cinéma et la science*. Paris: cnrs éditions.
Medeiros, Débora (2015), 'Vilém Flusser in Brazil: Media and the New Human', *Flusser Studies*, 20, pp. 1–19.
Merleau-Ponty, Maurice (1968), *The Visible and the Invisible*. Evanston, IL: Northwestern University Press.
Montani, Pietro (2018), 'L'Art comme expérience technique', in Christa Blumlinger and Mathias Lavin (eds), *Geste filmé, gestes filmiques*. Paris: Mimesis, pp. 215–25.
Nagib, Lúcia and Stefan Solomon (2019), 'Intermediality in Brazilian Cinema: The Case of Tropicália', *Screen*, 60:1, pp. 122–71.
Schelling, Vivian (2001), *Through the Kaleidoscope: The Experience of Modernity in Latin America*. London: Verso.
Scholar, Richard (2005), *The Je-Ne-Sais-Quoi in Early Modern Europe: Encounters with a Certain Something*. Oxford: Oxford University Press.
Simondon, Albert (1958), *Du mode d'existence des objets techniques*. Paris: Aubier.

Part II

The Empire of Music

CHAPTER 6

Watson Macedo's Aviso aos navegantes *(1950): Reflections on the Musical Numbers of a Brazilian* Chanchada[1]

Flávia Cesarino Costa

This chapter will explore the Brazilian musical comedy (or *chanchada*) *Aviso aos navegantes* (*Calling all Sailors*), directed by Watson Macedo in 1950 at the Atlântida studios in Rio de Janeiro. I argue that the film stands as an emblematic production in the heyday of musical comedies and provides a telling example of the intermedial connections that shaped Brazilian cinema between the 1930s and the 1950s. My analysis will stress the need to move away from the usual considerations of the relationship between musical numbers and plot so as to focus on the intermedial features of these numbers in terms of their ties with other cultural traditions, industries and practices, including theatre, carnival, the music industry and radio performances. Many studies of Brazilian cinema of the first half of the twentieth century overstate the centrality and specificity of cinema while downplaying the interference of other media. My aim is to demonstrate that we need to relativise the importance of cinema in the media landscape of that time.

As a research method, intermediality will be adopted here to examine the relationship between different media within filmic products. Musical numbers in *chanchadas* usually interrupt the narrative flow with song-and-dance spectacles that directly reference radio performances and theatrical revues, confirming these films' status as a complex intermedial mixture. In her book *Cinema and Intermediality* (2011: 4–6), Ágnes Pethő aligns film intermediality to techniques and devices that break the transparency of the filmic image. In her account, intermediality can be understood as a repetition or reinscription of a medium inside the form of other media, as a result of which the intermedial process becomes noticeable and refers back to itself. In the following sections I will argue that the musical numbers of the *chanchadas* are privileged moments when, either deliberately or because of production problems, the inscription of strategies from other media are made visible and gain in significance.

Before the advent of radio, *teatro de revista* (theatrical revue) was the main vehicle for musical releases in Rio de Janeiro, eclectically showcasing musical numbers teeming with double entendres and comic sketches featuring both popular and erudite musicians. In addition to commenting on daily life and current affairs, the revues produced around the end of the year often launched new songs ahead of Brazil's traditional carnival festivities, held annually between the preceding Friday and Ash Wednesday. Between the 1930s and 1950s the new musical releases and parades constituted an important part of carnival in its connections with radio and the phonographic industry. From 1934, Brazil witnessed an increase in the number of radio stations, which began to incorporate singing numbers previously performed in theatres. The popularity of radio programmes in the 1940s propelled singers, musicians and arrangers to stardom, especially as they now featured on the soundtrack of films, the same being of true of the actors and comedians of the theatrical revues.

Although largely frowned upon by critics, the *chanchada* was one of Brazil's most popular genres between the 1930s and the late 1950s. *Chanchadas* comprised humorous sketches and musical numbers strung together by a flimsy plotline, the choice of numbers often being indebted to the music and radio commercial network surrounding carnival, including many of its distinctive features (Vieira 2012: 141–2). As Vieira (142) notes, *chanchada* films are 'linked to the large universe of Carnival, in that they incorporate the social inversions typical of Carnival and develop, like Carnival itself, an implicit social critique'. In the heyday of these musical comedies, carnival acted as the nucleus around which radio hits, the theatrical revue and the *chanchada* revolved, with the presence of radio singers constituting a crucial feature of the films' popular mixture of music and humour. Initially employed as a derogatory adjective by critics, the word *chanchada* was rehabilitated by historians in the 1970s, at which point it started to be used more widely as a genre descriptor (Freire 2011: 103).

Important studies of *chanchadas* have noted the heavy influence of different cultural practices and other media, as well as the carnival culture in general, on the films produced between the 1930s and the 1950s (see Vieira 1984, 1987, 2012; Augusto 1989; Lenharo 1995; Shaw 2000 and 2003; Dennison and Shaw 2004; Schvarzman 2008; Freire 2011). In tune with these studies, this chapter focuses on the way in which the entertainment industry often dictated the configuration of specific musical numbers of *chanchadas*, as seen in *Aviso aos navegantes*, which will be analysed here not only as a text but also and especially in its context. My aim is to follow in the footsteps of scholars such as Ciocci (2010) and Araújo (2015, 2018), who argue for the need to remove cinema from a position of absolute centrality so as to examine its wider intermedial connections. Ciocci has shown how Atlântida *chanchadas* produced during the 1940s and the 1950s were influenced by both Brazilian music and Hollywood standards, while Araújo, though focusing on Brazilian silent cinema, deploys an intermedial approach to study the interplay between popular theatre and Hollywood, as well as the intermingling of stage attractions and screen practices in specific film theatres in São Paulo.

In what follows I first consider *Aviso aos navegantes* in relation to both Watson Macedo's career as a *chanchada* director and its production context at Atlântida, Brazil's biggest film production company at the time. I then move on to look more closely at some of the film's musical numbers as privileged examples of intermedial interactions between film and other contemporaneous media, including popular theatre, radio and the illustrated press, all of which carried a greater aesthetic weight in the film's final outlook than film-specific procedures themselves. My hope is to demonstrate that these numbers were conceived according to staging practices, illustrated magazines and the economic imperatives of the music industry in the wider context of a Brazilian star system.

WATSON MACEDO AND THE ATLÂNTIDA CINEMATOGRÁFICA

The 1940s and 1950s were dominated by films from the Atlântida Cinematográfica company, founded in 1941 in Rio de Janeiro. In 1947, one of the most powerful commercial exhibitors in Brazil, Luiz Severiano Ribeiro Junior, became its major shareholder and started producing films at low cost and with popular appeal, thus ensuring large profits until the late 1950s. Although *chanchadas* often relied on a small group of technicians working in modest studios and using second-hand equipment (including a large dose of improvisation), the films were highly profitable at the domestic box office. Between 1945 and 1960, Watson Macedo (1918–81) was one of the most prolific directors of *chanchadas*. He worked for Atlântida from 1944 to 1951, and became an independent film producer thereafter. At Atlântida he had garnered huge success directing four other *chanchadas* before *Aviso aos navegantes*. Despite the popularity of his films, Macedo was considered by many critics to be the most 'Americanised' of the directors in that period. This was because he was seen to adhere less strictly to the rules of parodic criticism, a feature of the *chanchadas* privileged by other directors, including José Carlos Burle and Carlos Manga. Moreover, unlike those directors, Macedo was concerned with embellishing and visually improving the musical numbers in order to enhance their appeal. While the majority of these numbers in the 1940s and early 1950s tended to preserve the immobility of radio performances and the frontality of theatrical staging, Macedo was particularly skilful at making them more dynamic and cinematic.

Macedo was aware that the inclusion of the year's greatest musical hits in the *chanchadas* was a highly lucrative business for the record companies, and Atlântida accordingly charged those companies for each and every song in his films. The choice of musical attractions in the *chanchadas* was always based on the popularity of radio songs, and the plots were often adapted to the songs rather than the other way around. Moreover, as Lenharo has noted (1995: 116), the recruitment of singers to perform acting roles in these films increased just before carnival. To have an acting part in those movies was highly significant for these singers' careers – as important as being hired by big record companies or invited to tours around the country (Lenharo 1995: 115). Yet the goal of these singers was simply to appear in the films as a marketing strategy to boost image popularity: indeed, they never turned into actors, in the same way that actors and actresses rarely turned into singers.

From the 1940s onwards, Hollywood cinema started to bridge the gap between musical performances and plots with more tightly integrated narratives, which soon became an established pattern of the genre. In the Brazilian *chanchadas*, conversely, the move towards more coherent plots did not completely eliminate a certain gap between the narrative and the musical numbers, which, for many critics at the time, was evidence of the poor quality of these films. In her book on the Hollywood musical, Jane Feuer comments that the genre fostered an organic mise-en-scène whereby singers and dancers smoothly blended in with settings and objects to the point that spectators would forget all the planning and deliberations that sat behind the numbers. She notes:

> The engineering, as the mode of production of the Hollywood musical, is cancelled by a content relying heavily upon bricolage. We lose all sense of the calculation lying behind the numbers and we gain, as a bonus, the aura of absolute spontaneity. (Feuer 1993: 7)

In other words, the musical scenes are still perceived as seamlessly integrated within the film as a whole, despite the fact that they break the narrative flow, thus enabling the audience to focus entirely on the numbers rather than on the work that made them happen.

In the Brazilian musical numbers of that period, the opposite was true: the acting often drew attention to itself and the connections with other media at the basis of the production process were made apparent, as we will see in the next section. This was different from American films, where the visual content of the musicals seemed so spontaneous and natural. There was another logic in place, one connected to wider mechanisms dictating Brazilian mass culture until the late 1950s, as described by Lenharo (1995: 135):

> After the casinos were closed down [in 1943], the appearance of theatrical revues and the *chanchadas* formed with radio a triad of mass culture production,

but the radio always retained a more wide-ranging and concentrated role. The phonographic industry, music publishers, specialised magazines and publicity all gravitated around that triad. The musical life in Rio de Janeiro and other Brazilian capital cities relied on that triad as a reference point for their activities. Singers, composers, musicians, vaudeville actors, radio actors, in one way or another, circulated around these cultural spaces.[2]

Similarly, Luis Rocha Melo (2017: 153–4) has noted the defining relationship between film and a wider cultural context:

> The interactions between radio, the record industry and the cinema illustrate that in Brazilian popular musical comedies stardom cannot be understood at a strictly cinematic level. It is a wider phenomenon, the result of the interplay between the cinema and a nascent 'culture industry', which included not only the radio and the record industry, but also the press and, from the second half of the 1950s, television.

If radio took on a central role in Brazilian mass culture in the 1940s and 1950s, the *chanchadas* participated in this phenomenon through their musical numbers. In particular, the presence of radio singers was essential to lend the *chanchada*'s blend of music and humour a popular appeal. While many critics condemned the comedies due to their precarious mode of production, this is because, as Lenharo notes, they 'did not realise the originality of the phenomenon and insisted on reducing Atlântida to an underdeveloped copy of the American cinema' (1995: 116). Let us now look at some musical numbers in *Aviso aos navegantes* in order to explore these intermedial relations.

AVISO AOS NAVEGANTES AND ITS MUSICAL NUMBERS

Released in 1950, *Aviso aos navegantes* survives in different and conflicting copies. My analysis will be based on the DVD version launched in 2000, which was put together from footage extracted from different versions, all of which remain more or less incomplete. It is therefore impossible to ascertain if the 2000 version is entirely faithful to the original.

Aviso aos navegantes is set aboard a steamship that leaves Buenos Aires heading towards Rio de Janeiro. Some of the musical numbers take place on a fictitious stage in Buenos Aires, others inside the ship, and yet others stand in for the characters' dreams. A chase plot involving a dangerous spy and a series of romantic mishaps are interspersed with the musical numbers. Although the numbers are often performed on an actual stage, Macedo employs fluid camerawork, with the camera moving across the set and among the performers. Macedo's first films were crucial for creating the formula of the triangle involving a good girl, a good guy and a bad guy that helped establish a local star system in Brazilian cinema, in turn increasing audience identification and boosting film production at Atlântida (Vieira 1987: 161).

The most important comic actors from theatrical revues of the time, Oscarito and Grande Otelo, star in the film alongside other famous actors, such as Anselmo Duarte, who plays 'the good guy' Alberto, the ship's captain, and Eliana Macedo as Cléia, the captain's sweetheart. An important feature of the *chanchadas* is that they often mixed actors from different backgrounds and contexts. *Aviso aos navegantes* was no different, also featuring aspiring actors, theatrical revue starlets such as Virgínia Lane, and professional singers who, as noted earlier, appeared in films to disseminate their songs, including Francisco Carlos, Emilinha Borba, Jorge Goulart, Linda Batista and Dalva de Oliveira. In the musical numbers, the diverse artistic backgrounds and skills of the cast are all made visible rather than effaced, and I will come back to this.

In contrast with the comedian actors, Eliana Macedo did not have an acting background, nor was she a professional dancer or singer to start with. Being white and blonde, however, Eliana did become the most popular Brazilian star of the period, with her unassuming beauty and her way of mingling Hollywood-inspired elements with local popular music and culture. Despite her lack of training, Eliana managed to act, sing and dance like no other actress or actor at the time, emerging as a hybrid figure straddling a real and an idealised Brazil. As João Luiz Vieira (2012: 148) explains, she 'would embody the ideal of the archetypal nice girl next door in musical numbers that would frequently quote Carmen Miranda gestures, choreographies and, especially, the stylized baiana costume'.

Although often set on a stage within the diegesis, none of the musical numbers in *Aviso aos navegantes* has content that is tightly related to the plot. They are all, in fact, inspired by contemporaneous musical hits, thus evidencing the film's subordination to the phonographic market. In the version of the film under discussion, there are 17 musical numbers in total: 7 *marchinhas* (classic carnival songs), 2 *baiões* (a typical northeastern musical genre), 2 country waltzes, 3 rumbas, 2 sambas, and even a number that mixes Tchaikovsky's Concerto No. 1 with *gafieira* (a samba subgenre). There is also a scene where the diegetic music played in the background is the famous song 'Paraíba', which is also an important musical moment in the film, as we will see.

Most musical numbers are performed by radio singers. Ruy Rey, a Brazilian who had earned success singing in Spanish, delivers the rumbas, in tune with the Latin rhythm craze of the time. Ivon Curi plays French foxtrot songs. Adelaide Chiozzo plays the accordion and sings folk music, performing two pieces with Eliana: 'Recruta biruta' (Mad Rookie) and 'Beijinho doce' (Sweet

Table 6.1 Musical numbers of *Aviso aos navegantes* (1950). Developed from author's research on the film copy, at Cinemateca Brasileira (Brazilian Film Archive) and the online archive of Brazilian phonograms at the Moreira Salles Institute, <http://acervo.ims.com.br>

	Time played on the film	Music name	Genre	Release date	Singer or performer	Record company
1	2m42	Bate o bombo (Hit the Bass Drum)	*Baião*	1950	Eliana Macedo	Continental
2	5m44	Marcha do neném (Baby's March)	March	1950	Oscarito	Capitol
3	11m12	Mercê	Rumba	29 Jan 1951	Ruy Rey and his band	Continental
4	12m52	A romper el coco (Breaking the Coconut)	Rumba	Unreleased, recorded for the film (1950)	Ruy Rey and his band, and the rumbera Cuquita Carballo	Performed for the film
5	22m15	Toureiro de Cascadura (Cascadura Bullfighter)	March	1950	Oscarito	Sinter and Capitol
6	25m54	Sereia de bordo (Mermaid on Board)	Waltz	Unreleased, recorded for the film (1950)	Adelaide Chiozzo	Performed for the film
7	28m52	Beijinho doce (Sweet Little Kiss)	Waltz	1950	Adelaide Chiozzo and Eliana Macedo	Continental
8	31m42	C'est si bon (It Is So Good)	Foxtrot	1951	Ivon Curi	Continental
9	37m09	Piano Concerto No. 1 in B-flat minor, Op. 23 (Pyotr Tchaikovsky)	Classic / Samba	Composed in 1875, samba version not released, recorded for the film (1950)	Bené Nunes and his orchestra, samba version arranged by Lindolfo Gaya	Performed for the film

Table 6.1 (Continued)

	Time played on the film	Music name	Genre	Release date	Singer or performer	Record company
10	43m00	Não vivo bem (I'm Not Well)	Samba-canção	Unreleased, recorded for the film (1950)	Francisco Carlos	Performed for the film
11	46m43	Sereia de Copacabana (Copacabana's Mermaid)	March	1950	Jorge Goulart	Continental
12	51m00	Tomara que chova (Let's Hope It Rains)	March	1950	Emilinha Borba	Continental
13	55m00	Paraíba	Baião	1950	Bené Nunes and his orchestra	Continental
14	1h09m56	Recruta biruta (Mad Rookie)	March	1950	Eliana Macedo and Adelaide Chiozzo	Todamerica
15	1h16m14	Cubana (Cuban Girl)	March	1950	Ruy Rey and his band	Continental
16	1h17m32	Na Candelária (At Candelaria)	Rumba	Unreleased, recorded for the film (1950)	Oscarito, Ruy Rey and his band	Performed for the film
17	1h26m56	Marcha do caracol (Snail March)	March	1950	Quatro Ases e um Coringa (Four Aces and a Joker)	RCA Victor
18	1h53m50	Rio de Janeiro	Samba	1944	Francisco Carlos, Eliana Macedo, Oscarito	Performed for the film (Odeon released a version with Dalva de Oliveira in 1951)

Little Kiss). The group Quatro Ases e um Coringa (Four Aces and a Joker) plays a carnival *marchinha*, as do famous radio singers such as Emilinha Borba, Jorge Goulart and Francisco Carlos. Bené Nunes, a well-known pianist, appears not only in the Tchaikovsky number but also in the ballroom scenes, including one in which Eliana fights with another woman to the sound of the aforementioned 'Paraíba'.

As we can see in Table 6.1, most songs were released in 1950 and 1951, many of them by Continental, which indicates a close relationship between the film producers and this record company. In fact, the majority of the songs premiered in *Aviso aos navegantes*, which was shot in 1950, and were then released for the 1951 carnival. All songs featured in the film were new releases, except for the last one, 'Rio de Janeiro', originally composed by Ary Barroso for the American film *Brazil* (Joseph Stanley, 1944). Yet even here it is no coincidence that the song was released in a 1951 version by the Odeon record company with the voice of superstar singer Dalva de Oliveira, showing how *chanchadas* capitalised on musical hits, with no generic bias, as a way of boosting their popularity and profitability. Let us now look more closely at some musical numbers so as to examine the way in which the connections with the entertainment industry played themselves out in the mise-en-scène alongside features borrowed from the Hollywood musical.

The film's opening number features the *baião* 'Bate o bombo' (Hit the Bass Drum), with Eliana singing and dancing, accompanied by performers at the back of the stage on an inclined ramp. The performance blends Brazilian rhythm with elements from the Hollywood musical, some of which, such as the ramp, had been reworked by theatrical revues and then translated back into the cinema. As another Atlântida director, Carlos Manga, would note years later, the rapport with Hollywood cinema in this and other musical numbers was intentional, yet adapted to a Brazilian context: 'That is what I always say: the Americans used to make their stars descend a footbridge of 180 meters. We used to put Eliana descending a footbridge of 1.8m. But it was the influence of American cinema! This little ramp had a classical touch' (Ciocci 2010: 67). In addition, the camerawork and the multiplication of geometric forms on screen recall Busby Berkeley's numbers, with a lively effect achieved by highlighting the mobility of dancers within the frame, rather than moving the camera. The dance is framed in such a way as to stress the dynamism of circular forms and the contrasting black-and-white colours in the spiral figures dotting the objects and clothes (Figure 6.1).

As for the number's choreography, it was crafted by Juliana Yanakiewa, an important figure on the vaudeville scene and in the musical films of the period. The scene alternates shots of Eliana's direct address to the camera, surrounded by male dancers, with shots of the lateral movement of female dancers, led

Figure 6.1 Eliana sings and dances in the musical number 'Bate o bombo' (Hit the Bass Drum) in *Aviso aos navegantes* (1950).

by Yanakiewa herself, over the inclined platforms that cross the frame diagonally. An Austrian-born ballet dancer who lived in Bulgaria, Yanakiewa came to Brazil in the 1940s and was unable to return home because of the war. By 1950, Yanakiewa was already a recognised choreographer on the Rio de Janeiro theatrical revue scene. She circulated between the classical and the popular with ease, and worked in both films and revues, as well as in ballet presentations where she mixed classic dance with Brazilian rhythms. The presence of Yanakiewa and her dancers in this number is therefore evidence of the complex intertwining of cinema and theatrical presentations at the time.

Another telling intermedial example is the musical finale of *Aviso aos navegantes*, when Eliana and Oscarito celebrate national identity as encapsulated in the lyrics of Ary Barroso's aforementioned 'Rio de Janeiro' song, here interpreted by radio singer Francisco Carlos:

> Para cantar a beleza
> A grandeza
> De nossa terra
> Basta ser bom brasileiro
> (To sing the beauty
> The grandiosity
> Of our land
> It is enough to be a good Brazilian.)

This number features Rio's Sugar Loaf as the background scenery and begins with Francisco Carlos, framed in a medium shot, singing melancholically.

As the orchestra starts up with the brass section and the camera retreats, we then realise that the singer, standing still, is surrounded by cheerful dancers in the background, whereas Eliana and Oscarito, respectively a film actress and a theatrical revue star, play their parts, Cléia and Frederico, in the foreground. The proximity of these three figures and the institutions they represented – radio, cinema and theatre – within the scene is an important cross-medial feature of the *chanchadas* that distinguishes it from the integrated American musicals. The diversity of stage practices finds a spatial translation in the visual arrangement, with a motionless Francisco Carlos at the back standing as he would in a radio auditorium, the dancers behind him prancing around as though in a Hollywood-inspired revue presentation, and the actors at the front clearly at ease playing their parts.

Indeed, the elements of the 'mass culture triad' defined by Lenharo (theatrical revues, *chanchada* films and radio) are in full evidence here: a radio singer who does not dance or act very well, a film star who dances and sings in the cinema but not on the radio, and a vaudeville comedian who does everything demanded by the scene, since that theatrical genre required multiple skills from actors, including singing, comic acting and 'film' acting. Macedo wisely placed Francisco Carlos, with his lack of dancing skills, in the background in order to foreground the acting by Oscarito and Eliana. Moreover, in addition to different acting styles and narrative levels (the plot and the performance), carnival themes and references added a further layer and dictated the tone of performances. In the plot, the characters of Cléia and Frederico dance happily in the foreground, and this diegetic event is itself the performance of a famous musical hit from 1944, now played by a contemporaneous radio singer.

The case of Francisco Carlos is telling when it comes to the different concerns on the part of singers and actors populating the *chanchadas*. He had risen to fame the year before with the song 'Meu brotinho' (My Little Girl). This had featured in Macedo's previous *Carnaval no fogo* (*Carnival in Flames*, 1949) but was released months after the film itself came out: that is, after Carlos had gained a public following and become a recurrent presence in the illustrated magazines (as with many radio attractions, he had been chosen for his handsome looks) (Ciocci 2010: 94). As one 1951 article featured in the magazine *A Cena Muda* (*The Silent Scene*, 1952: 10–11) reported, following his appearance in *Carnaval no fogo*:

> Such was his success and so great the interest on the part of the public and the critics that [film director] José Carlos Burle himself offered him the main role in a forthcoming Atlântida film. Francisco Carlos declined the invitation as he was not interested in pursuing a career in acting, accepting only roles that would allow him to appear in musical numbers. And so it was that he went on

to appear in two other films from that company: *Não é nada disso* [*That's Not at All the Case*, 1950] and *Aviso aos navegantes*.³

Atlântida thus represented for singers a precious opportunity in terms of publicity, so much so that, even if they could not act and rarely turned into actors, they were willing to appear in the musical numbers. Conversely, the so-called *vedettes*, or theatrical revue stars, such as Virgínia Lane, as well as film actresses such as Eliana Macedo – who, as mentioned earlier, had great singing skills – never built a career as singers. Similarly, when singer Ivon Curi or musician Bené Nunes performed acting roles, they were far from convincing, but then again that was not really their goal in the first place.

Another example of a musician unconcerned by her lack of acting skills is Adelaide Chiozzo, originally an accordionist and singer who played the role of the protagonist's best friend in several films, but who never became an accomplished actress. In *Aviso aos navegantes*, Chiozzo plays the accordion and sings 'Beijinho doce' together with Eliana; she also plays the guitar in a scene set in a restaurant. 'Beijinho doce' went on to become Chiozzo's biggest ever hit. Both Chiozzo and Eliana also sing 'Recruta biruta', a popular carnival *marchinha* whose placement in the film no doubt spoke to its current popularity. Macedo knew the audience would sing along in cinemas, and the presence of these singers, largely advertised on the radio and in the press, was a sure way to lure the public despite the singers' poor acting skills. Unlike the Hollywood model, then, the *chanchadas* star system was dictated by the radio and phonographic industries, both of which were far more powerful and lucrative businesses than cinema at the time. Film numbers featuring radio singers thus served the function of showing the face of these popular performers, who also featured in theatrical revues and illustrated magazines.

Yet another example of this phenomenon in *Aviso aos navegantes* concerns the *marchinha* 'Toureiro de Cascadura' (Bullfighter from Cascadura), recorded by Oscarito in 1950 with the 1951 carnival in mind. In the film, he performs a comic number alongside chorus girls dancing in the *vedette* style typical of theatrical revues. The camera moves sideways while the scene alternates between long shots and close-ups of the actor. Oscarito released this song alongside 'Marcha do neném' (Baby's March), which appears in the film in a typical revue skit with the actor dressed as a baby and surrounded by girls in skimpy skirts. Disguised as a rumba dancer, Oscarito imitates a dancer in the number 'Na Candelária' (At Candelária), performing a hilarious scene in the film, followed by Ruy Rey and his (not quite) Latino band. Rey also plays in three more musical numbers, pretending in two of them that he is a real Latino artist, singing 'Mercê' and 'A romper el coco' (Breaking the Coconut), then performing the march 'Cubana' (Cuban girl) in Portuguese, also released that year.

Another musical hit featured in the film is 'Sereia de Copacabana' (Copacabana's Mermaid), by Jorge Goulart, who appears in the film in a number filmed in a lateral tracking shot complete with beachgoers and beach-related visual elements, including a ramp emulating Copacabana's famous pavement. Not a professional actor himself, Goulart, dressed up as a tourist, simply walks in and sings, with the camera following his slow gestures. The song was a huge success that year on the radio. As with the aforementioned 'Toureiro de Cascadura', Goulart had launched the song in the film as a publicity strategy for carnival, backed up by the Continental record label. 'Sereia de Copacabana' came third in the 1951 Rio city hall annual song contest.

The choice of singers who appeared in the *chanchadas*, as well as the details of their performances (which could be stilted or visually uninteresting), were therefore the result of deals struck between film producers and directors, according to the rules of the music market. For most of these *chanchada* performers, cinema was an *additional* breadwinning activity, since their main income derived from live presentations in circuses and theatres around the country. As Stephanie Dennison and Lisa Shaw note, 'many of them went on tours of the countryside with their own stage shows, often in the wake of the first screening of their latest film' (2004: 63). Many actors, singers, composers, musicians, choreographers and costume designers who worked in the *chanchadas* and who had come from the radio and vaudeville quite often continued to live off their original professional activities. This demands that we relativise the importance of cinema in the analysis of *chanchadas*, as artists working in different milieux continued to do so for income while bringing their medium-specific talent and craft to the medium of film. As Oscarito, one of the greatest ever *chanchada* actors, once summarised in an interview: 'What I earned in the cinema was only to survive. Real money I made with the shows I presented in the countryside' (Augusto 1989: 194).[4]

AVISO AOS NAVEGANTES AND THE *MUIÉ MACHO SIM SINHÔ* REVUE

As well as relying on the phonographic and radio industries, *chanchadas* depended on the production of theatrical revues. In this last section, I will explore one such revue, *Muié macho sim sinhô* (*Yes, Sir, I'm a Macho Woman*), in connection with *Aviso aos navegantes*, paying particular attention to the precarious production conditions besetting the film, which distinguished it from the seamlessly integrated Hollywood musicals.

In the 1940s and 1950s the theatrical revues in Rio de Janeiro were under the influence of producer Walter Pinto, who blended the erudite and the popular in stunning shows featuring classical ballet dancers, chorus girls, naked models, singers and *vedettes*, with visual effects and settings modelled on the sophisticated Ziegfeld Follies Broadway productions. These lucrative productions, moreover, featured the salacious themes and double entendres typical of revue scripts, involving beautiful, scantily clad women dancing to carnival songs on ramps and platforms lifted straight from Hollywood cinema.

The year 1950, when *Aviso aos navegantes* was shot, marks a specific transitional moment when the interchange of actors and technicians across revues and cinema was in full swing, as abundantly documented in the illustrated magazines. *Aviso aos navegantes* in many ways profited from *Muié macho sim sinhô*, then on at the Teatro Recreio in Rio (Figure 6.2). For this production, Walter Pinto had deployed sophisticated scenic effects such as rose petal showers, smoke curtains and exuberant costumes, all culminating in a dazzling finale. Some cast members from *Aviso aos navegantes*, such as Grande Otelo and Oscarito, also featured in this revue, alongside singer

Figure 6.2 The façade of Teatro Recreio in Rio de Janeiro, where the revue *Muié macho sim sinhô* was shown between 1950 and 1951. Image from Walter Pinto Archives. Courtesy of the Centre of Documentation and Art / National Foundation of Arts (Cedoc/Funarte), Brazil.

Figure 6.3 Oscarito and Juliana Yanakiewa rehearse for the theatrical revue *Muié macho sim sinhô* (1950). Image by Walter Pinto Archives. Courtesy of the Centre of Documentation and Art / National Foundation of Arts (Cedoc/Funarte), Brazil.

Dalva de Oliveira, dancers Edgardo Deporte and Marina Marcel, *vedette* Virgínia Lane, showgirls, and even Yanakiewa as the first dancer and choreographer (see Oscarito and Juliana Yanakiewa rehearsing for *Muié macho sim sinhô* in Figure 6.3). The soundtrack comprised popular and classical music, ranging from pieces by José Maria de Abreu, Rimsky-Korsakov and Khachaturian to the *baião* 'Paraíba' closing the show. In the space of five months there were over 300 shows of *Muié macho sim sinhô* concomitant to the making of *Aviso aos navegantes*, which incorporated formal elements, actors and songs from the theatrical revue, including the aforementioned 'Paraíba' (played in the scene where Eliana fights her rival on the dance floor).

One of the film's most memorable musical numbers is the well-known ballet piece where Yanakiewa dances to Piano Concerto No. 1 in B-flat minor, Op.23, by Pyotr Tchaikovsky, conducted by Bené Nunes and his orchestra. The presence of Yanakiewa in the film and in the theatrical show ensured a similar choreographic style in both. Halfway through the number, the film cuts from the classical piece to a shot of a couple dancing a Brazilian *gafieira* version of the same song, in a musical arrangement by Lindolfo Gaya. This unexpected mixture recalls the blending of *baião* with Rimsky-Korsakov in *Muié macho sim sinhô*, while further resonating with a scene from *The Barkleys of Broadway* (Charles Walters, 1949), in which pianist Oscar Levant plays the same extract from Tchaikovsky's concerto. In the Brazilian *chanchada*, however, the decorative smoke, intended as a minor detail, goes out of control and ends up obscuring both the pianist and the dancer; this leads us back to Feuer's reflections on the concealed 'engineering' of Hollywood musical numbers, which in the Brazilian case is often laid bare, thanks to its precarious mode of production.

This example further shows that the mixture of the erudite and the popular was not exactly a *chanchada* innovation but was a frequent practice in popular theatre. This question is also paramount when it comes to some Hollywood musicals, such as *Shall We Dance* (Mark Sandrich, 1937) and *The Band Wagon* (Vincente Minnelli, 1953), where Feuer (1993: 54–5) detects an 'opera versus swing' battle through which classical and popular cultures acquired visibility as central elements of the plot, always with the final victory going to the popular style. A similar blending appears in many *chanchadas*, but in them the popular and erudite musical genres are not so much quarrelling but in the friendly mode of coexistence that had characterised Brazilian theatre since the nineteenth century.

Another musical number in the film that strips bare 'the engineering' behind the scenes has Emilinha Borba singing one of the greatest hits of that year, 'Tomara que chova' (Let's Hope It Rains), and the special effects disrupt the seamlessness of the number as a whole. She begins by singing under an umbrella on a set with artificially created wind, thunder and rain, water splashing on her face to such an extent that it cannot but detract attention from the song-and-dance performance. Then six ballerinas show up in transparent raincoats, dancing the simple steps choreographed by Yanakiewa. While the song's lyrics allude to water shortage in the city, a close-up of the singer reveals her water-soaked face while the wind blows seemingly uncontrollably. In the film, moreover, Emilinha Borba does not really dance; she only attempts a few little jumps here and there. Yet in the end that did not matter, given that she was singing a musical hit, launched in the film, as was the case with the songs examined in the previous section, with the forthcoming carnival in mind.[5]

These examples show the extensive net of underlying marketing and commercial interests dictating the choice of musicians to participate in the *chanchadas*, which often overrode the needs of naturalistic characterisation or even a connection with the plot of the films. They illustrate the many crossings between different practices that manifested themselves in the film's formal elements and mise-en-scène. The purpose of this chapter has been to demonstrate that it is necessary to take into consideration not only popular theatre but also carnival routines, the market logic of the phonographic industry and radio performances in order to displace the historiographic importance often attributed to cinema. I hope to have shown that it is limiting to study musical numbers in *chanchadas* separately from the various and varied staging practices of the 1940s and the 1950s, since looking at the practices, personnel and elements traversing these forms and media can help us better understand the performances in all their complex materialisations.

Notes

1. Research supported by grant #2014/50821-3, São Paulo Research Foundation (FAPESP). The opinions, hypotheses, conclusions or recommendations contained in this material are the sole responsibility of the author and do not necessarily reflect FAPESP opinion.
2. 'Depois do fechamento dos cassinos, o implemento do teatro de revista e das chanchadas cinematográficas formam com o rádio um tripé básico da produção massiva de cultura, mas o rádio sempre manteve um papel mais abrangente e concentrador. Ao redor desse tripé gravitavam a indústria do disco, as editoras de músicas, as revistas especializadas, a publicidade. A vida musical do Rio e das capitais tinha nesse tripé o ponto de referência de suas atividades. Cantores, compositores, músicos, artistas de teatro, radioatores, de uma forma ou outra, transitavam por um desses espaços culturais' (Lenharo 1995: 135).
3. 'O sucesso foi tanto e tamanho o interesse despertado pelo público e pela crítica que o próprio José Carlos Burle lhe ofereceu um papel principal num dos próximos filmes da Atlântida. Francisco Carlos rejeitou a proposta, pois não desejava seguir a carreira de ator, aceitando, apenas, quando tivesse a ocasião, de figurar em quadros musicais. Tanto assim que tomou parte em mais duas películas daquela empresa: *Não é nada disso* e *Aviso aos navegantes*' (*A Cena Muda*, 7 June 1951, pp. 10–11).
4. 'O que eu ganhava no cinema', contou também no seu depoimento ao MIS, 'só dava para me sustentar. Dinheiro, mesmo, eu ganhei com os espetáculos que dava pelo interior' (Augusto 1989: 194).
5. Originally composed by Paquito and Romeu Gentil, 'Tomara que chova' was launched in a successful revue by Luiz Peixoto at the Gloria Theatre, produced by Zilco Ribeiro and starring the famous actress Dercy Gonçalves. The song was an instant hit, the audience reportedly singing along loudly at presentations (Antunes 2004: 117).

References

Antunes, Delson (2004), *Fora do sério: um panorama do teatro de revista no Brasil*. Rio de Janeiro: Funarte.

Araújo, Luciana Corrêa de (2015), '*Augusto Annibal quer casar!*: teatro popular e Hollywood no cinema silencioso brasileiro', *Alceu*, 16:31, July/December, pp. 62–73.

Araújo, Luciana Corrêa de (2018), '"Cinema como evento": atrações de palco e tela no cineteatro Santa Helena em São Paulo (1927)', *Significação*, 45:49, January/June, pp. 19–38.

Augusto, Sérgio (1989), *Este mundo é um pandeiro, a chanchada de Getúlio a JK*. São Paulo: Cinemateca Brasileira/Companhia das Letras.

Ciocci, Sandra Cristina Novais (2010), *Assim era a música da Atlântida: a trilha musical do cinema popular brasileiro no exemplo da Companhia Atlântida Cinematográfica 1942/1962*. Master's dissertation, Universidade Estadual de Campinas.

Dennison, Stephanie and Lisa Shaw (2004), *Popular Cinema in Brazil, 1930–2001*. Manchester: Manchester University Press.

Feuer, Jane (1993), *The Hollywood Musical*, 2nd edn. Bloomington: Indiana University Press.

Freire, Rafael de Luna (2011), *Carnaval, mistério e gângsters: o filme policial no Brasil (1915–1951)*. PhD thesis, Fluminense Federal University, Niterói.

Lenharo, Alcir (1995), *Cantores do rádio*. Campinas: Editora da Unicamp.

Melo, Luis Alberto Rocha (2017), 'Radio Stars on Screen: Critiques of Stardom in Moacyr Fenelon's *Tudo Azul* (1952)', in Tim Bergfelder, Lisa Shaw and João Luiz Vieira (eds), *Stars and Stardom in Brazilian Cinema*. Oxford and New York: Berghahn, pp. 144–61.

Pethő, Ágnes (2011), *Cinema and Intermediality: The Passion for the In-Between*. Newcastle-Upon-Tyne: Cambridge Scholars Publishing.

Schvarzman, Sheila (2008), 'Cultura popular massiva no Brasil: o lugar do cinema sonoro e sua relação com a música popular', *Icone*, 10:1, pp. 77–99.

Shaw, Lisa (2000), 'The *Chanchada* and Celluloid Visions of Brazilian Identity in the Vargas Era (1930–45)', *Journal of Iberian and Latin American Studies*, 6:1, pp. 63–74.

Shaw, Lisa (2003), 'The Brazilian Chanchada and Hollywood Paradigms (1930–1959)', *Framework*, 44:1, Spring, pp. 70–83.

Vieira, João Luiz (1984), *Hegemony and Resistance: Parody and Carnival in Brazilian Cinema*. PhD thesis, New York University.

Vieira, João Luiz (1987), 'A chanchada e o cinema carioca (1930–1955)', in Fernão Ramos (ed.), *História do cinema brasileiro*. São Paulo: Art, pp. 129–87.

Vieira, João Luiz (2012), 'Brazil', in Corey K. Creekmur and Linda Mokdad (eds), *The International Film Musical*. Edinburgh: Edinburgh University Press, pp. 141–54.

CHAPTER 7

(In)Visible Musicians: Supporting Instrumentalists and their Intermedial Vocation[1]

Suzana Reck Miranda

In the 1930s Brazil was dominated by the US film industry. The arrival of sound held the promise of a tool to combat such domination and, like many Latin American countries, Brazil invested in the recipe of 'imitating' Hollywood musicals while emphasising local ingredients: 'our' language, 'our' music, 'our' artists. Urban popular music was central to this recipe, given its dissemination via radio and the record industry, as well as its popularity in entertainment venues, including revues, casinos and circuses.[2] In particular, radio played a fundamental role in the consolidation of a Brazilian star system: singers represented lucrative business not only for the recording companies and the aspirations of the nascent sound film, but also for the press, which started churning out publications aimed at fans.

Supporting musicians in filmic musical numbers are hardly ever noticed, either in the films themselves or in the corresponding critical literature. Ian Garwood's article 'Play It Again Butch, Cricket, Chick, Smoke, Happy ... The Performances of Hoagy Carmichael as a Hollywood Barroom Pianist' (2013) and accompanying audiovisual essay 'How Little We Know: An Essay Film about Hoagy Carmichael' (2013) are among the few studies that explore the theme.[3] In these, Garwood discusses the marginal role of the composer and pianist Hoagy Carmichael, with particular emphasis on *To Have and Have Not* (Howard Hawks, 1944). As Garwood shows, the musician plays the part of a pianist, Cricket, who, despite being a supporting role, interferes discretely in the interaction of the protagonists, Slim (Lauren Bacall) and Harry (Humphrey Bogart). One example – among many other memorable scenes – is when Cricket plays 'Am I Blue' (Harry Akst and Grant Clark) with Slim, alongside other musicians who are awarded even less importance than Carmichael. This chapter will focus on two of these musicians.

When Carmichael sings the phrase 'ain't these tears', with Bacall sitting still on the left-hand side of the frame, we are able to see two guitar players seated between them and waiting for their cue to play: these are the Brazilians José do Patrocínio Oliveira (or Zezinho) and Nestor Amaral. Marginal supporting actors, they are hardly noticeable in the scene. Nestor appears only briefly, playing a short solo.[4] Zezinho remains practically outside of the frame, playing a discrete musical accompaniment. Though almost invisible in this scene, back in Brazil Zezinho enjoyed an altogether different reality: he was a radio celebrity in the context of the burgeoning São Paulo music industry and equally known for his virtuoso skills as a multi-instrumentalist, playing the violin, guitar, *cavaquinho* (a small four-stringed guitar) and banjo. During the same period, Nestor Amaral also began to garner visibility on the São Paulo musical scene as both a vocalist and a versatile instrumentalist, deftly playing the mandolin, tenor guitar and violin.

This contrast in visibility becomes even more interesting when we consider that, in addition to *To Have and Have Not*, both musicians appeared in a number of other Hollywood films, many the result of the Good Neighbour Policy, implemented in the years of Franklin Roosevelt's presidency (1930–45) and deemed strategic for the US's relationship with Latin America. Political and economic solidarity with Latin American countries was fostered not only as a means of helping the US economy (ravaged by the 1929 depression) to recovering, but also as a curb on European influences on Latin American shores. This extended to the cultural realm, as the US film industry was now interested in spreading 'good values' and creating 'symbols' that expressed continental solidarity, including Carmen Miranda and the cartoon 'Joe Carioca' (in Brazil, Zé Carioca). The participation of Nestor Amaral and Zezinho in Hollywood films was therefore part and parcel of this phenomenon, and while their names often went uncredited in such films, in Brazilian magazines and newspapers of the time they were widely celebrated as examples of the success of 'our' music and musicians in Hollywood (see *A Scena Muda* 1945: 27; *Fon-Fon* 1946: 31, 70).

The aim of this chapter is to relocate these two secondary musicians (and their performances) from the margins and to chart their transnational movement across different media, such as cinema, radio and the press. Can their hitherto neglected intermedial crossings cast new light on the films themselves and thereby unveil new cinema histories? In order to answer this question, the concept of intermediality will be adopted here as an analytical and historiographic method that can uncover a variety of relations and crosspollinations between different artforms and media.

My use of intermediality in this chapter is especially in tune with Ana M. López's (2014: 137) view, via Jürgen Müller, that the notion 'has been most productively utilised as a "research axis" or "research concept" that cuts across several arenas and identifies issues to be explored', rather than being a 'theory per se'. In particular, López (139) notes that the idea of intermediality has been fruitfully deployed by researchers to re-evaluate the Latin American classic filmographies of the 1930s, especially as many studies have tended to privilege genre, stardom and national cinema frameworks to the detriment of intermedial relations between films and other forms.

In what follows, I begin with a brief survey of the careers of Zezinho and Nestor Amaral in Brazil, looking in particular at Zezinho's appearance in Brazilian musical films throughout the 1930s and the circumstances that propelled them both on to a 'transnational' career. The chapter then moves on to explore the duo's complex rapport with Hollywood cinema and its disproportionate coverage by the Brazilian press. My hope is to uncover not only aspects related to Brazilian popular music and cinema, but also the cultural capital of Hollywood in Brazil at the time, which accorded a newfound importance to both musicians.

ZEZINHO, THE DIABOLICAL

In the early 1930s, José do Patrocínio Oliveira worked at the São Paulo biological research centre, Instituto Butantã, classifying types of snake while devoting his spare time to music (Souto 1947: 3). Between 1929 and 1931, he featured on hundreds of recordings for Columbia Records, accompanying famous Brazilian artists such as João Pernambuco, Stefana de Macedo, Jararaca, Paraguassu and Batista Júnior, among others. At Columbia, he also joined the Colbaz Orchestra, known for its recordings of *chorinhos* (a popular Brazilian instrumental musical genre) and waltz. Yet it was Zezinho's flair with the banjo that propelled him to fame. This was especially so after he won the 1931 Grande Concurso de Música (Grand Musical Competition), sponsored by the newspaper *A Gazeta*, playing the instrument; and indeed, in Brazil he is still widely referred to as 'Zezinho do banjo' (Mello 2012: 25).

In 1931 Zezinho also starred in *Coisas nossas* (*Our Things*, Wallace Downey, 1931), the first fully synchronised Brazilian sound film – including voices, dialogue and ambient sound – thanks to the vitaphone system. Like foundational sound films such as *Fox Movietone Follies of 1929* (David Butler, 1929), *Coisas nossas* was not narrative-oriented, but rather a collection of humorous gags interspersed with musical numbers that included northeastern *batuques* (an Afro-Brazilian musical genre), serenades and regional songs. In turn, these numbers were performed by successful radio and theatrical revue singers whose appearance in the film was down to its producer, Alberto Byington Jr., who was also the Brazilian representative of Columbia, with which most singers had a contract.[5] In *Coisas nossas*, Zezinho both featured in numbers as a solo singer and appeared alongside other musicians; the film was a box-office hit, turning him into a household name across Brazil.[6]

It is perhaps helpful to note that the major box-office successes in Brazilian cinema at the time were musical films featuring singers, musicians and comedians from radio, theatrical revues and circuses, often recruited as a way to ensure the films' popularity (see Flávia Cesarino Costa's chapter in this volume). An example is the film *Alô, alô carnaval* (*Hello, Hello Carnival*, Adhemar Gonzaga, 1935), in which Zezinho plays in an orchestra accompanying the singer Alzirinha Camargo.[7] Unlike in *Coisas nossas*, however, he was not even credited here, and indeed, with the exception of this film, Zezinho's roles in Brazilian films ultimately did little to leverage his career. It was only when he joined the renowned Rio de Janeiro musical group Conjunto Regional da Rádio Mayrink Veiga in the mid-1930s that the local press began to advertise him as 'the man of seven instruments' (Mello n.d.), or Zezinho, the 'diabolical' (*Gazeta de Notícias* 1935: 10). With fame came new work opportunities and, from 1936 on, he joined many international artistic troupes travelling through Europe and Latin America, including Buenos Aires, where he first met and performed with sisters Carmen and Aurora Miranda (Castro 2005: 142).

In 1938, after travelling to the US with the Romeu Silva Orchestra for a six-month performance season at the New York World Fair, Zezinho decided not to return home. He remained illegally in New York, giving guitar lessons and playing at a church until 1940, when he was employed as a musician for the Brazilian Pavilion at the San Francisco World Fair, thus regularising his situation in the country (*Gazeta de Notícias* 1935: 10). Soon after he moved to Los Angeles, Zezinho embarked on a period of intense, though almost anonymous, musical activity. It was during this period that he again met Carmen Miranda, already a Hollywood star at this point, while reuniting with his countryman Nestor Amaral, who, as it turned out, had also been living in the US.

Nestor, a New Star

Nestor started his career in São Paulo at the Rádio Record in 1932, after which he and Zezinho became acquaintances, playing together on many occasions, including a duo performance of mandolins at Rádio Cruzeiro do Sul (*Correio de S. Paulo* 1934: 3). In 1935, Nestor was hired by Rádio Ipanema, in Rio de Janeiro, where he began to play in orchestras at the best casinos, but soon left the city to embark on a two-year tour as a singer at several radio stations in South America (Mello 2012: 82). After a brief return to São Paulo, Nestor then joined the cast of Rio's Rádio Nacional, which gave a much-needed boost to his career.[8] Indeed, by 1938, he was already advertised as the radio's newest star, 'a pleasure to hear' and a 'gift' to listeners (*O Malho* 1938: 7), going on to sign a contract with a record company. His stint at Rádio

Nacional turned out to be a brief one, however, and in the following year he was hired by the Rádio Clube do Brasil, whose director, Alberto Byington Jr., was trying to set up a permanent cast of renowned artists to attract greater audiences.

Nestor's goal was the radio star system and, unlike Zezinho, he does not seem to have appeared in Brazilian musical films.[9] Although his career prospects were not exactly dire, he struggled financially (*Correio Paulistano* 1949: 9), which explains why, in July 1940, he accepted an invitation to replace the guitar player Garoto in the group Bando da Lua.[10] Led by Aloysio de Oliveira, Bando da Lua was about to go on a US tour with Carmen Miranda as her supporting band, to appear in Broadway shows, film performances, radio programmes, recordings and tours. Perhaps unsurprisingly, the band was forced to gravitate around Carmen and lost the autonomy and fame it had enjoyed in Brazil during the 1930s.[11] This led de Oliveira to quit the band in 1942 and start working in *Saludos Amigos* (Wilfred Jackson et al., 1942), the first of two Disney films produced under the auspices of the Good Neighbour Policy. As a result, the band had its name and configuration changed several times, with Nestor now bandleader.[12]

BETWEEN THE FILMS AND THE LOCAL PRESS: THE 'MUSICAL' SUCCESS OF AN ANONYMOUS DUO

Zezinho was also invited to join Bando da Lua when Carmen Miranda moved to Los Angeles, becoming an official member of the group in 1941: that is, one year before de Oliveira left.[13] During this period, Zezinho would also become something of a 'star' as he ended up playing a central, if invisible, role in *Saludos Amigos*: namely, the voice of the animated cartoon character Joe Carioca, a Brazilian parrot.

Zezinho and Nestor can be seen alongside Carmen Miranda in a number of films, including *Week-End in Havana* (Walter Lang, 1941), *Springtime in the Rockies* (Irving Cummings, 1942), *The Gang's All Here* (Busby Berkeley, 1943), *Greenwich Village* (Walter Lang, 1944), *Something for the Boys* (Lewis Seiler, 1944), *Doll Face* (Lewis Seiler, 1945), *If I'm Lucky* (Lewis Seiler, 1946) and *Copacabana* (Alfred E. Green, 1947).[14] In the last film, Bando da Lua plays with the orchestra on stage with Carmen Miranda during two performances: Nestor is the conductor and Zezinho is among those playing the violin. They also performed with other musicians at Los Angeles bars and restaurants, as well in other films produced under the Good Neighbour Policy, often as a duo playing Latin-sounding rhythms.

One of these was *The Three Caballeros* (Norman Ferguson et al., 1944), another Disney production dedicated to the Latin 'neighbours': in addition to vocally impersonating the Brazilian parrot Joe Carioca (also a character in this film), Zezinho appears in the scene where Carmen's sister, Aurora Miranda, sings Ary Barroso's 'Os quindins de Yayá' next to Nestor, who, dressed as a Portuguese street vendor selling fruit, blends in with the other supporting musicians and dancers. Then, in a curious moment during the instrumental section of the performance, Zezinho simulates playing a percussive flute with a pencil while his voice gives life to Joe Carioca. In other words, in the same scene we see Zezinho on screen and hear his voice, but these are entirely detached from each other and appear as different entities. In the end, Zezinho embraced his identity as Joe Carioca, using it as his artistic name and performing the character in different contexts in Los Angeles (see Castro 2005: 413).

In *The Gang's All Here* Nestor played a more significant role than a fruit vendor, even if he still went unacknowledged in the credits. At the start of the film, his face, half in shadow, emerges at the upper-left corner of the frame against a black background, singing the first lines of Ary Barroso's 'Aquarela do Brasil'. As the camera closes in, his face gradually takes up the whole screen and becomes centralised, only to recede again as the camera moves on to the left so as to reveal diagonal bamboo struts and a Brazilian ship in a dock. As Gibbs and I have argued in the video-essay 'Playing at the Margins' (Gibbs and Miranda 2018), Nestor is the 'first' of many 'Brazilian imports' (including coffee, sugar and fruit) highlighted during this opening, even if, quickly afterwards, the singer returns to his habitual secondary position together with the other musicians surrounding Carmen Miranda.

To be sure, sometimes Zezinho and Nestor were given brief lines of dialogue, examples including *Carnival in Costa Rica* (Gregory Ratoff, 1947), where they perform 'local' music in a hotel bar at the request of Jeff Stephens (Dick Haymes), and *Romance on the High Seas* (Michael Curtiz and Busby Berkeley, 1948), more specifically in the scene where Georgia Garrett (Doris Day), at a bar supposedly in Havana, becomes entranced by the Spanish version of the song 'It's Magic'. Georgia asks Nestor: 'Pedro, you must teach me that song', to which he replies: 'Le gusta señora?' After the exchange of a few more words in English, Nestor then hands her a piece of paper with the English version of the song (the most important in the film); she then begins to sing it and the number ends with Nestor and her in a duet.

It must be noted, however, that even if Zezinho and/or Nestor had the opportunity to 'talk' with the leads, as in the examples given above, this was often part of a prosaic performance bearing no resemblance to the dazzling extravagance of choreographed musical or stage numbers. On the contrary, they were always the ordinary musicians playing background music at an ordinary bar in exchange for a few tips. Moreover, one issue that emerges when it comes to exploring these two musicians' performances in the films of the time is the fact that their names were not always listed in the credits, meaning it is difficult to ascertain exactly how many films they appeared in. To date, in addition to the films mentioned above, I have located the following: *Allergic to Love* (Edward C. Lilley, 1944), *Gay Senorita* (Arthur Dreiffus, 1945), *Pan-Americana* (John H. Auer, 1945), *The Thrill of Brazil* (S. Sylvan Simon, 1946), *The Time, the Place and the Girl* (David Butler, 1946), *Road to Rio* (Norman Z. McLeod, 1947), *A Song is Born* (Howard Hawks, 1948) and *Holiday for Lovers* (Henry Levin, 1959). Zezinho also appeared solo in *A Star is Born* (George Cukor, 1954) and *Hell's Island* (Phil Karlson, 1955), and Nestor in *Latin Lovers* (Mervyn LeRoy, 1953).[15]

Back then, however, the Brazilian press made sure that Zezinho and Nestor's 'acting' would not go unnoticed. While, in the 1930s, it was often their musical skills that received attention, in the ensuing decade it was their almost insignificant, fleeting appearance in Hollywood films that came up in popular newspapers and magazines rather than, for example, the quality of the duo's performances at bars, nightclubs, shows or recordings in the US.[16] The important thing was to celebrate their contribution to Hollywood cinema in overly patriotic articles whose exaggerated titles included 'O samba vence em Hollywood' (Samba Wins in Hollywood) (Guimarães 1945: 30), 'O Brasil em Hollywood' (Brazil in Hollywood) (*Revista Carioca* 1948: 35) and 'O pandeiro invade Hollywood' (The Tambourine Takes Over Hollywood) (Portela 1948: 35). This celebratory treatment was further cemented by Alex Viany and Gilberto Souto, both Hollywood correspondents in the 1940s who regularly wrote complimentary articles about the duo.[17]

And yet, the nationalist attention showered on both musicians had to turn a blind eye to the fact that their performances embodied a tropical mixed bag, both visually and musically. That is, the *paulistas* Zezinho and Nestor (hailing from São Paulo) were transmuted into Rio-born *cariocas*, Mexicans, Cubans, Costa Ricans or any other Latino type deemed necessary, confirming the confusing and inaccurate representation of Latino characters in films made under the auspices of the Good Neighbour Policy, as already pointed out by many scholars (Roberts 1993; López 2011, 2012; Sadlier 2012). Sandoval-Sánchez (1999: 23–4), for instance, locates an Anglo-American, stereotyped construction of the 'Latin other' and 'south of the border' in musicals with Hispanic characters who often appear as lazy rascals in a carnivalesque and sensuous atmosphere. My own contribution to this debate hopes to shed new light on the 'place' often reserved for the Latino presence in Hollywood films from the Good Neighbour Policy era by focusing on the context and movement of background musicians and their music, which can make us better equipped to examine the blurred lines between foreground and background, lead and backing singers, star and extras, and parody and representation in these films.

In some respects, Zezinho and Nestor, with their bodies, instruments and 'exotic' costumes, were the visual counterparts of the sonic transformation already in course in Hollywood films with regard to Latino melodies and genres. That is, rearrangements, hybridisations and alterations were the usual device to make the 'unusual' songs from neighbouring countries more readily accepted by US audiences, with terms such as 'latinoid' and 'latunes' recently adopted by scholars to account for the peculiar performances of the period (Herrera 2015: 20). In this context, did Hollywood also misrepresent the songs played by Zezinho and Nestor?

Anyone who defends the existence of uniquely Brazilian rhythmic and sound matrices would certainly say so. The historian José Ramos Tinhorão (2015: 12), for instance, has observed that, in the period under discussion in this chapter, there were few incursions of Brazilian urban music into the foreign market, since there was no way to conquer that market unless one complied with its cultural and economic imperatives. It followed that the desire for success abroad led many artists to sacrifice Brazilian musical 'peculiarities' so as to ensure they would achieve a so-called 'international standard'.

On the other hand, Humberto Franceschi reminds us that almost all of the popular music recorded in Brazil during the late 1920s and into the early 1930s (the period when Zezinho and Nestor Amaral started gaining visibility in Brazil) was arranged by Europeans, including Simon Boutman, Arnold Gluckmann and Isaac Kolman. As Franceschi notes (2002: 291), popular rhythms received 'arrangements with pseudo-erudite symphonic pretenses', due to these arrangers' disregard for local sonorities. Thus, 'the 1920s was dominated by jazz bands under the strong influence of foreign rhythms, particularly North-American' (Francheschi 2002: 291). Moraes (2000: 11–14) has also shown that a great number of musicians during this period became professionalised by joining musical groups on the radio (now a commercial rather than amateur enterprise) and/or at record companies (which had expanded since the appearance of electrical recording in 1927) – musical industries in which distinctly Brazilian popular genres such as sambas, *choros, toadas* and *modas de viola* coexisted with foreign ones, such as the tango and foxtrot.

Another point worth noting is the appearance in Brazil of Rio's Rádio Nacional (1936), where some programmes sponsored by large US corporations added symphonic orchestration to their renderings of Brazilian popular music, often by replacing percussion with brass. According to Franceschi (2002: 292–4), this strategy reduced the rhythmic force of samba and other local music styles when compared with the earlier days of radio, when modest stations hired small ensembles (known as *Regionals*) that performed Brazilian popular music with a more colloquial and native flair.[18]

As for the musicians under discussion in this chapter, their careers reveal a wide-ranging professional experience that covered a number of musical genres and styles promiscuously. Although Zezinho often played Brazilian music in regional bands, he was versed in many kinds of rhythms. At the São Paulo record company Columbia, for example, he was part of the Colbaz Orchestra, a jazz band, and also the Columbia Jazz Orchestra, which, as well as recording many international musical genres, performed regularly at theatres and radio stations with an ecletic repertoire. His transcultural musicality therefore antedated his move to the United States. Nestor was also versatile. Between 1934 and 1935 he directed a programme dedicated exclusively to jazz (*Correio Paulistano* 1934: 2; 1935: 4) at São Paulo's Rádio Diffusora, and in 1936, during the period he lived in Rio de Janeiro, he also played distinct musical styles in the casino orchestras, not to mention all the recordings he made as a rumba and waltz singer for Odeon (*Revista Carioca* 1936: 41).

This professional and musical elasticity leads us to infer that it must not have been so difficult for Zezinho, the *paulista*, to become Joe, the *carioca*. Or for Nestor, in the aforementioned *Romance on the High Seas*, to impersonate a Cuban singer that 'teaches' Doris Day the song that would eventually land her at the top of the Billboard chart in 1948 (see Gibbs and Miranda 2018). On the other hand, Zezinho and Nestor are often hardly noticeable on screen, overshadowed as they are by the main stars or the 'Latin others' acting as extras. One could even go so far as to say that the nearly imperceptible quality of these supporting musicians can be compared to the way that traditional background music is often perceived in so-called classical narrative cinema. In her book *Unheard Melodies* (1987), Claudia Gorbman argues that background music remains 'transparent' and unnoticed by the viewer for most of the time in the classical film. Although the music is important to the narrative and contributes to the dramatic structure, it remains subordinated to plot demands rather than drawing attention to itself.

Of course, this does not apply to the musical genre, where music often ceases to be the background and takes on a role of its own, breaking the narrative flow and becoming an attraction in itself. Given that Zezinho and Nestor Amaral always participated in musical numbers, the music they played cannot therefore be said to be 'transparent' in the sense proposed by Gorbman. Rather, here it is the secondary musicians themselves who are almost transparent and invisible, even if they do fulfill narrative and symbolic requirements when functioning as scenic and aural 'props' of a vague idea of Latin-ness. After all, as we saw earlier, Hollywood films had little concern with realism and verisimilitude, offering the sights and sounds of whatever they decided was 'authentically' Latino in terms of characterisation, choreography and musical arrangements.

Concluding Remarks

During their career in Brazil throughout the 1930s, Nestor Amaral and Zezinho already enjoyed recognition, especially in publications aimed at fans. Since Nestor was both an instrumentalist and a singer, his face was often stamped on the cover of these magazines, unlike that of Zezinho, who remained a talented musician and instrumentalist but *not* a singer, and was thus relegated to short notes or advertising columns. When they moved to the US, their songs and image publicity changed: after all, the artists were now part of international rather than national show business. Yet, as I hope to have shown, the nature of this change happened for other reasons as well: their minuscule parts in Hollywood films were celebrated in the local press as a source of pride and as undisputed proof of Brazilian music's international success. During this period, Zezinho in particular became far more widely known and admired throughout Brazil than when he regularly performed for Brazilian record companies, on stages and at radio stations, which reveals the crucial role of Hollywood films in boosting his career in Brazil.

In this context, it might be more productive to consider Zezinho and Nestor as part of a rather peculiar star system, one whose main purpose was to compensate, at least in these decades (1930s and 1940s), for Brazil's hopeless efforts to compete with Hollywood. Worthy of note here is the fact that the duo received uniformly positive coverage, which differs from the treatment given to Carmen Miranda, for example, who was already a famous star in Brazil before migrating to the US and whose success was received with mixed feelings. Though she was sometimes glorified in the Brazilian press as the 'samba ambassador' in Hollywood, others claimed that she had sold herself with distasteful musical performances and a stereotyped persona (see *A Scena Muda* 1943a: 20; 1943b: 6).

No doubt the attention lavished on Zezinho and Nestor cannot be compared to the avalanche of magazine and press attention devoted to the Brazilian bombshell. Yet whenever the duo featured in the press, a patriotic and exaggerated tone prevailed, as when one article noted that their film roles would make Brazilian popular music 'conquer' the American market (Cuesta 1941: 20). In other words, these secondary stars were endowed with a heroic aura, as if they were able, however briefly, to stand up to the foreign cultural domination embodied by Hollywood cinema. In this sense, we can say that there is a curious political dimension in the intermedial vocation of this musical duo: their promiscuous career pathways, which cut across a range of cultural, musical and medial forms and challenged traditional binarisms – visible and invisible, audible and inaudible, local and international – can provide us with a much richer perspective on the transnational relations between music and cinema in those decades.

Notes

1. Research supported by grant #2014/50821-3, São Paulo Research Foundation (FAPESP). The opinions, hypotheses, conclusions or recommendations contained in this material are the sole responsibility of the author and do not necessarily reflect FAPESP opinion.
2. Regional music was also important for the same reasons.
3. I would like to thank John Gibbs for introducing me to the work of Ian Garwood.
4. We hear and see Nestor playing on the guitar a sequence of chords that recalls a segment from Radamés Gnatalli's famous orchestration of 'Aquarela do Brasil', by Ary Barroso.
5. For more on Alberto Byington Jr., see Freire 2013.
6. According to a note published in the newspaper *Correio da Manhã* (1931a: 7), Zezinho made a parody of Ukulele Ike (Cliff Edwards) singing 'Singing in the Rain' in the film *Hollywood Revue of 1929* (Charles Reisner, 1929). The note also highlights that this is the only non-Brazilian song in *Coisas nossas*. Another article noted that Zezinho also participated in the film with his 'country music group' (see *Correio da Manhã* 1931b: 10) and also in the Jazz Columbia Orchestra, conducted by Gaó. See Miranda 2015.
7. In this musical number, Alzirinha sings the carnival march 'Cinquenta por cento' (Fifty Per Cent), a famous 1930s *marchinha* by Lamartine Babo, one of the greatest composers of the genre.
8. Founded in 1936 and overseen by a railway company that belonged to an American, Percival Farquhar, Rádio Nacional quickly became popular and caught up with its competitor, Mayrink Veiga, then number one in terms of audience in the city. In 1940 the station was taken over by the Brazilian government due to its alleged debts. With the aim of making the radio a strong propaganda tool, the then president, Getúlio Vargas, turned it into one of the best equipped in the world and its reach covered almost the entire Brazilian territory. Its programmes were very popular at the time, and could count on an excellent cast of musicians, singers and actors. See Calabre 2002.
9. To the best of my knowledge, there are no records of his acting in Brazilian films.
10. Garoto (the nickname of Aníbal Augusto Sardinha) was an extraordinary guitar player and had solo career ambitions that his contract with Bando da Lua prevented him from pursuing (see Mello 2012: 45; Castro 2005: 253).
11. Spanning ten years of existence and with forty albums to its credit, Bando da Lua was a highly successful and critically acclaimed musical group of the time.
12. Other names adopted by the group were the Samba Kings, Carioca Boys and Copacabana Boys (Francischini 2009: 37).

13. Zezinho replaced Hélio Pereira, who decided to leave Bando da Lua for good (Castro 2005: 327).
14. Nestor also features in *That Night in Rio* (Irvin Cummings, 1941).
15. In addition, Zezinho and Nestor also recorded songs that were played in many films. For example, Nestor played the guitar in songs for *Road to Zanzibar* (Victor Schertzinger, 1941), *The Man Behind the Gun* (Felix E. Feist, 1953) and *Rio Bravo* (Howard Hawks, 1959), among others.
16. Both recorded songs with important musicians such as Stan Kenton and played countless times in at least two of the most famous Los Angeles nightclubs: Ciro's and Trocadero Café. They also took part in performances with other musicians in US cities such as Chicago, Las Vegas and New York. Zezinho also played at the renowned Los Angeles restaurant Marquis, and was a member of the Desi Arnaz Orchestra in the TV series *I Love Lucy*.
17. Viany, an important writer, historian, screenwriter and Brazilian filmmaker, wrote the article 'Põe o chapéu, José' for *O Cruzeiro* magazine (Viany 1947: 77). Souto, who worked as a film critic and a translator for Disney films for Brazil, wrote 'A singular carreira de Joe Carioca' (The singular career of Joe Carioca) for *A Scena Muda* (Souto 1947: 3).
18. That said, Franceschi also notes that, in spite of these changes that occurred at many radio stations, groups and musicians working at Rádio Tupi (Tupi Radio Station) in the following decade, such as Pixinguinha (one of the greatest *chorinho* composers in Brazilian popular music) and the group O Pessoal da Velha Guarda, were able to maintain a 'Brazilian style' in their musical arrangements (Franceschi 2002: 93–4).

References

A Scena Muda (1943a), 26 January, p. 20.
A Scena Muda (1943b), 16 February, p. 6.
A Scena Muda (1945), 21 August, p. 27.
Calabre, Lia (2002), *A era do rádio*. Rio de Janeiro: Zahar.
Castro, Ruy (2005), *Carmen, uma biografia*. São Paulo: Cia das Letras.
Correio da Manhã (1931a), 25 November, p. 7.
Correio da Manhã (1931b), 1 December, p. 10
Correio de S. Paulo (1934), 17 April, p. 3.
Correio Paulistano (1934), 7 December, p. 2
Correio Paulistano (1935), 3 March, p. 4
Correio Paulistano (1949), 18 December, p. 9
Cuesta, Emanuel de la (1941), 'O batente de Hollywood é duro, mas rendoso …', *Revista Carioca*, 24 May, pp. 20, 21, 61.
Fon-Fon (1946), 5 September, pp. 31, 70.
Franceschi, Humberto (2002), *A Casa Edison e seu tempo*. Rio de Janeiro: Sarapuí.
Francischini, Alexandre (2009), *Laurindo Almeida: dos trilhos de Miracatu às trilhas de Hollywood*. São Paulo: Cultura Acadêmica.

Freire, Rafael de Luna (2013), 'Da geração de eletricidade aos divertimentos elétricos: a trajetória empresarial de Alberto Byington Jr. antes da produção de filmes', *Estudos Históricos*, 26: 51, pp. 113–31.

Garwood, Ian (2013), 'Play It Again Butch, Cricket, Chick, Smoke, Happy... The Performances of Hoagy Carmichael as a Hollywood Barroom Pianist', *Movie: A Journal of Film Criticism*, 4, pp. 29–39.

Garwood, Ian (2013) 'How Little We Know: An Essay Film About Hoagy Carmichael', *The Audiovisual Essay: Practice and Theory of Videographic Film and Moving Image Studies*, available at <https://reframe.sussex.ac.uk/audiovisualessay/reflections/intransition-1-3/ian-garwood> (last accessed 30 December 2020).

Gazeta de Notícias (1935), 27 June, p. 10.

Gibbs, John and Suzana Reck Miranda (2018), 'Playing at the Margins', *[in]Transition: Journal of Videographic Film & Moving Image Studies*, 5:2, available at <http://mediacommons.org/intransition/2018/05/01/playing-margins> (last accessed 14 December 2021).

Gorbman, Claudia (1987), *Unheard Melodies: Narrative Film Music*. Bloomington: Indiana University Press.

Guimarães, Celso (1945), 'O samba vence em Hollywood', *Fon-Fon*, 1 September, pp. 30–1.

Herrera, Brian Eugênio (2015), *Latin Numbers: Playing Latino in Twentieth-century U.S. Popular Performance*. Ann Arbor: University Michigan Press.

López, Ana M. (2011), 'Geographical Imaginaries', *Studies in Hispanic Cinemas*, 7:1, pp. 3–8.

López, Ana M. (2012), *Hollywood, Nuestra América y los Latinos*. Havana: Ediciones Unión.

López, Ana M. (2014), 'Calling for Intermediality: Latin American Mediascapes', *Cinema Journal*, 54:1, pp. 135–41.

Mello, Jorge (2012), *Gente humilde: vida e música de Garoto*. São Paulo: Edições Sesc.

Mello, Jorge (n.d.), 'Zezinho', *Dicionário do acervo digital do violão brasileiro*, available at <http://www.violaobrasileiro.com.br/dicionario/visualizar/zezinho-jose-do-patrocinio-oliveira> (last accessed 3 December 2018).

Miranda, Suzana Reck (2015), 'Que coisas nossas são estas? Música popular, disco e o início do cinema sonoro no Brasil', *Significação: Revista de Cultura Audiovisual*, 42:44, pp. 29–44.

Moraes, José Geraldo Vinci de (2000), 'Polifonia na metrópole: história e música popular em São Paulo', *Tempo*, 10, pp. 1–24.

Müller, Jürgen E. (2010), 'Intermediality and Media Historiography in the Digital Era', *Acta Univ. Sapientiae, Film and Media Studies*, 2, pp. 15–38.

'O Brasil em Hollywood' (1943), *Revista Carioca*, 1 May, pp. 18, 19, 62.

O Malho (1938), 14 July, p. 7.

Portela, Orlando (1948), 'O pandeiro invade Hollywood', *Revista Carioca*, 27 May, pp. 35, 36, 60.

Revista Carioca (1936), 11 April 1936, p. 41.

Roberts, Shari (1993), 'The Lady in the Tutti-frutti-Hat: Carmen Miranda, a Spectacle of Ethnicity', *Cinema Journal*, 32:3, pp. 3–23.

Sadlier, Darlene (2012), *Americans All: Good Neighbor Cultural Diplomacy in World War II*. Austin: University of Texas Press.

Sandoval-Sánchez, Alberto (1999), *José, Can You See? Latinos On and Off Broadway*, Madison: University of Wisconsin Press.

Souto, Gilberto (1947), 'A Singular Carreira de Joe Carioca', *A Scena Muda*, 8 July, p. 3.

Tinhorão, José Ramos ([1969] 2015), *O samba agora vai ... a farsa da música popular no exterior*. São Paulo: Editora 34.

Viany (1947), 'Põe o chapéu, José', *O Cruzeiro*, 4 April, p. 77.

CHAPTER 8

Music-video Aesthetics in Pernambucan Cinema[1]
Samuel Paiva

Many films produced in the state of Pernambuco, Brazil, from the 1990s onwards present aesthetic features associated with the Manguebeat musical genre, especially those directed by the filmmakers who took part in the so-called Árido Movie movement. Music video was a key medium in the interaction of film and music in these films. In this chapter, I will examine musical moments in Pernambucan films as the result of a dialogue between film and music videos. Tensions between fiction and documentary, as well as pop references, will be explored by means of an intermedial method that enables reflections on historical developments and meanings, taking into account the film supports available in a moment of transition between analogue and digital technologies.

Manguebeat exploded in the media as a musical phenomenon in the 1990s, paving the way for its cinematic counterpart, Árido Movie. Two decades had elapsed in Pernambuco, a state located in the northeast of Brazil, without a single feature film being produced. Then, the film *Baile perfumado* (*Perfumed Ball*, Paulo Caldas and Lírio Ferreira, 1996) was released, becoming a landmark of the so-called Retomada do Cinema Brasileiro (Brazilian Film Revival), after the crisis in the early 1990s, when President Fernando Collor de Mello's government dismantled Embrafilme, the agency supporting film production and distribution in the country. In a bid to overcome the crisis, the interaction of cinema with other media became a way of getting up to speed with the political and social reality of Brazil.

Both phenomena – Manguebeat and Árido Movie – emerged in the city of Recife, Pernambuco's capital. At origin, both can be understood as a response to the city's problems, as can been gleaned from the manifesto 'Caranguejos com cérebro' (Crabs with Brains) (Vargas 2007: 66), launched in 1991 as a press release by Manguebeat member Fred Zero Quatro (from the band Mundo Livre S/A) and supported by several other musicians and artists from Recife. 'Mangue', meaning 'mangrove', is a feature of Recife's natural landscape and defines the three parts of the manifesto. Part I, 'Mangue, the Concept', refers to Recife's ecosystem, which is characterised by a web of rivers and the sea, metaphorically suggesting cultural hybridisation. Part II, 'Manguetown, the City', refers to Recife's economic stagnation and the dire living conditions of its poor population. Part III, 'Mangue, the Scene', defends pop culture and mass media as channels for local artistic expression. The latter is symbolised by the image of a parabolic antenna stuck in the mud, connecting technology with the local geography characterised by mangroves. According to the manifesto:

> In mid-1991, centres for research and production of pop ideas started to emerge and articulate in various parts of the city. Their goal is to create an 'energy circuit', capable of connecting the good vibrations of the mangroves with an international network of pop concepts. Image-symbol: a parabolic antenna stuck in the mud. (Vargas 2007: 66)[2]

At the time, Recife's living conditions were so appalling that an item in the news stated: 'November 1990. The *Washington Post* published that Recife was the fourth worst city in the world to live in, according to the Population Crisis Committee. The committee reached that number after evaluating social indicators in 45 countries' (Passos 2020).[3]

Needless to say, in a situation like that, conditions for making films were also very difficult. However, after Collor de Mello's impeachment in 1992, the provisional government of Itamar Franco created the Prêmio Resgate do Cinema Brasileiro (Brazilian Cinema Rescue Award), which redistributed the assets from the extinct Embrafilme. This was followed by the Audiovisual Law, in the subsequent government of Fernando Henrique Cardoso, creating fiscal incentives for the production of films in Brazil and triggering a cinematic boom in the country. *Baile perfumado* was one of those films that benefited from this new context, becoming a foundational work of both the Pernambucan and the Brazilian Film Revival.

Before the crisis of the early 1990s, Pernambucan cinema history had been marked by moments of glory, including what is known as the 'Recife Cycle' in the 1920s and the 'Super-8 Cycle' in the 1970s. In the 1980s, there were shorts produced in 16mm and 35mm and, most of all, works in the new medium of video, which had a decisive impact on the 1990s mediascape, entering into immediate dialogue with film production and constituting a decisive aesthetic influence on Árido Movie.

At the same time, the new Pernambucan cinema jumped on the bandwagon of local music, which already benefited from a strong presence in the media, in particular television, in the form of music videos. Directly or indirectly, *Baile perfumado* relates to many music videos which were launched at that time. Examples include, among others, *Homero o junkie*, directed by Dolores and

Morales, who, using video formats such as Hi8 and U-Matic, created a narrative for the song by the band Mundo Livre S/A, 1992; *Maracatu de tiro certeiro*, Dolores and Morales, Hi8/U-Matic, with the band Chico Science & Nação Zumbi, 1993; *Samba esquema noise*, Dolores and Morales, Hi8/Betacam, with the band Mundo Livre S/A, 1995; *Se Zé Limeira sambasse maracatu*, Dolores and Morales, Betacam, with the band Mestre Ambrósio, 1996; and *Sangue de bairro*, Lírio Ferreira and Paulo Caldas, 35mm, with Chico Science & Nação Zumbi, 1997 (see Nogueira 2009: 192–193).

Though drawing aesthetically on contemporaneous influences, the story of *Baile perfumado* is situated in the 1930s and focuses on the real character of Benjamin Abrahão, a Lebanese photographer and cinematographer who became famous for capturing moving images of Lampião and his gang of *cangaceiros* (northeastern outlaws), the most notorious bandits at that time in Brazil. Retrospectively, these images by Benjamin Abrahão can be related to a film genre, the *cangaceiro* film, which would later prosper in Brazil and include masterpieces such as *O cangaceiro* (*The Bandit*, Lima Barreto, 1953) and *Deus e o Diabo na terra do sol* (*Black God, White Devil*, Glauber Rocha, 1964), among many others. However, in terms of aural and visual aesthetics, spectators of *Baile perfumado* are vividly situated in the 1990s, mostly thanks to the aforementioned music videos. In 2016, Caldas and Ferreira's film celebrated its twentieth anniversary after its launch in 1996 at the Brasília Film Festival. To commemorate the event, Amanda Mansur Nogueira and Paulo Cunha (2016) compiled a book which brings together various testimonies from the film crew, including my own, as I worked as a video assistant within the film's cinematography department. The work of a video assistant in a film production is in itself an indicative factor of intermediality between the two mediums of film and video for a specific purpose, the cinematographic image. However, the testimony I would like to quote here is from Paulo Caldas, who reflects on the work with the soundtrack:

> Not everyone knows, but the soundtrack was recorded a year before the film was shot. [. . .] Despite preceding the film by a year, the soundtrack was not altered. We recorded it beforehand to instigate the production, and to instigate ourselves during the process. And then the soundtrack remained the same for the film, hardly anything was recorded after the shoot. (Nogueira and Cunha 2016: 27).[4]

Here, Caldas is referring to the work of Manguebeat bands, in particular Chico Science & Nação Zumbi, Mundo Livre S/A and Mestre Ambrósio, some of whom feature in the film. For instance, Siba and other members of Mestre Ambrósio play the roles of musicians in several scenes, including the iconic one of the 'perfumed ball' itself. Fred Zero Quatro, Mundo Livre S/A band leader, in turn, plays a journalist interviewing the protagonist Benjamin Abrahão.

One example of the music-video effect on the film is the scene in which Lampião, his wife and the gang are on a boat and he asks a musician to play a beautiful song. The musician is Siba, then Mestre Ambrósio's band leader, who goes on to play the film's title song, 'Baile perfumado', on a *rabeca* (fiddle), a musical instrument of Arab origin which was a precursor to the violin. Although its origins date back to the Middle Ages, *rabecas* are widely used in the present day by popular artists in Brazil, especially in the northeast. When the music begins, the whole mise-en-scène changes: the music becomes louder and is picked up by the non-diegetic track, becoming the main attraction. The images in turn slow down, changing the classical montage into music-video style.

Here, the narrative 'crisis' (Nagib 2014) created by the interference of music is typical of an intermedial dialogue in cinema. Thiago Soares (2013) calls attention to the importance of the presence of an artist in a music-video scene, which is very much the case of Siba in the aforementioned sequence, affording a kind of recognition that also has an advertising side to it, a kind of cultural marketing of Manguebeat within an Árido Movie film. Thus, film and music feed off each other, both profiting from the commercial power of the Brazilian phonographic industry.

Still, according to Soares (2013: 106), 'music videos enable the "visualisation" of the scenario in which the diction of a song evolves'.[5] Thematic, rhythmic and melodic patterns constitute the diction of a song, which enables us to distinguish, for example, between heavy metal and hip hop, through their stylistic and generic traits. In the case of music videos, the diction of a song is paired off with visual correspondents: for instance, night life for heavy metal or street scenes for hip hop. In the scene in question, in *Baile perfumado*, Siba's *rabeca* becomes the visualisation of Manguebeat. In this musical movement, the *rabeca* is related not only to Siba, but also to other artists, such as Mestre Salustiano, who became well known for his mastery of this musical instrument. Thus, the *rabeca* provides the diction in the song, which in turn gives the film its title.

Music Video in Films

Michel Chion (1994: 166) states that 'The music video has invented and borrowed an entire arsenal of devices; it's a joyous rhetoric of images.' And it engages with changing speeds and stop-action in addition to other features which are rarely present in films, at least in its dominant forms. Other authors (Vernallis 2004; Oliva 2017) also interested in the relationship between films and music videos make similar propositions. For most of them, while films in general are related to the editing process of continuity, music videos present discontinuity as an important feature, with fragmented frames changing in varying speeds to connect with the music rhythms, melodies and harmonies. Therefore, in the remediation between video and film, these differences become noticeable, as in the aforementioned *Baile perfumado* scene, when Siba starts playing the *rabeca* and the image changes to slow motion.

My aim is to highlight this perceptible *difference* not only as a (dis)order in the film narrative and discourse but also as an index of media archaeology implicated in the remediation of one medium into another, in a process which becomes evident through intermedial strategies revealed in some music-video scenes in films. These strategies are simultaneously related to historiographic and geographic dimensions. In other words, music-video effects in films can be understood as a worldwide phenomenon. However, there are implications involving each case study. In the case of Pernambucan cinema, music-video effects can be found in films by many directors active from the 1990s, including Adelina Pontual, Hilton Lacerda, Marcelo Gomes, Renata Pinheiro and others. Not by chance, some of them were working on both film and video productions, including music videos. Hence the following questions arise: given that film and music have historically been in dialogue throughout Brazilian film history, what would be specific to the Pernambucan case? How did technologies which expanded or converged at that moment, including video and television, affect cinema?

To answer these questions, it is necessary first of all to consider the Brazilian context. Thiago Soares (2013: 228) highlights that 'some experiences with filming live musical performances had taken place in Brazil since the late 1960s, with artists such as Raul Seixas, Novos Baianos and Maria Bethânia, among others'.[6] However, it was only in the following decade that the first Brazilian music video to be called by this name was recorded: *América do Sul*, with Ney Matogrosso, in 1975, for a television programme of Rede Globo, Brazil's biggest media network.

With this, Globo launched a dynamic that would increasingly bring mainstream television closer to the music and advertising industries. This is especially true in the southeast of Brazil, where cities such as Rio de Janeiro and São Paulo are the traditional hubs of the national cultural industry. Therefore, a market for music video was already in place when MTV arrived and was installed in São Paulo. The arrival of MTV in Brazil was a turning point in TV marketing, aesthetics and techniques. Since then, music video has increasingly become an important tool for positioning artists in the music market, including musicians from other regions of the country, the northeast among them. Such positioning was reflected, for example, in the creation of the VMB-Video Music Brasil award in 1995, with an impact on the country's audiovisual production, including cinema, as many music video producers also began to produce films inflected by an aesthetics that MTV helped to disseminate.

Some critics argue that, in 1990s Brazil, a kind of genre emerged based on this relationship between film and music video. A case in point is Ivana Bentes (2007), who, in an article entitled 'Vídeo e cinema: rupturas, reações e hibridismo' ('Video and film: breaks, reactions and hybridity'), provides a broad overview of the relationship between film and video, including a discussion of what she calls *filmeclipes* ('music-video films'). Bentes draws attention to a number of film companies that, historically, had a strong relationship with advertising and music videos, such as Conspiração, O2 and Videofilmes, and to directors who stood out in this scenario, such as Beto Brant, Vicente Amorim, Andrucha Waddington and Kátia Lund, most of them from the southeast of the country. However, much of her attention is focused on the production from Pernambuco and the work of Paulo Caldas and Lírio Ferreira. Bentes's emphasis on the production of these two directors is due to the impact of the film *Baile perfumado*, but she also looks at the music video *Sangue de bairro*, for a song by Chico Science & Nação Zumbi, directed by Caldas and Ferreira, with scenes from *Baile perfumado*. In fact, *Sangue de bairro* was shown several times on MTV, therefore promoting the film and the band at the same time.

As regards Pernambucan cinema and its relationship with music video, Nogueira (2009), identifies 'musical moments' in what she defines as a 'new wave of cinema from Pernambuco', which are particularly notable in *Baile perfumado*, but also in a host of other films, including *Amarelo manga* (*Mango Yellow*, Cláudio Assis, 2003), *Árido Movie* (Lírio Ferreira, 2005), *Deserto feliz* (*Happy Desert*, Paulo Caldas, 2007), *O rap do Pequeno Príncipe contra as almas sebosas* (*The Little Prince's Rap Against the Wicked Souls*, Paulo Caldas and Marcelo Luna, 2000), *Baixio das Bestas* (*Bog of Beasts*, Cláudio Assis, 2006), *Cartola: música para os olhos* (*Cartola: Music for the Eyes*, Lírio Ferreira and Hilton Lacerda, 2007) and *O homem que engarrafava nuvens* (*The Man Who Bottled Clouds*, Lírio Ferreira, 2009).

To understand exactly what characterises the musical moments in these films, Nogueira's method consists in studying sequences which acquire greater autonomy in relation to the dramatic action, or a certain 'displacement' from the plot. In her view, these 'sequences are characterised by adapted "pop" moments whereby the film gives way to the music (in an exhibition mode)' (Nogueira 2009: 125).[7] In other words, these musical moments are comparable to music videos. They are moments in which music, be it from a source in the diegesis or incidental, drives the dramatic action and even the movements of the characters. Besides, they are moments of attractions in the sense of a 'cinema of attractions', as proposed by Eisenstein to highlight the possibility of scenes that could cause a kind of sensory shock in the viewer (Nogueira 2009: 130). Then Manguebeat arises in Árido Movie with songs whose themes and sounds refer to local landscapes (for instance, mangroves as a geographic marker) and issues of cultural identity (mostly related to the city of Recife and its historical and contemporary contexts), contributing to the formation of a cinematic style.

Following Nogueira's insights, I argue that remediation between music video and cinema can elicit a variety of effects depending on their archaeologies, implying different forms of perceptible attractions. Let us look, for example, at the documentary *O rap do Pequeno Príncipe contra as almas sebosas*. Filmed in Camaragibe, in the outskirts of Recife, it tells the story of two young men from that community: Garnizé, the percussionist of the band Faces do Subúrbio; and the vigilante Helinho, famous for murdering other thugs. The film intersperses Garnizé and Helinho's views on urban violence as opposing ways of thinking and acting to transform that reality, the former through art and the latter through violence. Garnizé playing his drums serves as a recurrent leitmotif. In one of these scenes, however, the music-video effect becomes apparent. It is the moment when musicians from the Faces do Subúrbio band, from Pernambuco, meet others from the Racionais MCs band, from São Paulo. They discuss discrimination against black communities in Brazil, at which point, as Nagib (2018: 36) describes, the rap 'Salve' (Edy Rock and Mano Brown, from Racionais MCs) is played over an aerial long take of around 2 minutes showing the never-ending favelas around Recife. The lyrics, uttered from the perspective of someone behind bars, salute the populations of favelas in São Paulo, Rio de Janeiro, Belo Horizonte and Brasília, unifying by means of the music-video form the entire population of Brazil, through its underbelly of poverty.

In terms of media archaeology, this scene evidences the importance of MTV at that time, not only for musicians from São Paulo (where the television company was based), but also for other artists coming from other cities, including Recife. It is thus not surprising that Racionais MCs won the audience's award at VMB in 1998 with the music video *Diário de um detento* (*An Inmate's Diary*), produced in São Paulo and directed by Maurício Eça and Marcelo Corpani for a song by Jocenir, who reports on his own experience in prison. The music genre is rap, an ideal genre to express the plights of black people in the prison system. As an innovative feature, the music video presents an array of documentary scenes, which certainly influenced the film by Caldas and Luna released in 2000.

On the other hand, as discussed by Paulo Caldas in the film that Lúcia Nagib and I directed, *Passages: Travelling in and out of Film Through Brazilian Geography* (2019), rap is related to rhythm and poetry and in this sense it evokes an *embolada*, a popular musical genre in the Brazilian northeast, consisting of singers who improvise with fast, metrical verses. The music-video scene described above also evokes the *embolada* genre. In Caldas and Luna's film, this archaeological aspect is explained by Garnizé himself when he states that Nelson Triunfo is one of the most important connections between rap and *embolada*. Indeed, Nelson Gonçalves Campos Filho, a.k.a. Nelson Triunfo, was born in 1954 in the Pernambucan city of Triunfo and migrated to São Paulo in the 1970s. Working as a musician and a dancer, he became an icon of hip-hop culture inspired by rhythms of the Brazilian northeast.

LOCAL TV AND SHORT FILMS

The bands that stood out the most in the context of Manguebeat were offered contracts with major companies in the music industry. As a result, they received attention in certain spaces, such as MTV. This was the case with Chico Science & Nação Zumbi, who were contracted by Sony Music and started to work with directors from the southeast in music videos, such as *Manguetown* (Gringo Cardia, 1996) and *Maracatu atômico* (Raul Machado, 1996). However, this was not a reality for most local Pernambucan bands, and even for Chico Science and his collaborators it was not so until a certain stage in their careers. This fact leads us to consider other possibilities of media archaeology, drawing on remediation in the limited scope of Pernambuco, including TV channels that existed outside of the dominant broadcasting model and basically relied on video, and the local production of short films. Very often, these two areas would combine: for instance, in the case of TV Viva, one of the most emblematic examples, because it involved many artists from Manguebeat and Árido Movie, as in the case of the short film *O mundo é uma cabeça* (*The World is a Head*, 2005), co-directed by Cláudio Barroso (one of the founders and coordinators of TV Viva) and Bidu Queiroz. This film brought together musicians from the most important bands of the Mangue movement at that time, including Chico Science & Nação Zumbi, Mundo Livre S/A and Mestre Ambrósio.

O mundo é uma cabeça follows Chico Science's journey, filmed in a car driven by Roger de Renor (a multimedia artist) through the streets of Recife at night, when he talks randomly about the city, music, festivals and so on. Interspersed with this, there are testimonies by Fred Zero Quatro and Otto (Mundo Livre S/A) and by Siba (Mestre Ambrósio), as well as by veteran composer and singer Gilberto Gil. Originating from a background as a tropicalist musician and making connections with this new post-tropicalist generation, Gil sings songs such as 'Maracatu Atômico' and 'Macô' with Chico Science, in scenes from a show, among many others who appear in this film. The editing style sits entirely within music-video patterns.

In fact, *O mundo é uma cabeça* follows a trend that had started a long time before, with films such as *Maracatu, maracatus* (Marcelo Gomes, 1995) and *Punk rock hardcore – Alto José do Pinho é do caralho!* (*Punk Rock Hardcore – Alto José do Pinho is Fucking Great!*, Adelina Pontual, Cláudio Assis and Marcelo Gomes, 1995) both produced by Parabólica Brasil, owned by filmmakers Adelina Pontual, Cláudio Assis and Marcelo Gomes. *Maracatu, maracatus* discusses connections between traditional musical forms such as *maracatu* and pop music, something that was investigated in depth by Chico Science & Nação Zumbi, a band which can be heard on the soundtrack. The interbreeding, but also tensions, between local culture and the pop industry become evident in an initial scene in which Mestre Salustiano turns away a television crew wanting to film his *maracatu* piece.

Punk rock hardcore, in turn, presents a technological question related to the act of musical creation even in precarious situations. Alto José do Pinho is a neighbourhood on the outskirts of Recife where, despite the economic difficulties of its population, several bands appeared at that time, such as Primeira Dama, Faces do Subúrbio, Matala na Mão, III Mundo and Devotos do Ódio, all of which are introduced in the film. The film documents how musicians make their instruments using recyclable materials, record their albums with their own money and, thanks to the diffusion and recognition of their music, create a new, artistic image for the place where they live, beyond poverty. The scene in which the band Devotos do Ódio plays the song 'Punk Rock Hard Core', in the neighbourhood itself, shows evidence of music-video effects as its montage is dictated by the music. With lyrics that report on the existential problems of the population, the song is inspired by diverse punk-rock references, including bands from UK and especially from São Paulo at that time (for instance, Inocentes). At the same time, it reveals the trends locally prevalent: for example, in the scene in which two musicians sing, with a tambourine, *a rap-embolada* which is interspersed with images of daily life in the community.

As far as short films are concerned, the Super-8 format is an important device in the history of Pernambucan cinema, which developed parallel to and in tune with the music-video format. A specialist on the subject, Figueirôa (1990) defines the period between the 1970s and the early 1980s as the peak of a Super-8 movement that brought many filmmakers together. In Figueirôa's view, Super-8, more than a format for domestic use, became an expressive possibility for many artists at that time when Brazil was living under a military dictatorship. Prominent among these Super-8 makers were directors such as Fernando Spencer, Geneton Moraes Neto, Jomard Muniz de Britto and Amin Stepple, some of them also being responsible for extending the discussion about that type of cinematic production to newspapers, such as *Diario de Pernambuco* and *Jornal do Commercio*. This was part of an effervescence that included film festivals, courses, political associations and other initiatives involving various themes and forms of filmmaking. According to Araújo (2000: 425), 'around 200 films were made in this period, following various approaches: documentaries with regional themes, experimental films, fiction, satire, travelogues'.[8]

For the purpose of this chapter, there are at least two relevant aspects to be considered, regarding this type of production. Firstly, the last film of the Super-8 cycle in Recife was *Morte no Capibaribe* (1983), directed by Paulo Caldas (I myself was a member of the crew as assistant producer), which, inspired by a true story, tells the tale of a shoemaker who, lacking the money to feed his children, decides to throw them into the Capibaribe river. The film establishes a direct connection between the Super-8 generation of the 1970s and early 1980s and that of the Penambucan Film Revival of the 1990s. This connection also includes references to the local geography, including the city's rivers and mangroves. Secondly, Super-8 has restricted technical possibilities for image and sound when compared to other gauges such as 16mm or 35mm. However, its portability opened up a wealth of opportunity for artists who would subsequently turn to videoart and music video.

This is certainly to be felt in *Tatuagem* (*Tattoo*, 2013), directed by Hilton Lacerda with a soundtrack by DJ Dolores, a duo that has been working together since the origins of Manguebeat, when they were graphic designers creating covers for music bands, working at parties as DJs and directing music videos. The film pays homage to the Super-8 generation and combines with music-video effects inserted throughout. Thus, *Tatuagem* expresses a historical awareness which lends itself to a media-archaeological approach. Several musical moments in this film, as well as its aesthetic conception in general, emulate Super-8 productions, with references to the tropicalist artist and Super-8 filmmaker Jomard Muniz de Britto. It remediates his multimedia work, especially the Super-8 films he created with the troupe Vivencial Diversiones, fictionalised in Lacerda's film via the characters of Professor Joubert and the theatre troupe Chão de Estrelas. In *Tatuagem*, there is even an experimental short film, *Ficção e filosofia* (*Fiction and Philosophy*), which brings in the photographic texture of the Super-8 format.

Attractions in the Post-television Era

The most recent stage of music-video effects in cinema concerns digital. In Pernambuco, this factor has been present since the 1980s. The emergence of new digital technologies, such as computers, influenced the aesthetics of the album covers, the bands' costumes and even the song lyrics launched in the 1990s. An example is the cover of the album *Samba esquema noise*, by Mundo Livre S/A, on which we see a photograph of a man with a digital system glued to his bare chest; or the lyrics of the song 'Computadores Fazem Arte' (Computers Make Art) by Fred Zero Quatro, which was first recorded by Chico Science & Nação Zumbi. In the case of Pernambuco, digital technology has enabled the emergence of bands defined by Soares (2013) as 'post-Manguebeat'. Soares recognises that the term can be controversial, as there are several connections between the 'post-television' and the 'television' generations. In the transition from analogical to digital formats, he perceives intersections, among other possibilities, in relation to a production based on a collaborative system among artists of multiple generations, including musicians, videomakers and filmmakers, making it hard to define boundaries between languages and periods. In Recife, this system of mutual collaboration is defined as *brodagem* (yet another English–Portuguese combination, meaning 'brotherhood') and is characteristic of the 1990s generation, as discussed by Nogueira (2009; 2020).

Thanks to the Internet, the contemporary system of *brodagem* has considerable independence in relation to the audiovisual and music industries. A Pernambucan band such as Mombojó, for example, launched its first album – ironically entitled *Nada de novo* (*Nothing New*, 2004) – independently, on the Internet. Juliano Dornelles, who directed the music video for the song 'Deixe-se acreditar' (Let Yourself Believe, 2004), by Mombojó, became a collaborator of internationally acclaimed filmmaker Kleber Mendonça Filho, with whom he co-directed the Cannes award-winning film *Bacurau* (2019).

One interesting case of the combination of music video and the internet involves the film *Tatuagem* and the singer Johnny Hooker. In an analysis of Hooker's work, Janotti Jr. and Alcantara (2018: 36) perceive him as someone who moves between different gender and musical identities. It was certainly this aspect that led Hilton Lacerda to invite Hooker to compose a song for the soundtrack of *Tatuagem*, a film structured around genre and gender tensions. Hooker composed the song 'Volta', which he himself performs in a scene in the film. In addition, he also produced a music video of the song, with the participation of the film cast. The music video went viral on the internet, and thus helped to promote both the musician and the film simultaneously, as stated by Lacerda and producer João Vieira Jr. in the film *Passages*.

Another example of post-television music videos in films is *Amor, plástico e barulho* (*Love, Plastic and Noise*, 2013), directed by Renata Pinheiro. Focused on the dispute between two female singers in search of celebrity, the film is a constant meandering between television and the internet. Its aesthetic conception, including the soundtrack (by DJ Dolores and Yuri Queiroga), pertains to the so-called *brega* and *tecnobrega* music genre. *Brega* refers to a very popular and melodramatic genre in Brazilian music, whose lyrics are mostly related to love stories and disappointments. The Pernambucan musician Reginaldo Rossi (1944–2013) is considered one of its creators, and it is an indispensable part of Recife's musical landscape. Alongside concerts put on in many places, Rossi's work is very much dependent on television. In turn, *tecnobrega* is associated with more recent popular musicians whose careers exist predominantly on the web. Mixing these genres and alluding to their relationship with television and the internet, the fictional narrative of *Amor, plástico e barulho* is placed on the outskirts of Recife, in a poor neighbourhood near the mangroves, where we can follow the band Amor com Veneno (Love with Poison) and the professional and personal rivalries between the two singers, as well as their boyfriends and co-workers, all involved in popular show business. By focusing on this intermedial environment, Renata Pinheiro's film presents a kind of music-video archaeology that describes the whole process of remediation embedded in the film itself. The battle between the two singers mimics the dispute between the various media in the film. The whole process of music production is described on screen, including the shooting of a music video and studio recording. The focus then turns to street vendors who take part in the system of relaying the recorded materials to the audiences. There are also the band's trips to nearby cities to put on shows. The apex is attained when they reach television programs, but they are able to achieve this only thanks to the internet, which has paved their way to success. Despite the difficulties of the process as a whole, the two singers, regardless of their ages and talents, find ways to balance themselves in the midst of many disputes.

To conclude, *Amor, plástico e barulho*, as much as the other films discussed here, is an eloquent example of intermediality between film and music, which relies on music-video aesthetics for its completion. The result is the 'music-video effects' pervading Pernambucan cinema since the 1990s. Having music as their primary material, music videos have become a powerful expression of Manguebeat that went on to shape the cinematic style of Árido Movie. In the films discussed here, as well as in many other Pernambucan films, music from the region becomes an element of visual attraction, thanks to the remediation of music videos, which in turn articulate with other media, such as mainstream television, videoart, and experimental works in Super-8 and on the internet, facilitating their intermedial connections with film. Music video thus allows us to understand the media archaeology embedded in Pernambucan cinema, including media convergences, clashes and ruptures. These effects emerge from the local reality and its material conditions, as propounded in the manifesto 'Crabs with Brains', which left its imprint on some of the most creative songs, videos and films in Brazil.

Notes

1. Research supported by grants #2014/50821-3 and #2018/05762-0, from the São Paulo Research Foundation (FAPESP). The opinions, hypotheses, conclusions or recommendations contained in this material are the sole responsibility of the author and do not necessarily reflect FAPESP opinion.
2. 'Em meados de 91 começou a ser gerado e articulado em vários pontos da cidade um núcleo de pesquisas e produção de ideias pop. O objetivo é engendrar um 'circuito energético', capaz de conectar as boas vibrações dos mangues com a rede mundial de circulação de conceitos pop. Imagem símbolo: uma antena parabólica enfiada na lama.' Unless indicated, all translations are by the author.
3. 'Novembro de 1990. O *Washington Post* publicava que o Recife era a quarta pior cidade do mundo para se viver, de acordo com o Population Crisis Committee. O comitê chegou a esse número depois de avaliar indicadores sociais em 45 países.'
4. 'Nem todos sabem, mas a trilha foi gravada um ano antes do filme ser rodado. [. . .] Mesmo tendo antecedido em um ano as filmagens, a trilha não foi alterada. Gravamos antes inclusive para nos instigar na produção, e para nos instigar nas filmagens. Mesmo assim a trilha foi daquele jeito para o filme, pouquíssimas coisas foram gravadas depois das filmagens.'
5. 'O videoclipe permite a "visualização" de um cenário em que a dicção da canção se desenvolve.'
6. 'É relevante destacar que algumas experiências com registros de atos performáticos ao vivo já eram realizadas no Brasil desde o final dos anos 60, em suporte fílmico, para artistas como Raul Seixas, Novos Baianos e Maria Bethânia, entre outros. No entanto, somente com a gravação de "América do Sul" [com Ney Matogrosso, em 1975], o Brasil teria seu "primeiro" videoclipe.'
7. 'Em filmes como *Baile perfumado*, *Amarelo manga*, *Árido Movie*, *Deserto feliz*, observamos, recorrentemente, a existência de sequências que poderíamos chamar de "momentos musicais". Estas sequências podem estar incorporadas ao enredo (como parte do percurso narrativo geral) ou podem ser dotadas de maior autonomia em relação à própria ação dramática (marcadas por um certo "deslocamento" do enredo. Em uma ou outra situação, as sequências se caracterizam por

atualizarem momentos "pop" em que o filme pára em função de mostrar a música (exibir).'
8. 'Cerca de 200 filmes foram realizados no período, seguindo abordagens diversas: documentários com temas regionais, filmes experimentais, ficção, sátiras, impressões de viagem.'

References

Araújo, Luciana (2000), 'Pernambuco', in Fernão Ramos and Luiz Felipe A. de Miranda (eds), *Enciclopédia do cinema brasileiro*. São Paulo: Editora Senac, pp. 424–5.

Associação Cultural Videobrasil. 'TV Viva', available at <http://site.videobrasil.org.br/acervo/artistas/artista/93884> (last accessed 20 January 2019).

Bentes, Ivana (2007), 'Vídeo e cinema: rupturas, reações e hibridismo', in A. Machado (ed.), *Made in Brasil: três décadas do vídeo brasileiro*. São Paulo: Iluminuras/Itaú Cultural, 2007, pp. 111–28.

Chion, Michel (1994), *Audio-vision: Sound on Screen*. New York: Columbia University Press.

Eisenstein, Sergei ([1924] 1998), 'The Montage of Film Attraction', in R. Taylor (ed.), *The Eisenstein Reader*. London: BFI, pp. 35–52.

Figueirôa, Alexandre (1990), *O cinema super-8 em Pernambuco – do lazer doméstico à resistência cultural*. Master's thesis, University of São Paulo.

Janotti Jr., Jeder and João André Alcantara (2018), *O videoclipe na era pós-televisiva: questões de gênero e categorias musicais nas obras de Daniel Peixoto e Johnny Hooker*. Curitiba: Editora Appris.

Nagib, Lúcia (2014), 'The Politics of Impurity', in L. Nagib and A. Jerslev (eds), *Impure Cinema: Intermedial and Intercultural Approaches to Film*. London and New York: I. B. Tauris, pp. 21–39.

Nagib, Lúcia (2018), 'Passages: Travelling in and out of Film through Brazilian Geography. *Rumores: Revista Online de Comunicação, Linguagem e Mídias*, 12:24, pp. 19–40, doi: http://dx.doi.org/10.11606/issn.1982-677X.rum.2018.148836.

Nogueira, Amanda Mansur Custódio (2009), *O novo ciclo do cinema em Pernambuco: a questão do estilo*. Recife: Editora da UFPE.

Nogueira, Amanda Mansur Custódio (2020), *A brodagem no cinema pernambucano*. Recife: Editora Massangana.

Nogueira, Amanda Mansur Custódio and Paulo Cunha (eds) (2016), *A aventura do Baile Perfumado: 20 anos depois*. Recife: CEPE.

Oliva, Rodrigo (2017), *Interconexões de poéticas audiovisuais: transcineclipe, transclipecine e hiperestilização*. Curitiba: Editora Appris.

Paiva, Samuel (2019), 'Sobre intermidialidade: cinema, maracatus, *Tatuagem* e pós-tropicalismos', *Contracampo – Brazilian Journal of Communication*, 38:2, pp. 147–60. Available at <https://periodicos.uff.br/contracampo/article/view/27106/pdf> (last accessed 4 September 2020).

Paiva, Samuel (2020), 'Cinema and its Intermedial Passages to Reality: The Case of the Árido Movie', *Alphaville: Journal of Film and Screen Media*, 19, pp. 81–100. Available at <http://www.alphavillejournal.com/Issue19/ArticlePaiva.pdf> (last accessed 2 August 2020).

Passos, Paula (2020), 'O cinema intermidiático', *Revista Continente*, 235, January. Available at <http://www.revistacontinente.com.br/edicoes/230/o-cinema-intermidiatico> (last accessed 2 August 2020).

Soares, Thiago (2013), *A estética do videoclipe*. João Pessoa: Editora da UFPB.
Vargas, Herom (2007), *Hibridismos musicais de Chico Science & Nação Zumbi*. Cotia-SP: Ateliê Editorial.
Vernallis, Carol (2004), *Experiencing Music Video: Aesthetics and Cultural Context*. New York: Columbia University Press.

CHAPTER 9

Possessing Archival Images: Ghosts, Songs and Films in Cartola – música para os olhos *(2007)*[1]
Albert Elduque

> 'In *Ganga Zumba* I was the master's trusted slave. Then I betrayed him and was tortured to death. There might be some photos around. In *Os marginais* I was a police rat and got killed going up the hill. I was only kept alive in *Orfeu Negro*.'
>
> Cartola (cited in Silva and Oliveira Filho 1983: 109)[2] (Figure 9.1)

Cartola – música para os olhos (*Cartola – Music for the Eyes*, 2007) is a music documentary by Lírio Ferreira and Hilton Lacerda dedicated to Cartola, one of the most important samba singers and composers of the twentieth century. Cartola was born Angenor de Oliveira in 1908 Rio de Janeiro, the grandson of a senator's cook in the brand-new Brazilian Republic. However, following the death of his grandfather and the decline of their economic situation, the family moved from the middle-class neighbourhoods of Catete and Laranjeiras to the

Figure 9.1   Cartola is shot dead in Moisés Kendler's episode 'Papo amarelo', in *Os marginais* (1968).

favela of Mangueira. In 1928, Angenor, who had been interested in carnival parades since an early age, became one of the founders of Estação Primeira de Mangueira, a prominent samba 'school' in the city.[3] The songs he composed in the 1930s and 1940s became quite popular, but they were recorded only by white singers, such as Francisco Alves and Carmen Miranda. This inequality between poor black or mixed-race composers and middle-class white singers was the rule at that time and one of the biggest contradictions in the history of Brazilian popular music. In the late 1940s, Cartola experienced personal problems and disappeared from the artistic scene, but in the late 1950s, young left-wing artists and intellectuals brought him back to public attention, which allowed him to open a short-lived restaurant in the 1960s and record a few albums in the 1970s. He died in Rio in 1980, by which point he was already a national symbol (see Silva and Oliveira Filho 1983).

The project *Cartola – música para os olhos* began as an invitation from the cultural institute Itaú Cultural to Ferreira and Paulo Caldas to write a fictional script about Cartola. Lacerda soon joined the project, encouraged by his colleagues, and Caldas eventually dropped out due to other commitments. The Rio de Janeiro-based company Raccord then stepped in and Ferreira and Lacerda developed the project, now to be produced as a documentary. Following the model of the book *Please Kill Me: The Uncensored Oral History of Punk* (1997), the filmmakers structured the film as an essayistic patchwork of images and sounds (Lacerda in Nagib and Paiva 2017a). Edited by Mair Tavares and Lessandro Sócrates, the film includes conventional interviews with experts and acquaintances, footage from fictional films, documentaries, newsreels and television, still photographs and album covers, as well as the re-enactment of carnival dances and a few sequences featuring the young Marcos Paulo Simião as Cartola in his childhood years.

In this chapter I aim to approach *Cartola – música para os olhos* from an intermedial perspective by following two interrelated threads: the work done with repurposed archival images and the role of the lyrics of the songs as narrative agents. In both cases I will build on Ágnes Pethő's (2011) take on the concept of 'metalepsis', which for her is defined by leaps between different narrative levels as produced by intermedial occurrences. The dichotomy between life and death serves as a metaphor to explore how the story and context of a deceased artist are retrieved from the archives: I argue that in proposing unexpected relations between film footage and recorded songs, intermediality acts as a historiographic tool through which these two media are given a 'new life'. To explore how these interactions are produced, my essay is divided into four parts. I first briefly introduce the concept of metalepsis and its relation to intermediality, as well as its relevance for *Cartola – música para os olhos*. Sections two and three are respectively dedicated to an analysis of the intermedial and narrative roles of fiction film excerpts and song lyrics in the documentary. In the last section I shall bring these two elements together to explore the intermedial relation between documentary film footage and the lyrics of the songs.

METALEPTIC LEAPS

Gérard Genette defines the notion of metalepsis from a narratological point of view in his book *Narrative Discourse*, first published in 1972. According to him, metalepsis refers to transgressions across different narrative registers that produce a disturbing effect on the reader:

> any intrusion by the extradiegetic narrator or narratee into the diegetic universe (or by diegetic characters into a metadiegetic universe, etc.), or the inverse (as in Cortázar), produces an effect of strangeness that is either comical (when, as in Sterne or Diderot, it is presented in a joking tone) or fantastic. (Genette [1972] 1980: 234–5)

Among other examples, Genette quotes Lawrence Sterne's *Tristram Shandy* (1759–67), in which the narrator asks the reader to give him a hand to close a door, and Julio Cortázar's short tale *Continuidad de los parques* (*The Continuity of Parks*, 1964), where a character is about to kill the man who is reading his story (Genette [1972] 1980: 235–6). Genette's definition is broad enough to include leaps in both directions (from the extradiegetic into the diegetic and vice versa) and across distinct diegetic levels (extradiegetic, diegetic and metadiegetic). Crucially, for him, there is a separation between two different narrative levels marked by 'a boundary that is precisely the narrating (or the performance) itself: a shifting but sacred frontier between two worlds, the world in which one tells, the world of which one tells'. In metalepsis, the separation between these levels is put into crisis (Genette [1972] 1980: 237).[4]

In her book *Cinema and Intermediality*, Pethő argues that this crossing of narrative borders can be put on an equal footing with the crossing of media borders that intermediality entails:

> sequences that suddenly step from the medium of cinema into the realm of another medium and/or apparently employ the language of another art are conventionally markers of a metaleptic crossing from the narrative level of 'reality' into one of subjective consciousness (dream, phantasy, memory flash-back, altered mental state, etc.). (Pethő 2011: 128)

Her examples include the dream sequence designed by Salvador Dalí in Alfred Hitchcock's *Spellbound* (1945), and song-and-dance numbers within classic musicals (2011: 128), as well as the documentary essays by Agnès Varda. According to Pethő, in films such as *Les Glaneurs et la glaneuse* (*The Gleaners and I*, 2000) and *Les Plages d'Agnès* (*The Beaches of Agnès*, 2008), metaleptic leaps produce a two-way interaction between Varda's reality and a variety of media. In the latter, for example, Varda's memories are presented via film clips, photographs and installations, as well as re-enactments using props and painted scenery, thus shifting 'from immediacy to hypermediacy,[5] from discursive to figural, from transparent to opaque, from real to fantastic, and back'. This playful approach to media culminates at the end of the film with the 'house of cinema', a 'first-person installation' which consists of a construction built out of celluloid film stock from her film *Les Créatures* (*The Creatures*, 1966) (Pethő 2011: 382–3).

In the remaining sections I will argue that in *Cartola – música para os olhos* intermedial relations produce metaleptic leaps between the real and the mediated that invite new readings of the repurposed original materials. Lírio Ferreira states that he is fascinated by the blurred boundaries between truth and falsification, documentary and fiction, which may explain his devotion to Orson Welles (Nagib and Paiva 2017b). In fact, Cartola's final statement in the documentary, which is heard over an image of a cemetery fence ('I'd like to leave my best regards to all of you, and thank you for choosing me to chit-chat with you to tell some lies and a few truths'),[6] is reminiscent of Welles's final confession in *F for Fake* (1973): 'I did promise that for one hour I'd tell you only the truth. That hour, ladies and gentlemen, is over. For the past seventeen minutes, I've been lying my head off.' Throughout the film, the truthfulness of Cartola's story is constantly questioned: while images from newsreels and documentaries are intercut with excerpts from fictional films, the patchwork of voices from interviews is interrupted by recordings of specific songs. In both cases, the documentary narration gives way to fictional parentheses and the film leaps into a different register. Let us now explore these intermedial metaleptic crossings.

LIVING IN THE MOVIES

In her essay 'Border Talks: The Problematic Status of Media Borders in the Current Debate about Intermediality', Irina Rajewsky distinguishes between intramedial and intermedial references. According to her, intramedial referencing 'remains within *one* medium and consequently does not involve any kind of medial difference'; this is the case of intertextuality, for example, when a film quotes another film. Conversely, 'in the case of *inter*medial references a medial difference *does* come into play' (Rajewsky 2010: 62). Dagmar Brunow explores the use of such concepts in relation to archival images, arguing that the mixture of different film formats, even if it is restricted to the film medium, may be considered intermedial instead of intramedial: '[Rajewsky's distinction] does not account for the materiality of film footage. For instance, remediating 8mm or 16mm footage in a feature film can foreground a medial difference' (Brunow 2015: 48). Brunow (2015: 48–9) exemplifies this 'media specificity of repurposing' with three examples: in *Deutschland bleiche Mutter* (*Germany Pale Mother*, Helma Sanders-Brahms, 1980), an archival newsreel creates a disruption in the narrative, becoming 'a self-reflexive device, breaking the illusion, disrupting continuity and breaking into the diegesis', while in *Milk* (Gus Van Sant, 2008) and *Saving Private Ryan* (Steven Spielberg, 1998) specific staged sequences are artificially altered to give them a different texture and therefore a higher effect of 'authenticity'.

Whether archival footage constitutes a medial difference is not an easy question to answer. According to Rajewsky (2010: 62), what ultimately distinguishes one medium from another, and therefore what allows us to consider whether two objects are part of the same medium or not, are 'material and operative restrictions': 'painting ... can never become genuinely photographic, even though this is suggested at times by photorealistic painting. Here medial specificities and borders emerge, which make clear that certain basic medial constraints must be considered.' In her argument Brunow takes these material conditions into consideration, but it may be argued that the visual textures she describes do not match the material restrictions described by Rajewsky. Nonetheless, as Brunow's examples prove, considering archival footage as a different medium might be useful in specific cases, for example, when archival images introduce a disruption into the narrative flow, or when a simulacrum of texture is purposely created. I consider the excerpts from fictional films in *Cartola – música para os olhos* to fall into the first of these categories, even if they contribute to narrate Cartola's life. In the remainder of this section, I will focus on the ways in which these excerpts are used in the documentary, and how their obvious difference from the documentary footage produces a metaleptic leap that transgresses medial borders and, in doing so, breaks with the homogeneity and linearity of the narrative discourse.

In *Cartola*, numerous short clips from Brazilian fiction films are intercut with the narration of Cartola's life. They help to define the cultural, political and social context in which the singer developed his career, including three features where he played small parts: *Orfeu negro* (*Black Orpheus*, Marcel Camus, 1959), *Ganga zumba* (Carlos Diegues, 1963) and Moisés Kendler's episode 'Papo amarelo' in *Os marginais* (*The Outsiders*, 1968).[7] However, the most interesting cases are those where the link between Cartola and a given film is not a historical fact, but a poetic insight created by Ferreira and Lacerda. Throughout the documentary, images that bear no relation to Cartola are repurposed to complement, illustrate or parody the story of his life. Thus, the brothel in *Perdida* (*A Lost Woman*, Carlos Alberto Prates Correia, 1976) features as the imaginary place of his sexual initiation; the social-realist *Rio,*

40 graus (*Rio, 40 Degrees*, Nelson Pereira dos Santos, 1955) and the comedy *Aviso aos navegantes* (*Calling All Sailors*, Watson Macedo, 1950) are used to inject humour into his affair with a married woman; and the unequal deals between black samba songwriters and white singers are explained using images from *Quem roubou meu samba* (*Who Stole My Samba*, José Carlos Burle, 1959), *O mandarim* (*The Mandarin*, Júlio Bressane, 1995) and *Rio, Zona Norte* (*Rio, Northern Zone*, Nelson Pereira dos Santos, 1957). The chronological correspondence between these films and the biographical events is not always accurate: for example, *Perdida* is set in the 1970s but is used to illustrate a story set in a 1920s brothel. However, this anachronism never comes to the fore, nor does it hinder the excerpts' narrative and comical effect.

Scenes from *Orfeu negro* and *Os marginais* also appear as visual records of Cartola's work in the film industry, but at the same time they are used as metaphors for specific biographical episodes. To the best of my knowledge, Cartola's cameo in *Orfeu negro*, which took place at the time of his comeback to public life, is the second record of him on film, after his elusive appearance in *O descobrimento do Brasil* (*The Discovery of Brazil*, Humberto Mauro, 1937, see note 7). In *Cartola – música para os olhos* this moment is highlighted by the fact that it is the first time we see a moving image of Cartola, after 33 minutes of still photographs of him and his disembodied voice as an old man, telling the story of his life. With *Orfeu negro* we can, at last, see him in motion. His resurrection as an artist therefore coincides with his aparition as a cinematic figure, and his wife, Dona Zica, knotting his tie, seems to be preparing him to perform his rebirth as a public persona. On the other hand, the excerpt from *Os marginais* is placed to illustrate a difficult moment in Cartola's life, when he had to close down his restaurant and move into his father's house due to financial problems. In the film, Cartola is chased by two men who shoot him down, thus aligning a moment of decline in his life with his literal fall.

Unlike the previous examples, Júlio Bressane's literary adaptation *Brás Cubas* (1985) bears no relation to Cartola's life nor to his socio-cultural context.[8] Immediately after an introductory sequence featuring a burial (more on which shortly), the off-screen voice of singer Jards Macalé recites the first words from Machado de Assis's novel *Memórias póstumas de Brás Cubas* (*The Posthumous Memoirs of Brás Cubas*), first published in 1881: 'For some time I debated over whether I should start these memoirs at the beginning or at the end, that is, whether I should put my birth or my death in the first place' (Machado de Assis [1881] 1997: 7). A dead man telling his life is not a rigorous example of metalepsis, but its narrative paradox has a similarly disturbing effect, which Bressane brings to the fore by highlighting a technical mediation: his film shows a sound engineer roving his microphone over a skeleton, then scraping it on its surface, even digging it into its eye socket in order to produce raw, irritating sounds. Ferreira and Lacerda reframe the original footage in panoramic format, change it from colour into black and white, and superimpose on it Cartola's recorded voice from an interview in which he tells the story of his life.

A complex intertextual play between films and characters is thus established here: in the film, Cartola seems to open his posthumous memoirs as if he were Brás Cubas as read by Jards Macalé. The filmmakers have acknowledged that the deceased Cartola mirrors not only the ghostly narrator Brás Cubas, but also Machado de Assis, because the singer was born the year the writer died, and each of them became the symbol of a particular level of Brazilian culture: popular culture in the case of Cartola, and highbrow culture in the case of Machado de Assis (Vianna 2007), bearing racial undertones in both instances because Machado de Assis and Cartola were black. Apart from this rich cultural interplay, the microphone entering the eye socket (which in Bressane's film is appropriately dubbed a 'necrophone') suggests that Cartola's voice is emerging from beyond the grave. It is not surprising, then, that Ferreira and Lacerda's original project included spiritualism and reincarnation, thus emphasising a crucial idea that I will pick up on later on:

> In the first screenplay, which was much more fictional . . . we intended to do a spiritualist film. Cartola would be a spirit embodied by actress Marieta Severo, actor Paulo José, the footballer Vampeta, a child, and other people. . . . A few years later, I saw a film about Bob Dylan with the same idea. (Ferreira in Nagib and Paiva 2017b)[9]

From *Orfeu negro* to *Brás Cubas*, a playful cross-pollination between the life of the singer and the history of Brazilian cinema takes place. Most of the short excerpts are brought to the fore to parody or highlight specific biographical passages, and they become new versions of Cartola's life; at the same time, the singer's story brings new meanings to the images of well-known films. Starting with the skeleton at the beginning of the film, the spirit of Cartola acquires a new life in the bodies of the movie characters from the past, and in a way he becomes a new historical thread weaving through Brazilian cinema and arts.

Throughout this journey, which also includes newsreels and TV programmes,[10] the heterogeneity of the repurposed works is never concealed, and their differences in colour pattern and preservation state are apparent. Grainy images from old films and analogue video from television broadcasting stand in stark contrast with the new footage's crisp digital image. Rather than effacing the contrast, the film highlights it: for example, the fictionalised train trip of Cartola as a kid to Mangueira, which is filmed with soft colours, is intercut with black-and-white images from different sources, including grainy excerpts of the documentary film *Conversa de botequim* (*Bar Talk*, Luiz Carlos Lacerda, 1970) and some poorly preserved TV images of a homage to samba songwriter Donga. In fact, the contemporary images of the train encapsulate and reframe the footage from the past.

Following Brunow's suggestion of a 'media specificity of repurposing', it is possible to argue that the relevance given to different textures within this archival footage highlights medial differences between digital, film print and television. From this perspective, Cartola's life as presented in these materials becomes an intermedial journey through the audiovisual history of Brazil, one that transgresses medial and material borders as well as traditional historiographic hierarchies.

LIVING IN THE SONGS

As much as the use of fiction film clips, the inclusion of songs performs a metaleptic leap by highlighting a medial difference.[11] A film focused on the life and work of an artist is a privileged space for intermedial effects, and indeed, recent scholarship on the biopic has been interested in the ways in which the work of painters, poets and singers can be integrated into the fabric of film (Brown and Vidal 2014; Andrews 2013; Minier and Pennacchia 2014). For example, in a fine analysis of the biopics *Ray* (Taylor Hackford, 2004), *Walk the Line* (James Mangold, 2005) and *Beyond the Sea* (Kevin Spacey, 2004), Jesse Schlotterbeck argues that these films break with the tradition of most musical biopics by integrating the lyrics of the songs into the story in order to express the emotions of characters (Schlotterbeck 2008).

Cartola – música para os olhos is structured as a biopic, however, and unlike other music documentaries where songs are played for just a few seconds or used as background music, it allows the spectator time to listen to long sections of these songs and to enjoy their specificity as a medium. As a result, on many occasions Cartola's lyrics become the main narrative voice of the film, performing an intermedial interference that is also a metaleptic leap. For a moment, the songs break away from their condition as objects in focus to become storytelling narrators in and of themselves. By these means, Ferreira and Lacerda produce poetical versions of facts that are otherwise relayed via conventional oral accounts by the interviewees or Cartola's own voiceover.

A large number of Cartola's compositions are included, most of them from old records, though a few are sung anew by members of the Mangueira community. Unlike the use of fiction films, where a movie from the 1970s could be used to narrate an event from the 1920s, compositions are often played following a chronological order, and sung by the artists that made them popular. For this reason, in the section that spans from Cartola's birth until his late recognition in the early 1960s, most of the songs are performed by other artists, including Francisco Alves. Later in the film, once Cartola returns to the public eye and is recognised as an artist, his renditions take on a central role, as seen in the TV programme *Ensaio* or heard in the recordings of his own albums. In addition, his late popularity is attested by the multiple performances of 'O sol nascerá' (The Sun's Gonna Rise) and 'As rosas não falam' (Roses Don't Talk), which are sung both by Cartola and by younger singers who pay homage to him, such as Nara Leão and Beth Carvalho.

Songs are therefore artistic creations inherent in the main story, which is Cartola's life story. They are objects in which the documentary is interested. However, from the very beginning they are also given a narrative function in the storytelling,[12] given that a significant part of Cartola's lyrics is concerned with his own experience and refer to specific episodes in his life. For example, 'Sim' (Yes) was composed following the death of his first wife, Deolinda (Silva and Oliveira Filho 1983: 86), and 'Nós dois' (Both of Us) in anticipation of his long-lasting marriage to Dona Zica (Silva and Oliveira Filho 1983: 106). It is unsurprising, then, that in *Cartola – música para os olhos* these two songs are used to complement or even replace those specific biographical episodes, sometimes keeping the original facts somewhat unexplained but offering instead a more intimate, poetical view of them. Songs, in the film, thus fulfil the role Hannah Andrews (2013: 366) ascribes to poems in some poet biopics, in which 'the poems are both themselves the subjects of the adaptation process and are simultaneously used in these films to support, underline or illustrate the adapted narrative of the life of the poet that the film proposes'.

In other cases the songs' evocations become even more complex due to the displacement of their object: that is, the person to whom they were originally addressed. The most eloquent example is the song 'Festa da vinda' (Welcome Party), which is performed by Elza Soares at the narrative point when Cartola returns to the public eye. The first verses read: 'Eu e meu violão / vamos tocando em vão / o seu regresso' (Me and my guitar / we're playing in vain / your return). In the original song the lyrics ask for a love reconciliation, but here, thanks to the editing, they seem to address Cartola himself and ask him to come back to the stage.

The primary role of songs in *Cartola – música para os olhos* is to stand as examples of his artistic production, but the fact that long sections of them are played, combined with their specific location within the film, alters and amplifies their significance. In a way, songs produce an intermedial intrusion of fiction (the artist's creation) into a constructed reality (the documentary approach), and therefore they enact a metaleptic leap into a more subjective, mediated and self-reflexive space, blurring narrative borders and performing the role of a narrative voice in and out of the story.

LIVING IN THE ARCHIVES

The previous section looked at the ways in which song lyrics shape *Cartola*'s temporal structure. However, these songs are often played back over archival footage, establishing a dialogue with it. The film's title, 'music for the eyes', an expression borrowed from Arnold Schönberg, is an explicit reference to this dialogue. It is also reminiscent of Abel Gance's definition of cinema as 'the music of light', a formula he used to legitimise cinema as an autonomous medium in the context of the 1920s avant-garde (Bordwell 1980: 155). Júlio Bressane, a key influence on Ferreira and Lacerda, has also invoked Gance's formula with reference to his own experimental combination of image and music (Bressane 1996: 24). As we will see in this section, in *Cartola* the idea of 'music for the eyes' is closer to Bressane than to Gance because it does not aim to legitimise cinema as a pure art with a distinct language, but to encourage the spectator to watch the film as a space for synaesthetic experiments.

In the film, as well as providing contextual information, music and images are often combined in unexpected ways, producing new meanings via intermedial relations. This is especially visible in two groups of sequences: those concerned with historical political facts and those related to Cartola's death. In both cases, as we will see, the interaction between songs and images triggers an intermedial leap that challenges and reconfigures narrative borders.

While both social and cultural lives are given pride of place throughout the film, the political context takes on greater importance in the sequences devoted to the period between 1950 and the 1970s, from the era of President Juscelino Kubitschek's policy of developmentalism to the military dictatorship. As a result, the songs heard offer personal, subjective comments not only on biographical episodes, but also on historical facts. For example, the cheerful 'O sol nascerá' (The Sun's Gonna Rise) is played over the images of the optimistic Kubitschek government of the late 1950s and early 1960s: shots showing Brasília, the President greeting crowds, people walking in the street and a carnival parade are combined with the lyrics 'A sorrir / eu pretendo levar a vida / pois chorando / eu vi a mocidade perdida' (Always smiling / I intend to live my life / because crying / I've seen my youth go to waste), thus suggesting a new political hope for the country. On the other hand, the conformist and defeatist 'Acontece' (It So Happens) illustrates the 1964 coup. In this case, images of a military parade are superimposed with a photo of Cartola's wedding, thus bringing together his personal life and the political events. Although the images of the parade are subverted by being played in slow motion and backwards, its drama is kept and even heightened by the song lyrics: 'Acontece que meu coração ficou frio / e nosso ninho de amor está vazio' (It so happens that my heart grew cold / and our love nest is empty). As a result, the cold heart and the empty love nest from 'Acontece' are linked with political disenchantment. In both examples, Cartola's intimate feelings are used to connote historical images, giving them a personal tone, and images work in turn as metaphorical illustrations of Cartola's feelings of joy, despair and sorrow. There are leaps between the subjective and the collective in which both songs and historical facts acquire new meanings and undertones, thanks to the intermedial contact with each other.

In an essay on Brazilian music documentaries, Tatiana Heise (2012) explores *Cartola* alongside films on Vinicius de Moraes, Tom Jobim and Caetano Veloso, to show how the contemporary depiction of these artists is strongly concerned with the concept of *brasilidade*, or Brazilianness. In her view, these films reinforce the sense of national identity provided by Brazilian popular music and its singers. I would add that the most accomplished expression of *brasilidade* in *Cartola* is the connection it produces between lyrics, personal life and national history, as seen in the interaction between songs and archival footage.

Another kind of archival images affected by their contact with the songs can be found in three sequences focusing on Cartola's death, burial and afterlife. At the film's opening, the song 'Divina dama' (Divine Lady), sung by Cartola, is heard over images from *A morte de um poeta* (*The Death of a Poet*, 1981), directed by Aloysio Raulino (who, as it happens, is also cinematographer on the documentary), a black-and-white film focusing on the singer's burial in 1980. First recorded by Francisco Alves in 1933, 'Divina dama' talks about the end of a ball in a melancholic tone: 'Tudo acabado / e o baile encerrado' (Everything's over / the ball has ended). Set over images of a cemetery, the closing moments of the party in the song become linked with the end of Cartola's life, equalling the sorrowful end of dancing with death.

At the end of the film, Cartola bids farewell twice, as follows. After a TV news report, which shows him in poor condition after some days in hospital, the song 'O inverno do meu tempo' (Winter of My Days), which he wrote at the end of his life,[13] is first heard over a sunset in Rio de Janeiro, which stands as an obvious metaphor for his death. However, once the sky turns black and only the lights from Central Station are visible, the film fades to images from Leon Hirszman's *Rio, carnaval da vida* (*Rio, Carnival of Life*, 1978), while the song continues to play on the soundtrack. In these images, Cartola does not

Figure 9.2 Cartola in *Rio, carnaval da vida* (Leon Hirszman, 1978).

look sick any more, and, together with other important Mangueira composers, leads Mangueira's carnival parade in front of the crowds (Figure 9.2). The shots are in slow motion and have a dreamlike quality, and their placement just after a sunset makes them evocative of an afterlife. The images from *Rio, carnaval da vida*, crowded with dancers, take on a nostalgic quality, while 'O inverno do meu tempo' becomes brighter, thanks to the joy of the carnival parade.

A little later, other images from Raulino's *A morte de um poeta* are included, now showing some men drinking in a bar next to the cemetery. Over these images we hear 'Fiz por você o que pude' (I've Done What I Could For You), a song composed by Cartola in 1957 to mark his comeback to the artistic scene (Silva and Oliveira Filho 1983: 92). However, here this song is placed at the very end of his life and repurposed as a farewell to Mangueira, the lyrics suggesting the arrival of a new songwriter: 'Surge outro compositor / jovem de grande valor / com o mesmo sangue na veia' (Another songwriter comes / so young and full of worth / with the same blood in his veins). The melancholic drinking scene thus becomes full of promise.

Nuno Ramos, in a compelling essay on the works of Nelson Cavaquinho, a samba singer and composer who was also a member of Mangueira, points out that Cavaquinho and Cartola started to record albums in their old age, and that this fact is reflected in their lyrics. According to Ramos, their point of view is 'the perspective of a life lived. There is accumulated experience here, which results in a certain restraint and sobriety, and a weariness that comes with it' (Ramos [2009] 2017: 38).[14] In the three songs mentioned above, which are played in their entirety, Cartola's sober, aged voice sings from the grave and gives new meanings to the images filmed by Raulino and Hirszman, to the point of slowing down the speed of the parade in *Rio, carnaval da vida*. Songs create an intermedial rupture, opening up a subjective, fictional space within the documentary.

In the quote at the beginning of this chapter, Cartola makes fun of the fact that he was killed in most of his film roles. However, the quote ends with his mention of *Orfeu negro* as the film where he survived, thus evoking that musician from Antiquity who travelled to hell to bring his lover back to life. *Cartola – música para os olhos* replies to this by showing how his spirit and tunes can possess characters and spaces from old comedies, social dramas, propaganda newsreels and carnival parades, and transform them with his heartfelt lyrics and tender voice in the process. Cartola mobilises the archive, embodies it, and in so doing injects new life into a section of Brazil's artistic history.

Notes

1. This chapter is the result of research conducted as part of the AHRC–FAPESP-funded project *Towards an Intermedial History of Brazilian Cinema: Exploring Intermediality as a Historiographic Method* (short title: IntermIdia). Previous versions were presented at the conference 'A Europa e os impérios coloniais dos séculos XVI, XVII e XVIII na literatura e no cinema' (Universidade do Algarve, 2016); the I IntermIdia Conference (Universidade Federal de São Carlos, 2016); and 'Symbiotic Cinema: Confluences Between Film and Other Media. 24th Sercia Conference' (Linnaeus University, 2018). *Cartola – música para os olhos* was also discussed in the Sewing Circle (University of Reading, 2016) and with my students at the seminar 'Cinema e Intermidialidade' (Universidade Federal de São Carlos, 2017) and the extension course 'Brazilian Music and Film' (University of Reading, 2018). I am indebted to the organisers of and the participants at all those events. I am also grateful to all my colleagues on the IntermIdia Project for their help and to Nicolau Bruno de Almeida Leonel, who, during my stay in Brazil, generously shared with me his passion for and knowledge of Brazilian music and cinema.
2. 'No *Ganga Zumba* eu era o escravo de confiança do senhor. Pois traí o senhor e morri torturado no tronco. Tinha até umas fotos por aí. Em *Os marginais* eu era "cagüete" da polícia, me assassinaram na subida do morro. Só fiquei vivo no *Orfeu*.' Unless indicated, all translations are by the author.
3. Samba 'schools' ('escolas de samba' in Portuguese) is the name given to the samba groups that compete in Rio's annual carnival parade contest. According to composer Ismael Silva, author of the most accepted explanation, the term 'samba school' came into existence in 1928, when pioneer samba group Deixa Falar was created in the Estácio neighbourhood. At that time a teacher training school, which in Brazil was known as a 'Normal School', was running nearby.

The term 'samba school' was then coined as a playful contrast with 'Normal School' to stress the difference between community parties and formal education. Historian Sérgio Cabral (1974: 22) explains Silva's version but says that he has not found any evidence of it.

4. Genette further developed his works on metalepsis in his book *Métalepse: de la figure à la fiction* (2004). For a discussion of the use of metalepsis in media other than high-brow literature, see Wolf 2005.
5. Pethő refers here to the double logic of remediation as theorised by Jay David Bolter and Richard Grusin (1999).
6. Unless otherwise indicated, the quotes from the film, as well as the lyrics and titles of the songs, follow the English translations on the DVD.
7. In addition, Cartola claimed that he also played a part in *O descobrimento do Brasil* (*The Discovery of Brazil*, Humberto Mauro, 1937) (Silva and Oliveira Filho 1983: 71). The website *Catraca Livre* states that in that film Cartola 'played an indian among a crowd and it is almost impossible to recognise him' (2019). I have not been able to find any further details, and Mauro's work is not used in Ferreira and Lacerda's documentary.
8. It is important to mention that Júlio Bressane is a crucial model for Ferreira and Lacerda. Throughout his career, Bressane has consistently explored the relationship between image and recordings of old Brazilian songs in films such as *Tabu* (1982) and *O mandarim* (*The Mandarin*, 1995).
9. Ferreira is obviously referring to Todd Haynes's *I'm Not There* (2007). Apart from that, the cemetery also features prominently in *O homem que engarrafava nuvens* (*The Man Who Bottled Clouds*, 2009), directed solely by Ferreira and devoted to *baião* lyricist Humberto Teixeira. The film bears a strong relation to *Cartola – música para os olhos* for its similar patchwork structure and creative use of archival images.
10. The creative use of still photographs in the film is also worthy of note but I am unable to consider it here for reasons of space.
11. Here I will focus on the songs themselves rather than the use of sounds or voices throughout the documentary. A very interesting analysis that includes noises and silences can be found in Puccini 2015.
12. Fortunately, the DVD edition of the film provides subtitles with translation of the lyrics.
13. Cartola's biographers call this song 'a samba-synthesis of that moment of his life' (Silva and Oliveira Filho 1983: 122).
14. The original reads: 'o ponto de vista de quem já viveu. Há uma experiência acumulada aqui, que obriga a uma contenção e sobriedade, e a um cansaço de fundo que vem dela'.

REFERENCES

Andrews, Hannah (2013), 'Recitation, Quotation, Interpretation: Adapting the Oeuvre in Poet Biopics', *Adaptation*, 6:3, pp. 365–83.

Bolter, Jay David and Richard Grusin (1999), *Remediation: Understanding New Media*. Cambridge, MA, and London: MIT Press.
Bordwell, David (1980), 'The Musical Analogy', *Yale French Studies*, 60, pp. 141–56.
Bressane, Júlio (1996), *Alguns*. Rio de Janeiro: Imago.
Brown, Tom and Belén Vidal (eds) (2014), *The Biopic in Contemporary Film Culture*. New York: Routledge.
Brunow, Dagmar (2015), *Remediating Transcultural Memory: Documentary Filmmaking as Archival Intervention*. Berlin and Boston: De Gruyter.
Cabral, Sérgio (1974), *As escolas de samba: o quê, quem, como, quando e por quê*. Rio de Janeiro: Fontana.
Catraca Livre (2019), 'Zicartola no cinema: descubra os filmes estrelados pelo sambista e sua esposa', 9 May, available at <https://catracalivre.com.br/samba-em-rede/zicartola-no-cinema-descubra-os-filmes-em-que-o-sambista-e-sua-esposa-estrelaram-2/> (last accessed 20 August 2020).
Genette, Gérard ([1972] 1980), *Narrative Discourse*, trans. Jane E. Lewin. Ithaca, NY: Cornell University Press.
Genette, Gérard (2004), *Métalepse: de la figure à la fiction*. Paris: Seuil.
Heise, Tatiana Signorelli (2012), 'Sounds from Brazil: *Brasilidade* and the Rise of Music Documentary', in Lisa Shaw and Rob Stone (eds), *Screening Songs in Hispanic and Lusophone Cinema*. Manchester: Manchester University Press, pp. 249–63.
Machado de Assis, Joaquim Maria ([1881] 1997), *The Posthumous Memoirs of Brás Cubas*, trans. Gregory Rabassa. New York and Oxford: Oxford University Press.
Minier, Márta and Maddalena Pennacchia (eds) (2014), *Adaptation, Intermediality and the British Celebrity Biopic*. Farnham and Burlington, VT: Ashgate.
Nagib, Lúcia and Samuel Paiva (2017a), Interview with Hilton Lacerda for the film *Passages*, available at <https://research.reading.ac.uk/intermidia/passages> (last accessed 21 January 2019).
Nagib, Lúcia and Samuel Paiva (2017b), Interview with Lírio Ferreira for the film *Passages*, available at <https://research.reading.ac.uk/intermidia/passages> (last accessed 21 January 2019).
Pethő, Ágnes (2011), *Cinema and Intermediality: The Passion for the In-Between*. Newcastle-Upon-Tyne: Cambridge Scholars Publishing.
Puccini, Sérgio (2015), 'As vozes e o silêncio em *Cartola, música para os olhos*', *RuMoRes*, 9: 18, pp. 72–85. Available at <https://www.revistas.usp.br/Rumores/article/view/90107> (last accessed 10 January 2022).
Rajewsky, Irina O. (2010), 'Border Talks: The Problematic Status of Media Borders in the Current Debate about Intermediality', in Lars Elleström (ed.), *Media Borders, Multimodality and Intermediality*. Basingstoke: Palgrave Macmillan, pp. 51–68.
Ramos, Nuno ([2009] 2017), 'Wrinkles – About Nelson Cavaquinho', trans. Roderick Steel, in Albert Elduque (ed.), *Contemporary Brazilian Music Film*. Reading: University of Reading, pp. 35–45.
Schlotterbeck, Jesse (2008), '"*Trying to Find a Heartbeat*": Narrative Music in the Pop Performer Biopic', *Journal of Popular Film and Television*, 36:2, pp. 82–90.
Silva, Marília T. Barboza and Arthur L. de Oliveira Filho (1983), *Cartola: os tempos idos*, Rio de Janeiro: FUNARTE/INM/DMP.
Vianna, Luiz Fernando (2007), 'Samba na veia', *Folha de S. Paulo Ilustrada*, 6 April, available at <https://www1.folha.uol.com.br/fsp/ilustrad/fq0604200707.htm> (last accessed 21 January 2019).

Wolf, Werner (2005), 'Metalepsis as a Transgeneric and Transmedial Phenomenon: A Case Study of the Possibilities of "Exporting" Narratological Concepts', in Jan Christoph Meister, Tom Kindt and Wilhelm Schernus (eds), *Narratology Beyond Literary Criticism: Mediality, Disciplinarity*. Berlin and New York: De Gruyter.

Part III

Entertainment Circuits

CHAPTER 10

Intermediality in Brazilian Silent Cinema: Luiz de Barros's Works and Intermedial Strategies[1]

Luciana Corrêa de Araújo

Luiz 'Lulu' de Barros was one of Brazil's most prolific filmmakers. Between 1916 and 1977 he directed over 100 films, which included features and shorts, fiction and non-fiction films. Barros also worked extensively with theatre and scenography, as director, set designer, playwright and impresario, in theatres, casinos and other entertainment venues. His constant transit across different types of media and forms of entertainment contributed to the construction and viability of a career that spanned no fewer than seven decades.

Although intermedial strategies, alongside constant dialogues with foreign cinema, characterise his entire career, this chapter will focus on the period between the 1910s and 1920s. This is because the study of Barros's activities in that period can enlighten us on some significant intermedial dynamics pertaining to Brazilian silent cinema as a whole.

There are no known surviving film elements of Barros's silent films. Albeit distressing, this does stimulate an analysis of intermedial relations beyond film texts. Following Rick Altman (1992: 6–7), who proposes the concept of cinema as 'event' rather than as 'text', this chapter aims to consider 'a broad spectrum of objects, processes, and activities'.

In Brazilian cinema scholarship, a key reference over the past decades has been Jean-Claude Bernardet's book *Historiografia clássica do cinema brasileiro* (*Classical Historiography of Brazilian Cinema*), published in 1995. Although it does not deal directly with the concept of intermediality, the book leans towards this field of enquiry. Its methodological proposals aim at dismantling and refuting the classical historiography that tends to isolate film production from other related arenas. By suggesting a series of 'research itineraries', Bernardet (1995: 85) argues that the 'crossover of diverse territories can enrich the way in which each one of them is understood'.[2] Avoiding nationalistic and overgeneralised approaches, he analyses the production of the so-called Bela Época (*Belle Époque*) of Brazilian cinema, between 1907 and 1911, by means of transversal cuts or 'veins' (*filões*, in the original) and draws several comparisons: between the most successful genres back then (crime films, sung films and revue films) and other fields such as the press and the theatrical revues of the year; between Brazilian and foreign cinema; and between film production and film exhibition and reception. If we are to understand Bernardet's 'crossover of diverse territories' as encompassing intermedial relations, it is fair to state that the methodological proposals, as well as the analyses he undertakes in *Historiografia clássica do cinema brasileiro*, constitute a ground-breaking application of intermediality as a historiographic method to Brazilian cinema.

This chapter also draws on Charles Musser's (2004a) concept of 'theatrical culture'. Considering 'both the central role of theatre in Western culture throughout most of the nineteenth and twentieth century and the commonalities of stage and screen' (12), Musser proposes that 'we might profitably seek to write an integrated history of theatrical entertainment which includes both live stage performance and the cinema' (2004b: 4).

Combining the concept of 'theatrical culture' formulated by Musser with Bernardet's methodological proposals, this chapter establishes as its main 'vein' or axis of analysis the relations between stage and screen which proved to be central to both Luiz de Barros's career and Brazilian silent cinema in general.[3] It will address Barros's activities chronologically, considering 'the relationship between stage and screen on many levels: that of personnel, subject matter and treatment, production methods, distribution of productions, advertising and promotion, as well as spectatorship' (Musser 2004b: 8).

CIRCULATION OF THEMES AND PERSONNEL

By the early 1910s Lulu de Barros already showed combined interests in theatre, painting and cinema. His passion for theatre prompted him to drop out of law school in Rio de Janeiro to study scenography and decorative painting in Europe, where he attended art schools in Milan and Paris (Heffner 2012: 66). As Barros (1978: 40) himself recalls in his autobiography *Minhas memórias de cineasta* (*My Filmmaker Memoirs*), he was drawn to cinema after he saw a film being shot on a Parisian street, featuring comedian Max Linder. He would go on to find his way into Gaumont Studios, where he acquired his first notions of filmmaking (1978: 41). With the outbreak of World War I, he returned to Rio and began to make films, becoming in the following ten years one of the most active and best-known professionals of Brazilian cinema, while at the head of his own production company, Guanabara-Film.

Stage elements punctuate his cinema from the outset. His first commercially released film, *Perdida* (*Misguided*, 1916), featured actor Leopoldo Froes in one of the leading roles. Although he was already well known as a stage actor, it was only in the following year, 1917, that Froes would become the most prestigious and commercially successful actor of his time (Ferreira 2004). When *Perdida* was released, the theatre professional garnering the most attention in the film's adverts and in the articles published in the press was Oscar Lopes – a writer, playwright and journalist, often credited as the film's 'author' (*A Noite* 1916: 5). The premiere at Cinema Pathé, in Rio de Janeiro, brought together journalists and a group of Rio's elite families, eliciting mentions in the press that mixed film commentary and social chronicle (*Revista da Semana* 1916: 17–18). Although there is no extant print of this film, this kind of response clearly testifies to the ambition of producing a film in Brazil in the style of the European *film d'art* (Freire 2018: 261). The 'intellectual contribution' (*Revista da Semana* 1916: 18) of a renowned writer and stage author was an efficient strategy to gain prestige for both *Perdida* and Guanabara-Film, as well as to validate Barros's artistic intentions. The strategy of seeking prestige for Brazilian films through collaboration with renowned writers had been at work since the period of the Bela Época. Two good examples are Raul Pederneiras, writer and caricaturist, and José do Patrocínio Filho, writer and journalist, both of great prominence in Rio's cultural life at the time, whose collaboration is credited in the films *O cometa* (*The Comet*, Empresa F. Serrador, 1910) and *Paz e amor* (*Peace and Love*, William e Cia, 1910), respectively (see Conde 2007).

In Barros's following film, *Vivo ou morto* (*Dead or Alive*, 1916), other theatrical elements are activated to reinforce links with the *film d'art* genre. The protagonist is played by Tina D'Arco, an operetta singer who was performing in Rio with the Italian company Maresca-Weiss; the set design was created by Angelo Lazary, who was very active in Rio's theatre circles. As in *Perdida*, D'Arco and Lazary's participation in *Vivo ou morto* points to one of the most important aspects of the dynamic relationship between stage and screen: the constant professional exchange between the two media. The stage works by these two artists, however, suggest an additional kind of intermedial relation.

Both D'Arco and Lazary worked on plays in which cinema was central to the plot and the staging. D'Arco was in the cast of the operetta *A menina do cinematógrafo* (*The Cinematograph Girl*), staged in Rio de Janeiro a few months before the film's release, and focusing on a series of events triggered by indiscreet film footage of a young man who is soon to be married, captured in a romantic situation with another woman (*O Paiz* 1916: 5). And Lazary, in the following years, would do the set design for such plays as *Cinema-troça* (*Cinema-mockery*) and *Brutalidade* (*Brutality*), staged in Rio de Janeiro in 1917 and 1921, respectively. The *Cinema-troça* prologue recreated on stage a cinematic projection, with the actors positioned behind a diaphanous veil that simulated a cinema screen, while *Brutalidade* was a stage adaptation, within the operetta genre, of the successful American western

The Beast (Richard Stanton, 1916) (*O Imparcial* 1917: 7; *Palcos e Telas* 1921: 6). On one hand, Brazilian film production used stage elements as a way to gain prestige and attract patrons; on the other hand, some plays staged in Brazil incorporated cinematic references, thus taking advantage of cinema's growing popularity. The cross-cultural dialogues of the 1920s between Rio's *teatro de revista* (the Brazilian theatrical revue) and Hollywood cinema, as pointed out by Lisa Shaw (2015: 80), were already under way in the previous decade regarding foreign cinema more broadly: 'In spite of the apparent threat posed by the movies to the commercial survival of popular theater in Brazil, the *teatro de revista* found ways to co-exist and mutually promote the silent cinema.'

In the late 1910s, fiction film production in Rio de Janeiro and São Paulo focused on themes considered to be distinctively Brazilian as a way to stand out in a market dominated by foreign production – initially European, then, after World War I, American. Many of these titles were literary adaptations of novels by nineteenth-century Brazilian writers or were based on plots that focus on customs and characters from the country's rural regions. Luiz de Barros was no stranger to this trend. He addressed the regional universe in films he directed such as *A derrocada (A vingança do peão)* (*The Downfall: The Peasant's Revenge*, 1918), based on the novel by Teixeira Leite Filho; *Coração de gaúcho* (*Gaucho's Heart*, 1920); and *Alma Sertaneja* (*Country Soul*, 1919), produced by Alberto Botelho, for which Barros was hired as director. In 1919, he adapted for the screen José de Alencar's indigenist novel *Ubirajara*. These films too incorporate stage elements. *Ubirajara* and *Alma sertaneja* both star Ottilia Amorim and Antonia Denegri – the latter also appearing in *Coração de gaúcho* – two of the best-known actresses from the popular *teatro de revista*. In the absence of its own film stars, Brazilian cinema made use of the established theatrical star system to cast artists who were already familiar to the audience.

The professional links with popular theatre in Barros's film career were strengthened in 1923, when *Augusto Annibal quer casar!* (*Augusto Annibal Wants to Get Married!*) and *A Capital Federal* (*The Federal Capital*) were produced and released. Well aware of the appeal of stage attractions to audiences, Barros used it in exemplary fashion in *Augusto Annibal quer casar!* The comedian Augusto Annibal not only stars in the film but also lends his name to its title, testifying to the actor's great popularity as a *teatro de revista* star. In the previous year, he had performed the lead role in the play *Aguenta, Felipe!* (*Hang in There, Felipe!*), which ran for over seven months in Rio de Janeiro and became the genre's biggest success of the decade (Gomes 2004: 139).

Dancers from the French revue company Ba-ta-clan, then on its second tour of Brazil, also participate in the film. An artistic and cultural phenomenon, the company, led by Madame Rasimi, featured visually appealing shows with luxurious sets and costumes, elaborate lighting designs and very risqué exposure of the female body. While Lulu de Barros cast Ba-ta-clan dancers for his film, taking advantage of the company's popularity, Brazilian revues were resorting to a corresponding move. As Lisa Shaw (2015: 85) observes, 'the impact and controversies caused by the performances of Madame Rasimi's troupe in Brazil in 1922 and 1923 led to its name entering the zeitgeist'. In several revues the name Ba-ta-clan and neologisms derived from it were often mentioned or even incorporated into their titles, 'in what was undoubtedly an attempt to cash in on its popularity with local audiences' (86).

Another stage artist cast in *Augusto Annibal quer casar!* was Darwin, celebrated as 'the king of the imitators of the fairer sex', who used to perform on stage in Rio's *cineteatros* – cinemas that also programmed stage shows (*Gazeta de Notícias* 1922: 8).[4] The film's female lead, Yara Jordão, who would start performing in *cineteatros* soon after the film's release, had participated in a beauty contest, in which she was elected 'the queen of Copacabana', a title that was widely used in the film's promotional campaign.

This unpretentious comedy, therefore, articulates a fascinating network combining different media and cultural practices. It stands out as a powerful example of Luiz de Barros's remarkable ability to bring together from the emerging entertainment industry a wide range of attractions that had already engaged and captivated audiences (Araújo 2015).

In *A Capital Federal*, Barros adopted a different strategy. Instead of casting well-known stage attractions, he relied on the popularity of the original play on which the film was based. Written by Arthur Azevedo, the musical revue *A Capital Federal* was staged regularly from its debut in 1897, enjoying great public acclaim. A successful restaging in 1920 by the Companhia de Teatro São Pedro prompted Barros to adapt it for the screen (Barros 1978: 62). Although he brought it up to date and added new scenes and locations, Barros seemingly made no significant changes to the original play. A review in the magazine *Para Todos* . . . criticised the film for lacking a proper cinematic script: the 'concern with fidelity to the revue's plot caused great harm to the film's action' (1923: 46).[5] The review further criticised the reproduction of dialogue extracts from the revue in the intertitles, pointing out they could be understood only by those already familiar with the play. Barros's intention, however, seems to have been to narrow the divide between the film and the play, which, incidentally, constituted a key selling point in the film's promotional campaign (Vasconcellos 2014: 7). While critics called for originality and purely cinematic approaches, Barros was more interested in connecting his film productions with the growing Brazilian entertainment industry, taking advantage of media, products and practices that were already popular with the audiences.

MIXED STAGE AND SCREEN PROGRAMMES

By adapting *A Capital Federal* into a silent film, Luiz de Barros lost one of the play's main attractions: the songs. However, while the film lacked musical numbers, the same cannot be said of the film screenings. When *A Capital Federal* made its debut at the Rialto cinema in Rio de Janeiro, it shared the programme with two stage attractions: a ballet starring actress Yara Jordão and a singing number performed by Italian artist Dina Aprile. Writing about the film and its exhibition, Evandro Vasconcellos (2014: 11) emphasises how dance and music interacted with the film, even though there was no thematic link between them. Absent from the film text, musical numbers were nevertheless provided by the mixed stage and screen programme, which drew the film nearer the musical revue on which it was based.

Stage and screen relations are one of the practices mentioned by Rick Altman (1992: 6) in his concept of 'cinema as event', which advocates the 'recognition of the heterogeneous natures of the cinema experience'. Regarding exhibition, he draws attention to the use of presentational differences 'as a prime method of product differentiation' (1992: 8). In Brazil, given the unequal competition between local and foreign productions, such methods were resorted to in order to increase the appeal of Brazilian films, while also strengthening local exhibition circuits. Therefore, when studying the first decades of cinema in Brazil through a methodology based on intermedial relations, exhibition practices cannot be ignored.

While, in the case of *A Capital Federal* at the Rialto, the live shows were separate from the film screening and not thematically related to it, a different strategy was applied to *Alma Sertaneja*, whose regional storyline inspired the film's presentation. In screenings held in Rio de Janeiro and Recife, the film was accompanied by an orchestra or musical ensemble that played regional music. In Recife, besides the orchestral accompaniment, a singer placed behind the screen performed the songs, whose lyrics were reproduced in the film's intertitles (*Jornal do Recife* 1920: 3). It is interesting to notice how a successful presentational practice from early Brazilian cinema was resumed in 1920. In Brazilian cinema's Bela Época, cinema owners such as William Auler in Rio de Janeiro and Francisco Serrador in São Paulo invested in the production of films that featured music and sound performed live by artists positioned behind the screen. Adopting this practice, many *filmes cantantes* (sung films) and *revistas* (revue films) were released between 1908 and 1911, attracting thousands of patrons, especially to Auler's Cinematógrafo Rio Branco (Souza 2004). Auler produced two of the most successful titles of the time, the operetta *A viúva alegre* (*The Merry Widow*, 1909) and the revue *Paz e amor* (1910), the latter filmed by the cinematographer Alberto Botelho, who would be the producer of *Alma Sertaneja* almost a decade later.

While *filmes cantantes* were not a long-term presentational practice, enhanced film exhibition through simultaneous live performance was a constant throughout the silent period. The strategy used in *Alma Sertaneja* screenings had been triggered a few months earlier by Luiz de Barros with *Carnaval* (*Carnival*, 1919), a non-fiction film on the 1919 festivities, whose screenings in Rio were accompanied by an orchestra and members of the Ameno Resedá carnival group, who sang the songs (Vasconcellos 2015: 45). Barros's *Carnaval* resorted, on a smaller scale, to presentational practices that had turned *O carnaval cantado* (*The Sung Carnival*, 1918) into probably the most successful Brazilian film of 1918, screened in several cities with musical accompaniment by a large orchestra and chorus that sang and danced to that year's most popular carnival songs (*Jornal do Recife* 1918: 2). Throughout the 1920s, other carnival films would be presented in a similar fashion. With the coming of sound, those intermedial relations, reached through the combination of films and live stage shows, were largely absorbed by the film text, as proved by the popular musical comedies and *chanchadas* from the 1930s up to the 1950s, released around carnival time and featuring dance and musical numbers as well as the most successful songs of each year's carnival season.

Cinema on Stage

From 1924 on, Luiz de Barros's connections with theatre became more intense. During this year he took part in two works that combined stage and screen shows.

Along with Italian actor and filmmaker Carlo Campogalliani, Barros directed *Rosa de sangue* (*Blood Rose*, 1924) a short film that integrated the eponymous play starring the Italian actress Letizia Quaranta, Campogalliani's wife and partner. Quaranta and Campogalliani, with long track record in Italian cinema, would star the following year in the film *A esposa do solteiro* (*The Bachelor's Wife*, 1925), directed by Campogalliani and co-produced by Paulo Benedetti, an Italian cinematographer and producer based in Brazil. The play *Rosa de sangue* was advertised as a 'modern screen and stage action piece' (*Correio da Manhã* 1924: 16), performed by the 'Italian–Brazilian *cinemímica* troupe' (*Gazeta de Notícias* 1924: 4).[6] No further details are relayed about the play and how stage and screen were integrated in the so-called *cinemímica* (film mimicry).

Gwendolyn Waltz (2012: 360) draws attention to the fact that projections were incorporated into stage shows only months after cinema was introduced to the public, adding that 'motion pictures were embraced immediately as a means to reshape and revitalize live performance experiences, as well as to navigate nascent intermedial relationships'. In Brazil, although detailed research is still needed, this particular film-and-theatre hybrid format had already attracted audiences since at least the late 1910s.

Soon after his work with Campogalliani and Quaranta, Luiz de Barros took part in a peculiar stage and screen show, which was probably decisive in shifting his career to theatre over subsequent years. Barros was invited by his long-time friend Jardel Jercolis, impresario and stage actor, to collaborate on the third and final sketch of a variety show performed in São Paulo by the Jercolis-Villar troupe in June 1924. With the title *Como se faz um filme cinematográfico* (*How to Make a Movie*), the sketch involved the filming of a scene on stage, using people chosen from the audience as actors. The footage, showing both the scene and the audience watching it, was screened the following evening, when another shoot would take place (*A Plateia* 1924b: 2). In this brief experience over five evenings, first at the Casino Antarctica and then at Teatro São Paulo, Barros coordinated the lighting and filming on stage, besides developing and editing the films himself (Barros 1979).

According to the advertisements, four short plots were filmed: the dramas *Amor de apache* (*Apache's Love*) and *Adultério* (*Adultery*), and the comedies *Vocação irresistível* (*Irresistible Vocation*) and *O homem mosca* (*Fly Man*), the latter inspired by the Harold Lloyd hit *Safety Last!* (Fred C. Newmeyer and Sam Taylor, 1923), which had premiered in the city just a few days earlier (*A Plateia* 1924a: 3; 1924b: 2; *A Gazeta* 1924: 5; *O Estado de S. Paulo* 1924: 26). The attraction had a distinguishable popular appeal, as Barros recalled later in an interview (1979). Jercolis sought to draw laughs from the audience by creating comic gags from the patrons' rehearsals on stage before shooting.

Although the attraction lasted only a few days, it served to strengthen Luiz de Barros's ties with theatre and in particular with Jercolis, who carried out an ambitious project the following year: the creation of the revue company Tro-lo-ló. Barros was then invited to work as set and costume designer, and remained in the company from October 1925 to February 1926. Up to 1929, theatre would prevail over cinema in Lulu de Barros's career, although films continued to be a reference in his works, as exemplified by his staging of film prologues.

Film Prologues

After leaving Tro-lo-ló and before setting up his own stage company, the Ra-ta-plan Company of Sketches and Ballets, Barros was invited by film exhibitor Francisco Serrador to stage film prologues in the Odeon and Gloria theatres (Figure 10.1). With these two venues, together with Imperio and

Capitolio cinemas, all of them inaugurated between 1925 and 1926, Serrador created a new entertainment area in downtown Rio de Janeiro, which soon came to be known as Cinelândia (Filmland). To attract the audience to his new, lavish cinemas, one of the novelties prepared by Serrador was film prologues: stage presentations based on theme, characters, dialogue and/or scenes from the feature film they preceded. At Imperio and Capitolio, prologues were produced by Benjamin Fineberg, Annibal Pacheco and Celestino Silveira, publicists from the Rio de Janeiro office of Companhia Películas de Luxo da América do Sul, Paramount's Latin American division.

Live film prologues were a common practice on the North American exhibition circuit from the late 1910s and also became an attractive feature in British theatres in the first half of the 1920s (Koszarski 1994; Hediger 2004; Brown 2013). Cinelândia's film prologues were related to the US model, as implemented by showmen such as Sid Grauman, in Los Angeles, and especially Samuel 'Roxy' Rothafel, in New York, with their 'lavish productions on the scale of contemporary Broadway musicals' (Hediger 2004). When adapting the foreign model, Brazilian film prologues also called upon local stage traditions, namely the *teatro de revista*, incorporating song and dance numbers; using characters and themes typical of the revues; and casting performers (actors, singers, dancers) known for their work on stage. In Rio,

Figure 10.1 Prologue to *Orphans of the Storm* (D. W. Griffith, 1921), staged by Luiz de Barros in 1926 at the Gloria theatre. Courtesy of Cinemateca do Museu de Arte Moderna do Rio de Janeiro.

film prologues were considered stage plays and, as such, their scripts had to be submitted to censorship prior to staging. This authoritarian requirement has ultimately allowed access today to several prologue scripts, which are preserved in a collection held by the Arquivo Nacional (National Archive) in Rio de Janeiro (*Fundo: Delegacia Auxiliar* . . . 2017).

In his prologues, Luiz de Barros had the opportunity to draw on his skills and experience with stage direction and set design, as well as cinema. Testament to this is the prologue to *The Lost World* (Harry O. Hoyt, 1925), the adventure film adapted from Arthur Conan Doyle's eponymous novel, known for its innovative stop-motion effects that recreate prehistoric creatures (Figure 10.2). Set in the Amazon jungle, the prologue begins with Roberto Vilmar delivering a song previously performed by the famous singer Vicente Celestino in the operetta *O mano de Minas* (The Brother from Minas Gerais), staged in 1924. Vilmar and the actress Carmen Azevedo then share the stage with three other actors, delivering short dialogues adapted from scenes from the film. Meanwhile, chorus girls, led by Austrian dancer and choreographer Valery Oeser, enter the stage to perform what is called in the script 'a dança do macaco' ('the monkey dance'). At the end, the script

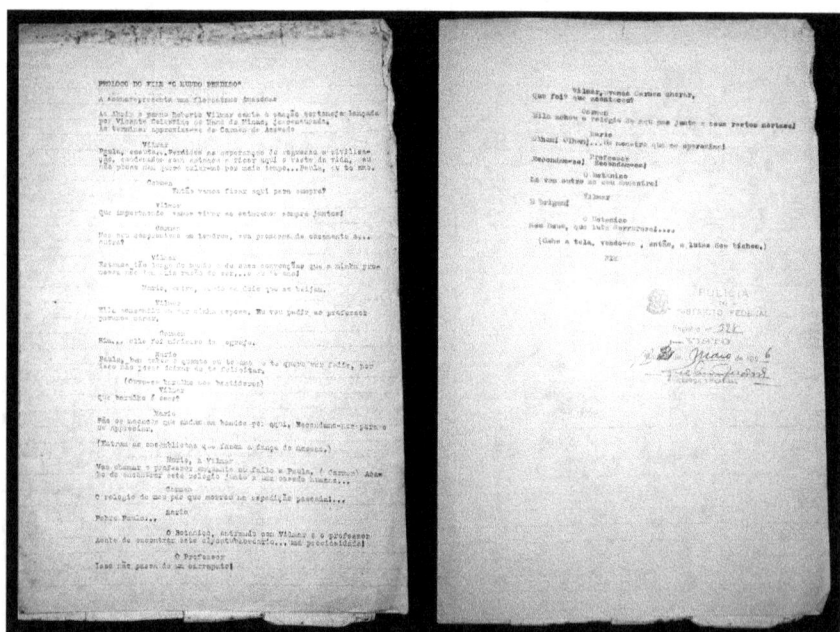

Figure 10.2 Prologue to *The Lost World* (Harry O. Hoyt, 1925), which was subjected to censorship. Courtesy BRASIL. Ministério da Justiça e Segurança Pública. Arquivo Nacional. Fundo Delegacia Auxiliar de Polícia, BR_RJANRIO_6E_CPR_PTE_0826.

indicates that the screen is lowered and a horrible fight between two monsters is shown (*Prólogo do filme* 'O mundo perdido' 1926).

The prologue to *The Lost World* is an eloquent example of the dynamics of this promotional practice in Brazil. Some professionals involved in the production of prologues used to work in both theatre and film. As a film exhibitor, Francisco Serrador often mixed stage and screen attractions, such as the combination of projection and live musical performances in the *filmes cantantes* he had produced years before. In October 1925, a few days after opening the Gloria as a cinema to an enthusiastic reception from the press, Serrador did not hesitate to turn it into a live theatre house, where Jardel Jercolis's Tro-lo-ló debuted to critical and public acclaim (*Para Todos . . .* 1925a: 45; *Para Todos . . .* 1925b: 22).

For Lulu de Barros, in turn, film prologues allowed for a different approach to the combination of cinema and theatre. The dialogue with foreign productions, a notable feature of the films he had directed thus far, gained new contours in the prologues he staged at Cinelândia, with references and rereadings directly connected to the foreign films projected. His experience with *teatro de revista* paved the way for the hiring of artists such as Roberto Vilmar, with whom he had previously worked in the Tro-lo-ló company, and Valery Oeser, who soon after would join the Ra-ta-plan troupe. Many of Barros's prologues presented singing and dancing numbers, a combination directly linked to *teatro de revista*. His talents as a set designer and decorative painter were also resorted to. The set for *The Lost World* prologue was painted by Barros himself and featured 'the banks of a river, with huts surrounded by dense forest, the virgin forest of the Amazon's hinterlands' (*Gazeta de Notícias* 1926: 10).[7]

In production terms, film prologues required large investments to put together short plays that sometimes featured over ten performers on stage with sets and costumes linked to the film's theme – and all that to run for a few days only. High production costs certainly contributed to the short life-span of film prologues at Cinelândia, which lasted only from March to around August 1926. The prologue to *The Lost World* was presented over a week at the Odeon, as an introduction to the film, from 10 to 16 May 1926. *Cinearte* magazine reported that Serrador had spent more than 40 *contos* a month on the production of Odeon prologues (*Cinearte* 1926a: 27). Even if the costs were overestimated, given the magazine's avowed dislike of those prologues, this was still a significant amount of money. A far smaller sum could have covered the production of a feature film, the kind of investment *Cinearte* would have valued.

Although expensive, film prologues helped create a unique programme that audiences would not find in competing cinemas, as a press release for *The Lost World* makes clear:

> And if it is true that you will be able to see the film later on in another cinema, bear in mind that the Odeon offers unique and incomparable comfort, and not only that: you may be able to see the film [elsewhere], but without the prologue, which is a gem. (*Gazetas de Notícias* 1926: 10)[8]

Advertisements and promotional material often established comparisons between the Hollywood actors in the films and the Brazilian actors starring in the prologues. *Cinearte* magazine rejected such comparisons, on the assumption that 'any film actor is ten times more popular and loved than an entire theatre company' (*Cinearte* 1926b: 28).[9] This statement, however, did little justice to Rio de Janeiro's vibrant entertainment circuit. Well aware that local stage artists were an attractive selling point for the prologues, Serrador and the Paramount publicists did not hesitate to compare, for example, Arthur Oliveira with Buster Keaton, when the Brazilian played the American comic star in the prologue to the movie *Go West* (Buster Keaton, 1925) (*Correio da Manhã* 1926: 5).

Far from treating film and theatre audiences as separate entities, both the prologues and their publicity targeted a 'theatrical spectator knowledgeable of contemporary key works on stage and screen', to borrow Charles Musser's (2004b: 15) words in his analysis of African-American theatre and film in the 1920s. Most spectators of Odeon's mixed programmes would certainly have recognised both stage and film references. In addition, the practice of presenting a prologue thematically linked to the film made way for modes of exhibition and reception that reconfigured the foreign product, opening a variety of interpretations and connections for the spectator that the film alone may not have triggered. At the Odeon theatre, *The Lost World* offered Rio locals a fanciful view of the Amazon, which *Cinearte* judged to be 'admirably well-groomed ... except for the "Hawaiian" skin and attire of some of the "natives"' (*Cinearte* 1926b: 27).[10] The prologue also took liberties when approaching both the Hollywood film and the representation of the Amazon jungle, with a painted set and Brazilian music and chorus girls in *teatro de revista* style, for instance, thus providing 'a kind of creative interference' (Musser 2004b: 10) with regard to how the film would be received by local audiences.

Ross Melnick stresses 'the meanings transacted during the live and filmed programming available to audiences during this period that had a tremendous influence on audience comprehension and on the original experience of any silent film' (2012: 14). Addressing the combined stage and screen programmes at American neighbourhood theatres, Miriam Hansen (1991: 100) argues that the live portions 'shaped the way mainstream films could be received – and reinterpreted – by nonmainstream audiences'. After watching the 'monkey dance' performed by chorus girls in the prologue to *The Lost World*, one wonders how Odeon patrons might have reacted to the film scenes showing monkeys or to the elaborate special effects that recreate prehistoric monsters.

The Brazilian live number might have worked as a parody of the foreign film, much as popular film comedies (*chanchadas*) would do a few decades later, whether through musical numbers and comic sketches, or by reference to the whole plot, as in *Nem Sansão nem Dalila* (*Neither Samson Nor Delilah*, Carlos Manga, 1954) and *Matar ou correr* (*To Kill or to Run*, Carlos Manga, 1954), parodies of *Samson and Delilah* (Cecil B. DeMille, 1949) and *High Noon* (Fred Zinnemann, 1952; released in Brazil with the title *Matar ou morrer/To Kill or to Die*), respectively.

CROSSOVER ENTERTAINMENT

The work of impresarios and entertainment companies is key to understanding the dynamic intermedial nature of 'theatrical culture'. In this sense, Luiz de Barros's career is equally exemplary. His relationship with film exhibitors and owners of theatres and other entertainment venues was one of the decisive factors in securing his long, uninterrupted artistic career.

The invitation to stage prologues at Cinelândia was certainly triggered by his previous connections with Serrador while working with the Tro-lo-ló Company at Gloria theatre. After his contract with Serrador's Companhia Brasil Cinematográfica (Brazil Film Company), Barros developed a fruitful partnership with Empresas Cinematográficas Reunidas (Reunidas Film Companies), which dominated theatre and cinema businesses in São Paulo. This relationship had been established at least as early as 1924, when the sketch with the troupe Jercolis-Villar was presented in two Reunidas theatres. In 1927, after performing Ra-ta-plan revue plays in Reunidas venues, Barros was put in charge of the 'special *mise-en-scène*' at *cineteatro* Santa Helena, in São Paulo city centre, where he created either stage shows or appropriate set designs and lighting for the film screenings. His skills as a stage director and set designer were also drawn upon to modify and decorate the front of the stage of the Cineteatro Coliseu, in the city of Santos (Barros 1978: 85), and to provide decoration and lively attractions during the carnival ball promoted at Santa Helena (*Diário da Noite* 1928: 6).

In 1928, with the end of Ra-ta-plan, he went on to direct stage shows at Moulin Bleu, a small vaudeville venue located in the basement of *cineteatro* Santa Helena (Freire and Souza 2018: 314). Comedians Tom Bill and Genésio Arruda performed there before starring in *Acabaram-se os otários* (*Gone Are the Morons*, 1929), the first Brazilian sound film, directed by Luiz de Barros. His relationship with Reunidas, which financed and exhibited both the feature film and a few short sound films, allowed Barros to resume his filmmaking career.

Tracing Barros's commercial and artistic partnership with Reunidas points to how the same company invested in different types of attractions, from films and stage shows to carnival balls. These activities were not isolated from each other but integrated into the entertainment circuit. In the films, plays and activities covered in this chapter, a business model emerges, grounded in intermedial crossovers and embedded in the very dynamics of Rio and São Paulo's growing entertainment industry, which constantly crossed boundaries and categories in order to explore connections that were both artistically and commercially attractive.

Given that personnel tended to circulate across different professional fields and mediums, Jean-Claude Bernardet argues that those who are now called 'filmmakers' might not, in the Bela Época period, have thought of their work in terms of cinema, but in terms of the show, which could be either a cinematic or theatrical attraction, so long as they had an audience and made money. 'Perhaps they were not men of cinema, but men of entertainment,' concludes Bernardet (1995: 106).[11] In this sense, it is as men of entertainment that artists and businessmen of the silent period, such as Luiz de Barros, Francisco Serrador and many others, can be best understood, insofar as they systematically brought together different media and cultural practices. Guided by talent and also by a keen sense of topicality and opportunity, Barros made use of intermedial exchanges as a key strategy of his career in entertainment as filmmaker, set designer, film technician, stage director, playwright and impresario.

Barros's film career during the silent period is undoubtedly a fruitful object of study. But when investigated in terms of 'theatrical culture', encompassing his diverse stage and screen work as well as his business partnerships, his career sheds light on the numerous, dynamic intermedial relations within the entertainment circuit of which films and film activities were part.

Notes

1. Research supported by grant #2014/50821-3, São Paulo Research Foundation (FAPESP). The opinions, hypotheses, conclusions or recommendations contained in this material are the sole responsibility of the author and do not necessarily reflect FAPESP opinion.
2. 'Pretendo apenas sugerir itinerários de investigação e como o cruzamento de territórios diversos pode enriquecer a compreensão de cada um deles.' Unless indicated, all translations are by the author.
3. Other intermedial relations in Brazilian silent cinema have been addressed in recent works. On relations between film and press, see Freire (2011), Conde (2012) and Navitski (2017). On relations between film and music, see Pereira (2014) and Souza (2014). On relations between film, music, theatre and circus, see Carvalho (2017; 2018).

4. 'Rei dos imitadores do belo sexo'.
5. 'Esta preocupação de seguir à risca o enredo da revista muito prejudicou a ação do filme.'
6. 'Uma ação moderna na tela e no palco'; 'Estreia da trupe cinemímica ítalo-brasileira'.
7. 'Luiz de Barros nos pinta as margens de um rio, com cabanas cercadas pela floresta densa, a mata virgem dos nossos sertões da Amazônia.'
8. 'E se é verdade que mais tarde poderão ver o filme em outro cinema, é bom que se lembrem que a comodidade que oferece o Odeon é toda sua, própria e inimitável; e não é só isso: poderão ver o filme, mas não terão o prólogo que é um encanto.'
9. 'Qualquer artista de Cinema é dez vezes mais popular e querido do que uma companhia teatral inteira.'
10. 'E o Amazonas, a não ser na tez e na vestimenta de "havaí" de alguns "nativos", está admiravelmente bem ambientado.'
11. 'Talvez não tenham sido homens de cinema, e sim homens de espetáculo.'

REFERENCES

A Gazeta (1924), 21 June, p. 5.
A Noite (1916), 13 October, p. 5.
A Plateia (1924a), 14 June, p. 3.
A Plateia (1924b), 17 June, p. 2.
Altman, Rick (1992), *Sound Theory, Sound Practice*. New York: Routledge.
Araújo, Luciana Corrêa de (2015), '*Augusto Annibal quer casar!*: teatro popular e Hollywood no cinema silencioso brasileiro', *Alceu*, 16, pp. 62–73.
Barros, Luiz de (1978), *Minhas memórias de cineasta*. Rio de Janeiro: Artenova.
Barros, Luiz de (1979), Interview recorded on tape with the Museum of Image and Sound of Rio de Janeiro/MIS-RJ.
Bernardet, Jean-Claude (1995), *Historiografia clássica do cinema brasileiro*, São Paulo: Annablume.
Brown, Julie (2013), 'Framing the Atmospheric Film Prologue in Britain, 1919–1926', in J. Brown and A. Davison (eds), *The Sounds of the Silents in Britain*, New York: Oxford University Press, pp. 200–21.
Carvalho, Danielle Crepaldi (2017), 'O cinema silencioso e o som no Brasil (1894–1920)', *Galáxia*, 34, pp. 85–97.
Carvalho, Danielle Crepaldi (2018), 'D'*O Guarani* de José de Alencar e Carlos Gomes aos *Guaranis* do *clown* Benjamin: diálogos entre literatura, cinema, circo e música', *ANIKI*, 5, pp. 78–104.
Cinearte (1926a), 7 July, p. 27.
Cinearte (1926b), 9 June, pp. 27–8.
Conde, Maite (2007), 'Exposing the Illusions of Modernity: Literary Society and the Belle Époque of Brazilian Cinema', *Chasqui*, November 2007, pp. 98–115.
Conde, Maite (2012), *Consuming Visions. Cinema, Writing and Modernity in Brazil*. Charlottesville: University of Virginia Press.
Correio da Manhã (1924), 20 May, p. 16.
Correio da Manhã (1926), 13 May, p. 5.

Diário da Noite (1928), 16 February, p. 6.
Ferreira, Adriano de Assis (2004), *Teatro Trianon: forças da ordem x forças da desordem*, Master's dissertation, Universidade de São Paulo.
Freire, Rafael de Luna (2011), *Carnaval, mistério e gangsters: o filme policial no Brasil (1915–1950)*, PhD thesis, Fluminense Federal University, Niterói.
Freire, Rafael de Luna (2018), 'O cinema no Rio de Janeiro', in S. Schvarzman and F. P. Ramos (eds), *Nova história do cinema brasileiro*. São Paulo: Edições Sesc, pp. 266–7.
Freire, Rafael de Luna and Carlos Roberto de Souza (2018), 'A chegada do cinema sonoro ao Brasil', in Sheila Schvarzman and Fernão P. Ramos (eds), *Nova história do cinema brasileiro*. São Paulo: Edições Sesc, pp. 294–343.
Fundo: Delegacia Auxiliar de Polícia, 2ª: inventário dos documentos textuais, seção Censura Prévia: série Peças Teatrais e série Avulsos. Rio de Janeiro: Arquivo Nacional, 2017, available at <http://www.arquivonacional.gov.br/images/conteudo/servicos_ao_cidadao/instrumentos-de-pesquisa/pdf/DELEGACIA_AUXILIAR_POLICIA_2.pdf> (last accessed 23 January 2020).
Gazeta de Notícias (1922), 8 August, p. 8.
Gazeta de Notícias (1924), 12 June, p. 4.
Gazeta de Notícias (1926), 15 May, p. 10.
Gomes, Tiago de Melo (2004), *Um espelho do palco*. Campinas: Editora Unicamp.
Hansen, Miriam (1991), *Babel and Babylon*. London and Cambridge, MA: Harvard University Press.
Hediger, Vinzenz (2004), 'Putting the Spectators in a Receptive Mood', in V. Innocenti and V. Re (eds), *Film's Thresholds*. Udine: Forum, pp. 291–308, unpaginated PDF available at <https://www.academia.edu/11011915/_Putting_the_Spectators_in_a_Receptive_Mood_Stage_Prologues_and_other_Thresholds_of_Film_in_American_Movie_Theaters_of_the_Silent_Era> (last accessed 20 June 2020).
Heffner, Hernani (2012), 'Barros, Luiz de', in F. Ramos and L. F. Miranda (eds), *Enciclopédia do cinema brasileiro*, 3rd edn. São Paulo: Senac, p. 66.
Jornal do Recife (1918), 18 August, p. 2.
Jornal do Recife (1920), 22 July, p. 3.
Koszarski, Richard (1994), *An Evening's Entertainment. The Age of the Silent Feature Picture: 1915–1928*. Berkeley: University of California Press.
Melnick, Ross (2012), *American Showman: Samuel 'Roxy' Rothafel and the Birth of the Entertainment Industry, 1908–1935*. New York: Columbia University Press.
Musser, Charles (2004a), 'The Hidden and the Unspeakable: On Theatrical Culture, Oscar Wilde and Ernst Lubitsch's *Lady Windermere's Fan*', *Film Studies*, 5, pp. 12–47.
Musser, Charles (2004b), 'Towards a History of Theatrical Culture: Imagining an Integrated History of Stage and Screen', in J. Fullerton (ed.), *Screen Culture: History & Textuality*. Eastleigh: John Libbey, pp. 3–19.
Navitski, Rielle (2017), *Public Spectacles of Violence: Sensational Cinema and Journalism in Early Twentieth-Century Mexico and Brazil*. Durham, NC: Duke University Press.
O Estado de S. Paulo (1924), 22 June, p. 26.
O Imparcial (1917), 12 April, p. 7.
O Paiz (1916), 26 April, p. 5.
Palcos e Telas (1921), 17 March, p. 6.
Para Todos... (1923), 17 November, pp. 46–7.
Para Todos... (1925a), 10 October, p. 45.
Para Todos... (1925b), 7 November, p. 22.

Pereira, Carlos Eduardo (2014), *A música no cinema silencioso no Brasil*, Rio de Janeiro: Museu de Arte Moderna.

Prólogo do filme 'O mundo perdido' (1926), Censorship Visa 328, 12 May, Conjunto documental da 2ª Delegacia Auxiliar da Polícia do Rio de Janeiro (Índice das peças, gêneros e onomástico). 1917–1940. Rio de Janeiro: Arquivo Nacional.

Revista da Semana (1916), 21 October, pp. 17–18.

Shaw, Lisa (2015), 'The *Teatro de Revista* in Rio de Janeiro in the 1920s: Transnational Dialogues and Popular Cosmopolitanism', *Luso-Brazilian Review*, 52:2, pp. 73–98.

Souza, José Inácio de Melo (2004), *Imagens do passado*. São Paulo: Senac.

Vasconcellos, Evandro Gianasi (2014), '*A capital federal* e *samba em Berlim*: o teatro de revista em filmes de Luiz de Barros', *Imagofagia*, 9, pp. 1–23.

Vasconcellos, Evandro Gianasi (2015), *Entre o palco e a tela: as relações do cinema com o teatro de revista em comédias musicais de Luiz de Barros*, Master's dissertation, Universidade Federal de São Carlos.

Waltz, Gwendolyn (2012), '"*Half Real-Half Reel*": Alternation Format Stage-and-Screen Hybrids', in A. Gaudreault, N. Dulac and S. Hidalgo (eds), *A Companion to Early Cinema*. Malden, MA: Wiley-Blackwell.

CHAPTER 11

'Synchronised Film Fever' amid the 'Gramophonoradiomania': Record, Radio and Cinema at the Dawn of the 'Talkies' in Rio de Janeiro
Rafael de Luna Freire

The cartoonist Max Yantock (or Yantok), the nickname of Nicolau Cesarino, was a regular contributor to the illustrated magazine *O Malho*, published in Rio de Janeiro. His contributions included the section 'A Trip to Pandegolandia',[1] in which he satirised the federal capital through drawings and texts. In *O Malho* from 15 February 1930, his last square section featured the illustration of a man with earplugs and an ice pack on his forehead, holding a protest sign that read: 'Protest league against all devices that end with "phone"' (Figure 11.1). The caption said ironically: 'I had occasion to note that people are very fond of jazz and cinema, especially when their ears are properly corked' (Yantock 1930: 4).[2]

Some months before, the same Yantock had published, also in *O Malho*, a comic strip occupying a full page of the magazine, addressing the same subject of the city's excessive noise resulting from new sound technologies. Named 'Gramophonoradiomania', the story featured a man who wandered through the streets of the city, disturbed by various sounds, especially those emanating from record players and radios that permeated the urban public space (Figure 11.2). Not even in death, inside a coffin, was he free from that unwanted soundscape (Yantock 1929: 69).

This chapter will draw on these two similar comments on the modern, urban and intermedial soundscape of Rio de Janeiro in order to launch a discussion of the intermedial character of sound cinema at the time when this technology was being introduced into the Brazilian film market. I adopt Emily Thompson's definition of soundscape as an 'auditory or aural landscape', which differs slightly from Murray Schaefer's, who coined the term: 'Like a landscape, a soundscape is simultaneously a physical environment and a way of perceiving that environment; it is both a world and a culture constructed to make sense of that world' (Thompson 2008: 1). My discussion will first consider how late 1920s Rio de Janeiro, then Brazil's main metropolis, was consistently represented as a 'noisy city' – an old appellation that gained a new lease of life at the time. The noises then invading the capital came,

Record, Radio and Cinema at the Dawn of the 'Talkies'   195

Tive ensejo de notar que a população gosta muito do jazz e do cinema, especialmente quando o ouvido está devidamente arrolhadoo.

Figure 11.1 A humorous cartoon comments on the noise produced by modern electrical sound technologies. Source National Library, Brazil.

above all, from the exponential growth of new electrical technologies of sound reproduction: phonograph, radio and sound cinema.[3] Or, as Yantock's cartoon shows, from the various devices that ended with 'phone', such as the gramophone, the 'radiophone' and the vitaphone.

The idea that, between 1929 and 1930, Rio de Janeiro experienced a certain 'gramophonoradiomania', then, lends itself perfectly to an intermedial analysis inspired by the very combination of different media, as per the title of the comic story. Media historian Jonathan Sterne has argued that various sound media, such as telephony, sound recording or radio – and sound cinema, we could add – should be understood not as separate phenomena but as institutionally and economically interrelated, as they emerged from a shared cultural and industrial context (Sterne 2003: 184).

Focusing on the Rio soundscape in the late 1920s, I will reflect on how phonographs, radio sets and sound-film apparatus benefited from the convergence of sound reproduction technologies and interacted in an urban space increasingly dominated by electrically amplified sounds. My aim will be to investigate the ways in which the production and exhibition of some early Brazilian sound films established a relationship with radio and the record

Figure 11.2 'Gramophonoradiomania': a comic strip depicts Rio de Janeiro's noisy soundscape. Source National Library, Brazil.

industry which was at once technological, economical and aesthetic, catering both for the educational ambitions of the elites and for mass culture.

My intention is to demonstrate the advantages of an approach to Brazilian cinema history based on media archaeology through a detailed analysis of the economic, technological, cultural and aesthetic relations between record, radio and cinema in Rio de Janeiro at the beginning of the exhibition of sound films. Addressing this moment in the late 1920s from a non-medium-specific vantage point allows us to identify better the wide-ranging intermedial interactions embedded in 'talking cinema' – which traditional and teleological historiographic approaches usually miss. As Thomas Elsaesser has defined it, 'the activity of recovering this diversity and to account for such multiplicity, to trace these parallel histories and explore alternative trajectories, is what is meant by "film history as media archaeology"' (Elsaesser 2016: 25).

Elsaesser argues that 'besides the history of photography, the histories of the telegraph, the radio, the gramophone, and the telephone have always been much more intertwined with that of cinema than the specialists of the respective media felt comfortable with' (24). Rather than isolating film from other media forms (which is often the case in histories of Brazilian cinema), I intend to look at all of them in combination, as an attempt to 'uncover links previously missed' (Elsaesser 2016: 24).

'Rio, the Noise City'

Magazine illustrators may be among the best chroniclers of Rio de Janeiro in the 1920s. Alongside Yantock, another equally talented illustrator was Raul Pederneiras. In one of his illustrated books, published in 1930, Pederneiras commented on what he had seen and heard on trips to different European countries, always comparing their habits with those of Rio de Janeiro. In one passage, he shows confidence in the primacy of the former Brazilian capital in one aspect: 'Rio is undoubtedly the city of noise. The other cities we visited do not suffer from the pestering of horns, loudspeakers and street hawkers' cries' (Pederneiras 1930: 47).[4]

The excessive noise of Rio de Janeiro was notorious, particularly in its central area, which had been undergoing radical urban reforms – and noisy construction work – from the beginning of the twentieth century (Vieira 2006). In 1924, a cartoon by another celebrated illustrator, J. Carlos, titled 'The Noise City', was also published in *O Malho*. The image carried a representation of a street in Rio de Janeiro besieged by the sound of car horns, bells and hammers (Carlos 1924: 23). In the 1920s, comments on the noise caused by cars, trams and trains, partying in clubs or on the streets, and the shouting of street vendors in the most diverse public spaces were common.

Some noises harked back to the city's colonial soundscape, such as dogs barking in the streets, serenades at dawn or the bell ringing of many Catholic churches scattered throughout Rio de Janeiro. By the end of the 1920s, however, in addition to the noise produced by modern means of transport, complaints about the sounds of the new media had been added to those in the 'noise city'.[5] In September 1929, one publication described the widespread perception that 'the city has an increasing number of establishments selling noisy things and has greatly increased the number of pianolas, "loud-screamers" and gramophones in private households' (Duque 1929: 5).[6] It was the result of the 'radiomania' and 'victrolamania' that plagued the 'noise city', to which, in the second half of 1929, 'synchronised film fever' was added.

Radiomania

The first experimental radio broadcasts in Brazil took place in Rio de Janeiro in 1922. From then on, the earliest radio stations in the city started sprouting up, but in the form of societies or clubs for educational, cultural and scientific purposes. Initially, the stations tried to pay their expenses by collecting monthly fees from their associate members.[7] But their educational–cultural aims and scarce resources limited their schedules, which were restricted to a few hours a day and were dedicated, above all, to the reading of the news from the printed press, lectures by guest academics and pieces of classical music transmitted live from theatres or studios.

Slowly, radio started to gain in popularity, initially among the elite and the growing urban middle class. However, the 'radiomania' (or 'radiophilia', as some preferred) that was now being trumpeted in the Brazilian press referred mainly to radiotelephony – or TSF (*telegrafia sem fios*, meaning wireless telegraphy), as it was also called: that is, point-to-point communication, from one ham operator to another. Radio amateurs were fascinated by their ability to contact the world via the radio waves, overcoming long distances, contacting colleagues from other cities or states and, given the precarious scheduling of local broadcasters, attempting to capture broadcasts from Buenos Aires, New York or London radio stations.[8] The serial publications that soon appeared targeting this amateur readership had a strong technical character, with instructions on how to build, upgrade or adapt the receiving and transmitting devices to the possibilities and interests of ham radio.

In the second half of the 1920s, however, a change in the use of radio technology would occur in Brazil: 'what was previously thought to interconnect, wirelessly, two points, both sending and receiving messages, is then used for the traffic of information, by electromagnetic waves, from a broadcasting station to listeners scattered in the most diverse places' (Ferrareto 2013: 11).[9] The intermedial relations between radio and electrical recordings still need to be thoroughly studied, as the way they took place in Brazil was different from elsewhere. However, we can state that the advent of electrical recording was a relevant factor in the development of Brazilian radio as a medium of mass communication, as it evolved from the preponderance of radiotelephony to the hegemony of broadcasting.[10]

In 1926 the first discs recorded abroad using the recently developed process of electrical recording began to be sold in the country. But a new era for the Brazilian record industry would start in earnest the following year, when Odeon installed in the country the first studio and factory for recording and manufacturing discs by the electrical process. In 1928, it was Parlophon's turn to settle in Brazil with the new technology, with Columbia, Victor and Brunswick following suit in 1929. Although historians point out the marked commercial development of Brazilian radio since 1932, thanks to the regulation of radio advertising,[11] by the end of the 1920s an increase in the number of listeners can already be noticed, coinciding with the arrival of electrical recording.

The novelty of the electrical recording process resulted in a great increase in the sale of records, and also of phonographs. The development of the record industry provided a huge boost for the Brazilian music market and, consequently, for radio broadcasters, who were able to extend the duration of their daily programming by broadcasting records in the last years of the 1920s.

Radios and Record Players Joined by Electricity

After the introduction on the market of the new electrically recorded records, it was the turn of the 'improved phonographs' (that is, new mechanical phonographs), with metal diaphragms and longer folded acoustical horns, which increased the quality of the sound reproduced ('Gravações elétricas . . .' 1926: 10). By the end of the 1920s, the first phonographs powered by electricity had begun to be publicised and sold as obtaining better and, above all, more powerful results.[12] The introduction of electricity into the sound amplification mechanism made it possible to combine the record-playing device and the radio receiver, which had been sold and used as separated apparatuses up until then.

The novelty of electrical amplification had a huge impact on the quality of sound recording and reproduction. Biased radiophiles, however, attributed the improvement in the quality of records by the electrical process to the radio, which, after all, had always used electricity to receive, transmit and reproduce sound across space (Sterne 2003: 276). The Brazilian magazine

Radiocultura, published from June 1928 onwards, strongly championed electrical technology – at the base of radio microphones and loudspeakers – emphasising how it contributed to the record industry: 'Unquestionably, the phonograph owes to radiotelephony its recent extraordinary development' ('Phonographos e discos' 1928: 16).[13] In addition to the sale of the then very expensive electrical phonograph–radio receiver combination in the form of luxurious wooden cabinets,[14] there were highlights in the announcements and reports on how radio sets could easily be used to electrify ordinary (that is, non-electrical) record players already owned by the customer. The replacement of the mechanical phonograph arm by the connection of an electrical 'pick-up' to a radio receiver allowed its owner to listen to records through the radio's loudspeakers rather than the acoustic diaphragm and horn of the old record player.[15]

Advertisements that described how a radio could serve as a 'gramophone amplifier', as well as instructions and diagrams to enable radio amateurs to electrify their phonograph themselves, became commonplace in Rio's newspapers and magazines. Mechanical sound-reproducing gadgets, in general, became outdated things to be mocked, as in this sexist joke from *Careta* magazine: 'Women's intelligence is like cheap victrolas: we have to wind them from time to time . . . ' ('Verdades e mentiras' 1930: 26).

In this media convergence context, rather than there being competition between radio and phonograph, in the opinion of the editor of *Radiocultura* the opposite was true: there was a combination beneficial to both. 'It is a common occurrence [today] that radio and phonograph [are] conjugated, in the same box, one supplying for the other: the radio supplying energy and amplitude of sound, and the phonograph the record, in the intervals of the irradiations' ('Phonographos e discos' 1928: 16).[16] Thus, the magazine *Radiocultura* insisted on the positive influence of one medium on the other: 'The radio has also been contributing to a greater dissemination of records, considerably increasing their sales, a proof being the expansion of this business, now spread all over the globe' (16).[17]

For radiophiles emphasising the technological connection between the two mediums, 'victrolamania' was merely a product of the radio. However, a view that privileged the economic side of things would establish other hierarchies.

VICTROLAMANIA

'Victrolamania' was, in fact, the title of an article that described such a phenomenon as the result of the 'great development here of the sales and use of radio devices'. There followed the multiplication of stores selling records and record players – the so-called 'victrola houses': 'They appear in every part of the city, in an extraordinary proportion, every day easily observed . . . It is, therefore, the great business of today. The great trade' (Freitas 1929: 10).[18]

The sales of records exploded, thanks to the proliferation of cheaper mechanical phonographs, especially in the form of portable cases. The new electrical records could also be played on these common phonographs. However, the more expensive and robust electrical sound reproduction devices, such as the Victor-Radio-Electrola, were favoured by wealthier elites and business people for collective auditions in their establishments, such as shops, theatres, clubs and cafes. As the comic strip 'gramophonoradiomania' implies, it was impossible to go to any bar or restaurant in the city where there was no sound system in operation. The streets of central Rio, now occupied by record stores, were dominated by their sounds.

Studying the city of São Paulo, Camila Koshiba Gonçalves has called attention to complaints about the so-called *basbaques das victrolas* (victrola idiots), who used to stop in front of the windows of record stores to enjoy the music, disrupting pedestrian traffic on the pavements (Gonçalves 2006: 61–9). The same happened in Rio de Janeiro, as observed in a January 1929 article:

> Do you want proof? Let's take an excursion . . . to Ouvidor Street, one of the busiest Rio arteries (if not the busiest). And we will see, here and there, a compact crowd parked in front of the music houses, attracted by the sounds that a victrola, placed at the door of each of them, radiates outwards. (Santiago 1929: 33)[19]

The sounds and the crowds provoked governmental reaction. Repeating what had happened in São Paulo in 1927, a municipal law was approved in Rio de Janeiro, in 1930, to stop record and victrola stores from displaying at their doors sound devices aimed 'to amuse or delight passersby' (Réo 1930b: 49).[20] This notwithstanding, the songs on the records could be heard everywhere, including on the radio stations, which started to privilege programmes that played back records to expand and diversify their offering. Some elitist supporters of radio's 'education and literacy' principles initially accused certain record companies of paying for record diffusion, blaming them for the proliferation of light commercial music on the broadcasts, such as the 'dissolute music of the Favelas' ('música vadia da Favela'), in an allusion to samba ('Phonographos e discos' 1929: 18). Record lovers, on the other hand, would claim that radio stations were the main beneficiaries of the radio broadcasting of records acquired free of charge from record companies: 'First, because they do not buy records to promote them; second, because they do not have to hire artists to make their programmes; third, because they have a growing clientele, given the advantages they offer' (Réo 1930d: 52).[21]

The inevitability of this alliance was expressed from the first issue of the São Paulo magazine *Radio Phono* in August 1929. According to its editorial, the phonograph was a companion to the radio, which took advantage of the progress of the record 'because it would be impossible to have extensive, high-quality programming if phonographic recordings were left out' (*Radio Phono* 1929).[22] But another important public space that was not immune to the victrolamania was the cinema.

RECORDS IN CINEMAS

The presence of phonographs and gramophones had been recurrent since the first film exhibitions in Rio de Janeiro, especially in the *cinematographo fallante* seasons – a generic name given at the time to any synchronic sound and moving image experiments – carried out during the first decade of the twentieth century (Costa 2008: 19–36). However, these were sparse exhibitions, special attractions existing amid a variety of forms of sound accompaniment to the films of that period. Like other countries, Brazil also underwent a process of standardisation of the sound accompaniment of films, which, in the 1920s, made live music a hegemonic presence during the projections (Altman 2004).

At the time, in Brazil, both business people and fans had heard about the success of the first sound films made by Warner Bros. in the US through the vitaphone system of synchronising films and records using the same record industry technology developed by Western Electric. However, the novelty of the electrical recording and reproduction of records was gradually incorporated by Rio exhibitors in the late 1920s, both inside and outside the auditorium. In 1926, the Odeon Theatre had already installed two Marconi loudspeakers on its façade to attract patrons among passersby in the Floriano Peixoto Square (Denada 1926: 9). In June 1928, Victor and its Brazilian representative, the Paul J. Cristoph company, organised a week of record auditions at the Phenix Theatre, enabled by the Victrola Ortophonica Auditorium, a fully electrical enlarged record player with an automatic record changer and enough power to replace orchestras in 'clubs, casinos and theatres' ('Aspectos do Theatro . . .' 1928: 44). After these concerts, the Victrola Ortophonica Auditorium was shown at the Capitólio Theatre, this time to replace its small orchestra at certain moments of the projection of the feature film *Doomsday* (Rowland V. Lee, 1928). Then the aviation film *Wings* (William A. Wellman, 1927) was synchronised with air battle noise records played on the same device, during the projection, also at the Capitólio.

Special projections accompanied by records were occasionally held until June 1929, when the first screening of sound films finally took place with the movietone (sound on film) and vitaphone (sound on disc) systems at the Palacio Theatre in central Rio. Sound cinema had premiered in Latin America two months earlier, at the launch of the Paramount Theatre in São Paulo. This successful innovation encouraged other powerful Brazilian exhibitors to bear the high costs for the installation, in their picture palaces, of the new technology of sound film reproduction.

The first wired cinemas in Brazil chose to buy exclusively from Western Electric, whose equipment was compatible with both vitaphone and movietone, entailing high costs for the purchase and transportation of equipment from the US. Moreover, the wiring also required the adaptation of electrical installations in order to connect the projection booth to loudspeakers close to the screen. Despite the financial costs and technical difficulties, the best cinemas in Rio were quickly wired. In just over three months, between June and September of 1929, the six best cinemas in the city were already equipped to project the images and sounds of the latest Hollywood hits. The attraction of this innovation justified the high investment, since musical films like *The Broadway Melody* (Harry Beaumont, 1929) or *Fox Movietone Follies of 1929* (David Butler, 1929) hit box-office records in that period.

In the midst of gramophonoradiomania, the 'synchronised film fever' and the novelty of sung and spoken films began to be trumpeted by the press.

RECORDS AND CINEMA

As we have seen, before and also after the arrival of sound cinema, cinemas had become some of the spaces available to enjoy the electrical recording novelty, especially for the vast majority of its audiences, who were not able to afford a record player at home, let alone an electrical one. According to the September 1929 issue of *Phono-Arte* magazine, which specialised in record music, it was common at that time for the half-dozen wired cinemas in Rio de Janeiro to play phonograph records through the vitaphone system's loudspeakers, with music related or not to the sound films programmed, before the lights were turned down and the projection began ('Cinema fallado' 1929: 28).

It is also worth noting that, according to a photograph published in a 1929 issue of *Fox Magazine* (Figure 11.3), the Odeon cinema, the second cinema to be wired for sound in Rio de Janeiro, continued to display horns facing outwards (perhaps the same ones installed three years before). Apparently, the cinema sought to attract audiences by advertising the novelty of *cinema fallado* – 'talking films', as literally announced on the signs – similarly to record stores, and, in so doing, contributing to the aforementioned loud soundscape in central Rio.

Figure 11.3 Rio de Janeiro's Odeon showing its first 'talkie': *Fox Movietone Follies of 1929*. Author's private collection.

As a matter of fact, cinemas, record companies and victrola stores had established a fruitful commercial collaboration. On the one hand, sound films increased the sales of records of hit songs from Hollywood musicals, boosting the popularity of American artists and music genres such as jazz and foxtrot. On the other hand, records of film songs frequently came into stores before the films premiered, thus helping to promote their future release. The 'Music and Records' column, in *O Malho*, regularly addressed this mutually beneficial relationship:

> The advent of sound cinema, as we never tire of repeating, brought an extraordinary boost to the phonographic commerce in this Capital, so that nothing can be written about songs and records without alluding to the novelties ushered in by the recently screened 'talkies'. (Vaz 1929: 53)[23]

In that period, virtually all record companies set up in the country were releasing records of the most successful film songs, with some boasting that theirs were the only ones featuring the same artists as in the film. At the same time, rerecording by Brazilian artists, with lyrics translated into Portuguese, of the musical successes from Hollywood sound films became very common. An example of the impact of sound cinema on the record market is singer Francisco Alves, who recorded versions of the most popular songs from virtually all the Hollywood musical films released between 1929 and 1930. Similar to traditional complaints about the quality of translation of the titles and intertitles of foreign films, criticisms were frequently levelled at the Portuguese translations of song lyrics from Hollywood musicals (Réo 1930c: 51).

To keep up with synchronised film fever, the more modest Rio de Janeiro cinemas replaced their orchestras with electrically amplified phonographs, contributing to the mass unemployment of musicians, victims of both sound films and records. Instead of projecting sound films accompanied by the special 33⅓rpm vitaphone discs provided by film distributors, the exhibitors themselves started to synchronise silent prints with 78rpm phonographic records of music and sound effects. To that end, they used the new and powerful electrical record players, replicating the 1928 phenomenon of the Victor Ortophonica Auditorium. It was a less expensive way to take advantage of the success of both sound cinema and victrolamania, which the trade magazines called 'tapeaphone' ('bogusphone'), a pun on the Brazilian slang word *tapeação*. These intermedial borrowings inflected not only the modes of film presentation during gramophonoradiomania, but also the films themselves, as Brazil moved into producing films spoken and sung in Portuguese.

'ILLUSTRATED RECORDS'

The musical feature films produced in the 1930s by major Rio studios, such as Cinédia, Brasil Vita-Filmes or Sonofilms, featured some of the best-known radio singers. Film production at the time was under the influence of radio, as has been noted by many film scholars, and is apparent in films such as *Alô, alô, carnaval* (*Hello, Hello, Carnival*, Adhemar Gonzaga, 1936), the oldest surviving Brazilian musical feature film starring Francisco Alves and Carmen Miranda, among other famous singers. But this turns out to be only part of the picture, when we consider the early sound films made in Brazil in 1929 – almost all of them believed lost – whose relationship with the record industry was equally as important as, or even more important than, the growing but still restricted medium of radio.

One of the earliest synchronised films, following the arrival of vitaphone and movietone, was the short *Casa de caboclo*, produced by the Circuito Nacional de Exibidores (CNE, or National Exhibition Circuit), which was filmed and screened in sync with a 78rpm phonographic record.[24] Probably directed by Vittorio Verga, the film showed the singer Gastão Formenti interpreting the eponymous song by Heckel Tavares (tune) and Luiz Peixoto (lyrics). The record featuring this song, released in 1928, had been a bestseller, turning the composers and performer into stars.[25]

First exhibited on 23 August 1929 in Rio, at the modest Guarani Theatre, *Casa de caboclo* was announced as 'the first Brazilian film sung and synchronised with national equipment' (*Correio da Manhã* 1929a: 7).[26] Initially programmed to precede the feature-length film *The Divine Lady* (Frank Lloyd, 1929), its success seems to have been immediate, as an announcement two days later printed the title of *Casa de caboclo* much more prominently in the press than the Hollywood film (*Correio da Manhã* 1929b: 7). The following week, the CNE announcements did not even mention the title of the feature film on show, only *Casa de caboclo*, which was running in two theatres, the Guarani and Polytheama (*Correio da Manhã* 1929c: 11).

The Guarani's owner, Justino do Amaral, states that he used an adapted electrical record player to accompany the projection (*Correio da Manhã* 1929d: 7). *Casa de caboclo* and the other CNE films that followed, shorts produced on a weekly basis in which singers like Laís Areda and Vicente Celestino lip-synched their own phonographic recordings of Brazilian and foreign songs, were screened at different unwired cinemas in Rio de Janeiro.[27] Scorned by *Cinearte* film critic Pedro Lima as mere 'illustrated records' (Lima 1929: 14), they were attractive as a kind of local version of the short sound films that regularly accompanied Hollywood feature-length films. They also represented a novelty to the large number of fans of Brazilian songs and artists: instead of jazz and foxtrot, *modinhas* and *sambas*. As an alternative or complement to Hollywood sound films, spectators could enjoy Brazilian illustrated records.

At first glance, films by CNE and other producers resorting to the same expedient – such as the musical shorts made by Paulo Benedetti (Souza and Freire 2018: 313–314) – may be considered attempts to compete with the novelty of foreign sound cinema. Yet a film like *Casa de caboclo* can also be understood as a further development in the Brazilian music market of the enormous success of Heckel Tavares and Luiz Peixoto's song, which, from the first (but not last) phonographic record, began to be sold and also explored in sheet music, radio broadcast, musical theatre plays and, finally, the cinema.

Filmed Speeches

It should be noted, however, that *Casa de caboclo* and the other short films that followed it were not the first Portuguese-spoken sound films available to Brazilian audiences. Since the first exhibitions of the new technology in the country, Hollywood distributors in Brazil had focused on enhancing their programmes with special attractions for local audiences. At the premiere of Brazilian sound cinema, in São Paulo, as early as 13 April 1929, the film screened before the main feature, *The Patriot* (Ernst Lubitsch, 1928), was a short produced by Paramount, shot in its studios on Long Island and entitled *Saudação à cidade de São Paulo* (*Greetings to the City of São Paulo*); it presented a speech by the Brazilian Consul General in New York, Sebastião Sampaio.

In the case of this movietone short of about 4 minutes, probably consisting of a single shot,[28] there is an intermedial relation with radio, the emphasis being on speech rather than music. The similarity of *Saudação à cidade de São Paulo* to a radio broadcast was highlighted by Sampaio's emphasis on bridging distances, by using words like 'trip', 'far' and 'distant'. The film's first sentence introduces the new technology and seems to highlight, deceptively, a quality associated more with a transmission medium (the liveness of radio) than with a storage medium (such as sound film): 'Here I am, ladies and gentlemen, not having left New York at all, but at the same time before your eyes and speaking to your ears – opening the São Paulo Paramount Theatre together with you.'[29] Indeed, according to newspaper comments, this filmed speech received warm applause from the elite audience in the luxurious new theatre, as if Sampaio were there in the flesh.

In fact, the ideas of simultaneity ('at the same time') and of seeing and hearing from a distance ('before your eyes and speaking to your ears'), suggested by Sampaio's words, seem to reposition this film in a long and neglected history of the televisual, as suggested by William Uricchio: that is, 'within a trajectory of technologies that sought to connect two distant points in real time' – the camera obscura, telescope, telephone, telegraph and, of course, radio and television (Uricchio 2008: 287).

These radio-toned 'filmed speeches' were shown at other premieres in first-run theatres, as in the first sound-cinema premiere in Rio, on 20 June 1929, which featured a new speech by Sebastião Sampaio. On 6 September, at the sound-cinema premiere at the Capitólio Theatre, the fourth Rio de Janeiro cinema to be wired, the feature film *The Wedding March* (Erich von Stroheim, 1929) was preceded by a filmed speech in Portuguese by the Deputy Consul of Brazil in New York, David Moretzsohn, and a musical prologue performed by a pianist from Rio, Dyla Josetti, both pieces shot in the US (Freire 2012: 260). The music performed was the 'Grande Fantasia Triunfal sobre o Hino Nacional Brasileiro' (Grand Triumphal Fantasy on the National Anthem), composed by Louis Moreau Gottschalk. Combining a speech and an instrumental concert, this short sound film adopted an erudite, elitist and nationalist tone, linked to the educational–cultural aims of the early radio stations, and with a quite different perspective from the commercial appeal of the phonographic records made of popular songs in the CNE films shown in second-run theatres.

FILM DISCS AND RADIO TECHNICIANS

One example of a film marked by hybrid relations between radio and record, in terms of both production and exhibition, is the first Brazilian feature-length sound film, released on 2 August 1929. Produced in São Paulo while the CNE was shooting its 'illustrated records' in Rio de Janeiro, *Acabaram-se os otários* (*No More Suckers*), directed by Luiz de Barros, has been studied more attentively in recent times (Freire 2013a; Freire 2013b; Souza and Freire 2018: 314–6).

As with the CNE films, the director and producer of *Acabaram-se os otários* filmed the musical numbers with singers lip-synching 78rpm records that were later synchronised with the projector at the time of screening. But in addition to using pre-recorded discs – such as those of Columbia singer Paraguassu – Barros also specially recorded dialogue discs for this musical comedy at the Parlophon studios (Freire 2013a: 107–9). Unlike the 'filmed speeches' already mentioned, some scenes from the film resembled 'filmed sketches'. The recordings of the dialogued scenes, played in sync with the film projections, were curiously marketed by Parlophon as comic albums, revealing an autonomy of the sound component of *Acabaram-se os otários* as an independent phonographic work.[30] The fact that the records did not carry any indication of their original connection with the film meant that they were not recognised until recently as the only preserved elements from the recordings originally made for the first Brazilian sound feature film.[31]

As well as enlisting the help of a record company studio for the production of his film, Barros turned to radio technicians for help with its exhibition. In order to screen *Acabaram-se os otários* in sync with the 78rpm discs in unwired theatres, the producers developed their own equipment, called Sincrocinex, which synchronised a silent 35mm film projector with an electrical phonograph. Built in the workshops of the Empresa Cinematográfica Pathé, owned by Gustavo Zieglitz, the mechanical component of the Sincrocinex was devised by company technicians who manufactured and repaired film projectors. But as reports in the press make clear, sound cinema demanded an expertise outside film. Thus, 'the spoken and sound part' of Sincrocinex – that is, the electrical amplification and the connection with the loudspeakers – was in the charge of 'well-known radio technicians Moacyr Fenelon and Romeu Muniz Barreto' ('A fita nacional falada' 1929: 10).

This was Fenelon's (1903–53) first job in the film business. Originally a radio and sound specialist, he would go on to direct and produce films, becoming one of the most important Brazilian film professionals of all time. However, to date, almost nothing has been written about his previous work in the radio sector.[32] Luiz de Barros recounts in his autobiography that he asked Fenelon to join the *Acabaram-se os otários* team due to his previous experience at a 'radio store' in central São Paulo and his 'understanding of amplifiers' (Barros 1978: 105–6). But Fenelon was not a mere radio salesman; in fact, he was an active radio expert in São Paulo. In April 1927, he had joined as partner and managing director of the magazine *Radio Paulista: Revista Mensal de Divulgação Radio-Technica*, in which he even published an article, 'Radio Futurista', as collaborator (1927: 160–1).

He left the magazine a few months and four issues later, launching, in December 1927, the first issue of *Radiomania* magazine, with himself as director. A 'radiorabid' ('radioferina')[33] magazine, *Radiomania* did not last for many numbers, as Fenelon was prosecuted – and convicted – for insulting his former *Radio Paulista* partner, Euripedes Fomm Pereira, in one of his articles (*Radio Paulista* 1928). Thus, in mid-1928 he was already at the head of a new magazine, dedicated to the 'radio-electric sciences', entitled *TSF*, of which Radiomania became a section (*Diário Nacional* 1928: 6). In July 1929, Fenelon closed the programme of the 'Radio Club de Amadores' festival, broadcast by Radio Record station, from São Paulo, speaking as president of that association (*Correio Paulistano* 1929d: 14).

Fenelon was therefore already a well-known, active – and perhaps controversial – name on the radio scene in São Paulo when he took his first step towards what would be a long career in Brazilian cinema. As such, before the stars of the radio broadcast era were cast by Brazilian film producers to act and sing in their films, radio technicians were employed to allow Brazilian films to talk through the electrical loudspeakers. But to record the dialogues, filmmakers such as Luiz de Barros had to resort to phonographic studios. As for the songs, Barros, CNE and his competitors used phonographic records that had already been released, taking advantage of their popularity amid the victrolamania.

Adopting an approach inspired by media archaeology, an analysis of the intermedial context of the arrival of sound cinema in Brazil, focusing on the Rio de Janeiro soundscape, allows us to understand the combination of technologies, the cross-polination of different practices, and the trajectory of many professionals, enriching our understanding of this crucial moment in the history of Brazilian cinema. Expressions used to characterise some of the films discussed in this chapter, such as 'illustrated records', 'filmed speeches' or 'filmed sketches', emphasise the diversity of early Brazilian sound films and their strong ties with different media. Media archaeology stands out, therefore, as a privileged means to revitalise the historical narrative of a national cinema. As regards Brazilian cinema history, I firmly believe that it is more important (even if more difficult) 'to be doing media archaeology rather than merely using it as a conceptual tool' (Elsaesser 2016: 353).

After all, as this chapter has demonstrated, the intermedial relationship between cinema, record and radio in late 1920s Rio de Janeiro was evident in technological (expertise and equipment), economic (sales and marketing), cultural (audience niches and circuits) and aesthetic (modes of representation and address) terms, revealing a landscape of convergence that prefigures the contemporary digital mediascape.

Notes

1. 'Pandegolandia' is a neologism for the land of the *pândegos*, or playful persons.
2. 'Tive ensejo de notar que a população gosta muito do jazz e do cinema, especialmente quando o ouvido está devidamente arrolhado.' Unless otherwise indicated, all translations are by the author.
3. At the time, phonograph, victrola and gramophone were terms routinely used in Brazilian Portuguese in an interchangeable way, although originally the phonograph referred to the apparatus for recording and reproducing sound in cylinders and the gramophone, on discs. Victrola, in turn, was the trademark of the Victor company, that had already become a generic term for record players.
4. 'O Rio é sem dúvida a cidade do barulho. As outras que visitamos não sofrem a azucrinação de buzinas, alto falantes e pregões.'
5. Although studying the soundscape of cities in the US, Thompson notices something similar in the same period: 'While the noise of traffic had gradually crept up on listeners over the course of a decade or more, a new noise that announced its presence far more abruptly was the amplified output of electroacoustic loudspeakers' (Thompson 2008: 149).
6. 'A cidade tem um número cada vez maior de estabelecimentos que vendem coisas ruidosas e tem aumentado muito o número de pianolas, altos berrantes e gramophones nas residências particulares.'
7. Because commercial advertisement was forbidden and there were no public radio stations in Brazil, the country's first radio stations were established as associations maintained by fees paid by their members, who were willing to contribute to the development of radio. However, the money collected was usually insufficient and sponsorship from shops selling radios soon became another source of income for the stations.
8. 'The fetish of distance listening was both cosmopolitan (how *many* different places a listener could pick) and exploratory (how *far* a listener could hear)' (Sterne 2003: 209).
9. 'O antes pensado para interligar, sem fios, dois pontos, ambos enviando e recebendo mensagens, passa a ser empregado para o tráfego de informações, por ondas eletromagnéticas, de uma estação emissora para ouvintes distribuídos nos mais diversos locais.'
10. I argue that this development in Brazil differs from that in other countries, such as the US, where the radio boom affected the record industry: 'The "radio craze"

was a devastating blow to an already depressed industry which had barely survived the postwar depression of the early 1920s' (see Millard 2005: 136).
11. Through the Decree-Law No. 21.111, of 1 March 1932, which regulated radio communication services in the national territory.
12. Contemporaneous accounts highlight a radical difference: 'The phonograph itself reproduces and amplifies the sound mechanically, while the new system reproduces and amplifies the sound electrically. The only common point is that they both play songs recorded on discs' (Denada 1926: 17). Electrical record players began to be widely marketed in Brazil only in 1929 through models such as Victor Electrola, Columbia-Kolster, Panatrope Electrica (from Brunswick) and Polyfar (from Polydor).
13. 'Incontestavelmente, à radio-telefonia deve o fonógrafo o desenvolvimento extraordinário dos últimos tempos.'
14. 'The exterior of the talking machine might not have changed much, but inside was an amplifying unit, with its vacuum tubes, and other electrical devices. The mysterious innards of the talking machine had been transformed from polished brass and oiled gear wheels to wires and glowing tubes' (Millard 2005: 144–5).
15. In the mechanical phonograph, the hollow tone arm transmits the motions of the stylus to a reproducing diaphragm. In the electrically amplified phonograph, the arm just supports the pick-up or phonograph cartridge that works as an electromechanical transducer, converting mechanical vibrations into electrical signals. Nevertheless, a mechanical phonograph in which a pick-up was installed and connected to a radio receiver could still have a wind-up turntable, for example.
16. 'É coisa comum rádio e fonógrafo conjugados, na mesma caixa, um suprindo o outro: o rádio fornecendo energia e amplitude de som, e o fonógrafo o disco, nos intervalos das irradiações.'
17. 'O rádio tem concorrido ainda para maior divulgação dos discos, aumentando-lhes consideravelmente a vendagem, e a prova está na ampliação deste comércio, hoje espalhado por todos os cantos.'
18. 'Grande desenvolvimento que tomou aqui a instalação e venda de aparelhos de rádio (. . .) elas aparecem em todos os pontos da cidade, numa proporção extraordinária, cada dia facilmente observada (. . .) É, pois, o grande negócio de hoje. O grande comércios.'
19. 'Querem uma prova? Façamos uma excursão (. . .) na rua do Ouvidor, uma das artérias mais transitadas, ou, talvez, a mais transitada artéria carioca. E veremos, aqui e ali, uma compacta multidão estacionada em frente das casas de músicas, atraída pelos sons que uma victrola, colocada a porta de cada uma delas, irradia para o exterior.'
20. The same magazine columnist, a critic of the law, celebrated its annulment a few months later: 'The absurd measure of the City Hall of this capital . . . has already been revoked, fortunately . . . you can already see the crowds in front of music stores, delighted with the pieces in vogue, sambas, waltzes or foxtrots' (Réo 1930a: 12). On São Paulo, see Gonçalves (2006: 63–5).

21. 'Primeiro, porque não compram discos para irradiá-los; segundo, porque não precisam contratar artistas para formar os seus programas; terceiro, porque assim conseguem uma clientela cada vez maior, dadas as vantagens que oferecem.'
22. 'Pois impossível seria ter-se um programa extenso, de alta qualidade, se se prescindisse das gravações fonográficas.' A symbol of this alliance was the creation, in 1930, of the Brazilian Association of Phonography and Radio (Associação Brasileira de Phonographia e Rádio). The history of this entity is yet to be researched.
23. 'O advento do cinema sonoro, como não nos cansamos de repetir, trouxe para o comercio phonográfico desta Capital, um impulso extraordinário, de maneira que nada se pode escrever sobre músicas e discos sem aludir às novidades lançados pelos "*talkies*" recém-apresentados.'
24. On the beginning of the CNE, see Freire (2018: 283).
25. Parlophon record, n. 12883, 21 September 1928. The track 'Casa de Caboclo', on the A side of the album, can be heard on the website of the Instituto Moreira Salles, available at <http://www.discografiabrasileira.com.br> (last accessed 22 July 2020).
26. 'O primeiro filme brasileiro cantado e sincronizado, por aparelhos nacionais.'
27. 'In the following weeks, *Casa de caboclo* was replaced in the Politheama and Guarani display with other films made from popular songs: *Sublime canção*, performed by Laís Areda and Vicente Celestino; *Feijoada*, by Laís Areda; *Baianinha*, by Laís Areda; *Il Pagliacci* (The Clown), by Vicente Celestino; and *Romanza*, by Vicente Celestino' (Souza and Freire 2018: 312).
28. According to the press, the speech was filmed four times and the best reel was then chosen (Freire 2012: 249).
29. 'Aqui estou, minhas senhoras e meus senhores, sem sair de Nova York, mas ao mesmo tempo diante de vossos olhos e falando aos vossos ouvidos – inaugurando convosco o Theatro Paramount de São Paulo.' For the complete transcription of Sebastião Sampaio's speech, see Freire (2012: 249–50).
30. One of the albums recorded especially for the film, with the tracks 'Tangomania' and 'A quadrilha', considered 'of easy understanding and something funny', was reviewed by the magazine *Phono-Arte* (Freire 2013a: 110).
31. These records had already been digitised and were available on the Instituto Moreira Salles website when, in 2012, I discovered they were recordings originally made for the film. In 2019, I participated in a reconstruction of the film *Acabaram-se os otários*. See <http://www.cinevi.uff.br/lupa/reconstituicao-do-filme-acabaram-se-os-otarios-dir-luiz-de-barros-1929/> (last accessed 20 June 2020).
32. Miranda (1990: 138) reports that Fenelon took a course at the Radio Institute in the US in the early 1920s, without giving further details; Souza repeats the information (2000: 233). In a 1952 interview, Fenelon says that he started working on films with *Acabaram-se os otários*, 'precisely on 17 October 1927'. Twenty-five years later, he certainly mixes up the date (Alencar 1952: 8–9).
33. According to competing magazine *Antenna* (1927: 289).

REFERENCES

'A fita nacional falada' (1929), *Correio Paulistano*, 17 July, p. 10.
Alencar, Renato de (1952), 'Falam os técnicos. O que todos devemos saber sobre o cinema nacional. Tem a palavra Moacyr Fenelon'. *A Cena Muda*, 32:35, 29 August.
Altman, Rick (2004), *Silent Film Sound*. New York: Columbia University Press.
Antenna: Rádio Para Todos (1927), 2:21, January, p. 289.
'Aspectos do Theatro Phenix na ocasião da primeira audição da Victrola Ortophonica Auditorium' (1928), *Fon-Fon*, 22:27, 7 July, p. 44.
Barros, Luiz de (1978), *Minhas Memórias de Cineasta*. Rio de Janeiro: Artenova: Embrafilme.
Carlos, J. (1924), 'A cidade barulho'. *O Malho*, 23:1129, 3 May, p. 23.
'Cinema fallado' (1929), *Phono-Arte*, 15 September, p. 28.
Correio da Manhã (1929a), 23 August, p. 7.
Correio da Manhã (1929b), 25 August, p. 7.
Correio da Manhã (1929c), 30 August, p. 11.
Correio da Manhã (1929d), 4 August, p. 7.
Correio Paulistano (1929d), 2 July, p. 14.
Costa, Fernando Morais da (2008), *O Som no Cinema Brasileiro*. Rio de Janeiro: 7letras.
Denada (1926), 'Discos e machinas falantes'. *O Paiz*, 31 October, p. 17.
Diário Nacional (1928), 10 July, p. 6.
Duque (1929), 'Gabino. Fox-Trot'. *Jornal do Brasil*, 17 September, p. 5.
Elsaesser, Thomas (2016), *Film History as Media Archaeology: Tracking Digital Cinema*. Amsterdam: Amsterdam University Press.
Fenelon, Moacyr (1927), 'Radio Futurista'. *Radio Paulista*, 4, May, pp. 160–1.
Ferrareto, Luiz Artur (2013), 'De 1919 a 1923, os primeiros momentos do rádio no Brasil'. *Revista Brasileira de História da Mídia*, 3:1, January–June, p. 11.
Freire, Rafael de Luna (2012), 'A febre dos sincronizados: os primeiros meses da exibição de filmes sonoros no Rio e em São Paulo em 1929', in Gustavo Souza, Laura Cánepa, Mauricio de Bragança and Rodrigo Carreiro (eds), *XIII Estudos de Cinema e Audiovisual Socine*, vol. 2. São Paulo: Socine, pp. 388–99.
Freire, Rafael de Luna (2013a), '*Acabaram-se os otários*: cinema e disco na chegada do filme sonoro', in Stephanie Dennison (ed.), *World Cinema: As novas cartografias do cinema mundial*. Campinas: Papirus, pp. 105–15.
Freire, Rafael de Luna (2013b), '*Acabaram-se os otários*: compreendendo o primeiro longa-metragem sonoro'. *Rebeca*, 3:3, January, pp. 104–28.
Freire, Rafael de Luna (2018), 'O cinema no Rio de Janeiro (1914–1929)', in Sheila Schvarzman and Fernão Ramos (eds), *Nova história do cinema brasileiro*, vol. 1, São Paulo: Edições Sesc, pp. 252–92.
Freitas, Luis Paula (1929), 'Victrolamania'. *Fon-Fon*, 23: 41, 12 October, p. 10.
Gonçalves, Camila Koshiba (2006), *Música em 78 rotações: 'discos a todos os preços' na São Paulo dos anos 30*. PhD dissertation, University of São Paulo.
'Gravações elétricas e phonographos aperfeiçoados' (1926). *O Paiz*, 29 August, p. 10.
Lima, Pedro (1929), 'Cinema brasileiro'. *Cinearte*, 4:192, 30 October, p. 14.
Millard, Andre (2005), *America on Record: A History of Recorded Sound*, 2nd edn. Cambridge: Cambridge University Press.
Miranda, Luiz Felipe (1990), *Dicionário de Cineastas Brasileiros*. São Paulo: Art Editora.
Pederneiras, Raul (1930), *Nós pelas costas: notas de um caderno de viagem*. Rio de Janeiro: Oficinas Gráficas do Jornal do Brasil.

'Phonographos e discos' (1928), *Radiocultura*, 5, p. 16.
'Phonographos e discos' (1929). *Radiocultura*, 14, July, p. 18.
Radio Paulista (1927), 3, April.
Radio Paulista (1928), 15, July-August.
Radio Phono (1929), 1:1, August.
Réo, Tom (1930a), 'Músicas e discos'. *O Malho*, 29:1447, 7 June, p. 12.
Réo, Tom (1930b), 'Músicas e discos'. *O Malho*, 29:1428, 15 January, p. 49.
Réo, Tom (1930c), 'Músicas e discos'. *O Malho*, 29:1440, 19 April, p. 51.
Réo, Tom (1930d), 'Músicas e discos'. *O Malho*, 29:1456, 9 August, p. 52.
Santiago, Oswaldo (1929), 'Os vagabundos da cidade'. *O Malho*, 28:1376, 26 January, p. 33.
Souza, Carlos Roberto and Rafael de Luna Freire (2018), 'A chegada do cinema sonoro ao Brasil', in Sheila Schvarzman and Fernão Ramos (eds), *Nova história do cinema brasileiro*, vol. 1. São Paulo: Edições Sesc, pp. 294–341.
Souza, José Inácio de Melo (2000), 'Moacyr Fenelon', in Luiz Felipe Miranda and Fernão Ramos (eds), *Enciclopédia do cinema brasileiro*. São Paulo: Senac, pp. 233–4.
Sterne, Jonathan (2003), *The Audible Past: Cultural Origins of Sound Reproduction*. Durham, NC: Duke University Press.
Thompson, Emily (2008), *The Soundscape of Modernity: Architectural Acoustics and the Culture of Listening in America, 1900–1933*. Cambridge, MA: MIT Press.
Uricchio, William (2008), 'Television's First Seventy-five Years: The Interpretive Flexibility of a Medium in Transition', in Robert Kolker (ed.), *The Oxford Handbook of Film and Media Studies*. Oxford: Oxford University, pp. 286–305.
Vaz, Reto (1929), 'Músicas e discos'. *O Malho*, 28:1416, 2 November, p. 53.
'Verdades e mentiras' (1930). *Careta*, 23:1154, 2 August, p. 26.
Vieira, Michele Cruz (2006), *A Belle Époque sonora: o rádio como fruto de novo ambiente dos sons do Rio de Janeiro no início do século xx*. PhD dissertation, Fluminense Federal University, Niterói, pp. 22–56.
Yantock (1929), 'Grammophonoradiomania'. *O Malho*, 28:1402, 27 July, p. 69.
Yantock (1930), 'Uma viagem a Pandegolandia'. *O Malho*, 29:1431, 15 February, p. 4.

CHAPTER 12

The Singer, the Acrobats and the Bands: A Study of Three Brazilian Films and their Intermedial Characters

Alfredo Suppia

Studies providing a comprehensive overview of the intersections between cinema and television are scarce in Brazil. One of the first and few works by a Brazilian scholar which cuts across different media is José Mário Ortiz Ramos's *Cinema, televisão e publicidade* (2004). Ortiz Ramos analyses what he calls the Brazilian audiovisual 'borderlands', offering a thorough account of underrated films starring Os Trapalhões (The Goofies), the famous Brazilian quartet of comedians. Following in the footsteps of Ortiz Ramos's sociological and intermedial approach to the Brazilian audiovisual production, I will address in this chapter three Brazilian popular films released between the 1960s and 1980s. Brazilian cinema was particularly thriving in that period – despite the spurious military dictatorship imposed on the nation from 1964 onwards – and this lasted until the latest major crisis in the history of Brazilian cinema, brought about by the shutdown of the state production and distribution company Embrafilme, in 1990.[1] Throughout those three decades, a number of Brazilian films succeeded in communicating effectively with wide audiences, with major box-office hits such as Bruno Barreto's *Dona Flor e seus dois maridos* (*Dona Flor and Her Two Husbands*, 1976), with more than 10 million spectators, or J. B. Tanko's *Os saltimbancos trapalhões* (*The Goofy Acrobats*, 1981) and *Os trapalhões na Serra Pelada* (*The Goofies in Serra Pelada*, 1981), both with more than 5 million spectators.

Many films from the 1970s and 1980s featured parodies of American blockbusters, attempting to recreate popular US film genres with local colour. This is the case with Brazilian adventure films targeted at juvenile audiences, and one can think of titles as varied as Roberto Farias's *Roberto Carlos em ritmo de aventura* (*Roberto Carlos at Adventure Rhythm*, 1968); Adriano Stuart's *Os Trapalhões na guerra dos planetas*, a.k.a. *Brazilian Star Wars* (*The Goofies in the War of the Planets*, 1981) and *O incrível monstro trapalhão* (*The Incredible Goofy Monster*, 1981); Ivan Cardoso's *O segredo da múmia* (*The Secret of the Mummy*, 1982) and *As sete vampiras* (*The Seven Vampires*, 1986); and Francisco de Paula's *Areias escaldantes* (*Scalding Sands*, 1985). Some of these films are of particular interest for an intermedial approach, insofar as they are musicals starring popular Brazilian singers or rock bands or featuring popular showbiz artists. These films, which lured generations of young spectators, are 'hybrid' in the sense that they amalgamate different languages and aesthetics from both cinema and television, but also from radio shows, the circus and pop music. They were often written by professionals with careers in different media (theatre, TV, film, the advertising industry), or cast stars whose popularity was achieved first and foremost in media other than film. The films also have in common the presence of 'intermedial bodies': that is, characters played by artists whose popularity was achieved via another medium or different mediums.

The predecessor of the aforementioned films can be found in the Brazilian *chanchada*. Usually regarded as a mixture of musical and comedy, the *chanchada* is a genuinely Brazilian film genre, deep-rooted in popular culture and the traditions of radio and vaudeville theatre – in addition to the circus and other non-cinematic forms of popular spectacle. The *chanchada* drew wide audiences in Brazil. It fed on Brazilian popular culture, thus delineating a mediascape full of inputs from circus, the Brazilian *teatro de revista* (vaudeville theatre), carnival and radio. As a result, a cinematic star system emerged that allowed producers and exhibitors to make a profit with national cinema.

The three films in focus in this chapter, *Roberto Carlos em ritmo de aventura*, *O incrível monstro trapalhão* and *Areias escaldantes*, follow in the footsteps of this *chanchada* tradition and are privileged examples of cinematic intermediality.

THE SINGER: *ROBERTO CARLOS EM RITMO DE AVENTURA*

Ortiz Ramos (2004: 201) refers to Roberto Carlos's films as a blend of action movie, detective film and musical, all adapted for the Brazilian context. *Roberto Carlos em ritmo de aventura* (1968), the first of a trilogy written and directed by Roberto Farias,[2] is a parody of the James Bond films with a touch of nonsense and a local reading of the American musical. Roberto Carlos, known as 'Rei' (King) and the most successful popular composer and singer of all time in Brazil, is featured in risky stunt scenes such as getting into a car hanging on a crane or crossing through the Pasmado Tunnel, in Rio de Janeiro, with a helicopter. The film had 2.5 million spectators in theatres at the time.[3] As noted by Ortiz Ramos (2004: 199), *Roberto Carlos* is punctuated by narrative breaks in which the characters speak about the film as a work in progress, thus dismantling narrative illusionism, an effect accrued with the use of the metalanguage typical of the cinema of the time. The Beatles films, such as Richard Lester's *A Hard Day's Night* (1964) and *Help!* (1965), had already resorted to a similar strategy. One example of this procedure is the sequence in which the character of a director, played by Reginaldo Faria (Roberto

Farias's brother), discusses his art and craft on the rooftop of a building, his face appearing alternately bearded and shaved in consecutive shots. As Ortiz Ramos (2004: 199) comments:

> *Roberto Carlos em ritmo de aventura* tried to dodge difficulties inherent in Brazilian film production by resorting to parody and following in the footsteps of the *chanchada*, where Roberto Farias made his début. But the film also tried to escape from pure entertainment, through the use of deconstruction and doses of cinematographic erudition, like the sequence in which the director of the film inside the film appears spinning and yelling, in a clear reference to the character of Corisco in the classical sequence from *Deus e o diabo na terra do sol* [*Black God, White Devil*, Glauber Rocha, 1964].[4]

Roberto Carlos benefited from a huge amount of media attention and publicity from the beginning of its production. One example was a public TV and magazine contest aimed at selecting girls for the film who would resemble the James Bond women. Needless to say, even though cinema was a 'new frontier' for him, Roberto Carlos already had an extremely successful career on radio and TV behind him. Let us have a quick look at some of that history. The early 1960s saw the launch of great radio hits by Roberto Carlos and Erasmo Carlos (Roberto's long-time friend and collaborator). By 1964, Roberto Carlos was already a star. The Jovem Guarda (Young Wave) movement, led by Roberto, gained momentum with the launch of the television show of the same name, first aired by TV Record in São Paulo on 22 August 1965. *Jovem Guarda* was broadcast on Sundays at 5pm, presented by the trio of artists Roberto, Wanderléa and Erasmo, and featured many other musicians. The show lasted for three years. When his film premiered in 1968, Roberto had just left the TV show.

The success of the Roberto Carlos films, and particularly *Roberto Carlos em ritmo de aventura*, cannot be fully understood out of the broader context of an 'alliance' involving the Brazilian music scene, the ascending TV industry, and cinema. In the film, Roberto Carlos appears singing hits such as 'Namoradinha de um amigo meu' (A Friend of Mine's Girlfriend), 'Negro gato' (Black Cat), 'Eu te darei o céu' (I'll Give you Heaven) and 'Eu sou terrível' (I'm Terrible). In fact, Farias's film is a kind of cinematic 'spin-off' from Roberto Carlos's eponymous album released in November 1967, featuring twelve songs, including some of his most famous hits. As in 'The Twelve Works of Hercules', *Roberto Carlos em ritmo de aventura* features the actor engaging in a number of disconnected action scenes, with little and sometimes no narrative transitions and without the usual cause–effect logic verified in classical film storytelling. It is as if the film were following the format of the disconnected tracks of a music album, some of which play in the film's background, and in so doing, constituting a music video *avant la lettre*. It seems, therefore, that the intermedial relationship with the music industry, more precisely with Roberto Carlos's eponymous album, directly affected the language and structure of Farias's film.

THE ACROBATS: *O INCRÍVEL MONSTRO TRAPALHÃO* (1980)

Another heir to the *chanchada* tradition consists of the films starring Os Trapalhões (The Goofies), a very popular group of comedians who had an extremely successful career at Rede Globo – the most powerful TV network in Brazil, hegemonic from the 1970s onwards, and only now challenged by other media or platforms such as social media, internet TV, streaming services and YouTube. With a successful TV show on air at Globo every Sunday at 7pm, Os Trapalhões targeted children and teenagers as their prime audiences. Initially consisting of a duo, Didi (Renato Aragão) and Dedé (Manfried Santana), the team soon welcomed a third member, Mussum (Antônio Carlos Bernardes Gomes), and finally a fourth character, Zacarias (Mauro Faccio Gonçalves).

The show that would later become a huge success at Globo was born from the show *Os insociáveis* (*The Unsociable Ones*), broadcast by TV Record between 1972 and 1974.[5] Directed by Wilton Franco, *Os insociáveis* featured Renato Aragão (Didi), Manfried Santana (Dedé) and Antonio Carlos (Mussum) as a trio of troublemakers involved in comic sketches. The show already featured actresses and actors who would follow the comedians into further projects: for example, the singer Vanusa, whose early career was linked to the Jovem Guarda, and the comedian Roberto Guilherme. In 1974, Franco and the comedians left Record; the show, then renamed *Os Trapalhões* (*The Goofies*), premiered at Rede Tupi, and finally acquired its fourth member, Zacarias. In 1976, *Os Trapalhões*' high audience rates at Tupi started to pose a threat to the variety show *Fantástico*, broadcast by Globo on Sunday nights. As a result, Globo bought the show from Tupi and *Os Trapalhões* premiered at Globo on 13 March 1977. It was on air until 27 August 1995, always preceding the variety show *Fantástico* (Castro 2015).

The films featuring Os Trapalhões represent one of the first consistent cases of box-office success in tandem with the rise of television as the hegemonic media industry in the country. From the mid-1960s onwards, the number of residences with a TV set escalated. Throughout the 1960s, only 4.6 per cent of residences had a TV set – the southeast, the most urbanised and industrialised region, accounted for 12.4 per cent of the total. By the end of the 1980s, the average number of TV sets in the country had increased to 56.1 per cent. In 1991, 71 per cent of Brazilian homes had a TV set and, by 2006, this number had risen to 93 per cent (Cesário 2010: 139).

Between 1978 and 1990, the quartet starred in no fewer than twenty feature films, plus a documentary and an animated feature, attracting more than 74 million viewers to theatres. Unsurprisingly, the film considered to be the first feature with Os Trapalhões, *Na onda do Iê-iê-iê* (*In the Rhythm of Iêiêiê*, 1966), directed by Aurélio Teixeira and starring the duo Didi (Renato Aragão) and Maloca (Manfried Santana), takes advantage of the pop music scene, notably the Jovem Guarda movement.[6] The relationship with the Jovem Guarda would continue through the work at TV Record, when the group performed alongside singer Vanusa. After leaving the Jovem Guarda, Roberto Carlos occasionally performed with Os Trapalhões.[7]

From *Na onda do iêiêiê* in 1966 until the dissolution of the quartet in the late 1990s, all the films bearing the Os Trapalhões brand were top hits in Brazilian cinema. In total, approximately 120 million spectators have watched films by Os Trapalhões. According to a list published recently by the National Cinema Agency (Ancine), between 1971 and 1991, the Trapalhões films, featuring either the whole quartet or only Renato Aragão, placed no fewer than thirteen titles in the top twenty box-office successes in Brazil. Over those twenty years, each of the thirty-two feature films starring the group surpassed the landmark of 1 million viewers (Moser 2014).

A huge TV success, Os Trapalhões also stand out in the history of Brazilian film industry for their power to communicate with audiences of all age groups. Experienced directors such as Carlos Manga, J. B. Tanko, Adriano Stuart, Daniel Filho and Roberto Farias helped to turn the group into an unprecedented cinematic phenomenon in Brazil, with more than forty feature-length films. Unlike Roberto Carlos, whose cinematic career was rather short in comparison and followed in the wake of his fame on radio and television and at music festivals, the career of Os Trapalhões was propelled by both TV and film. The group also spread their tentacles over the music industry, having released no fewer than twenty-three albums. Some of these albums are derived from their films and were also hugely successful, scoring big hits for children and youngsters, as in the case of 'Hollywood' and 'A história de uma gata' (The Story of a Cat),[8] two songs written and composed by Chico Buarque de Holanda, Sergio Bardotti and Luis Enriquez Bacalov, and performed by Lucinha Lins for the soundtrack of J. B. Tanko's *Os saltimbancos trapalhões* (*The Goofy Acrobats*, 1981), one of the quartet's greatest box-office hits, with more than 5 million spectators. Inspired by Chico Buarque, Sergio Bardotti and Luis Enríquez Bacalov's play *Os saltimbancos*, this film is canonical of Os Trapalhões' overall cinematic style, drawing on the legacy of the Brazilian *chanchadas*. Lucinha Lins appears in at least one unforgettable musical number, when Os Trapalhões, in awe, are visiting the sets of the popular American TV show *Battlestar Galactica*.[9] One of the best

Brazilian soundtracks ever – the LP, released by Ariola, opens with Chico Buarque's famous song 'Piruetas' (Twists) – *Os saltimbancos trapalhões* established a welcome and successful dialogue between the quartet and MPB (Brazilian Popular Music).[10]

Among Os Trapalhões' films, there are many parodies which took advantage of profitable American blockbusters – such as Franklin J. Schaffner's *Planet of the Apes* (1968), George Lucas's *Star Wars* (1977 onwards) and Steven Spielberg's *Jaws* (1975). Good examples are J. B. Tanko's *Os Trapalhões no planalto dos macacos* (*The Goofies on the Ape's Plateau*, 1976), Adriano Stuart's *Os Trapalhões na guerra dos planetas* (*The Goofies in the War of the Planets*, 1978) and *O incrível monstro trapalhão* (*The Incredible Goofy Monster*, 1980), among other titles.

O incrível monstro trapalhão features a modest Brazilian scientist called Dr Jegue (Renato Aragão), who works with Dedé, Mussum and Zacarias as mechanics for the racing driver Carlos (Eduardo Conde). A pun on Robert Louis Stevenson's character Jekyll, 'jegue' means 'donkey' in the northeast of Brazil. Jegue's hobby is chemistry and he has been doing some research on a ground-breaking type of fuel derived from the quince tree. Jegue is in love with Ritinha (Alcione Mazzeo) but his affection is not requited. Inspired by a Superman picture pinned to a wall in his laboratory, the fumbling scientist decides to invent a substance that could make him strong and handsome. However, after drinking his potion for the first time, Jegue temporarily transmutes into a giant caveman, ugly but gifted with superhuman strength. The quid pro quos continue, and towards the end of the film, the heroes head to Playcenter to rescue Ritinha and Carlos's girlfriend, kidnapped by Russian villains interested in the formula. Playcenter was an iconic amusement park in São Paulo in the 1980s, rivalled only by Tivoli Park in Rio de Janeiro at the time, and offers the perfect medium to underscore the corporeal humour of Os Trapalhões, in particular that of Renato Aragão. One of their most frequent sketches on TV had Carlos Kurt's or Roberto Guilherme's characters reacting to a mischievous Didi, who, from a porch or window on a second floor, threw water or bricks (fake, of course) at the heads of his poor victims. Didi himself constantly overreacted to props and characters featuring in the comic sketches on TV, as much as in the films, in the form of slapstick comedy. Moreover, *O incrível monstro trapalhão* takes advantage of the Playcenter setting to pay homage to Konga, a famous circus character and a hit in Brazilian itinerant circuses and amusement parks. Playing a woman who turns into a gorilla, Konga finds a kind of *doppelgänger* in Renato Aragão's Jegue character.

Even though Stevenson's novella *Strange Case of Dr Jekyll and Mr Hyde* (1886) gave origin to the plot, one of the film's most visible reference is Jerry Lewis's *The Nutty Professor* (1963), alongside comic books such as Stan Lee and Jack Kirby's *The Incredible Hulk* (1962) and its American TV adaptation. Created by Kenneth Johnson and broadcast by CBS from 10 March 1978 to 12 May 1982, *The Incredible Hulk* featured actors Bill Bixby and Lou Ferrigno as Dr Banner and Hulk, respectively. In Brazil, the series was broadcast by Globo, starting on 25 January 1978, at prime time, remaining extremely popular into the early 1980s. The 'goofy monster' in Stuart's film, played by the *capoeira* master and actor Mestre Touro (Antônio Oliveira Bemvindo), was clearly inspired by Lou Ferrigno's Hulk.

THE BAND: *AREIAS ESCALDANTES* (1985)

In the early 1980s, Brazil underwent some important socio-political transformations with the national campaign in favour of direct elections and the redemocratisation process that finally brought the military dictatorship to an end in 1985. In the same year, *Areias escaldantes* – produced, written and directed by Francisco de Paula – featured a generation of artists from theatre, music, visual arts, cinema, poetry, fashion and television. Director de Paula himself was part of that young generation, having previously worked as assistant director to directors Ozualdo Candeias, Neville de Almeida (who is part of the cast of *Areias escaldantes*) and Carlos Diegues.[11] Somewhat recalling the aesthetics of *Roberto Carlos em ritmo de aventura*, *Areias escaldantes* focuses on rock bands and musical hits of its time, with a vague and thin storyline: in a near future (probably the 1990s), in the fictional country of Kali, a group of young terrorists carry out subversive missions which include robberies, kidnappings and assassinations at the behest of a mysterious boss known as the 'Entity' (Figure 12.1). The rebel group is constantly escaping from the pompous and inefficient Special Police.

Francisco de Paula is hesitant about labelling *Areias escaldantes* a sci-fi film. According to him, if there is any link to science fiction iconography in the

Figure 12.1 In *Areias escaldantes* (1985) the 'terrorists', Vinícius Kishi ('Vini', Diogo Vilela) and Verônica Pinheiro ('Verrô', Regina Casé), carry out subversive actions.

film, that should be ascribed to the work of the art director, Arturo Uranga (Suppia 2013: 138). As a film animator, Uranga introduced certain visual-effect techniques in Brazil (notably glass painting), while collaborating with directors such as Cacá Diegues, Bruno Barreto, Zelito Viana, Geraldo Viana, Paulo Thiago and Carla Camurati, among others. He made a number of storyboards, worked as a production designer and created countless animation works for Brazilian TV and the advertisement industry before directing his first feature film, *Era uma vez* (*Once Upon a Time*, 1994). Uranga introduced the glass-painting technique into Globo TV, and he also worked as set and costume designer in Brazilian theatre. Directing a truly independent and low-budget film, de Paula resorted to Uranga's alluring illustrations to achieve the futuristic atmosphere in *Areias escaldantes*. The drawings appear from time to time as brief transitions between action scenes, thus suggesting that the characters inhabit a futuristic metropolis. The dystopian atmosphere and Uranga's art provide the association between this film and sci-fi, whereas the story is completely focused on the Brazilian pop music scene.[12]

Areias escaldantes was originally based on a detailed storyboard, made by Uranga and the comic-book designer Otto Dumovich. De Paula recalls that '[t]he film was shot in 30 days, with two hours of 35mm negative stock. Almost everything was used, and there was no take 2.'[13] Post-production was done in partnership with Sky Light Cinema and Álamo studios. The director comments that distribution and exhibition were disastrous because two actors in the film were arrested for drug possession. However, de Paula himself took the film to festivals in Portugal, Spain and France, and, according to him, it was well received abroad. He adds that 'the film's cinematography, cast, art direction, set design, costumes, makeup, editing and soundtrack were carried out in an authentic way, in tune with the independent film-making style of the time',[14] given that there had been no direct funding from Embrafilme. Recently rediscovered as a cult film, *Areias escaldantes* has been invited to a number of film festivals in Brazil.

As well as the eponymous hit song by Lulu Santos, 'Areias escaldantes', the film features no fewer than seventeen hits of the 1980s, mostly performed by acclaimed rock bands, including 'Inútil' (Useless) and 'Jealousy' (Ciúme), by Ultraje a Rigor; 'Núcleo base' (Base Nucleus) and 'Longe de tudo' (Far from Everything), by Ira; and 'Massacre' (Massacre) and 'Televisão' (Television), by Titãs. Titãs are particularly in the spotlight in *Areias escaldantes*, but the film also features other Brazilian rock/pop bands, such as Metrô, Lobão e Os Ronaldos, and Capital Inicial. Retrospectively, *Areias escaldantes* can be regarded as a true cinematic inventory of the Brazilian pop-music scene in the 1980s. The film also features Brazilian musician Jards Macalé in the role of Macau, the rock star Lobão as Médio Moura, and the Brazilian filmmaker Neville de Almeida as 'the Spy'. As well as the abundant musical performances, *Areias escaldantes* had among its cast some key figures who straddled music and theatre. They were artists who had their careers launched by the theatre troupe Asdrúbal Trouxe o Trombone (Asdrúbal has Brought the Trombone), the 'young terrorists' Regina Casé as Verrô, Luiz Fernando Guimarães as Marcelo Matos and Diogo Vilela as Vini.[15] Regina Casé won the Best Supporting Actress Award from the APCA (São Paulo Academy of Art Critics) for her role in the film, and in its wake some of the aforementioned artists would enjoy successful careers in the advertising industry and TV, Casé, Guimarães and Vilela becoming core members of Guel Arraes and Cláudio Paiva's popular TV show *TV Pirata*, a major success aired by Globo from 1988 to 1992.

Like *Roberto Carlos em ritmo de aventura* and *O incrível mostro trapalhão*, *Areias escaldantes* benefited from the presence of its stars on television. The mid-1980s set the scene for the ascending art of music video, and nearly all of the singers and bands in de Paula's film had significant exposure on Brazilian television, mostly on the aforementioned variety show *Fantástico*, produced and broadcast by Globo from 5 August 1973 to today. Throughout the 1980s, musical numbers were one of the flagships of *Fantástico*, and every Sunday night the show presented music videos or acoustic concerts by national and international artists. Music stars took advantage of this audiovisual showcase to disseminate their new albums while newcomers saw an opportunity to make their first hit. The concerts were often directed by professionals from Globo, on the stage of the Phoenix Theatre.[16] Not only *Fantástico*, but a number of 1980s TV shows in Brazil featured rock or pop bands, such as Globo's *Clip-Clip* (1984), *Videoshow* (aired from 1983 to 2019) and *Mixto-Quente* (1986); Bandeirantes' *Super Special* (1985) and *TV da Tribo* (1989); Manchete's *FMTV* (1984) and *Milk-Shake* (1988); Cultura's *Fábrica do Som* (1983) and *Matéria-Prima* (1990); and TVE's *Som Pop* (1982) and *Cabeça Feita* (1988), among several others (Caminha 2010: 202).

It is worth noting that *Areias escaldantes* may well owe some of its status as a cult movie to radio. Likewise, bands such as Ultraje a Rigor and Titãs, as well as singers such as Lulu Santos, had a privileged window for their work on the soundtracks of Globo's soap operas, which produced some long-lasting hits also available on LP, cassette tape and later CD, by Globo's subsidiaries Som Livre and Globo Discos.

Concluding Remarks

Despite attempts to find cinema's alleged purity at different times in film history, an intermedial approach appears to be useful for a vast number of films, among them the three case studies in this chapter, *Roberto Carlos em ritmo de aventura*, *O incrível monstro trapalhão* and *Areias escaldantes*. Not only do these films feature intermedial characters and actors, but they can also be seen as representative of a moment in film history when television becomes the new hegemonic audiovisual medium, occupying the forefront of the Brazilian cultural industry. These three films straddle media borders for both commercial and cultural reasons: if, on the one hand, they respond at a cinematic level to the rise of a new media industry, on the other they capitalise on intermedial characters, and this fact has an impact on their own film language. By intermedial characters I mean, here, something perhaps a little more radical: these three films feature *intermedial* bodies: that is, artists whose own styles and skills condense a combination of media and artistic heritages. None of them was 'born' as a cinematic character. Instead, their cinematic birth coincides with the rise of television in Brazil, and the growth (from the late 1960s onwards) of the Globo Network, which became hegemonic with the blessing of the military dictatorship. Most artists in all these films owe much of their success to television, and mostly Globo. Thus the actor's body, perhaps more than any character per se, stands out as a key element in all the three films discussed in this chapter, as the link and intersection between cinema and other media – and one might wonder whether this is not the case with the bulk of Brazilian popular film production since the *chanchada*. The bodies of Roberto Carlos, Renato Aragão, Os Trapalhões and Os Titãs are not 'purely' cinematic bodies; they bear the gifts and marks from other arts and media. They are bodies that circulated across circus, vaudeville theatre, the music stage, radio and television before migrating to film.

I use the 'singer', the 'acrobats' and the 'band' as metaphors in the title and subheadings of this chapter because these terms not only stress body talents or body configurations, but also allude to three possible phases in the complex history of Brazilian cinema from an intermedial perspective. In all three films, the body, or we could even say the 'Brazilian body', endures and stands out as a privileged locale of authenticity. The pioneering success of a voice made audiovisual body (Roberto Carlos) paves the way for the success of a quartet of comedians (when television had already become hegemonic in the Brazilian mediascape). Finally, several voices turned into 'electronic flesh' (on TV) move on to film, as with the rock bands featured in *Areias escaldantes*. In terms of box office, Os Trapalhões occupy the peak as the most successful intermedial characters in film as compared to all others cited here. Today, the media industry's configuration in Brazil is rather different, as new media (the internet) and political factors have placed Globo's power and hegemony in jeopardy. Despite Globo's enduring power and the foundation of Globo Filmes in 1998, the company would struggle to produce cinematic phenomena such as *Roberto Carlos em ritmo de aventura* or *O incrível monstro trapalhão* today.

Therefore, these three films can be extremely revelatory of a certain era of Brazilian popular culture within a broader perspective that takes into account the constant exchanges, fluxes, intersections and overlaps which have been taking place in the Brazilian mediascape over the years. The histories of Brazilian cinema and television have, for decades, exposed a belligerent scenario, with 'film people' marking their territory against 'TV people' and vice versa. The fact remains, however, that many artists and technicians have migrated from film to TV and the other way around, at the rhythm of the market, and the same can be said about radio and film between the 1930s and 1950s. The creation of Ancine, the National Film Agency, in 2001 took into account the media convergence that gained momentum in the early 2000s, but up until now Brazil is still far from having an audiovisual industry that fully articulates film and television to get the best of these two worlds. Despite some positive developments, the gaps, setbacks and disputes involving these two realms remain. By the same token, Brazilian scholarship remains prone to isolate mediums, and little exchange seems to be the norm between film and media scholars as a whole. Yet, this chapter hopes to have done justice to ongoing changes on that front.

Notes

1. With hindsight, we might say that the shutdown of Embrafilme in 1990 is no longer the latest crisis in Brazilian cinema. We are now facing a similar, if perhaps even more drastic, dismantling of the Brazilian film industry and culture under the presidency of Jair Bolsonaro, in power since 1 January 2019.
2. The two other films in the trilogy, both also directed by Roberto Farias and starring Roberto Carlos, are *Roberto Carlos e o diamante cor-de-rosa* (*Roberto Carlos and the Pink Diamond*, 1970) and *Roberto Carlos a 300 km/h* (*Roberto Carlos at 300 Km/h*, 1972).
3. See <http://www.adorocinema.com/filmes/filme-136252/curiosidades/> (last accessed 28 December 2020).
4. '*Roberto Carlos em ritmo de aventura* tentava driblar as dificuldades para se realizar um produto bem confeccionado, devido às deficiências da produção nacional, utilizando a ironia da paródia, caminhando nas pegadas da chanchada, gênero do início da carreira de Roberto Farias. Mas também fugia do registro popular do puro divertimento, recheando a narrativa com o recurso da desconstrução e pitadas de erudição cinematográfica como a sequência em que o diretor do filme dentro do filme aparece girando e gritando, numa referência clara a Corisco na clássica sequência de *Deus e o diabo na terra do sol*.'
5. See <https://www.youtube.com/watch?v=dNJk-9TmnT4> (last accessed 28 December 2020).

6. The term 'iêiêiê', an example of onomatopoeia, was then used to refer to Brazilian rock'n'roll in the 1960s. It came from the English 'yeah, yeah, yeah', as in the lyrics of the Beatles song 'She Loves You'.
7. See, for example, the 'Café da manhã' (Breakfast) sketch, available at <https://www.youtube.com/watch?v=hpDXz98iPyQ> (last accessed 28 December 2020).
8. See <https://youtu.be/eLgXFbixYDY> (last accessed 28 December 2020).
9. See <https://www.youtube.com/watch?v=AMBuvP1026w> (last accessed 28 December 2020).
10. MPB is an acronym that stands for Música Popular Brasileira, or Brazilian Popular Music, a post-bossa nova trend in Brazilian popular music that revisits typical Brazilian styles such as samba, samba-canção, bossa nova, baião and other national or regional music styles and rhythms, occasionally combining these with foreign genres such as jazz or rock'n'roll. This movement is represented by a number of renowned Brazilian composers and performers, such as Elis Regina, Gal Costa, Maria Bethânia, Alceu Valença, Moraes Moreira, Rita Lee, Arnaldo Baptista, Wilson Simonal, Jair Rodrigues, Geraldo Vandré, Jorge Benjor, Ivan Lins, Belchior, Caetano Veloso, Gilberto Gil, Chico Buarque and many others, whose individual styles generated their own trends within the genre. The term MPB is also used to label any kind of music with Brazilian origins and 'voice and guitar style' that appeared in the late 1960s.
11. Information obtained via an email from Francisco de Paula, dated 22 February 2019.
12. Interestingly, another science fiction-inflected film benefiting from handmade illustrations would appear much later in 2014: Adirley Queirós's *Branco sai, preto fica* (*White Out, Black In*), whose final sequence relies on drawings by the artist Shockito.
13. 'O filme foi rodado em 30 dias, com duas horas de negativo 35mm. Quase tudo foi usado, e não houve take 2.' This and the other quotes in this paragraph were obtained via the same email message from Francisco de Paula, dated 22 February 2019.
14. 'A fotografia do filme, elenco, direção de arte, cenografia, figurinos, maquiagem, montagem e trilha sonora foram desenvolvidos de forma autêntica, em sintonia com o cinema independente da época.'
15. Led by Regina Casé and Hamilton Vaz Pereira, the theatre troupe Asdrúbal Trouxe o Trombone was founded in Rio de Janeiro in 1974. It revealed a new generation of young talent that left an indelible mark on Brazilian dramaturgy, especially on stage and in TV comedies. Under the influence of the British group Monty Python, Asdrúbal Trouxe o Trombone had, among its most famous members, actors Patrícia Pillar, Luiz Fernando Guimarães, Patrícia Travassos, Evandro Mesquita, Nina de Pádua, Cacá Dionísio, Cazuza and Gilda Guilhon. Diogo Vilela was not a member of the original group, but soon joined colleagues from the troupe in TV shows such as *TV Pirata*.
16. See <http://memoriaglobo.globo.com/programas/jornalismo/telejornais-e-programas/fantastico/fantastico-musicais-e-videoclipes.htm> (last accessed 28 December 2020).

References

Caminha, Mariana (2010), 'A teledramaturgia juvenil brasileira', in Ana Paula Ribeiro, Igor Sacramento and Marco Roxo (eds), *História da televisão no Brasil: do início aos dias de hoje*. São Paulo: Contexto, pp. 197–215.

Castro, Thell de (2015), 'Em 1976, Os Trapalhões ameaçaram o Fantástico e foram contratados pela Globo', *Notícias da TV por Daniel de Castro*, 12 October, available at <https://noticiasdatv.uol.com.br/noticia/televisao/em-1976-os-trapalhoes-ameacaram-o-fantastico-e-foram-contratados-pela-globo—9428?cpid=txt> (last accessed 8 August 2020).

Cesário, Lia Bahia (2010), 'Majors e Globo Filmes: uma parceria de sucesso no cinema nacional', in Mariarosaria Fabris, Gustavo Souza, Rogério Ferraraz, Leandro Mendonça and Gelson Santana (eds), *Estudos de cinema Socine*. São Paulo: Socine, pp. 135–49, available at <https://www.socine.org/wpcontent/uploads/2015/11/X_ESTUDOS_SOCINE_b.pdf> (last accessed 8 August 2020).

Moser, Sandro (2014), 'Quando Os Trapalhões eram os reis do cinema', *Gazeta do Povo*, available at <https://www.gazetadopovo.com.br/caderno-g/quando-os-trapalhoes-eram-os-reis-do-cinema-ebw6ow1z75q9cdsi1pr96g47i/> (last accessed 8 August 2020).

Ortiz Ramos, José Mário (2004), *Cinema, televisão e publicidade*. São Paulo: Annablume.

Suppia, Alfredo (2013), *Atmosfera rarefeita: a ficção científica no cinema brasileiro*. São Paulo: Devir.

CHAPTER 13

Gilda de Abreu's O Ébrio *as a Unique Intermedial Project*

Margarida Maria Adamatti

Released in 1946, Gilda de Abreu's *O Ébrio* (*The Drunkard*) is one of Brazil's biggest box-office hits of all time, reaching the mark of 8 million spectators by the end of that decade (Paiva 1989; Pizoquero 2006). Featuring Abreu's husband, the tenor Vicente Celestino, in the title role, *O Ébrio* resulted from a partnership between the couple and the production company Cinédia. The company was owned by Adhemar Gonzaga, filmmaker and editor of the famous magazine *Cinearte*, and was the first major Brazilian studio to be built on the industrial model of Hollywood. It produced Brazilian classics, such as *Ganga bruta* (*Rough Gang*, Humberto Mauro, 1933) and *Bonequinha de seda* (*Silk Little Doll*, Oduvaldo Vianna, 1936), as well as successful carnival comedies. The *O Ébrio* project satisfied Cinédia's key industrial demands, by consolidating Vicente Celestino's position in the star system, meeting the highest technical level in the hands of Brazil's top film professionals (including the experienced cinematographer Afrodísio de Castro) and paying back the major investment with popular acclaim.

The film's storyline revolves around the fortunes and misfortunes of Gilberto (Vicente Celestino). A voiceover introduces him as an impoverished medical student, wandering aimlessly through the streets of Rio de Janeiro, hungry and homeless. His relatives have turned their backs on him, yet, thanks to the help of a priest, he manages to win a musical contest and become a radio star. After graduating, Gilberto marries the opportunist nurse Marieta (Alice Archambeau), who flirts continuously with his cousin José (Rodolfo Arena). José seduces Marieta, with an eye on Gilberto's fortune, and persuades an accomplice, the dancer Lola (Júlia Dias), to pass herself off as Gilberto's lover. As a result of this set-up, Marieta leaves her husband for José, who steals her money and flees to the US, leaving her and Lola behind. In his despair after finding himself abandoned and betrayed by his wife, the doctor–singer swaps his identity with that of a recently deceased homeless man and goes back to roaming the streets, now as a drunkard. At the film's end, José's three victims meet at a dingy bar. Gilberto sings the film's theme song, telling the story of his life. On encountering Marieta, now penniless, he forgives her but decides to follow his own path, in solitude and poverty.

The film and its melodramatic story constitute one of the most successful intermedial projects in the history of the Brazilian entertainment industry, being, as it is, the result of transpositions across five different media over the space of thirty years: radio, theatre, cinema, literature and television. And yet, the film's intermedial trajectory has remained largely unexplored, even if this is in line with the scarce attention devoted to film's relationship with other media in dominant Brazilian cinema histories. However, when it comes to a film such as *O Ébrio*, which builds directly upon the different media of its previous versions, intermedial interaction cannot be ignored, as it is key to understanding the film's aesthetic features. The intermedial historiographic method is thus ideally suited to an analysis of this 'impure' film.

My use of 'impurity' draws on André Bazin's (1967) coinage of this term, which will serve here as the conceptual basis for an analysis of the mise-en-scène and scenic strategies deployed in *O Ébrio*. For Bazin, the 'impurity' of cinema, as observed in its propensity to usurp and commingle with other media, rather than detracting from film's aesthetic integrity, is part of the very 'evolution' of filmic language. While *O Ébrio* has often been taken as the work of a first-time director that simply adapted a successful play for the screen, my aim here will be to explore the ways in which Abreu, in her film, deliberately and explicitly resorted to formal devices from theatre and musical performances. Thus my goal is to explore the traces from other media, inherited from previous versions of the work, within the film's stylistic choices. To that end, I will draw on intermediality, understood as an 'in-between' space (Pethő 2011), defined by fluid and porous borders, in order to show how *O Ébrio* is situated at the interstices of other mediums. Accordingly, rather than on plot or narrative strategies, my focus will be on the film form.

While early studies of intermediality highlight the crossing between media, Pethő's concept of 'in-between', following up on Raymond Bellour's idea of the space 'between the images' (1997; 2012) in videoart, sheds light on the existence of liminal spaces through which such media cross-pollinate and interact. In his study, Bellour (2012: 7) reflects on the existence of multiple sites that serve as passages connecting otherwise disparate mediums, thus giving rise to a multiplicity of overlaps and largely unforeseen configurations. Broadly speaking, this description can be applied to the sites of exchange between theatre, music and cinema in *O Ébrio*: that is, to passages in which multiple overlaps between media appear more or less visible in a number of procedures, in particular framing, sound design, editing and an acting style inflected by the actors' theatrical and musical training. In order to address these features, my analysis will start by focusing on the intermedial career of the Celestino–Abreu couple and their involvement in different medial versions of *O Ébrio*. It will progress to an analysis of the final musical scene, looking at the porous borders between actor and character, documentary and fiction, and diegetic and non-diegetic sound. Finally, I will consider the contamination of Celestino by his acting persona, which changes intermediality into real life itself.

The Intermedial Trajectory of Abreu–Celestino

The main source of intermediality in *O Ébrio* is the eclectic career of the Vicente Celestino and Gilda de Abreu couple. Both started as singers, performing predominantly in operettas. In 1933, Abreu made her artistic debut in the operetta *Canção brasileira (Brazilian Song)*, at Rio de Janeiro's Teatro Recreio, alongside the already experienced singer Celestino (Pizoquero 2006).

Born into a humble family, Antonio Vicente Felippe Celestino began to sing in church choirs early on as a child. First discovered at a bar, where he flaunted his musical flair, Celestino reached fame in 1914 by singing the waltz hit *Flor do mal (Evil Flower)* at Teatro São José, in Rio, owned by film pioneer Pascoal Segreto (Guerra 1994). As early as the 1920s, Celestino's name flashed on the neon signs outside the *teatros de revista* (revue theatres) in Rio's Tiradentes Square, a privilege afforded only to those talents able to attract large audiences. However, Celestino's dream of making it to the opera, with all its artistic prestige, had to be abandoned for more profitable activities. And indeed, as a popular singer, he remained at the top of record charts for several decades in Brazil. His trajectory through music, theatre and radio was actually common to many artists of the time. According to José Ramos Tinhorão (1981), releasing songs simultaneously on radio and theatre was a widely adopted marketing strategy to ensure immediate success.

Gilda de Abreu was born in Paris. Her mother was a lyrical singer and her father a doctor and diplomat. She also began her singing career as a child, on her return at the age of ten to Brazil, where she performed at charity parties. Against her family's will, Abreu debuted professionally in the operetta *Canção brasileira* in 1933, and in that same year married her colleague Vicente Celestino. In addition to her singing and acting careers, she was also a writer of plays and radio soap operas. In 1936, she became a film star at the company Cinédia, thanks to her role as the protagonist in *Bonequinha de seda*.

If intermedial crossings had always defined the trajectory of these two artists, they reached a new height with the ambitious production of *O Ébrio*. This was kickstarted with the release, in 1935, of the song 'O Ébrio' by Celestino at Guanabara Radio; it was arguably the biggest hit of his career and was turned into a disc in the following year. The song was then adapted for the stage by Celestino himself, with the play, inspired by the song, running for nearly five months in 1941 and then being successively restaged until the 1960s at a number of theatres and circuses. With a view to capitalising on the success of the play, Cinédia's owner, Adhemar Gonzaga, invited Abreu to adapt *O Ébrio* as a film, which was released in 1946. A year later, another stage adaptation, updated to match the filmic version, was launched at theatres in São Paulo. The literary adaptation of *O Ébrio* (n.d.) was then carried out by Abreu in an eponymous book that filled in some of the gaps in the story as portrayed in film and on stage. Later, the hero's misadventures were followed up in a rocambolesque novel, *Alma de palhaço* (*Clown Soul*, n.d.), also by Abreu, as well as in a radio soap opera at Tamoios Radio in 1952, when the hero was finally granted a happy ending, though not before going through a series of sorrowful events and plot twists. Finally, the serial adaptation of *O Ébrio* arrived on television, at TV Paulista, in 1965–6, directed by José Castellar and Heloisa Castellar, who invited Celestino to sing the musical theme in the first episode.

Given its various medial transpositions, *O Ébrio* must be considered an integrated project, the result of Celestino and Abreu's collaborative work over decades. As such, it deserves a special place on the Brazilian entertainment scene for having deployed the protagonist's story over various mediums whilst taking advantage of both the affinities and the specificities of these mediums, without ever losing sight of their popular appeal. This resulted in a long-lasting and profitable commercial career for the project. Its culmination, the film *O Ébrio*, is part and parcel of the musicals and theatre adaptations that flooded Brazilian screens throughout the 1930s and 1940s (Vieira 1987). However, whereas the majority of the films produced consisted of comedies, *O Ébrio* relied on melodrama, a genre in which the story as a song and a theatre play, as well as a key element in Celestino's career itself, had already attained ample public recognition. Contrary to the Latin American melodramatic tradition, which revolves around female protagonists, *O Ébrio*'s plot centres on a male character. The most important female figure is not in the cast, but in the post of director. Abreu became, with *O Ébrio*, the second woman ever to direct a feature-length fiction film in Brazil, after Cleo de Verberena, who had previously directed *O mistério do dominó preto* (*The Mystery of the Black Domino*, 1930).

Porous Borders: Actor and Character, Documentary and Fiction

In addition to the intermedial journey that both preceded and succeeded it, *O Ébrio* bears the marks of other media within its form at key moments. For example, the opening scenes establish a dialogue with radio broadcasting. A voiceover typical of radio is accompanied by images that simply duplicate the information it conveys. Some musical scenes can likewise be linked to radio, a case in point being the scene where the pauper becomes a music star, his glory filmed in a simulated radio station auditorium, where he supposedly performs live, including shot-reverse shots of the audience. The presence of the audience grants the scene a documentary quality, especially when considered in relation to the self-reflexive, confident performance of Vicente Celestino, who capitalises on his persona as a singer and displays his characteristic gestures and looks. After his wedding to Marieta, the intermedial relationship with music and radio migrates to theatre. Marieta's birthday party takes place in a space that recalls the theatrical stage, as I have discussed elsewhere (Adamatti 2019). Here, there is a preference for the long take with few camera movements and a reduced use of cuts. By using long takes, the montage seeks to adhere to the complete duration of the scene, with frontal shots that evoke the perspective of a theatre audience and avoid the need of shot-reverse shot editing.

In the final scene, set in a bar, the film once again flirts with the music show, though no longer through radio; this time, it is through a reference to the theatrical performance, as the simulation of a live performance. The scene brings the film to a climax, as Celestino finally performs the film's theme song. It is here that the borders between media in the film become particularly blurred, forking and multiplying in a number of directions in relation to diegetic and non-diegetic sound, actor and character, fiction and documentary, and affecting camera angle, sound design and editing.

Wandering through the streets, Gilberto arrives at the Café da Paz, where he meets two rich couples who offer him a bottle of spirits if he tells them his life story. Gilberto then borrows a guitar from a group of musicians and goes on to sing the story of his life (Figures 13.1 and 13.2). This is the point at which the character of Gilberto, the drunk, starts to fade and Vicente Celestino, the star, starts to emerge. When Celestino drops the drawling and staggering walk of the drunk, a process of uncoupling from the character he is playing occurs. The tenor grows and prevails, singing with his famous 'chest voice', leaving the poor alcoholic behind and becoming the great star in the costume of his most famous character (Figures 13.3 and 13.4). The star-system register starts here, when the camera closes in on Celestino, who sings the melodramatic lyrics with non-diegetic orchestral accompaniment, as a means to draw in and move the audience.

A full transcription of the lyrics is now in order because they sum up the melodramatic style of the film and of many other songs recorded by Celestino, which narrate, always in the first person, the suffering of a kind-hearted man, betrayed and abandoned by his beloved woman and despised by everybody else (Guerra 1994).

O Ébrio *as a Unique Intermedial Project*

Figures 13.1 and 13.2 Gilberto (Vicente Celestino) borrows a guitar and plays to the audience in the bar scene.

The Drunkard[1]
I became a drunkard and with drinking I seek to forget
That ungrateful woman whom I loved and who abandoned me.
Stoned in the streets I live a life of suffering
With no home or kin, all is over . . .
Only in the taverns do I find shelter.
Each fellow in suffering is a great friend,
Though they have their plights, like me,
They give me advice and relieve my torment.
I have been happy and received as a nobleman.

Figures 13.3 and 13.4 Vicente Celestino as the drunkard and the replica of his costume at the Museu Vicente Celestino.

> I revelled in gold and slept in satin.
> I trusted my close friends
> And also trusted my relatives, certainly!
> Today, in my misery, I understand everything:
> The false home I loved and abandoned in tears.
> Each relative, each friend was a thief!
> They left me and stole what I loved.
> Fake friends, I ask and implore you, in tears:
> When I die, don't add inscriptions to my tombstone.

> Let the worms slowly consume
> This sad drunkard and this sad heart.
> I only wish that in the grave where I will rest
> Mad drunkards like me will come to deposit
> Their secrets in my last abode
> And their tears in my friendly chest.

Up until now, suspense has been created in the expectation of this song, the central element of the film. Therefore, sound design is reinforced to help create the climax. The merging of the diegetic singing with the extradiegetic orchestra does not follow to the letter Rick Altman's (1987) description of audio dissolve, according to which the diegetic sound volume grows until it merges with that of the non-diegetic orchestra. Rather, in *O Ébrio*, there are some inversions or simplifications of this scheme, as follows.

Whereas in a typical American musical words would gain momentum until they changed into singing, before the extradiegetic orchestra joined in, Celestino starts to sing immediately, together with the extradiegetic orchestra, with no transition. He attempts some chords on the guitar, but his action finds no support on the soundtrack. Some shots of Celestino plucking the guitar strings show him out of synch with the orchestra. Soon after, the orchestral sound is turned down, and as Celestino's voice rises, so does the orchestra. Throughout the song, the sound design tries to avoid emphasising the orchestra above the singer's voice; however, at the beginning, the orchestra deserves equal attention to his singing, contrary to Altman's scheme. Visually, the strong lighting on Gilberto's face is an attempt at effacing the tenor's signs of age, while his powerful voice contrasts starkly with his ragged outfit and degradation through alcohol and age. His neckerchief constitutes the key costume prop, as it had already been consecrated as the character's distinctive symbol on and off screen.

Because it draws so much on Celestino's singing attributes, his eruption in the scene causes the film to oscillate between fiction and documentary registers. His charisma is incorporated into the film plot and, as in Hollywood musicals, his character is adulated by the diegetic audiences as a kind of celebrity. There is ample use of shot-reverse shots in order to highlight the presence of the diegetic audience. The cuts and changes in camera angle multiply the points of view in the bar space, while Gilberto continues to sing. By retaining the quality of a documentary of the singer, this scene highlights the exact moment when the audience in the film becomes entranced with the making of a star.

As Gilberto changes from a tramp to a celebrity, we are shown the mesmerised faces of the audience, many of whom are children outside the bar, watching him from behind a fence, shown through a tracking shot

Figure 13.5   Mesmerised children watch Gilberto/Celestino's performance.

(Figure 13.5). Through a series of cuts, the film reiterates how the song affects the bar clientele indiscriminately: the wealthy, the drunks, other musicians, the children and even an elderly couple peeping from outside through the window. Because these extras were drawn from the populace, the documentary character of the event is emphasised. At the song's dramatic climax, when Gilberto talks about his imminent death and last wishes, the camera captures a little girl, sitting on the floor. With her chin resting on her hand, she continuously stares at the camera, thus breaking the fourth wall and further heightening the documentary quality of the scene (Figure 13.6).

The presence of children in this scene attempts to underline Gilberto's kindheartedness. A recurring trope in the film, it testifies to a calculated media strategy to associate Celestino's star persona with children. In order to highlight the character's honesty and benevolence, and even a certain innocence, Gilberto is repeatedly depicted surrounded by children. This resonates with Celestino's star persona in other mediums. Singing on radio or at open-air concerts, he was always surrounded by a young audience (Figure 13.7).

Through this interplay with Celestino's star image, the narrative reinforces the stereotypical depiction of the good man who chooses to be a doctor in order to help the needy, even operating for free on a girl with a leg disability at one point in the film. Depicted as somewhat gullible, at the beginning, he does not even know how to flirt. He supports his opportunist relatives, even after they refuse to help him when he needed it most. Through subtle visual procedures, Gilda de Abreu draws a parallel between Celestino, the tenor,

O Ébrio *as a Unique Intermedial Project* 237

Figure 13.6 A little girl sitting on the floor breaks the fourth wall as she stares at the camera, reinforcing the documentary dimension of the film.

Figure 13.7 Singing on the radio or at open-air concerts, Vicente Celestino was always surrounded by a young audience.

and the character of Gilberto. Celestino was famously philanthropic: he sang at charity concerts, visited hospitals and comforted people on their deathbed (Guerra 1994; Abreu 2003). His star persona was built around what Dyer (2004) defines as one of the pillars of stardom: the idea of authenticity. In this case, 'the actor intervenes [. . .] between the *authenticity* of his own life, of his own self and its past as known to himself [. . .] and the *authenticated* life of the character he is playing' (Dyer 2004: 21). Both sincerity and spontaneity are among the desirable qualities for propagating the charisma of a star through the notion of authenticity. In the case of Celestino, the construction of the star system is focused on the attribute of kindness and sincerity as the main component, whether or not these were part of his real self. To reinforce this image, Abreu (2003) romanticised some aspects of Celestino's life in her husband's biography, creating parallels between the character and Celestino's moral dilemmas off screen.

The interstitial spaces in *O Ébrio* across three media allow us to draw a parallel between the film and the concept of intermedial reference (Rajewsky 2005). It relates to the cases in which an aggregated medium seems to contain an illusion of the qualities of the previous support, as an evocation (2005). As Pethő (2011: 40) explains, citing Jürgen Müller, a film's hybridity is not due to its content, but to medial interactions and interferences at various levels. It is the spectator's role, as the receiving consciousness, to build up multiple layers of signification. If theatre is not directly involved in the film, it is present through allusion to the organisation of the scenic space, which is reminiscent of the actual theatrical scene. Far from mere imitation, it is the 'expansion of the modes of representation of the referred medium' (Rajewsky 2005: 15).

In short, this final scene could be seen as an affective symbiosis across media. If the film's existence depends intrinsically on the previous supports in which the story was told, this is not due to Abreu's lack of ability as an author, but to an intentional choice, closely connected with her theatrical trajectory.

O Ébrio's Intermedial Life

The power of *O Ébrio*'s story and Celestino's star persona, as disseminated by Gilda de Abreu, endured throughout the decades, both in the imaginary of the press, with related cartoons and short stories contributed by readers, and in the countless submissions of musical pieces entitled 'O Ébrio' to the federal censorship office between the 1960s and early 1980s, explicitly citing sections of the original song. Even when the serenade genre, with which Celestino was associated (Guerra 1994), had started to decline, in the 1960s, the concert at the launch of *O Ébrio* TV soap opera in Belo Horizonte attracted 25,000 fans to the América football stadium. According to the magazine *Intervalo* ('Único vício' 1965), the audience requested endless encores of the title song. Such requests were a common occurrence in Celestino's career. During film screenings in 1946, the audience often asked the projectionist to replay the final scene containing the title song (Gonzaga 1987). Travelling around the country with the film, Celestino actively participated in its dissemination and sang the song live at the end of the screenings.

Given the character's poverty, Celestino rejected the tie in favour of the neckerchief and the rags to publicise the film in 1946. Nearly twenty years after the film's launch, he would resort to the strategy of boarding a flight from Rio to São Paulo dressed as a rough sleeper, to participate in the first episode of the TV soap opera launched in 1965, thus playing out in real life the trajectory of the fictional alcoholic figure. Echoes in the press of this episode included the intoxicated appearance not only of Celestino, but also of Ricardo Nóvoa, the actor who played the drunkard on TV (Figure 13.8) and who reportedly was almost barred from boarding the flight ('O Ébrio' 1965).

This strategy was not new in Celestino's career; in tune with the star-system dynamics (Morin 1989), he had, as early as in 1919, paraded in the streets dressed as a tramp with the full cast of the theatre play *Flor da noite* (Oduvaldo Vianna), in order to attract the attention of the press to the underworld represented in the play (Abreu 2003; Pizoquero 2006). As a filmmaker, actress and her husband's empresario, Abreu exploited to their advantage the fusion between character and actor, even when it came to alcoholism, considered a serious social illness in the 1940s. To the press, she used to guarantee that her husband was a teetotaller and showed concern with a possible negative image of her husband and with being perceived as the cause of his addiction, for the portrayal and publicity of a drunkard she had helped to create. Nevertheless, the strategy undoubtedly contributed to increasing Celestino's fame.

To sum up, *O Ébrio* draws its life from the interstitial spaces between documentary and the fictional modes, and between actor and character, created by the mixture of media at its base. The film's narrative and stylistic strategies are geared towards the blurring of boundaries and the exploration of intermedial relations, a process that also affected its circulation, with Celestino's live presentations after the screenings. The intermedial approach adopted in this chapter allowed for an analysis of the film beyond the frontiers of cinema, by taking into account the interactions and interferences across different artistic and medial forms.

Masterfully juggling radio, theatre, the record industry and cinema, Vicente Celestino and Gilda de Abreu left their mark on Brazilian film history as one of the most cogent and enduring cases of an intermedial life.

Figure 13.8 Vicente Celestino and Ricardo Nóvoa (who plays the drunkard in the TV version of *O Ébrio*) board a flight dressed as alcoholic tramps.

Notes

1. *O Ébrio*

> 'Tornei-me um ébrio e na bebida busco esquecer
> Aquela ingrata que eu amava e que me abandonou.
> Apedrejado pelas ruas vivo a sofrer.
> Não tenho lar e nem parentes, tudo terminou . . .
> Só nas tabernas é que encontro meu abrigo.
> Cada colega de infortúnio é um grande amigo,
> Que embora tenham, como eu, seus sofrimentos,

Me aconselham e aliviam o meu tormento.
Já fui feliz e recebido com nobreza. Até
Nadava em ouro e tinha alcova de cetim
E a cada passo um grande amigo que depunha fé,
E nos parentes . . . confiava, sim!
E hoje ao ver-me na miséria tudo vejo então:
O falso lar que amava e que a chorar deixei.
Cada parente, cada amigo, era um ladrão;
Me abandonaram e roubaram o que amei.
Falsos amigos, eu vos peço, imploro a chorar:
Quando eu morrer, à minha campa nenhuma inscrição.
Deixai que os vermes pouco a pouco venham terminar
Este ébrio triste e este triste coração.
Quero somente que na campa em que eu repousar
Os ébrios loucos como eu venham depositar
Os seus segredos ao meu derradeiro abrigo
E suas lágrimas de dor ao peito amigo.'

References

Abreu, Gilda de (n.d.), *Alma de palhaço*. São Paulo: Cupolo.
Abreu, Gilda de (n.d.), *O Ébrio*. São Paulo: Cupolo.
Abreu, Gilda de (2003), *Minha vida com Vicente Celestino*. São Paulo: Butterfly.
Adamatti, Margarida Maria (2019), 'Esboços intermidiáticos sobre teatro e cinema no *Ébrio* de Gilda de Abreu', in M. M. Adamatti, C. Aguiar, D. Carvalho, L. Monteiro and M. Villaça (eds), *Cinema, estética, política e dimensões da memória*. Porto Alegre: Sulina, pp. 63–78.
Altman, Rick (1987), *The American Film Musical*. Bloomington: Indiana University Press.
Bazin, André (1967), *What Is Cinema? Volume 1*, ed. Hugh Gray. Berkley, Los Angeles and London: University of California Press.
Bellour, Raymond (1997), *Entre-imagens: foto, cinema, vídeo*. Campinas: Papirus.
Bellour, Raymond (2012), *La Querelle des dispositifs – cinéma, installations, expositions*. Paris: P.O.L. Trafic, available at <http://flipbook.cantook.net/?d=%2F%2Fwww.edenlivres.fr%2Fflipbook%2Fpublications%2F143056.js&oid=16&c=&m=&l=fr&r=http://www.pol-editeur.com&f=pdf> (last accessed 9 April 2021).
Celestino, Vicente (1941), *O Ébrio*. Rio de Janeiro: Biblioteca Nacional.
Celestino, Vicente (1947), *O Ébrio*. São Paulo: Arquivo Miroel Silveira.
Dyer, Richard (2004), *Stars*. London: British Film Institute.
Gonzaga, Alice (1987), *50 anos de Cinédia*. Rio de Janeiro: Record.
Guerra, Guido (1994), *Vicente Celestino, o hóspede das tempestades*. Rio de Janeiro: Record.
Morin, Edgar (1989), *As estrelas – mito e sedução no cinema*. Rio de Janeiro: José Olympio.
'O Ébrio chega a São Paulo ganhando esmola' (1965), *Intervalo*, 146, pp. 20–1.
Paiva, Salvyano Cavalcanti de (1989), *História ilustrada dos filmes brasileiros*. Rio de Janeiro: F. Alves.
Pethő, Agnés (2011), *Cinema and Intermediality – The Passion for the In-between*. Newcastle-Upon-Tyne: Cambridge Scholars Publishing.

Pizoquero, Lucilene Margarete (2006), *Cinema e gênero: a trajetória de Gilda de Abreu (1904–1979)*. Campinas: Instituto de Artes, Unicamp.

Rajewsky, Irina (2005), 'Intermediality, Intertextuality, and Remediation: A Literary Perspective on Intermediality', *Intermédialités*, 6, pp. 43–64.

'Único vício de Celestino é ser ídolo eterno' (1965), *Intervalo*, 154, pp. 22–3.

Vieira, João Luiz (1987), 'A chanchada e o cinema carioca (1930–1955)', in F. Ramos (ed.), *História do cinema brasileiro*. São Paulo: Art Editora, pp. 131–87.

Tinhorão, José Ramos (1981), *Música popular – do gramofone ao rádio e TV*. São Paulo: Ática.

CHAPTER 14

Chanchada, *Samba and Beyond: From the Cinema of Radio to the Cinema of Television (1930s–1960s)*
João Luiz Vieira

This chapter will address the role of Brazilian popular music, specifically of certain generic samba forms, focusing on how their screen adaptations were inflected by a double process of cross-mediation.[1] It will demonstrate how cinema reconfigured Brazilian music via its intermedial connections with staged modes of production, representation and consumption, including radio auditoriums, casinos, nightclubs and other entertainment spaces, thereby incorporating audiences as part of the film's diegesis. Brazilian cinema, radio and television will be investigated in their many forms of interaction, from the moment synchronised sound was first introduced into Brazilian cinema until the late 1950s, when television gradually became the most popular form of audiovisual contact with audiences around the world.

Traditionally, there is a tendency among Brazilian film historians to subordinate musical comedies to the radio, in particular the *filmusical* of the 1930s and the *chanchadas* of the 1940s and 1950s. The same derivative approach has been more recently applied to contemporary Brazilian mainstream film production, with expressions such as 'a cinema of television' (*um cinema de televisão*), to justify the popularity of what has been defined as *neo-chanchadas* or *Globo chanchadas*, the latter term drawn from the dominant sitcoms produced by the Globo TV broadcasting network, which will not be covered here. Granted, narrative mainstream cinema has always been derivative. It has inherited, absorbed, shaped its forms and become popular in dialogue with amusement parks, circuses, vaudeville and theatre, among other forms of entertainment, as well as with other arts. Hence, I have opted in this chapter for a cross-media approach.

I will explore the period between the mid-1930s and the arrival of sound, and the late 1950s, when the traditional *chanchada* genre started to face the competition of other Brazilian film genres. Here it is important to note that the *chanchada* had a longer life than has been commonly assumed, having survived until the mid 1960s, when it coexisted with the more progressive, aesthetically provocative and politically committed films of the Cinema Novo movement, then at its peak.

In the first decade of the twentieth century, Brazilian cinema had a very brief period of visibility within its burgeoning internal market, known to some Brazilian film historians – notably Vicente de Paula Araújo, who coined the term, and Paulo Emilio Salles Gomes – as a sort of Golden Age, or 'Bela Época'. It was then superseded by European cinema and, later, Hollywood. For several years, Latin America became a major film consumer market, with Hollywood providing most of the entertainment fare. As in other Latin American countries, Brazilian filmmakers had to wait for the arrival of sound in order to envision the possibility of developing their own national cinema, by resorting to the power of their native language, Portuguese, or Spanish in the case of the rest of Latin America. In these countries, as elsewhere in the world, cinema became synonymous with classical Hollywood fiction film, which was posited as a 'universal' lingua franca and internalised by filmmakers, exhibitors, critics and spectators alike, though, of course, not without some degree of negotiation and resistance.

In the face of foreign domination, the visible presence of Brazilian cinema was mainly guaranteed in the post-sound era by the production of musical comedies. The first *filmusicais* were pioneered by the Cinédia Studios and Sonofilmes, among other less famous production companies. They were later pejoratively labelled as *chanchadas*, becoming the most popular genre ever produced in Brazil and, as I claim, the only true genre developed and consolidated in Brazilian cinema.

A derogatory epithet of controversial origin, meaning 'something of little value', the term *chanchada* was adopted by hostile mainstream film critics with reference to a body of films made between the mid-1940s and the mid-1960s. Although these films underwent formal changes through the decades, they usually featured comic plots, often (though not exclusively) interspersed with musical numbers that frequently disrupted the coherence and predictability of the storyline. Such a tendency was even more prevalent in the mid-1930s *filmusicais*, in which loosely connected narrative scenes were employed first and foremost as a pretext for the inclusion of hit musical numbers. Therefore, an intermedial approach seems ideally placed to allow us to understand properly the prevalence and popularity of the musical genre in Brazilian cinema. First, however, it is necessary to contextualise what I am calling a derivative *cinema of radio*.

A Cinema of Radio and Performance

The first dominant mode of the musical genre in Brazilian cinema, throughout the 1930s, was the revue film—or *filmusical*, a term which combines different media and immediately brings to mind the Hollywood matrix of the backstage musical, in which the narrative centred on the preparation of either a radio or a stage show. *Filmusicais* were, from their inception, linked to the world of radio and vaudeville and the then promising and ever-growing record/phonographic industry. Two classic titles from the beginning of the sound period in Brazil acknowledge the presence of and recognise the debt to radio: *Alô, alô, Brasil* (*Hello, Hello, Brazil*, Wallace Downey, João de Barro and Alberto Ribeiro, 1935) and *Alô, alô, carnaval* (*Hello, Hello, Carnival*, Adhemar Gonzaga, 1936). Both films allude to the common salutation by radio speakers to their audience.

Both *filmusicais* and *chanchadas* are linked to the large universe of carnival. Like carnival, they incorporate the social inversions and an implicit social critique of Brazilian society, which, in turn, projects a world whose utopian horizon appears upside down. According to Richard Dyer's (1993: 273) seminal argument, in his influential analysis of the musical genre, Hollywood musicals promise a utopian world through music, rhythm and camerawork, responding to certain necessities of the real world. In the universe of the *chanchada*, however, an idealistic vision of Brazil's relationship with Hollywood (and, by extension, the First World) might be constructed via inversions within the narrative plots. In general, *chanchadas* express the belief and desire that one day Brazil could be a great and better country.

Culture, and especially music, contaminated this popular genre with a strong feeling of joy and hope. The on-screen presence of marginal characters drawn from daily urban life offered a means of identification for the urban masses, who flocked into the cinemas. During three consecutive decades, from the 1930s to the 1950s, thousands of people in Brazil migrated from the countryside to the big cities, spurred on by the nationalist wave of industrialisation initiated by President Getúlio Vargas, in the early 1930s. This migration was further boosted by the developmentalist programmes implemented by President Juscelino Kubitschek, in the 1950s. It was also a time when going to the movies was a truly democratic habit, thanks to the proliferation of cinemas providing affordable entertainment for all audiences. The *chanchadas* succeeded in constructing a powerful imaginary dispositif for the working classes, who could now look at the elites in the movies with disdain. Previously seen as indicative of domination in their sophistication and cosmopolitanism, in these films they became the object of laughter and parody, key devices in the *chanchadas*.

Brazil's carnival traditions are among the most important elements in terms of cultural identification. In fact, the carnivalesque discourse permeates Brazilian cinema from its inception, from the first 'views' of Rio at the turn of the century, incorporating music and dance, up to Glauber Rocha's revolutionary Cinema Novo films, such as *Terra em transe* (*Entranced Earth*,

1967) and his last feature, *A idade da Terra* (*The Age of the Earth*, 1980), not to mention tacit allusions to carnival via music or costume, or carnivalesque strategies of inversion. It is worth noting that the very word 'carnival' figures prominently in the titles of a disproportionate number of Brazilian films, from early views such as *O carnaval de 1908 no Rio de Janeiro* (*1908 Carnival in Rio*) to the yearly film series of *carnavais cantados* (*Sung Carnivals*) from 1918 onwards. More than a strong cultural presence, the carnivalesque discourse, in different guises, informs, defines, structures and names an array of musical films and *chanchadas* from the sound era. These include the aforementioned *Alô, alô, carnaval* (1936), as well as *Carnaval no fogo* (*Carnival in Flames*, Watson Macedo, 1949), *Carnaval Atlântida* (*Carnival Atlântida*, José Carlos Burle, 1952), *Carnaval em Caxias* (*Carnival in Caxias*, Paulo Vanderley, 1953), *Carnaval em lá maior* (*Carnival in A Flat*, Adhemar Gonzaga, 1955), *Carnaval em Marte* (*Carnival in Mars*, Watson Macedo, 1955) and *Depois do carnaval* (*After Carnival*, Wilson Silva, 1959). It continues after the *chanchada* into the 1960s and beyond, with *Carnaval barra limpa* (*Groovy Carnival*, J. B. Tanko, 1967), *Carnaval de assassinos* (*Carnival of Murders*, Robert Lynn, 1969) the more experimental and independent work of Cinema Marginal director Rogério Sganzerla, with *Carnaval na lama* (*Carnival in the Mud*, 1970), and *Quando o carnaval chegar* (*When Carnival Comes*, Carlos Diegues, 1972), reaching the 1980s cycle of soft- and hard-core films such as *Carnaval das taras* (*Fetish Carnival*, Roberto Machado, 1983) and *Carnaval do Sexo* (*Sexy Carnival*, Nilton and Carlos Nascimento, 1986). From the late 1930s all the way to the early 1960s, a vast proportion of musical films were not only released just before carnival but especially produced to promote carnival songs. Some were even designated as *filmes carnavalescos*, or carnivalesque films.

The first successful sound film shown in Rio de Janeiro was *Broadway Melody* (Harry Beaumont, 1929), premiered at the Cine Palácio in the Cinelândia district, central Rio, in June 1929. It introduced Brazilians to the New York backstage through a lively portrait, centred on two sisters who want to work on Broadway but find romance instead. This plot was a narrative pretext for the insertion of several musical numbers, a pattern that was so successful that it was soon incorporated into Brazilian stage practices, such as the revue theatre, the vaudeville and the comic circus performances. The film also fed on the popularity of both the radio and the promising new phonographic industry, still in its infancy. This film inspired what is considered to be the first commercially successful Brazilian talkie, *Coisas nossas* (*Our Things*, Wallace Downey, 1931). This is also a foundational film in terms of how it established the interaction between cinema and other media practices connected with popular Brazilian music. Downey, a Columbia record company executive, was sent to Brazil in 1928 to identify business opportunities in the country's fertile musical scene, and, perhaps by accident, ended up introducing parody as a key feature of the *chanchadas*. In *Coisas nossas*, Downey presented a man singing in the shower mimicking the song *Singin' in the Rain*, performed by Cliff Edwards in *The Hollywood Revue* (Charles Reisner, 1929), a hit at that time. *Coisas nossas* also made the pages of *Cinearte*, a film magazine which was published from 1926 to 1942, modelled on the US magazine *Photoplay* in both content and form. An advert boasted patriotic pride associated with the production of a national cinema: 'Our customs, our music, our songs, our artists! A Brazilian film, a talkie, a musical, made here in Brazil!' (Cinearte 1931: 4). Though *Coisas nossas* was produced in São Paulo, it was in Rio that film musicals would thrive, for Rio was at that time not only the country's capital but also a Mecca for the interplay of music and film practices, as well as for the fusing and crossing of those two burgeoning media.

The advent of sound was instrumental for the visibility of already popular singers, as well as for the recording of the rich heritage of samba. It also permitted the showcasing on film of other popular musical genres not only from Rio and other urban areas, such as the *marchinhas* or sambas-*canções*, but also of regional musical expressions such as *baiões* and *frevos* from the northeast, among other rhythms, related or not to the universe of carnival. The merging of cinema and Brazilian popular music during the 1930s–1950s period was a guarantee of the regular presence and survival of Brazilian cinema in its own market. In addition, it underlined the strength, quality and vigour of the dawn of the rich cross-pollination and dynamic interplay between film, music and other media practices, whether designed to overtake foreign competition or to be an aesthetic proposition in itself.

Cinédia, considered the first film studio in the country to bear the definition of a real studio, capitalised on carnival and made its first sound film in the form of a semi-documentary entitled *A voz do carnaval* (*The Voice of Carnival*, Adhemar Gonzaga and Humberto Mauro, 1933). It was the first Brazilian feature to use movietone technology, a fact advertised in its publicity ('the first film in Brazil to record the real sounds of carnival'). In addition, it also launched the strategy of making the film release coincide with the carnival festivities, which, for the next two decades, would prove to be very successful in promoting songs and selling records. Interspersed with the songs and a very tenuous fictitious plotline shot in studio, *A voz do carnaval* included documentary footage of parades, confetti battles and revellers of all sorts and groupings, dancing and partying on the streets and in the clubs of Rio. It also included two musical numbers by a twenty-three-year-old Carmen Miranda, performing from the Mayrink Veiga radio station. Carmen already was a top-billing radio star, the most successful female singer in Brazil, then making her second screen appearance.

This combination of sound and image proved to be very fruitful and Cinédia, either independently or in co-productions, launched a series of musicals that supported the studio and motivated the production of a wide variety of films. Besides the carnivalesque films, Cinédia also ventured into the production of melodramas, costume comedies, literary adaptations, documentaries and newsreels. But those two major successes, *Alô, alô, Brasil* and *Alô, alô, carnaval* were instrumental in defining a foundational aesthetic for the first Brazilian *filmusicais*. Both are the result of a creative use of sound, made possible by the widespread popularity of Brazilian music and its most famous performers. They testify to the centrality of radio as an intermedial backbone of an incipient film industry in the face of the hegemonic presence of the American film, which, as a product, was then easily consumed in English, thanks to the use of Portuguese subtitles.

Displaying in their musical numbers a complete who's who of the first Brazilian radio singers, together with short humorous sketches, these two films and others – such as *Estudantes* (*Students*, Wallace Downey, 1935), a co-production between Cinédia and Waldow Films – were able to amplify the limited spaces of radio auditoriums, recording studios and even the larger settings of Rio casinos, nightclubs and theatre backstages.

As well as drawing on the creative and cultural power of carnival, Cinédia also ventured into other musical forms, including romantic tunes and the folk songs of the *festas juninas*—popular Catholic festivals held in June and devoted to Saints John, Anthony and Peter. At any given time of the year, the most visible form of Brazilian sound film was unabashedly transformed into a vehicle for monthly record releases and radio promotions, at a time when radio was beginning to gain wide access to homes, penetrating and inflecting popular culture in sprawling urban environments. These first *filmusicais* obviously found a ready-made cast of actors and performers amongst Brazil's radio stars, whose established appeal and popularity resulted in huge box-office draws. In addition to Carmen Miranda, other key names from that early convergence between cinema, radio, casinos and vaudeville included Miranda's sister, Aurora, Mário Reis, Aracy de Almeida, Francisco Alves, Irmãs Pagãs (the Pagan Sisters), comedians including Mesquitinha and Barbosa Júnior, and famous composers such as Alberto Botelho, João de Barro and Noel Rosa, among many others. Of course, the public responded well to the comic plots but those films' main appeal relied on their musical numbers. Even considering today's audiences, whenever *Alô, alô, carnaval* is shown in its pristine 35mm restored version, it is always and unsurprisingly a guaranteed success. The first Brazilian *filmusicais* therefore testify to a period when the plot was of little relevance to most audiences, whose major interest was in the musical numbers, widely promoted in the run-up to carnival, and whose list of songs was advertised widely. A large number of those songs became instant classics of the Brazilian popular songbook. Equally importantly, they promoted the feeling that spectators around the country were watching a musical live show broadcast directly from the stage of a radio station in Rio, fulfilling a ready-made cinema audience's longing to see their idols on screen.

CARMEN MIRANDA AND THE INTERMEDIAL BODY

Through these *filmusicais*, and especially the performance of some of their stars, the mediums of film and radio became inextricably connected. In the specific example of Carmen Miranda, the dynamics of music also contributed to liberate film from the then prevailing fixed and static camera position, as I explain below. It is argued that *Alô, alô, carnaval*, for example, contains a record of twenty-three musical numbers interspersed in the story of two adventurers trying to succeed in Rio. These scoundrels want to persuade a show-business impresario to produce and stage one of their revue shows at the fictitious Cassino Mosca Azul (Blue Fly Casino), in reality the sophisticated Cassino Atlântico, located at the far end of Copacabana beach, where some scenes of the film were actually shot. In her third appearance in film, Carmen already flaunts the performance style she would later import to Hollywood and would make her the first successful transnational (and *translatina*) Brazilian film celebrity. In *Alô, alô, carnaval*, Carmen performs two numbers. The first is a solo sequence in which she sings a carnival *marchinha* titled 'Querido Adão' (Dear Adam, 1936), by Benedito Lacerda and Oswaldo Santiago. The song was recorded on 26 September 1935, but only released to coincide with the film's premiere on 20 January 1936, at the Alhambra Theatre in Rio, again testifying to the commercial partnership between cinema and the recording industry. The second song is 'Cantoras do rádio' (Radio Singers, 1936), by Lamartine Babo, João de Barro and Alberto Botelho. In both numbers, Carmen Miranda seems to *embody* intermediality, as she mixes comedic elements from radio shows, vaudeville and the revue theatre. These are further combined with her particular way of singing a syncopated melody: speeding up the lyrics while exaggerating the specific pronunciation of the *rrrs* (as in *serpente*, serpent), which was meant to provide a comic commentary on the linguistic skills of the highly educated. In this sense, Carmen's exaggerated diction performs a self-conscious rewriting of different media, simultaneously reworking and incorporating into film traditions derived from more established media, such as theatre and radio. I have always had the impression that she is making fun of the stylised pompous theatrical pronunciation and declamatory style of Rio's and Brazil's classical theatre, as well as certain dramatic radio transmissions at the time when sound was being introduced in film. The 'Rs' had to be pronounced 'correctly' and Carmen is conscious of that. If this suggestion is true, she is transposing to film the same impulse of ridiculing 'high culture' in perfect symmetry with the popular roots of the revue theatre of which she was so fond, though she had never tried it herself.

By the mid-1930s, in Brazilian cinema, a time when musical performances and camera movements entailed a number of difficulties for sound recording, Carmen seemed to be always aware of the kinetic powers of cinema. During her brief film career in Brazil, she was already exploiting to the maximum the possibilities offered by framing when she appears in close-ups and medium shots, drawing the spectator's attention almost exclusively to herself. At a time when cameras seldom moved, remaining static for the most part, in long or medium shots of the performers, Carmen, as other singers, was probably given directions not to move around the stage so as to facilitate the shooting. However, as identified by Lisa Shaw (2013), she seems unable to resist the pleasure she derives from performing, moving from side to side, taking small steps in time with the music and forcing the cameraman to move with her. Her control of hand gestures with arms permanently in motion, together with her animated facial expressions, conveys contagious enthusiasm. Her self-awareness is apparent in the precision of her expression and movements, eyes wide open at specific moments suggested by the innuendo of the lyrics, glancing up and down, left to right and vice versa. At key points during the lyrics of 'Querido Adão', Carmen deliberately looks straight into the camera as if to address the spectator directly, creating a sense of complicity that would have been impossible with radio's remote listeners. Her facial expressions and hand gestures were imported from the live shows on the stages of the revue theatre, casinos and radio stations, with which she was very familiar. However, they were reworked via the intermedial fusion she was aware of, while performing. In its duration of two minutes and forty-one seconds, 'Querido Adão' sums up Carmen's performance, which is rich with innuendos, wide smiles, winking at the right times to expand the meaning of the lyrics and in total control of, and involvement with, the spectator. The humorous content of the song, in turn, launches a tone that will be embraced later on by the *chanchadas*. For example, in the second part of the song, she opens her arms and hands to emphasise Adam's original sin, as the lyrics say: *but in turn, your poor heart/which was poor, very poor of love/has grown and eternalised, my Adam,/your enchanting sin.* The sin eternalised refers to Adam's heart and emphasises Adam's original sin, tempted by the serpent, an obvious reference to the male organ.

Carmen Miranda's box-office appeal and star status mirror a successful and timely combination of cross-media references. She seemed to be the right performer at the right time, when the 1930s witnessed the rise of radio, the record industry and talking cinema in Brazil, thus summing up a veritable intermedial career. A few years later, in Hollywood, she would again be the right performer in the context of the growing impact and popularity of Technicolor films. She was able to cross any medial borders with total ease, as evidenced by her cinematic performance of 'Querido Adão' and other songs.

Three other actors deserve to be mentioned here in terms of their intermedial bodies: Oscarito, Ankito and Carequinha. The first two have already received a great deal of scholarly praise and recognition. This is especially the case with Oscarito, whose success as a comic performer stemmed from his background in the circus and his aptitude for physical clowning. His facial features, with special emphasis on his mouth, cheeks and nose, recalled the contours of the classic clown mask. Oscarito excelled at slapstick and visual humour, as can be seen in highly memorable *chanchadas*, either performing parodies such as a grotesque Latina *rumbeira* (rumba dancer) in *Aviso aos navegantes* (*Calling All Sailors*, Watson Macedo, 1950) or a serious professor of Greek Philosophy dancing mambo in *Carnaval Atlântida*, or, again in drag, imitating the affected manners of Madame Gaby (Eva Todor) in front of a fake mirror in *Os dois ladrões* (*The Two Thieves*, Carlos Manga, 1960).

Ankito, also from a circus family background (the son of famous clown Faísca and nephew of Brazilian clown master Piolim), moved from the circus to the stage of the Urca Casino, in Rio, at the age of eighteen. There he began his successful career, first as an athletic acrobat and then as comedian at the revue theatre. From 1952 onwards he adds film to his intermedial career and is successful in deploying his dynamic and malleable body to hilarious effect in many *chanchadas* during that decade.

However, the less famous Carequinha (real name George Savalla Gomes), although as important as the other two, is still in need of further attention. His emblematic persona as a performer coming straight from the circus subverts what had so far been considered the traditional trajectory of *chanchada* stars. I will return to him in the next section.

An Intermedial Negotiation with Television

By the end of the 1950s, television in Brazil (Rio, São Paulo and a few other state capitals) was finally booming. Inaugurated on 18 September 1950, first in São Paulo and then, on 20 January 1951, in Rio, it was a very elitist medium throughout most of the decade, with only a small percentage of the population able to own television sets. As Rodrigo Ricardo remarks, however, that situation changed as the decade advanced, with television losing its 'novelty for the wealthy' and becoming a household item, thanks to the mass-produced Invictus sets in the country. By the end of the decade, for example, television sets were common wedding presents.

In the 1950s, in Brazil and elsewhere, cinema was significantly impacted by the introduction of the new medium of television. It brought about an excitement with the new technology that, for the first time, competed with the novelty of film technology itself. Interestingly, however, the *chanchada* confronted this competition head on, by weaving it into its parodic style. As early as 1951, the presence of television makes its debut in the *chanchada Barnabé tu és meu* (*Barnabé You're Mine*, José Carlos Burle) as a novelty item in the living room of a scientist for whom Barnabé (Oscarito) works as janitor. The opening sequence begins with an establishing long shot of what could be the proverbial stage of a nightclub, as in many *chanchadas* before. The *rumbeira* Cuquita Carballo dances and sings the rumba 'A romper el coco' (Breaking the Coconut) by Otílio Portal with the Ruy Rey Orchestra. A cut takes us to the living room, where the scientist and the janitor are standing, watching the erotically charged rumba transmitted by a television set. Then another cut reveals that the characters and us, the spectators, are watching the musical number from the small screen of the TV set. Barnabé, a few steps behind his boss, is overtly excited, enjoying the transmission and moving his feather duster to the rhythm of the rumba in an explicit associative link between the feathers of the duster and the feathers of the *rumbeira* costume. The musical number shown on TV seems to be performed in the adult space of a nightclub or in a cinema featuring a *chanchada*, but here it is now available at home, for the pleasure of domestic spectators, who watch the spectacle standing. Suddenly, due to a technical problem, the televised transmission is interrupted and a close-up of a simple cartoon-like announcement within the frame of the TV set informs us that 'alguma coisa está errada! Voltaremos dentro de poucos minutos' ('something went wrong! We will be back in a few minutes'). In 1951, *Barnabé tu és meu* is quick in exposing the immediacy of TV transmission in real time, one of the most notable achievements of the new technology. In frontal opposition to film, the recurrent announcement, disrupting the televised audiovisual experience, evidences teething problems typical of the early period of television in Brazil and elsewhere. However, *Barnabé tu és meu*, the film, continues being projected to the non-diegetic spectators on the screen of the cinemas, signalling a technical superiority over the new medium.

Seven years later, the clown Carequinha, already a circus star, comes to film after a successful career on television, which started in 1950. *Carequinha's Circus* was his weekly show, popular with children, in which he paired with his partner Fred, another clown. Together, they pioneered circus on television. Both appear in a musical number of the *chanchada É de chuá* (*It's Super*, Victor Lima, 1958), which I consider a quintessential example of the impure nature of cinema discussed here. Its simple narrative of mistaken identities presents a couple of bizarre petty burglars, who dress up to sneak into a high-society party in order to steal a collection of jewels. At the party, out of nowhere, an MC on an improvised stage, painted to recall a radio studio, complete with a fake microphone, announces the presence of 'the greatest singer of the moment, Carequinha', who delivers the most famous *marchinha* of the 1958 carnival, 'Fanzoca de rádio' (Radio Fan, by Miguel Gustavo). The lyrics and its bizarre, almost surrealistic mise-en-scène, at an improbable high-society party in Rio, make fun of the radio star craze. This is demonstrated by an uncontrollable fan, who, according to the disparaging lyrics, spends her day listening to the radio and browsing the weekly illustrated magazine *Revista do Rádio* – the reason why 'ninguém arranja uma empregada' ('nobody gets a maid'). Carequinha sings the song in his traditional clownish manner among a group of dancers and to the accompaniment of a small orchestra. The woman in question repeatedly pretends to faint, holding an issue of *Revista do Rádio*, while Carequinha performs to the camera his signature somersault routine. The whole sequence demonstrates an awareness of mediation with a mobile juxtaposition defined by a space (a stage) on which the disposition and interplay of different media practices have been detached from their original contexts, to be recombined in a new form. The number materialises intermediality at its best in its polysemic interaction, mixture and contamination of circus, television, radio and cinema, as well as the illustrated press, all interacting simultaneously across different social classes.

Quem roubou meu samba (*Who Stole My Samba*), directed by José Carlos Burle, also dated 1958, emerges in the context of that specific intermedial convergence in Brazilian cinema, when radio and the record industry were still powerful and dominant media (Figure 14.1). That was about to change, however, as television was gradually working its way up to become the dominant medium in the country. Filmed during the decline of the *chanchada*, the film's main intertextual interlocutor was not Hollywood, as had been the case in countless *chanchadas* before, but Brazilian cinema: namely, the second feature film by director Nelson Pereira dos Santos, *Rio, Zona Norte* (*Rio Northern Zone*, 1957). Together with his landmark *Rio, 40 graus* (*Rio 40 Degrees*, 1955), dos Santos prefigured the arrival of Cinema Novo with his post-neorealist aesthetics and themes. In a detailed comparative reading of both *Quem roubou meu samba* and *Rio, Zona Norte*, Lisa Shaw (2007) points to the similarities between the two films. She explains that *Quem roubou meu samba* was not a conventional parody in the sense that, although it engaged in a dialogue with

Figure 14.1 Newspaper advert for the *chanchada Quem roubou meu samba* (1958), which was shown across twenty cinemas in Rio de Janeiro in advance of the 1959 carnival.

a recently released Brazilian film, it did not aspire to benefit from the fame or the box-office success of dos Santos's film, which was a commercial failure. The narrative of Burle's *chanchada* simply borrowed an idea from dos Santos's film about the common practice of fake songwriting partnerships within the universe of the popular music industry. In the plot, songs written by illiterate black composers from the favelas (shantytowns) are stolen by two unscrupulous and exploitative, middle-class white men who work for the music industry. However, despite some similarities, Shaw points out that Burle rather tastelessly trivialised its plot for popular audiences, despite efforts (on his and screenwriter Alinor Azevedo's part) to invest the *chanchada* tradition with social and racial concerns and thus reinvent or update the genre as the competition with television increased. Two excerpts from *Quem roubou meu samba* are of particular interest here, by way of conclusion.

The film starts with an extended long take of a radio station recording studio, where a record is being cut. The opening cast and crew credits are superimposed over the image of the actual manufacturing of a master being recorded directly on a record-cutting machine. It is an obvious stance of reflexivity that is not unusual in the *chanchada*. Although music had had such an emblematic presence in the genre, the actual material production of music is shown here for the first time, in a documentary-like style. Here the viewer is offered a privileged insight into the combination of three mediums – film, radio and the record industry – in a celebration of the labour behind them: the opening credits are superimposed over a close-up of a vinyl master being cut, followed by the actual work of two technicians handling and controlling the recording machines in the radio studio. His work is interspersed with the performance of the samba 'Você foi porque quis' (You Went There Because You Wanted To), by Armando Cavalcanti and Klecius Caldas, sung by Venilton Santos with backing vocals and orchestra.

The second sequence is of special interest here. Two characters played by Ankito (the trickster Leovigildo, a smuggler, fake detective and samba composer) and Maria Vidal (as Dona Aurora, the oppressive boss of a record company) are standing in front of a TV set in her office at Gravadora Aurora, listening to the orchestral introduction of a samba. After a shot of both characters' point-of view, a reverse shot shows singer Marion on a twenty-one-inch TV screen, dressed in a *baiana* costume, ostensibly modelled after Carmen Miranda but more restrained and stylised, performing the samba 'Não vou perdoar' (I Won't Forgive, 1958) by composer Almeidinha. After the first part of the song, another cut transitions from the screen of the TV set into the full frame of the film camera encompassing all the space of the carnival number in a TV studio. A crane shot slowly moves backwards in a long shot to reveal the orchestra and the choir of dancers and revellers singing the lyrics of the song's first section. Another cut presents Marion in medium shot, singing the second section of the song and moving her arms and head left and right in a clear reference to Carmen Miranda's performative style. Back in the office, Leovigildo and Dona Aurora continue to watch the number. She seems to be reflecting about what she sees, while Leovigildo is obviously enjoying the broadcast. Another cut brings us back to the TV set again occupying the entire film frame. Marion is brought down the stage and joins the other dancers below, with the camera following her body while she gracefully dances and sings among the dancers. One more cut returns us to the office and, finally, another cut repeats the medium shot of the TV set, concluding the number with it back at its much smaller television aspect ratio. Dona Aurora turns off the TV, remarking on how pleasing the musical number was.

In these scenes, the slow-moving camera closing in on the small television and then transposing the televised musical number into the world of film, now enlarged by the fully expanded frame, promotes an immediate comparison between different sizes – the small TV screen and the large cinema screen. It is an explicit reflexive process of remediation of the original broadcast now foregrounded in the film, where the juxtaposition of two types of screens paradoxically emphasises and erases their differences. The old film image (and screen) is offered as bigger and better while the new one seeks to remain faithful in content and mise-en-scène to the older medium. Following Bolter and Grusin (2000: 45), I would argue that *Quem roubou meu samba* ambiguously addresses the role of television in achieving cultural significance by refashioning the earlier medium of film. In the face of the eminently inescapable competition with television, *Quem roubou meu samba* would appear to reiterate cinema's superiority over the new medium, albeit well aware that cinema, and *chanchadas* in particular, depended upon the representational and aesthetic strategies of other pre-existing media. However, here, it eloquently looked with suspicion at the then new medium about to be popularised in Brazil, at the same time that it incorporates it in a reflexive manner, evidencing the process of remediation.

On the other hand, its narrative literally exposes the new medium of television, not only for the benefit of the record industry, as cinema had done in the previous two decades, but also for the development of new consumers and audiences. It may be argued that *Quem roubou meu samba*'s intermedial narrative acknowledges and naturalises the migration of the *chanchada* from one medium (film) to another (television), or that it surrenders to television what had been, until then, one of Brazilian cinema's most successful assets and faithful audiences. Indeed, the film suggests a recognition of television as the new medium to inherit and continue film's intermedial tradition, developed since the 1930s. At the same time, *Quem roubou meu samba* and *Barnabé tu és meu* demonstrate that the older medium cannot be entirely wiped out. In them, television remains dependent on film (and *chanchadas*). This reappropriation of discourses is much more than an intermedial process of transference. The explicit signs of negotiation on the part of the diegetic viewer, standing in for the general film/TV audience, produce meanings in which spectators (or rather, regimes of spectatorship) will always engage processes of mediation and resignification of whatever content new media are capable of offering.

On the eve of Cinema Novo, the case of *Quem roubou meu samba* exemplifies the process of transposition from the carnival-centred Brazilian filmic tradition to television, creatively representing the new medium. At the same time, with its emphasis on the spectacle of entertainment, it keeps a distance from the new movement of Cinema Novo, being announced as early as 1955 by Nelson Pereira dos Santos's innovative *Rio, 40 graus*. Dos Santos's second feature, *Rio, Zona Norte*, despite its subject being music as represented by a *chanchada* actor, Grande Otelo, in the role of a victimised samba composer, was even more politically radical and distant from the genre, as regards the meanings and role of samba (see Shaw 2007 in this respect).

Quem roubou meu samba is located at the crossroads of the decline of the *chanchada* and its migration to the new medium of television. As I have argued, the shrinking popularity of the *chanchada* went in tandem with the expansion of television, in the early 1960s. The negative reception of the *chanchada*, by critics who failed to appreciate the full implications of a subversive creative impulse embedded in its carnivalesque traditions, also accelerated its demise. Mainstream journalistic criticism became increasingly intolerant towards the genre as the decade came to a close. Hand in hand with a rising elitist middle class who could not sanction its vulgarity and embarrassingly inferior production values, a more nationalistic ideology, extremely preoccupied with a positive image of Brazil in both internal and external arenas, the country's internal and external image, considered unacceptable *chanchada*'s popular taste for its generic codes, laughter, debauchery, parodies of Hollywood and musical numbers, all of which favoured alienation versus political consciousness and engagement.

Note

1. I would like to thank David and Tania Shepherd for their useful advice on the first draft of this paper.

References

Araújo, Vicente de Paula (1976), *A bela época do cinema brasileiro*. São Paulo: Perspectiva.
Bolter, Jay David and Richard Grusin (2000), *Remediation: Understanding New Media*. Cambridge, MA: MIT Press.
Cinearte, 2 December, 1931.
Dyer, Richard (1993), 'Entertainment and Utopia', in Simon During (ed.), *The Cultural Studies Reader* (London and New York: Routledge, 1993).
Shaw, Lisa (2007), 'A imitação cultural na *chanchada*: o caso *Quem roubou meu samba?* e *Rio Zona Norte*', *ALCEU*, 8:15, July–December, pp. 69–81.
Shaw, Lisa (2013), *Carmen Miranda*. London: BFI/Palgrave Macmillan.

OTHER WORKS CONSULTED

Bernardet, Jean-Claude (1995), *Historiografia clássica do cinema brasileiro*. São Paulo: Annablume.
Castro, Ruy (2005), *Carmen: a vida de Carmen Miranda, a brasileira mais famosa do século XX*. São Paulo: Companhia das Letras.
Gonzaga, Adhemar and Paulo Emílio Salles Gomes (1966), *70 anos de cinema brasileiro*. Rio de Janeiro: Expressão e Cultura.
Mendonça, Ana Rita and Lisa Shaw (2017), 'Carmen Miranda: From National Star to Global Brand', in Tim Bergfelder, Lisa Shaw and João Luiz Vieira (eds), *Stars and Stardom in Brazilian Cinema*, pp. 73–92.
Nagib, Lúcia (2006), 'Towards a Positive Definition of World Cinema', in Stephanie Dennison and Song Hwee Lim, *Remapping World Cinema: Identity, Culture and Politics in Film*. London and New York: Wallflower Press, pp. 30–7.
Nagib, Lúcia and Ann Jerslev (2014), 'Introduction', in *Impure Cinema: Intermedial and Intercultural Approaches to Film*. London and New York: I. B. Tauris, pp. xviii–xxxi.
Pereira, Regina Paranhos (1967), 'Introdução ao filme musical brasileiro', *Filme Cultura*, I:6, September, pp. 42–50.
Souza, José Inácio de Melo (2018), 'Os primórdios do cinema no Brasil', in Fernão Ramos and Sheila Schvartzman, *Nova História do Cinema Brasileiro*, vol. 1. São Paulo: Edições Sesc, pp. 45–6.
Vieira, João Luiz and Leonardo C. Macário (2017), 'Oscarito and Grande Otelo: The Terrible Twosome', in Tim Bergfelder, Lisa Shaw and João Luiz Vieira (eds), *Stars and Stardom in Brazilian Cinema*. New York and Oxford: Berghahn, pp. 111–27.
Vieira, João Luiz and Robert Stam (1999), 'Parody and Marginality: The Case of Brazilian Cinema', in Manuel Alvarado and John O. Thompson (eds), *The Media Reader*. London BFI, pp. 82–104.

Part IV

From Impure Cinema to Cosmopoetics

CHAPTER 15

Impure Cinema as Method: The Last Films of Eduardo Coutinho

Consuelo Lins

> Purity doesn't exist. Purity and perfection are the only things that revolt me. Purity and perfection are fascist. My films are about life, because life will always be imperfect, because life will always be incomplete.
>
> Eduardo Coutinho (cited in Ramia 2013: 321)

Filmmaker Eduardo Coutinho (1933–2014) is a fundamental figure in Brazilian cinema.[1] His work contributed immensely to the consolidation of the documentary genre in Brazil. In the last fifteen years of his life, he produced almost a film every year, serving as a continuous stimulus to debate and critical thinking. Not only do Coutinho's films help us to understand Brazil better, but every one of them questions the very process of documentary making, raising issues around the possibilities and limits of the genre. His cinema can be seen as a corpus of films that forged, over the 2000s, a solid ground for other documentary productions to develop in different directions.

This chapter analyses the last phase of Eduardo Coutinho's production, encompassing *Jogo de cena* (*Playing*, 2007), *Moscou* (*Moscow*, 2009), *Um dia na vida* (*A Day in Life*, 2010) and *As canções* (*Songs*, 2011). Unlike his filming on real locations, which had come to a close with *O fim e o princípio* (*The End and the Beginning*, 2005), these last four works were shot in closed spaces, three of them in stage settings and based on unique strategies of interweaving artistic media and forms, as well as intensifying reflexive procedures already present in his previous work. The interpenetration of Coutinho's last films with theatre, television and music is so radical that it allows us to revisit his entire œuvre through the notion of 'impure cinema', the famous expression coined by André Bazin (1967) to signify the multimedia nature of cinema, which inspired generations of filmmakers and critics, and was more recently transformed into an analytical method by Lúcia Nagib and Anne Jerslev (2014).

Between Cinema, Video and Television

In late October 2010, filmmaker Eduardo Coutinho conducted an experiment that left a mark on the history of Brazilian documentary and astounded the audiences accustomed to his conversation-based films. In a surprise session at the São Paulo International Film Festival, Coutinho presented a ninety-six-minute film made entirely of recorded material from open Brazilian TV, with no commentary, interviews or any other interventions besides the montage itself. For this feat, the filmmaker recorded nineteen hours on a random day of television programmes, uninterruptedly taping religious programmes, TV journalism, reality shows, advertising, children's programmes, soap operas, variety shows, educational programmes and other attractions. He randomly zapped from one channel to another, from one programme to another, on the fly, without preset rules. Titled *Um dia na vida*, the film, or the 'stuff' as Coutinho used to call it, was screened publicly only a few times and was never presented as a proper film, due to the copyright imbroglio caused by the broadcast material.

To extract a film from Brazilian television was a provocative act. Coutinho used to complain about Brazilian artists and researchers looking down on the media that informed (and, according to them, deformed) the majority of the population. For him, to understand Brazil necessarily involved reflecting on open TV. Even though his own documentaries normally featured characters and testimonies that were never shown on TV, fragments of the televisual culture regularly emerged between the lines of the real-life characters he used to film. In a sense, in *Um dia na vida*, Coutinho decides to 'force' his viewers to withstand a concentrate of images and sounds that they might retreat from in other circumstances. Coutinho allowed *Um dia na vida* to be shown only in cinemas (or in auditoriums simulating them), followed by debate with the filmmaker himself. Unlike his previous works, Coutinho knew that this film would not survive as an entirely autonomous object for home or public consumption. This condition brought his 'TV film' in line with certain contemporary art installations that make sense only in specific spaces, such as museums or galleries. The characteristics of this 'impure' film, from its making to its screening, resonate with what Irina Rajewsky (2012: 66) defines as an 'intermedial experiment' with relation to artistic objects whose creative process is traversed by different art and medial forms.

Coutinho's iconoclastic gesture may have been just the most famous in a series of gestures of the same kind, pertaining to a profoundly impure *œuvre*, open to the world, to difference, to the imponderable. His first documentary film, *Cabra marcado para morrer* (*Twenty Years Later*, 1964/84), is considered a watershed in the genre in Brazil precisely for reclaiming a political event from the 1960s through a mixture of documentary aesthetics inspired by so-called 'modern cinema' and strategies from television reportage, in dialogue with Brazil's tradition of social documentary. The film narrates the search for (and re-encounter with) the actors that participated in the shooting of the first *Cabra marcado para morrer*, who were rural workers involved in the land struggle in northeast Brazil. Directed by Coutinho in 1964, the shoot was disrupted by the military coup that year. Various peasant leaders and members of the film crew were arrested. Seventeen years later, the original project of making a fiction film with peasant-actors became a documentary project, but of a new kind, without a preconceived screenplay or idea, but just a filming plan that consisted of searching out the peasant-actors from the original shoot, to see if they were still alive. The film that resulted from this process had an immediate impact on Brazilian audiences and critics, and enjoyed widespread acclaim on the international film festival circuit. 'It's reporting, reclaiming history, metacinema, the other's voice, intertextuality,' stated critic Ismail Xavier (2001: 124), according to whom the film brings to a close the most vigorous period in Brazilian filmmaking until then, marked by the tradition of modern cinema and inventively combining aesthetic and political concerns.

The decision to begin shooting on video after *Cabra marcado* was made in another unprecedented and surprising gesture by the filmmaker in the historical context of the mid-1980s. The film's success allowed Coutinho to continue to make films on acetate, but he refused to take the path of 'professional cinema' or conventional filmmaking. He wanted to practise what he had learned with the difficulties encountered with *Cabra marcado*. It was clear to him that he did not depend on acetate to make a film, an insight that predated the dissemination of digital technologies and proved correct, given what happened with cinema in the subsequent decades. Still, this prescient stance was actually a modest gesture of wanting to survive in the precarious arena of documentary-making in Brazil. Lightweight equipment and low-cost technologies would allow him to remain faithful to his own kind of cinema, characterised by pragmatism, small crews and 'minor themes', focused on poor communities: a cinema of his encounter with real-life characters, who at the same time displayed 'an element more theatrical and televisual than cinematographic', as Esther Hamburger (2013: 429) has aptly put it.

This openness of his filmmaking to television and video, and later to theatre and music, brought Coutinho closer to Jean-Luc Godard, who, at least in France, in the words of critic Serge Daney (1993: 296), 'made all the decisive gestures before the others' of linking devices, practices and reflections from different artistic fields. Perhaps the fact that Coutinho had lived in Paris at the very beginning of the Nouvelle Vague and studied at the prestigious IDHEC film school from 1957 to 1960 drew him closer to an idea of cinema aligned, on the one hand, with the open and adventurous approach of the filmmakers and critics from the *Cahiers du Cinéma*, and, on the other, with André Bazin's notion of 'impure cinema' (1967). Elaborated by the critic in 1951 to address the relations between cinema, literature and theatre, the concept of 'impure cinema' offered a path for cinema to interact with other media and arts in subsequent decades. Bazin died in 1958 when Coutinho was already living in Paris, and certainly imbibing those ideas. More than a few times in his life, the filmmaker spoke emphatically and with his characteristic wit against the notions of purity and perfection: 'When people talk to me about perfection and purity, I tell them, if you want perfection and purity, go to the cemetery' (Nader 2017: 72).

Perhaps I should mention here that, from 1999 on, I began to enjoy a work relationship and closer contact with Eduardo Coutinho, which made me experience his cinema differently, having already begun to analyse it in several articles. I was part of the team of researchers in two of his films in the early 2000s – *Babilônia 2000* (2001) and *Edifício Master* (*Master Building*, 2002) – a very rich experience that consolidated my knowledge of his creative process and working method, before, during and after filming. I followed from close up the making of all his subsequent films and wrote the first monograph on his work, published in Brazil in 2004. We remained close friends until his death in 2014, when he was in the middle of shooting his next documentary. I witnessed the enthusiasm this 'old dude' sparked in my students, having invited him numerous times to discuss his films in the School of Communications of the Federal University in Rio de Janeiro, where I have taught since the 1990s.

The last time Coutinho spoke with my students was precisely about *Um dia na vida*, debating seriously (but with boundless good humour) his views on television and observing something in 2010 that became clear only with Jair Bolsonaro's election as President of Brazil in 2018: the presence of pastors in 25 per cent of prime-time Brazilian TV, the force of Evangelical religion in Brazilian politics and its destructive power precisely in the name of a pure religious belief, and contempt and hate for other religions. 'The most dangerous fascism today is definitely Evangelical,' he foretold (Coutinho 2011b). Since then, the denunciations of attacks on other religions in the favelas and on the outskirts of Brazilian cities, particularly against African–Brazilian religions, have been a sad constant in the news. The same was observed in the speeches given by politicians in the notorious session on the floor of the Chamber of Deputies that voted for the impeachment of President Dilma Roussef in 2016 and often invoked the nefarious 'Christian purity' so presciently diagnosed by Coutinho in 2010.

Documentaries 'From Within'

Um dia na vida belongs to what is generally considered the director's final phase, beginning in 2007 with *Jogo de cena*, followed by *Moscou* and concluded with *As canções*. One last film, entitled *Últimas conversas* (*Last Conversations*, 2015), compiles the material that Coutinho was shooting when he died. It was edited by Jordana Berg – editor of all his films since *Santo forte* (*The Mighty Spirit*, 1999) – and finalised by producer and filmmaker João Moreira Salles, but it is less a film by Eduardo Coutinho and more a documentary on the filmmaker's state of mind in the few months before his tragic death.

The films in this last phase were shot in closed environments such as studios and theatres, indicating the filmmaker's abandonment of an apparently essential element of his cinema: the rootedness in an actual community, the interaction with residents in a 'single location'. He referred to this mode of single-location shooting variously as the 'spatial device' of his cinema or simply the spatial 'prison' that he invented with each film – certainly the most important principle until then in his filming method. *Santo forte* and *Babilônia 2000* are set in favelas, and *Edifício Master* in a middle-class building, all three in Rio de Janeiro. In *Peões* (*Metalworkers*, 2004) he shifted to the blue-collar cities close to São Paulo, and in *O fim e o princípio* to a rural village in northeast Brazil.

In *Jogo de cena*, *Moscou* and *As canções*, the filming process in a stage setting establishes a common ground across different interviewees and their life stories. There is no longer a geographic, social, economic or architectural backdrop to contextualise the characters and hold them together. In these films, all the wagers are on the fabulation by characters in the scene, on a 'performance of oneself' (Baltar 2019: 15) right there before the camera. The films' existence and force depend solely on their bodies at the moment of filming, on the way they narrate personal stories, on the way they express dramatic, tragic, comical or ordinary events in their lives. It is solely and exclusively each individual's speech that enables the spectator to draw connections between their private stories and social background.

In this new phase, the filmmaker radicalised the operation of subtraction that he had imposed on his work over the years, progressively eliminating voiceover narration, illustrative images, archival images, music track and effects of any kind. Thus his films moved increasingly towards an aesthetic minimalism, drawing on intermedial strategies, exploring procedures from theatre and television combined with documentary, and demonstrating an interest in the role of music and melodrama in the life story of his characters. What led the filmmaker to travel this path, no longer filming the world but the scene, arriving at a documentary form that we could call 'from within'? Coutinho always rejected the suggestion that his inventions had been conceived in advance, prior to making the films. There were concrete, personal reasons related to his health, increasingly delicate, that prevented him from making films that required great physical effort. Meanwhile, he did not want to repeat what he had already done; rather, he wanted to bring in professional actors, as in the case of *Jogo de cena* and *Moscou*, an idea that he had been cultivating for several years.

At any rate, regardless of the director's motives, what matters is what we can identify in the actual films. In them, we find common elements, such as single locations; a focus on characters' fabulation and self-theatricalisation; musical performances; and the use of colloquial and vernacular Portuguese. In *Jogo de cena*, after interviewing female volunteers, Coutinho invites actresses to perform their testimonials, thus bringing together the staged and the spontaneous. In *Moscou*, he progresses to filming exclusively professional actors in a rehearsal of Anton Chekhov's play *Three Sisters*. In *Um dia na vida*, as we have seen, he records a random day on open Brazilian television and brings to the fore the parlance typical of Brazil's audiovisual culture. In *As canções*, musical renditions, which had cropped up in the middle of interviews with real-life characters in his previous films, now become the film's very reason of being, the justification for bringing the characters before the camera. What Coutinho appears to be making in his final years of life are essay films based on his previous works, producing a new fold in the reflexive dimension that permeates his documentaries. He not only immediately reveals the principles of the making of his films, but lends new contours to the tacit dialogue between the works themselves. His previous films thus become a sort of grand audiovisual, methodological and procedural archive that he could draw on (if he had not died) to select elements endlessly for in-depth exploration and reorganisation in new film experiments.

JOGO DE CENA: THEATRE, REALITY, REFLEXIVITY

The single location for *Jogo de cena* is a real theatre stage – the Glauce Rocha Theatre, in Rio de Janeiro – with the characters sitting on black chairs, their backs turned to an empty auditorium of red seats. They reach the scene via a spiral staircase that leaves many of them short of breath. They are all women. Coutinho's decades of practice in conversation with individuals from different walks of life gave him the certainty that women speak of their pains and joys much more easily than men. Here, they speak undisturbed by their work, daily life, close relations and especially their children. *Jogo de cena* features stories of love, care and difficulties; they are narratives of loss, pain and suffering, but also of coping and moral recovery; many are stories of children brought up without their fathers around.

Coutinho spoke first with women who answered a classified advert in a Rio newspaper inviting volunteers to tell their stories on camera. Next, he invited actresses (some well known, others unknown to the general public) to portray the women whose testimonials he had already recorded. He then edited professional and non-professional testimonials together. By dissolving the distinctions between the staged and the real, the film is a source of constant surprises and bewilderment for viewers. Seeing the familiar faces of famous actresses in Brazil, we are initially tempted to judge their performance. But *Jogo de cena* offers a removal from this vantage point and invites another kind of experience, that of sharing, with talented and well-known actresses, the inherent angst and challenges of playing real-life characters. At many moments there is a touching short circuit between the actresses' feelings and those of the characters they are striving so hard to portray. One of them, Fernanda Torres, well known among Brazilians, interrupts her performance several times to tell Coutinho that she sounds as if she were lying. She explains the difficulty of playing a real-life character by saying: 'Reality rubs in your face how far you could have gone, but fell short.' *Jogo de cena* exhibits various forms of theatricality, conveying an understanding of the art of performance as something unstable, unsafe and exposed to risks: that is, close to documentary practice as conceived by Coutinho.

There are other issues arising from the use of actresses who are unknown to the general public and real-life characters, in *Jogo de cena*. Before our eyes, anonymous women narrating intimate moments before Jacques Cheuiche's camera acquire the force of truth, calling for our belief in the documentary image. Yet bits of stories already narrated begin to return in a phrase, a rap, a tale, gradually introducing doubt as to whether this is a real-life volunteer telling her story or an unknown actress performing.

Authentic, true and spontaneous, adjectives that had always accompanied the reception of Coutinho's documentaries, are now shattered one by one. The uncertainty permeating the film touches both the famous and the anonymous, and we ultimately never discover the real source of the famous actresses' hesitations and silences. We lose control over what is staged and what is not, and in fact the clues that the film is 'fooling' us constitute the core of the film's proposal. As highlighted by Robert Stam (2000: 175), 'Realism and reflexivity are not strictly opposed polarities, but, rather, interpenetrating tendencies quite capable of coexistence in the same text.' In *Jogo de cena*, we are asked to empathise twice with the same case, which removes the clues as to which woman is the story's 'true' owner. There is no guarantee, as both can be actresses playing the role of a third person who is not in the film. What turns out to be the film's focus of interest is the place for dramatisation and organisation of the lived experience, where dramatic forms of 'real narratives' appear as an inexhaustible source for fiction.

When the film was released in 2007, it sparked awe, fascination, bewilderment. Jean-Claude Bernardet (2012: 105,106), one of the foremost scholars on Brazilian cinema, called it 'a seismic shock, seven degrees on the Richter scale, for documentary cinema in general, or more precisely, for speech-based documentary film'. According to the critic, the film may represent a conclusion to 'a cinematic cycle that Jean Rouch began half a century ago with *Moi, un noir*' (106). The film yielded an immediate and voluminous critical response, and its effects are still being felt in the Brazilian filmmaking scene. It brings into question not only Coutinho's own previous work, but also 'all speech-based documentary films as the discourse of subjectivity and life stories'.

Moscou: Chekhov and Coutinho

The success of explicit theatricality in *Jogo de cena* encouraged Coutinho to up the stakes and take further steps towards staging. In his following work, he filmed over the course of three weeks a private rehearsal of *Three Sisters* (1900), by Russian playwright and author Anton Chekhov, with thirteen actors from the Galpão Troupe, directed by Enrique Diaz. This may have been the riskiest gesture of his career, foregoing what he knew how to do best: interacting with the characters, whether actors or not. He left it up to director Enrique Diaz to relate to the actors and direct them on the stage where the troupe usually rehearses its plays in the city of Belo Horizonte.

From the outset, Coutinho's idea was to stage a project that would remain unfinished one way or another. This did not scare him: quite the opposite, since he considered this an essential characteristic of Chekhov's plays, and especially *Three Sisters*. The short three-week rehearsal period was not aimed at an actual debut of the play on the stage, which would have been impossible for a group of actors who had never worked with the Russian author before and were being directed for the first time by Enrique Diaz. Instead, the rehearsal would exist only for the film, dispensing with a series of other important concerns if the play were aimed for the theatre stage. At the same time, neither was it about 'a play that looks like a play', as director Enrique Diaz recalls, or 'a rehearsal's making-of' (Diaz 2010). What was it about, then?

In one of the film's first takes, we witness a conversation between Coutinho, the actors and director Enrique Diaz, sitting around a table, reading excerpts from the play. At this moment, the filmmaker exposes his plan for the film, as he had done in previous films. Next, he practically exits the scene, something unprecedented in his work and surprising for critics and audiences alike. For those who claimed he had 'lost his touch', the filmmaker replied that he had created a device precisely to 'lose my touch' (Coutinho 2010). However, the adoption of a device that opens up so deeply to theatre still preserves for the director a number of other tasks: Coutinho was the one to invite the theatre actors and director and propose the project to them; he determined the space and time for filming, established the rules of the game, appointed the technical crew and took care of the editing, among numerous other responsibilities.

The film includes warm-up exercises with the actors and director Enrique Diaz, activities in the dressing rooms and backstage, recitation of scenes from the play in random order, pauses in the rehearsal, snack breaks with the actors interjecting Chekhov's lines, meetings, the actors chatting while looking into the camera, scenes in which the actors interact with the camera as if it were a character in the play, repetition of excerpts from the play in new dramatic situations, and various actors playing the same characters. As in *Jogo de cena*, many of the procedures proposed by Diaz end up producing a short circuit between what is staged and what is not – in this case, what is Chekhov's and what belongs to each actor's memories and personal dramas. It is as if there were an intermedial mirroring between Diaz's and the Galpão Troupe's conception of theatre and Coutinho's conception of cinema intertwining throughout the film.

The result, which was given the title of *Moscou* during the editing process,[2] is an experiment as unusual as his television film, *Um dia na vida*, but it ultimately failed to please Coutinho himself, even though he defended it, as he always did with his films: 'It was the most painful experience of my life. The film went wrong, but I still think it has an interesting mystery' (Coutinho 2013: 318). On the commentary track recorded in 2010 for the DVD version of *Moscou*, the director speaks of his anguish while making the film, but we can also feel his enthusiasm when discussing certain scenes with director Diaz, actor Eduardo Moreira and producer João Moreira Salles.

As canções: Music and Layers of Memory

In *As canções*, Coutinho left the professional actors aside and returned to filming real-life characters and their skills in storytelling and performance, this time evoked by songs that had marked their lives, bringing back memories of lost loves, past pains, unhealed wounds. The interweaving of film and music had been a constant in his work, and there are characters singing in nearly all of his films, but in this documentary the subject is amateur singing itself.

The opening of his work to a deeper immersion into the field of music is one more fold in the director's embrace of impure cinema. It was Coutinho's persuasion that, in a country like Brazil with high rates of illiteracy, music is much more efficient as a form of communication than literature, poetry or cinema. Music is capable of expressing visceral personal histories and of expanding on deeply rooted affective repertoires, offering a kind of pedagogy of how to deal with emotional occurrences such as unrequited love. Thus, in the film, characters use songs to evoke their personal dramas: for example, with a Mexican bolero from the 1930s, 'Perfidia' (Perfidy, sung twice in the film); the song 'Minha namorada' (My Girlfriend), composed by poet Vinícius de Moraes and Carlos Lyra, which opens the film; romantic hits by Roberto Carlos, the most well-known living Brazilian composer and singer; and a samba, 'Você me abandonou' (You Left Me), by the Old Guard of the Portela Samba School, suggesting an infallible method for dealing with lovelornness, among other musical pearls.

Although the stage setting from *Jogo de cena* is maintained here, the empty red seats are replaced by a huge black, draping curtain covering the backstage from floor to ceiling. In fact, this is no longer a real theatre, but a studio-built stage. Against this dark, neutral background, seventeen characters (nine women and eight men of various ages and social origins) converse and/or sing. We watch some of them enter and walk to the black chair in front of the filmmaker (who is always off screen) and exit towards the curtain.

The last scene in *Jogo de cena* could be the opening scene of *As canções*. In the 2007 film, a character who had already talked to the filmmaker asks to come back on stage to sing. She explains that her interview had been a 'downer', 'more tragic than comical', and that she 'didn't want to come across too sad'. She tells how her father used to sing carnival tunes and other lively rhythms, 'the songs of our life', but she ends up choosing a melancholic lullaby that moves her to tears again. This relationship between music and layers of memory permeates nearly all of the interviews and clearly reveals the affective and sensorial bond between the characters' past and present, right there before the camera. This coexistence of times, as the characters narrate their affective dramas, often brings tears to their eyes, underscoring what Mariana Baltar (2019: 15) calls the 'critical and taut' dialogue between Eduardo Coutinho's cinema and melodrama. For Baltar (17), Coutinho's cinema strikes a 'delicate balance' between a formal containment and 'the characters' melodramatic mode of self-fabulation'.

The fact that the characters knew that their musical performances would be the centre of the film led many of them quickly to adopt self-theatricalisation, especially the women. One of them tells of a turbulent relationship with a lover who supported her for a long time. 'He was very handsome, smelled nice of patchouli cologne.' Her story is full of dramatic pauses and formulations that intensify the self-staging: 'I had to serve eight plates of food a day, that is if I didn't eat anything, four for the kids for lunch, and four for the kids for dinner.' 'I was a black bombshell with bright-red lipstick, cruising in that tail fin Cadillac.' She sings 'O tempo vai apagar' (Time Heals All Things), a hit song by Roberto Carlos, and leaves to the end the story of how she nearly killed her lover, but that 'by the mercy of a God that I hated, the gun jammed'. At the end, she says that, despite it all, 'it was so good'. As she exits the stage, we can hear her copious weeping behind the curtain.

A male character confesses that he had been a scoundrel in his marriage, even as he pays homage to his wife (who had put up with his cheating ways), claiming that he is trying to redeem himself. As he exits, he asks the director to give him stage cues for leaving the scene: 'Should I go out sad or happy?' He himself decides to go out singing 'A volta do boêmio' (The Return of the Bohemian), a hit song from the 1950s, in the voice of crooner Nelson Gonçalves, and waves before disappearing behind the curtain.

When talking about the film, Coutinho aims his artillery at the mass-culture critics and their disregard for the world's impurities. 'This film would not exist if it weren't for radio since the 1930s,' he says: that is, if there were no radio theatre, *radionovelas* with melodramatic plots, and the propagation of music throughout most of Brazil's territory. 'This line of not accepting the changes introduced by mass culture – like jazz – which is Adorno's position, I consider abominable. These songs were created by mass radio. People recognise the melodrama of their own lives in these songs!' (Coutinho 2011a). Unlike *Moscou*, the making of which was very challenging for Coutinho, the shooting of *As canções* worked out well, and Coutinho rarely had as much fun making a film. In it, the marks of this pleasure appear in both the lively interactions with the characters and in the songs; in some cases, he even helps fill in the lyrics.

Final Remarks

When filmmaker Eduardo Coutinho died, he was in the middle of making a new film, this time with teenage secondary-school students in Rio de Janeiro. The conversations he had with the young people were filmed in the same studio as *As canções*, and the setting simulated a classroom, in line with the films he shot in stage settings. As frequently happened in his creative process, the director was not happy with the recorded material and was experiencing anxiety prior to the film's editing.

Coutinho was eighty years old and widely renowned. He had never stopped experimenting and pursuing new paths for his cinema. While, on the one hand, certain ethical and aesthetic principles were maintained from one film to the next, on the other, each of his documentaries brought subtle and gradual transformations that ended up forming a kind of fluid identity for his cinema, made of recognisable elements which emerged differently each time.

At the end of this analytical journey, in which the guiding thread was 'impure cinema' as a method, perhaps we can say, along with film critic Carlos Alberto Mattos, that 'Eduardo Coutinho was one of the most experimental Brazilian filmmakers of his time' (Mattos 2019: 255). His experimentalism translated, in the last films of his trajectory, into an even deeper investigation of procedures from theatre, television, music, melodrama, combined with documentary. Not only did he make films that allow us to understand Brazil better, but each of his films raised questions for documentary filmmaking itself, enquiring into the conditions for its possibility, its relationship with the 'other', with other media and artistic forms, and ultimately with the spectator.

The filmmaker died on 2 February 2014, leaving us some of the greatest films ever produced in Brazil.

Notes

1. Translation of this chapter by Christopher Peterson.
2. As suggested by producer João Moreira Salles, *Moscou* is the dream that never comes true, the sisters' aspiration to leave the province that never happens.

References

Baltar, Mariana (2019), *Realidade lacrimosa: o melodramático no documentário brasileiro contemporâneo*. Rio de Janeiro: EDUFF.

Bazin, André (1967), 'In Defence of Mixed Cinema', in *What Is Cinema?* Vol. 1, essays selected and translated by Hugh Gray. Berkeley, Los Angeles and London: University of California Press, pp. 53–75

Bazin, André (1967), 'In Defence of Mixed Cinema', in *What Is Cinema?*, vol. 1, essays selected and translated by Hugh Gray. Berkeley, Los Angeles and London: University of California Press, pp. 53–75.

Bernardet, Jean-Claude (2012), 'Jogo de Cena y Moscou', in Maria Campaña Ramia and Cláudia Mesquita (eds), *El otro cinema de Eduardo Coutinho*. Quito: Corporación Cinema, pp. 102–16.

Coutinho, Eduardo (2010), Commentary track on the DVD of *Moscou* (78'). Rio de Janeiro: Videofilmes.

Coutinho, Eduardo (2011a), Commentary track on the DVD of *As canções* (92'). Rio de Janeiro: Videofilmes.

Coutinho, Eduardo (2011b), Transcription of a conversation with students from the School of Communications/UFRJ.

Coutinho, Eduardo (2013), 'Não quero saber como o mundo é, mas como está', interview with Maria Campaña Ramia, in Milton Ohata (ed.), *Eduardo Coutinho*. São Paulo: Cosacnaify, pp. 307–21.

Daney, Serge (1993), *L'Exercice a été profitable, Monsieur*. Paris: P.O.L.

Diaz, Enrique (2010), Commentary track of the DVD of *Moscou* (*Moscow*). Rio de Janeiro: Videofilmes.

Hamburger, Esther (2013), 'Eduardo Coutinho e a TV', in Milton Ohata (ed.), *Eduardo Coutinho*. São Paulo: CosacNaify, pp. 414–31.

Lins, Consuelo (2004), *O cinema de Eduardo Coutinho: cinema, televisão e vídeo*. Rio de Janeiro: Jorge Zahar.

Mattos, Carlos Alberto (2019), *Sete faces de Eduardo Coutinho*. São Paulo: Boitempo.

Nader, Carlos (2017), 'No princípio era o verbo', in E. Altman and Tatiana Bacal (eds), *Ultimas conversas*. Rio de Janeiro: Editora 7Letras, pp. 47–117.

Nagib, Lúcia and Anne Jerslev (eds) (2014), 'Introduction', in *Impure Cinema: Intermedial and Intercultural Approaches to Film*. London and New York: I. B. Tauris, pp. xviii–xxxi.

Rajewsky, Irina (2012), 'A fronteira em discussão: o status problemático das fronteiras midiáticas no debate contemporâneo sobre intermidialidade', in T. F. N. Diniz and André Soares Vieira (eds), *Intermidialidade e estudos interartes: desafios da arte contemporânea*. Belo Horizonte: Rona editora, FALE/UFMG, pp. 51–73.

Ramia, Maria Campaña (2013), 'Não quero saber como o mundo é, mas como está', interview with Eduardo Coutinho, in Milton Ohata (ed.), *Eduardo Coutinho*. São Paulo: CosacNaify, pp. 307–21.

Stam, Robert (2003), *Introdução à teoria do cinema*. São Paulo: Papirus.

Xavier, Ismail (2001), *O cinema brasileiro moderno*. São Paulo: Paz e Terra.

CHAPTER 16

Queering Intermediality in Brazilian Cinema
Ramayana Lira de Sousa and Alessandra Soares Brandão

Queerness in Brazilian cinema has been explored in recent research from different perspectives, including film history and cultural studies.[1] Luiz Francisco Buarque de Lacerda Júnior (2015) argues that most of the studies on homoeroticism in Brazilian cinema up until the 2010s focused on the politics of representation and cinema's potential to resist/reinforce hegemonic heteronormative discourses. One good example of such approach can be found in Antônio Moreno's *A personagem homossexual no cinema brasileiro* (*The Homosexual Character in Brazilian Cinema*, 2001). In his book, Moreno catalogues a number of Brazilian films according to a (rather moralistic) scale of pejorative portrayals of lesbian, gay, bisexual and transgender (LGBT) characters and stereotyped gestures, in an attempt to compile the 'good' and the 'bad' representations of homosexual characters.[2] The shortcomings of Moreno's book seemed to have encouraged academics such as Lacerda Júnior (2015) and Mateus Nagime (2016) to design different approaches. Whilst Lacerda Júnior's study reviews the history of Brazilian cinema and its treatment of male homoeroticism, Nagime's thesis focuses on films made in the first five decades of the twentieth century, trying to point out the origins of a Brazilian queer cinema.

And yet, although these approaches are certainly welcome, the relationship between queerness and intermediality remains underexplored. For Carlos Rojas (2020: 175), intermediality is a 'weird concept', useful not only for 'thinking about processes of cultural production, but also for proposing a queer exploration'. This intersection is important because intermediality, as a critique of the notion of a 'pure medium', challenges the very concept of 'identity' and 'specificity', which is a similar theoretical position to queer studies. José Esteban Muñoz (2009: 116) has argued that:

> the intermedial process leads to a perpetual unfinished system that is by its very nature asystemological [. . .]. Intermedia is a radical understanding of interdisciplinarity. The usage of intermedia that I am suggesting is interdisciplinary in relation to both art-making protocols and taxonomies of race, gender, and sex.

Following Muñoz, our aim here is thus to highlight the protocols of intermedial citations and the taxonomies of race, gender and sex, in order to understand the two-way process through which queerness 'queers' intermediality and intermediality 'mediates' queerness.

In the history of Brazilian cinema, queerness and intermediality converge at various moments with diverse effects. Cross-dressing and the inversion of gender roles, for example, were common features of the *chanchada* genre, between the 1940s and early 1960s. A case in point is Watson Macedo's *Carnaval no fogo* (*Carnival in Flames*, 1949), where male actors Grande Otelo and Oscarito parody the balcony scene from William Shakespeare's *Romeo and Juliet*. Grande Otelo, a black man, plays the role of Juliet and briefly locks lips with Oscarito's Romeo. The language of theatre and the notion of 'playing a role', in this scene, provide a 'safe' space for the characters to 'enact' queerness.[3]

Then, from the late 1960s to the early 1980s, a wave of erotic films emerged, exploring non-normative sexualities, many of which were based on literary works, including *Histórias que nossas babás não contavam* (*Stories Untold by Our Nannies*, Oswaldo de Oliveira, 1979), *Dona Flor e seus dois maridos* (*Dona Flor and Her Two Husbands*, Bruno Barreto, 1976) and, as discussed later, *Ariella* (John Herbert, 1980). Antonio Moreno (2001) rightly argues that, in the process of adaptation, the homosexual characters in these films are often more elaborated and given a deeper psychological life, which he attributes to the literary construction on which they were based.

Even greater interaction between queerness and intermediality can be found in more recent Brazilian films, such as *Batguano* (Tavinho Teixeira, 2014), a queer reappropriation of the already camp 1960s *Batman* TV series; *Tatuagem* (*Tattoo*, Hilton Lacerda, 2013), a somewhat nostalgic rendering of 1970s free love seen through the lenses of theatrical and musical performance; and *Madame Satã* (Karim Aïnouz, 2002), the retelling of real-life queer João Francisco dos Santos, an icon of Brazilian counter-culture, also through the language of theatre and dance, to name just a few.

Common to the films mentioned above is the use of intermediality in order to engage creatively with TV, music and theatrical performance *and* to challenge normative figurations of Brazilian masculinity and femininity, as well as those of gender, sexuality and race. Given the limited scope of this chapter, rather than addressing the specificities of each medium contained in films, our focus will be on what happens 'in between' media, following Ágnes Pethő's (2011: 12) observation that

> cinema seems to consciously position itself 'in-between' media and arts, employing techniques that tap into the multimedial complexity of cinema, exploiting the possibilities offered by the distinctive characteristics of the

media components involved in the cinematic process of signification, and bringing into play the tensions generated by media differences.

Relying on the understanding of intermediality as 'medial transposition' and 'medial transformation' (Rajewsky 2010: 55), this chapter will explore 'inbetweenness' at a specific moment in Brazilian film history: namely the surge of erotic films in the 1970s–1980s and their intermedial dialogue with the literature of the period, which testifies to the circulation of queer desire between the two media. We will focus in particular on *Ariella*, a screen adaptation of Cassandra Rios's novel *Ariella, a paranóica*, which constitutes a fascinating example of queer intermedial interaction. As an emerging field of investigation, queer intermediality – or intermedial queerness – enables us to explore the politics of gender and desire beyond conventional disciplinarity, and embrace the refractions and distortions enacted by dissensual sexualities within media.

According to Judith Butler (1990: 136), gender is fictitious, incoherent, contingent, performative. In tune with Butler, we argue that intermediality operates in the space 'between' media, questioning the borders, in the same way that she first recognises the existence of gender borders (and the control exerted over them) then to debunk them. Irina Rajewsky (2010: 65) understands the concept of a border as the 'precondition for techniques of crossing or challenging, dissolving or emphasizing medial boundaries, which can consequently be experienced and reflected on *as* constructs and conventions'. Similar to Butler's critique of gender boundaries, Rajewsky's view of intermediality demands that we acknowledge that 'it is only due to our constructing borders in the first place that we are able to become aware of ways of transcending or subverting those very boundaries or of ways of highlighting their presence, of probing them, or even of dissolving them entirely' (2010: 65). Because (medial and gender) borders can, and often are, crossed, it is possible to assert their conventionality and constructedness.

In this chapter, we will analyse the role of intermediality in the process of adaption of a queer novel, paying close attention to the film *Ariella*'s ability to highlight, transform or erase the queerness of Cassandra Rios's novel: that is, the extent to which the (media and gender) borders are patrolled or blurred.

Literature and Film: Indecent Liaisons

From the late 1960s to the early 1980s there was an outpouring of erotic films in Brazil, often homogenised, erroneously, under the umbrella label of *pornochanchadas*. The term *pornochanchada* is derived from *chanchada*, and the prefix *porno* is meant to indicate its sexual content. However, the term can be misleading because not all *pornochanchadas* were overtly pornographic. Moreover, *pornochanchadas* and the more 'serious' erotic cinema of the time responded to structural changes in Brazilian society, which, by the late 1960s, was undergoing its own 'sexual revolution'. In tandem with the political struggles that marked the second half of the 1960s, which included the resistance against the newly installed military dictatorship, the questioning of sexuality opened society up for a wider range of experiences. A number of changes had led to the redefinition of gender roles and sexualities: the contraceptive pill, the devaluing of virginity, the understanding of sex as a source of pleasure rather than mere reproduction. Erotic films were, in this context, a celebration of this new social configuration, with sexuality seen as a battlefield for the redefinition of Brazilian culture and society. On the other hand, it is crucial to locate the production of *pornochanchadas* and erotic films (as well as historical narratives) within the context of the military dictatorship (1964–85) in Brazil, which welcomed the production of such films as a means to divert society's attentions from the myriad social, economic and political problems that marked the period.

The ambiguous aesthetics and politics of these popular film genres are visible in the prominent female characters and actresses. The actresses of the period were valued for both their beauty and their sensuality, but also degraded through a filmic form that blatantly privileged the male gaze. Claudette Joubert and Helena Ramos were two such actresses. Joubert, who was married to Tony Vieira (an actor, director and producer of many erotic pastiches of Hollywood westerns) and known for her screen persona as a resolute nymphette, was dubbed the 'erotic Eliana', in a reference to the 1950–1960s *chanchada* star Eliana Macedo, usually associated with juvenile, romantic roles (Ramos and Miranda 2000: 183). Helena Ramos also had a shy, reserved personality that contrasted with her luscious body, a feature that was fully explored in Silvio de Abreu's *Mulher objeto* (*Object Woman*, 1981), where she played Regina, a frigid housewife who can achieve pleasure only in her fantasies.[4]

A number of literary adaptations followed in the footsteps of this eroticisation of Brazilian cinema. *Dona Flor e seus dois maridos* is paradigmatic in this respect: based on Jorge Amado's novel first published in 1966 and directed by Bruno Barreto in 1976, it starred Sonia Braga as the recently remarried widow who is haunted by the seductive ghost of her late husband. *Dona Flor e seus dois maridos* is a light comedy that reconciles conservative customs (represented by the figure of the buttoned-up, living husband) and carnal pleasures (in the figure of the deceased husband, a Lothario), as Dona Flor decides not to choose between one or the other but instead to carry on with both husbands, in a humorous fantastic-realist style. The film went on to become the top-grossing feature in Brazil for more than three decades.

Equally paradigmatic of this trend, this chapter argues, is the literary work of Cassandra Rios (née Odete Rios, in 1932), a prolific writer who published over forty books in fifty years, selling more than a million copies in a country where illiteracy remained high. In a still modernising, peripheral country, Rios's writing, full of colloquialisms and plot twists in her exploration of sexuality, eventually brought her editorial success, though this was followed by social ostracism and intellectual marginality. The Brazil that read her novels was, to a certain extent, a country of a subterranean, outlaw pleasures, and her books helped imagine sex when this imagination was socially interdicted. While patriarchal morality conferred on her the dubious status of the 'most prohibited writer in Brazil', this epithet was paradoxically used as marketing strategy on book covers. Contributing, on the one hand, to the blossoming of the cultural industries in Brazil and the political transformation that eventually led to dictatorship, Rios was, on the other, herself the subject of veiled censorship practised by those resisting the dictatorship, who could not see political potential in her 'pornographic' novels – and indeed, this has been the most common approach to her writing as a pulp author (see Londero 2016; Trevisan 2018; Santos 2004).

And yet, in spite of her success in the editorial market, her books, it was believed, did not seem suitable for the cinema. After all, how could Brazilian cinema deal with themes such as incest, homosexuality, paedophilia and a whole catalogue of taboo subjects? This had to wait for a cinema that was itself ready to break taboos and in many ways be as strong as her writing. Even though she started to publish in the late 1940s, it was only in the early 1980s that three of her books were finally adapted for the screen: *Ariella* (1980), based on the novel *Ariella, a paranóica* (*Ariella, the Paranoid*), as we have seen, published in 1976 and re-edited in 1980 in the wake of the film's success; *Tessa, a gata* (*Tessa, the Hottie*, John Herbert, 1982), based on the 1974 eponymous novel and also re-edited after the film; and *O orgasmo da serpente* (*The Snake's Orgasm*, J. Marreco, 1983), based on *A serpente e a flor* (*The Snake and the Flower*, 1965). Rios wrote the script for *Ariella* and *Tessa*.[5] Unfortunately, there is little information about a fourth adaptation, *Muro alto* (*High Wall*, Luis Fernando Goulart, 1982): it is briefly mentioned on the Cinemateca Brasileira website (Filmografia Brasileira 2019) and in a short note in *Jornal do Brasil* (a popular Brazilian daily newspaper),[6] even though Rios's book, on which the film is based, is called *Muros altos* (*High Walls*, 1962), in the plural. Brazilian cinema was the subject of prejudice at the time, synonymous for a significant part of the spectators with *peito e bunda* (tits and butts). A conservative reception denied any political or artistic merit to the erotic wave, including on the part of the 'progressive' critics and filmmakers.

Adaptation studies often conflate aesthetics and politics, questioning notions such as 'originality', 'appropriation', 'fidelity' and 'hierarchy'. Rios's adaptations are implicated in these debates. One important aspect of the relationship between Rios's writing and the erotic films of the 1970s and 1980s is a lack of cultural hierarchy between the mediums of film and her literature, since both belong to mass culture. The transit between popular literature and popular cinema can thus be understood via the idea of reiteration: the negotiation with audience/readers who expect a number of repeated features; the need to infuse repetition with something new; the changes added to the reproduction of narratives from one medium to another. Linda Hutcheon (2006: 7) has called adaptation a 'repetition without replication' and Judith Butler (1990) defends the thesis that gender is based on the idea that all repetition carries within it the potential for subversion (as subversion itself depends on repetition). Taking these two ideas into consideration, it is possible to argue that the intermedial relationship between erotic films and literature in Brazil in this period has a queer dimension that has been overlooked. The result is the limited existing literature on a particularly interesting period of Brazilian cinema, which in turn asks for a revaluation of the ways in which a politics of bodies and (gender and sexual) identities can be foregrounded. After all, the notion of queer deconstructs the view of self as defined by essentialist approaches, going against claims of purity, which brings it provocatively close to the notion of intermediality.

When we consider the possibility of a queer intermedial approach it is possible to argue that, for example, the treatment given to the book cover of the second edition of the novel *Ariella* (Figure 16.1) indicates how the transit between the two media instils a crisis in the heteronorm that defines a patrilinear relation between book and film. Rios's novel was originally titled *A paranóica* (*The Paranoid*). It was only after the release of the film that the book was sold as *Ariella, a paranóica*, including the protagonist's name, undoubtedly to take advantage of the film's success. However, an unexpected result is also the fact that the 'lineage' is compromised, as the 'original' work loses its 'originality' and becomes a 'bastard child' of what it was supposed to create, the derivative film. One way to approach intermediality (and specifically, in our case, film adaptation) in this historical period is, then, to ask the question of the 'conceptual cooperations' which open up new dimensions of awareness and experience (Müller 1998: 31–2). A provisional answer can be found in the way popular cinema embraces, much like the first-person narrator in *Ariella, a paranóica*, a refusal to cure itself of a sexuality that is expressed in excesses and deviations. In Rios's novel the narrator asks: 'what is this disease

Figure 16.1 Book cover of Cassandra Rios's *Ariella, a paranóica* (*Ariella, The Paranoid*, 1980), 2nd edition. Authors' private collection.

that burns my body and disturbs my mind in hallucinations that celebrate sex as the force that moves life [. . .] as if the real sensations could never surpass the imaginary delirium?' (Rios 1980: 66).[7] Following this call, we argue that it is possible to think of intermedial links between film and literature through the lens of the circulating desires that both move and halt narratives. This will counter the prejudice against literary adaptations to the screen, a conventional critical language that tends to be, according to Robert Stam (2005: 4),

> profoundly moralistic, rich in terms that imply that the cinema has somehow done a disservice to literature. Terms like 'infidelity', 'betrayal', 'deformation', 'violation', 'bastardization', 'vulgarization', and 'desecration' proliferate in adaptation discourse.

It is revealing that the list of terms drawn up by Stam recalls popular parlance on the subject of sexual intercourse and family relations. The relationship between cinema and literature sounds similar to a conjugal relationship when the film is 'unfaithful', when it 'betrays' the original work, and reveals itself to be an ungrateful, 'bastard' offspring, whose existence vulgarises the novel. This language invites us to rethink the connection between film and literature from a queer point of view, one that posits 'an antinormative position with regard to sexuality' (Jagose 1996: 98). This critical perspective can contribute to overcoming the privilege of the patriarchal heterocisnormative family order and the patrolling of the circulation of desires. In this context, the question becomes: how to approach this specific moment of Brazilian cinema, when there was a proliferation of on-screen representations of desire, understanding adaptation as a queerly mediated process?

ARIELLA

In the novel, the narrative is centred around a rich family, which dictates, in the film, a refinement and the use of luxurious sets and costumes. The film translates Ariella's subjective point of view, her inner turmoil and frenzy, into an entrapment within the mansion's quarters. If, as readers, we are enmeshed in the narrator's delirious voice, as spectators we are caught up in the confined spaces where the drama unfolds. The outside world is rarely referred to, with a noticeable exception: a scene that takes place at the factory owned by Ariella's father, Rodrigo. The scene has the clear narrative function of constructing Rodrigo's licentiousness, as we see him interact in his office with a female employee who is wearing nothing but a pair of long, striped stockings. This semi-nakedness is rather gratuitous and in tandem with the exploration of female sexuality that was in vogue at the time. The employee is then told to 'try on' a new line of towels made in the factory. She is now fully naked and uses the towel to tease Rodrigo in a sort of striptease. This situation, however, is interspersed with a shot of the working women by the large industrial looms. The film effects a displacement of the visual pleasure by halting it with images of arduous labour, connecting the narrative with the outside world.

The book's narrative is presented in the format of a diary, where protagonist Ariella 'deposits' her thoughts (Rios 1980: 15). It is peppered with exclamation marks and words in capital letters, denoting overreaction and exaggerated awe. She says: 'This is my notebook. It represents who I am. In it I deposit my thoughts, drunk from LIFE or born from the MIND' (1980: 15).[8] The book is therefore announced as a representation, a mediation, a kind of caveat for the reader who might naïvely try to find some truth about Ariella. The first-person narrator declares its unreliability and oversentimentality, and rather than knowledge about the narrative world, she gives us the sense of excess, as feelings and thoughts circulate in a whirlwind.[9]

In the novel, the notion of a performative self is present from the beginning: for example, when Ariella imagines herself dying of leukaemia, fantasising the pain, tears and agony of her last days. Her imagination running wild, she begins to cry about her imagined death, performing the reaction she wants to elicit from the reader. But both she and the reader know that the book is just a 'representation' of who she is. Eventually, she calms down and stops crying, saying (both to herself and the reader): 'I've been an idiot! I shouldn't suffer this much! There was no one there to cry for me! No wonder ... I wasn't dying after all!' (1980: 18).[10] Rather than shying away from this melodramatic imagination, Herbert's film infuses it with queer sexuality. Ariella is a vaporous nymph with an appetite for revenge. She is a lonely young woman who feels alienated from her upper-class family. The awakening of her sexuality provokes a series of conflicts between her and her snobbish mother, Helena, and father, Rodrigo, as well as her brothers Alfonso and Clécio, both of whom are eventually seduced by her. She also becomes deeply involved with Mercedes, Clécio's fiancée. On overhearing a conversation between her siblings, Ariella learns that her biological father was, in fact, someone else; he was conned by Rodrigo, who stole his fortune and raised her as his own daughter. She then plots revenge against her family by using her body to reach that goal.

Much like in the novel, the filmic Ariella is ignored by her family: she is unloved, an intruder, 'unwanted, inopportune, a burden', as Rios (1980: 19) describes her in the book.[11] But whereas the book emphasises her inner life, the film focuses instead on her body. For example, her narcissism is visually highlighted in her intense encounters with her reflection in mirrors. In the novel she confesses: 'I spend most of my life immersed in [. . .] admiration for myself, for I'm able to see myself split into two, in a fantastic unfolding, facing life' (Rios 1980: 20).[12] The film makes the most of this doubling as though Ariella were fully aware that, as a woman, she is an image, much like the self-reflexive, unreliable first-person narrator in the novel. She rehearses in front of the mirror what would be expected from a feminine performance, but she is unable to find her true self.

Reflecting on women who flaunt their femininity in an exaggerated way in cinema, Mary Ann Doane (1982) suggests that such behaviour can be deemed a 'masquerade', or a mask adopted by certain women in order to conceal their masculine potential and avoid punishment. Doane recognises that, in films, female characters who masquerade are often punished – for instance, *femmes fatales* who try to usurp the masculine act of looking. No such punishment befalls Ariella. Not only does she use her bodily awareness to seduce her brothers and father, but she also exercises an active look towards Mercedes, who she desires. As both the object and subject of the gaze, Ariella thus confounds the patriarchal positions that, on the narrative level, she eventually debunks: she (falsely) accuses her father of trying to rape her, causing him to shoot her mother accidentally, and ends up as the sole heiress to the family's fortune.

As noted, the film *Ariella* gives centre stage to the problem of producing the (self-)image of the woman. This is, in fact, a recurrent feature in Rios's novels, which often unveil a woman's desire for other women, tearing apart moralities and standing in frank opposition to the censorship imposed by the dictatorship. In her books, troubling, non-normative identities frequently demand recognition by way of comparisons with the 'negative' or 'false' lesbians: married 'nymphomaniacs' who use other women to sate their sexual appetite, unredeemed prostitutes who exchange caresses for money, the big-bosomed 'butch' who wants to replace the male, and all the 'false' lesbians described in novels such as *As traças* (*The Moths*, 1975), *Um escorpião na balança* (*A Scorpio on the Scales*, 1975) and *Eu sou uma lésbica* (*I Am a Lesbian*, 1981). Flávia, a character from *Eu sou uma lésbica*, sums it up:

> My fingers chiselling my nipples. My tumescent young girl's breasts, in my hands, my hands going down, the guilty feeling, the revolt. I felt like a black woman in a blonde's festival, expelled, banished. I felt like a Jew at the time of Hitler, forced to walk in the middle of the road, banned from using the pavement. I felt as if I were inside an armour, with the helmet visor down, holding a sword to clear my way. I felt like a woman, not a girl, but a lesbian, a homosexual, a person with a defined character, with firm goals, no longer the rare cryptandra growing among false lesbians, the plant without visible male organs. What for? What are the bulge, the appendage, the penis, the vagina, the hymen for? It was all in the mind.[13] (Rios 2006: 72)

In *Ariella, a paranóica*, however, the narrator's unreliability, with her declared self-invention in the notebook, is much less assertive about her lesbian identity. The visual device used in the film, the mirrors, reinforce this lack of depth.

Ariella, the film, also confounds the limits of heteronormativity and jumbles generational familial hierarchy, as it ends with the protagonist alone in her mansion, a young sphinx eager to devour anyone willing to approach her riddles. The closest we come to an answer to Ariella's riddle is through Mercedes, even though here the film departs from the novel in the tone of their encounters. Like margarine ads or a TV commercial for the lesbian lifestyle, the images depicting the encounter between the two women are softly blurred, glossy, edited so as to show the idyllic nature of their rendezvous. In this sense, the film resists the pathologising of lesbian desire, describing instead the traditional family as cruel and opportunist towards non-heteronormative desire. In fact, Mercedes is Ariella's privileged interlocutor, though more so in the novel, since, unlike in the film, the story ends with their living together. It is the literary Mercedes that calls Ariella's attention to the existence of 'the devil', which she describes thus: 'It's not a person, it's not a beast, it's not an image, it's only an agitation in my body!' (Rios 1980: 73).[14] This is where film and literature merge, in the production of such demons, also known as 'affects', agitating the body with a desire that defies the laws of family bonds and society.

The difference in endings, however, suggests a cleavage in queer imagination as related to different mediums: whereas Rios's narrative creates a world where the melodramatic expectation for the lovers' union is met, Herbert's film constructs a much more self-centred character. In the filmic version, Ariella's trajectory revolves around her vengeance and destruction, and her propensity to use her sexuality to such ends links her to the figure of the *femme fatale*. In this sense, the film ends with a nod to conventional traditions in film history that deny resolution for this character type.

Although it is not possible to restrict the emergence of erotic films in Brazil to its connection to literature, it is interesting to notice what happens when film borrows narratives and a repertoire of non-normative desires from the literary medium. Books are consumed in a more or less solitary manner and are easily hidden, whereas cinema (watched in the traditional cinema, which was the practice at the time) provides a shared experience of looking. As the case of *Ariella* illustrates, by the early 1980s Brazilian cinema was keen to make visible a variety of desires, educating a whole generation on the pleasures and perils of looking, though adding clear limits to that experience.

Notes

1. For a discussion on queerness in Brazilian cinema see Nagime (2016), Lopes (2016), Marconi (2020), Bessa (2017) and Garcia (2004).
2. A clear indication of Moreno's dated approach is his use of the term 'homosexualism'.
3. Otelo and Oscarito will again kiss in Carlos Manga's *Matar ou Correr* (*To Kill or to Run*, 1954), a *High Noon* comedic parody. In this instance we could argue for an 'intramedial' connection between Fred Zinnemann's western and the Brazilian appropriation.
4. For some actresses, moreover, it was difficult to switch to more 'serious' works once their names were connected with *pornochanchadas* or erotic films. Adele

Fátima is a case in point. She was famous for her participation in films such as *Histórias que nossas babás não contavam* and had shot scenes as a Bond girl for the 1979 James Bond film *Moonraker* (Lewis Gilbert), but those scenes did not survive the final cut. Other actresses, such as Aldine Müller and Nicole Puzzi, migrated from film to television, taking advantage of their sophisticated looks to play secondary roles in soap operas.

5. For a discussion about Rios's authorship in the adaptation of *Ariella*, see Brandão and Sousa (2017).
6. The note, published on 9 February 1982 under the title 'Temporada de caça' (Hunting Season), mentions the search for a young actress to play the leading role in *Muro alto*. This has probably never seen the light of day.
7. 'Que doença me queima o corpo e conturba a mente, nessas alucinações que festejam o sexo como a força motriz da vida. [. . .] como se nunca as sensações reais pudessem superar os delírios imaginários.'
8. 'Este é meu caderno. Representa minha pessoa. Nele deposito meus pensamentos, bebidos da VIDA ou nascidos da MENTE.'
9. 'Cassandra Rios', the author, is also presented by Odete Rios (her real name) as a creation. In an interview given to *TPM Magazine* (2001), Odete Rios declares: 'When I speak of Cassandra, she is the one that I created, the one everyone sees' (Quando falo da Cassandra é aquela que criei, aquela que as pessoas vêem).
10. 'Que idiota fui! Eu não devia sofrer tanto! Ninguém estava ali a chorar por mim! Mas também . . . Afinal, eu nem estava morrendo!'
11. In the original, the full sentence reads: 'there always is the annoyed demonstration that my presence upsets and disturbs, that duties and obligations towards me are unwanted, inopportune, a burden' (Há sempre a irritada demonstração de que a minha presença perturba e atrapalha, que os deveres e obrigações para comigo são indesejados, importunos, um estorvo).
12. 'Vivo quase sempre mergulhada numa [. . .] admiração por mim mesma, pois sou capaz de me ver bipartida, num desdobramento fantástico, enfrentando a vida.'
13. 'Meus dedos burilando os bicos de meus seios. Os seios intumescidos de menina-moça, nas minhas mãos, as mãos descendo, o sentimento de culpa, de revolta. Me senti como uma negra num festival de loiras, expulsa, escorraçada. Me senti uma judia no tempo de Hitler, obrigada a andar no meio das ruas, proibida de subir pelas calçadas. Me senti dentro de uma armadura, a viseira do elmo descida, empunhando a espada para abrir caminho. Me senti uma mulher, não uma menina, uma lésbica, uma homossexual, uma pessoa de caráter definido, de objetivos firmes, não mais o raro criptandro crescendo entre falsas lésbicas, o vegetal sem órgão masculinos aparentes. Para quê? Para que a protuberância, o apêndice, o pênis, a vagina, o hímen? Estava tudo na mente.'
14. 'Não é gente, não é bicho, não é coisa, não é imagem, é só agitação do meu corpo!'

References

Bessa, Karla (2017), '"Como cheguei a ser o que sou"? Uma estética da torção em filmes das décadas de 60 e 70', *Revista Estudos Feministas*, 25:1, pp. 291–315.

Brandão, Alessandra and Ramayana Sousa (2017), 'Cassandra Rios e o cinema erótico brasileiro: autoria e performatividade', in K. Holanda and M. C. Tedesco (eds), *Feminino plural: mulheres no cinema brasileiro*. Campinas: Papirus, pp. 131–44.

Butler, Judith (1990), *Gender Trouble: Feminism and the Subversion of Identity*. New York: Routledge.

Doane, Mary Ann (1982), 'Film and the Masquerade: Theorising the Female Spectator', *Screen*, 23:3–4, pp. 74–88.

Filmografia Brasileira (2019), 5 September, available at <http://cinemateca.org.br/filmografia-brasileira/> (last accessed 27 September 2020).

Garcia, Wilton (2004), *Homoerotismo & imagem no Brasil*. São Paulo: FAPESP/Nojosa Edições.

Hutcheon, Linda (2006), *A Theory of Adaptation*. London: Routledge.

Jagose, Annamarie (1996), *Queer Theory: An Introduction*. New York: New York University Press.

Lacerda Júnior, Luiz Francisco Buarque de (2015), *Cinema gay brasileiro: políticas de representação e além*. PhD dissertation, Universidade Federal de Pernambuco.

Londero, Rodolfo Rorato (2016), *Adelaide Carraro, Cassandra Rios e o sistema literário brasileiro nos anos 1970*. Londrina: Eduel.

Lopes, Denilson (2016), *Afetos, relações e encontros com o cinema brasileiro contemporâneo*. São Paulo: Hucitec.

Marconi, Dieison (2020), *Ensaios sobre autorias queer no cinema brasileiro contemporâneo*. PhD dissertation, Universidade Federal do Rio Grande do Sul.

Moreno, Antônio (2001), *A personagem homossexual no cinema brasileiro*. Niterói: Editora UFF.

Müller, Jürgen E. (1998), 'Intermedialität als poetologisches und medientheoretisches Konzept: Einige Reflexionen zu dessen Geschichte', in J. Heibig (ed.), *Intermedialität: Theorie und Praxis eines interdisziplinären Forschungsgebiets*. Berlin: Schmidt, pp. 31–40.

Muñoz, José Esteban (2009), *Cruising Utopia: The Then and There of Queer Futurity*. New York: New York University Press.

Nagime, Mateus (2016), *Em busca das origens de um cinema queer no Brasil*. MA dissertation, Universidade Federal de São Carlos.

Pethő, Ágnes. (2011), *Cinema and Intermediality: The Passion for the In-Between*. Newcastle-Upon-Tyne: Cambridge Scholars Publishing.

Rajewsky, Irina (2010), 'Border Talks: The Problematic Status of Media Borders in the Current Debate about Intermediality', in L. Elleström (ed.), *Media Borders, Multimodality and Intermediality*. New York: Palgrave Macmillan, pp. 51–68.

Ramos, Fernão and Luiz Felipe Miranda (eds) (2000), *Enciclopédia do cinema Brasileiro*. São Paulo: Editora Senac/Edições Sesc.

Rios, Cassandra (1980), *Ariella, a paranóica*, 2nd edn. Rio de Janeiro: Record.

Rios, Cassandra (2001), interview with Fernando Luna. *Revista TPM*. 3, July, pp. 8–15.

Rios, Cassandra (2006), *Eu sou uma lésbica*. Rio de Janeiro: Azougue Editorial.

Rojas, Carlos (2020), '*Intermediality* – a "weird concept": queer intermediality in Dung Kai-cheungs' fiction', in H. Chiang and A. K. Wong (eds), *Keywords in Queer Sinophone Studies*. London and New York: Routledge, pp. 175–89.

Santos, Rick (2004), 'O mito de Cassandra: a gênesis da literatura gay e lésbica no Brasil', in D. A. Filho and R. M. A. De Maia (eds), *Livros e idéias: ensaios sem fronteiras*. São Paulo: Arte & Ciência Editora, pp. 159–88.

Stam, Robert (2005), 'Introduction: The Theory and Practice of Adaptation', in Robert Stam and Alessandra Raengo (eds), *Literature and Film: A Guide to the Theory and Practice of Film Adaptation*. Oxford: Blackwell, pp. 1–54.

Trevisan, João Silvério (2018), *Devassos no paraíso: a homossexualidade no Brasil, da colônia à atualidade*, 4th edn. São Paulo: Objetiva.

CHAPTER 17

The Humiliation of the Father: Theatrical Melodrama and Cinema Novo's Critique of Conservative Modernisation[1]
Ismail Xavier

In the late 1960s, a significant shift of focus occurred in Brazilian cinema from the public sphere to the private life and family dramas. In the previous decade, Brazilian cinema had primarily concerned itself with issues of labour exploitation, social movements, political history and allegories of national identity. Some Cinema Novo and post-Cinema Novo films provide compelling evidence of this change of emphasis. For example, *Copacabana me engana* (*Copacabana Deceives Me*, Antônio Carlos Fontoura, 1969) and *Brasil ano 2000* (*Brazil Year 2000*, Walter Lima Junior, 1969) focus on moral conflicts deriving from the generation gaps dividing petit-bourgeois characters; *Matou a família e foi ao cinema* (*Killed the Family and Went to the Movies*, Júlio Bressane, 1969) displays a series of criminal acts committed by passionate characters who, despite belonging to different social classes, present similar patterns of frustration and resentment developed within the private space of the family. The degeneration of traditional households is depicted in films that thematise the close connection between social changes and family decadence, as in *Os herdeiros* (*The Heirs*, Carlos Diegues, 1969), *A casa assassinada* (*The Murdered House*, Paulo César Saraceni, 1971), *Os deuses e os mortos* (*The Gods and the Dead*, Ruy Guerra, 1970) and *Os monstros de Babaloo* (*The Babaloo Monsters*, Elyseu Visconti, 1970). Significantly, psychoanalysis comes to the foreground as an overt guiding principle in the composition of many of these dramas, to such an extent that a film like *A culpa* (*Guilt*, Domingos de Oliveira, 1971) begins with a quotation from Freud that performs the same explanatory function which, in early 1960s Cinema Novo films, was fulfilled by social commentary and historical information.

From the late 1960s onwards, the experiences of the new generations, influenced by phenomena such as sexual liberation and other new codes of behaviour fostered by the development of mass-media culture, provided an impulse for films in which the concern with private life and sexual morality became a valid means of holding political debates, which, at that time, were suppressed elsewhere by the military regime. Strongly anti-Communist, the military endeavoured to support the West in the context of the Cold War and to accelerate the country's economic growth. On an ideological level, they adopted a staunch and symbolic defence of archaic moral codes, underpinned by the traditional family structure, even though these clashed with capitalist development and the consolidation of a consumer society in Brazil. Aware of this contradiction, artists searched for new ironic forms to express their distrust of the Brazilian conservative modernisation. To this end, some Cinema Novo filmmakers moved towards capturing the patriarchal ethos in its most modest manifestation, as found in petit-bourgeois households in disarray.

In composing their domestic tragedies, some filmmakers entered into dialogue with playwrights, a process which involved two different trends in modern Brazilian drama. The first of these trends regards the politicised realist aesthetic developed by the Arena Theatre troupe from the late 1950s onwards, as exemplified by the films *Em família* (*Inside the Family*, Paulo Porto, 1971), with a screenplay by playwright Oduvaldo Vianna Filho and writer Ferreira Gullar; and *Eles não usam black-tie* (*They Don't Wear Black-Tie*, Leon Hirszman, 1980), based on Francesco Guarnieri's 1958 eponymous play. Both films emphasise the relations between private dramas and class conditions, family affairs and economic crisis. Another trend was to focus on passion and desire, in an interesting dialogue with a melodramatic tradition which is best represented, in Brazilian modern literature, by the plays and novels of Nelson Rodrigues, whose work offers a rich stock of characters and dramatic situations for cinema to exercise a harsh critique of family life.

A notable feature of some Rodrigues's plays is their incorporation of space–time structures borrowed from cinema. His first play, *Vestido de noiva* (*Wedding Dress*), was hailed from its opening in 1943 as the inauguration of modern Brazilian theatre, thanks to the organisation of the action into three different lines which regularly alternate on stage. Each of these lines takes place in a distinct scenographic space, which alternates with the help of changes in lighting, light being directed to the space where action is taking place at a given moment, leaving the other two spaces in the dark. Rodrigues's play *Toda nudez será castigada* (*All Nudity Shall Be Punished*), written in 1965, is a good instance of his work with flashbacks and voiceover narration, two space–time organisation devices typical of cinema and an example of his intermedial process of creation. Right in the opening scene of the play, the female protagonist's voiceover sends the action back to the past, even before she is seen on the stage. This voiceover returns at regular intervals to comment on other passages of the enacted dramatic action.

Arnaldo Jabor, a leading Cinema Novo figure from the late 1960s onwards, played a key role in the intermedial dialogue between cinema and Nelson Rodrigues's plays. All his films present a bitter diagnosis of Rio de Janeiro middle-class conservatism, following the 1964 military coup. His first feature film, *A opinião pública* (*Public Opinion*, 1967), one of the best examples of the *Cinéma-Vérité* school in the Brazilian documentary tradition, launches an approach to the middle-class mind frame as expressed in everyday life and within the family context, anticipating some of the issues raised by his fiction films from the 1970s, including his Rodrigues's adaptations. Jabor adapted *Toda nudez será castigada* for the screen in 1972, and Rodriques's serial novel (*feuilleton*), *O casamento* (*The Wedding*, 1966), in a subsequent 1975 eponymous film. In the latter, he radicalised the ironic style already present in *Toda nudez*, taking advantage of the convoluted plot typical of serial novels. In both films, irony allows the director to posit bad taste, hysteria and family problems as historical symptoms of the decline of the patriarchy in Brazil. Jabor's aim was to expose the close connection between conservative thought and melodramatic imagination at that specific juncture. Melodrama is incorporated in his work to expose the contradictions of Brazilian modernisation during the most severe period of the authoritarian regime (1969–74). I shall examine his two Rodrigues adaptations in chronological order to highlight the gradual process of dramatic amplification within his filmmaking style. The focus on family dramas allows him to connect the way middle-class males handle their private traumas in that specific historical moment of Brazilian political life.

Toda nudez será castigada

In *Toda nudez será castigada*, Jabor signals a change in Cinema Novo's filmmaking style in the late 1960s and early 1970s. After being established via a coup d'état in 1964, the military dictatorship was then consolidated by Institutional Act Number 5 in December 1968, a highly repressive ruling aimed at extending the dictatorship for much longer than originally thought. In the film's very first shot, we follow the protagonist, Herculano, driving his car along the Flamengo beach in Rio de Janeiro, with the sky and the buildings lining the street in the background (Figure 17.1). This image recalls a nightmarish shot from Glauber Rocha's seminal film *Terra em transe* (*Entranced Earth*, 1967), a major allegory of the 1964 coup. In Rocha's film, the tracking shot along Flamengo beach, lined by Burle Marx gardens, works as an emblem of the rise of the conservative forces. In it, one of the protagonists, Porfirio Diaz, is seen from the same viewpoint and crosses the same space as in Jabor's opening sequence. In what is suggested as a triumphal parade, Diaz's countenance is presented as a fixed mask, his prominent, proud chin in profile; he is holding a dark banner in one hand and a crucifix in the other. The whole composition suggests the idea of an angel of darkness ushering in a new era in Eldorado (the imaginary state in which the story is set). Herculano's ride

Figure 17.1 Herculano in his car, with Piazzola's tango on the soundtrack.

in *Toda nudez* is a more prosaic, everyday event, highlighting the protagonist's self-assurance and enjoyment. The soundtrack sets a tone which is radically opposed to that of Diaz's parade. The ceremonial sounds and mythological associations suggested by the Afro-Brazilian *candomblé* ritual music in Rocha's film are replaced in Jabor's by Astor Piazzola's 'Fuga 9', a modern tango used as background to Herculano's entire story. With its at once passionate and 'cool' modernity, Piazzola's music anticipates the kind of sensibility privileged by Jabor's narrative style. However, while the music track contrasts with the tone adopted in *Terra em transe*, the shot's visual composition indicates a continuity of concerns between the portrayals of Herculano and Diaz. With this self-conscious acknowledgement of the earlier Cinema Novo masterpiece at the very beginning of his film, Jabor takes advantage of his medium to change the opening of *Toda nudez* completely when compared with theatrical performances of Rodrigues's play. Besides, with this clear reference to Rocha's film and recurrent nods to it throughout, Jabor expresses his basic assumption that family affairs constitute a hybrid domain, in the sense of Jacques Donzelot's (1997) concept of a 'hybrid sphere' as a meeting point for the public and private spheres, and for the confrontation between sex drives and moral codes, through which they acquire a clear political overtone.

Family melodramas, in Rodrigues's plays, combine comic and tragic elements deriving from his critical view of the failed father figure, a recurrent motif in his work. In Rodrigues, the downfall of the father is the result of his weakness, moral dissolution and waning authority, which prevent him from fulfilling the role of a traditional patriarch of the 'good old days'. In other words, Rodrigues is much more concerned with what he sees as morals than with politics. What Jabor does is reinforce the ironic view of the father figure in order to introduce a political critique of patriarchal tradition.

Jabor's protagonist Herculano is not parading towards a government palace to give an inaugural speech, like the powerful Diaz. He is going to his secluded villa, the private domain to which he has confined Geni, a former prostitute he turned into his wife in order to obtain a legitimate happy bourgeois marriage. He is in good humour when he arrives home, holding flowers and calling for Geni, but there is no answer. His attention is then drawn to the noise of a tape recorder, which turns out to be Geni's final message, recorded just before she committed suicide. This is the first scene of the play *Toda nudez será castigada*, one of the best examples of Rodrigues's exploration of the flashback as dramatic device. Geni's message takes us back in time, and her voiceover narration returns regularly throughout the film, always addressing her husband, up to the last sequence which returns us to the moment of Herculano's arrival at the villa. Geni's revelations function as a final gesture of desperate revenge, performed to denounce out loud how Herculano's whole life has been based on illusions about himself, about the character of his young son and about the very meaning of their marriage.

The flashback follows the pattern of a three-act play, full of intense conflicts and spectacular twists and turns as Herculano struggles between his desires and his moral convictions. As a spectacle, the film takes advantage of Nelson Rodrigues's dramatic toolkit, which competently and effectively combines different traditions (from Strindberg and O'Neill to popular melodrama), and which has proved extremely popular with Brazilian audiences since the 1940s. Within this context, Jabor launched a radically new approach that reads the play as a farce. In it, the victimisation of the characters elicits a tragicomic effect due to the gap between the way they see their dramas and the way the narrative presents them.

In its first stages, Herculano and Geni's love story is the result of a series of stratagems devised by Herculano's brother, Patrício, who lives at Herculano's expense. First, Patrício uses Geni, introduced as a prostitute friend, to save his brother from a state of mourning and melancholy caused by the death of his wife. Taken to the brothel while drunk, Herculano undergoes an auspicious rebirth of his sex life accompanied by requited passion (Figure 17.2). To soothe his troubled conscience about sleeping with a prostitute, however,

Figure 17.2 Geni sings at the brothel in *Toda nudez será castigada*.

Herculano masks this desire with the appearance of charity: he wants to redeem Geni. Meanwhile, on her part, Geni lives out her own fantasy of falling in love with a widower in order to save him from distress. After this first stage, Patrício instructs Geni to break his brother's last moral resistance by insisting on marriage as a condition for their sex life to continue. This, however, merely transfers the conflict from the widower's own conscience into his open, and comic, struggle with the rest of his family, who are not willing to accept Geni. Central to this struggle is the unflinching demand from Serginho – Herculano's son – that his father remains faithful to his late mother. Serginho enters the drama, then, as the agent of castration, switching roles with his father as he becomes the authority figure in the family, whose permission Herculano must obtain in order to marry Geni.

A central opposition between death – embodied by Herculano's family – and life – embodied by Geni's 'solar' figure – is clearly established throughout Rodrigues's original play. Jabor's film version translates this visually into a contrast between the restraint of the lugubrious family houses and the freedom, energy and sound of the colourful brothel. The space and light design thus symbolises the traditional duality at the heart of patriarchal Brazilian life: on the one hand, the family household and, on the other, the

Figure 17.3 Geni at Herculano's second family home, or the 'haunted house'.

brothel. They are the oppositional poles of an old social order, meant to be kept apart, but which are nonetheless brought together by the comings and goings of men. Given his family's conservative ethos, Herculano's mistake lies in his desire to connect these two worlds by integrating Geni, the prostitute, into the family realm. Even before he is granted permission to marry, he secretly confines Geni in his second family home, the old secluded villa, abandoned after the death of his first wife (Figure 17.3). Moved by jealousy of her life in the brothel, he installs Geni in his own domain and engages in a farcical game of seduction (fuelled by his desire) and restraint (caused by her strategic prudery) which seems completely out of place in a house haunted by his first wife's death. Geni's first contact with that space, her future tomb, already prefigures her ultimate misfortune.

To free the couple from the uncomfortable deadlock, a sudden and melodramatic turn precipitates Herculano's son's change of heart about granting permission for them to marry. Disturbed by his father's continued affair, Serginho starts to drink, is involved in a brawl and goes to jail, where he is raped by a cell mate, the so-called 'Bolivian thief'. When Herculano finds out about it, he blames Geni, and their whole affair seems ruined. But her rescue fantasy is displaced on to the victimised Serginho and coincides with the son's own plan of revenge on his father. Geni and Serginho start a secret love affair.

Meanwhile, the family and Serginho himself grant Herculano permission to marry Geni. Their wedding finally takes place, initiating a bizarre love triangle in which Serginho exacts his revenge by engaging in an incestuous love affair with his stepmother. On her part, Geni prefers Serginho, reducing Herculano to the comic role of a double victim, as the deceived husband and the father outwitted by his son. But Serginho's hatred for his father turns out not to exclude Geni.

In Jabor's film, when Serginho decides to go away on a trip to 'forget all his recent traumas', he makes Geni take him to the airport. Once there, they bid farewell and she goes to one of the airport windows to see him boarding his plane. Then a close-up of Geni's disfigured face while looking through the window reveals her despair. She leaves the airport sobbing uncontrollably in complete distress. That shot will only be complemented by its reverse shot at the very end of the film, when we go back to Herculano's villa to hear Geni's final message to her husband that closes the series of flashbacks. While her recorded voice is relating what happened at the airport and deeply shocked her, the film finally reveals Serginho getting on the plane with his real same-sex lover, the 'Bolivian thief', who addresses an ironical smile at her (Figure 17.4). It is a magnificent shot-(retarded) reverse shot effect that highlights the difference between film and theatre, an effect made possible because Jabor could film at the airport and radically change the ending of

Figure 17.4   Serginho and the 'Bolivian thief' go away together.

the story as compared to the original play. In the play Geni does not go to the airport; she knows nothing about it. She is sad and lonely at home, when Patrício comes to pay a visit and have a 'nice' chat with her. At a certain point, he looks at her and says, quite sadistically: 'Geni, I'm going to tell you something after which you will never be able to sleep again: Serginho has run away with the Bolivian thief.' This is the last of Patrício's blows in his melodramatic role as intriguer, the one who is behind the decisive twists in the plot, and a figure whose presence in the film strategically departs from Rodrigues's play. While, in Jabor's film, the irony comes from Geni's direct visual confrontation with the Bolivian's mischievous smile, in the play the irony takes place indoors and comes from the mouth of the intriguer as an efficient theatrical device.

In the film, Geni kills herself after recording her message for Herculano, in which she reveals all the stratagems that made him a puppet in the hands of his brother, Patrício, and his son, Serginho. Before she dies, she curses Herculano's entire family, and also her own breasts, her most cherished possessions, blaming her own vanity as the weakness that made her, at the beginning, accept Patrício's advice. By cursing her breasts, Geni reveals an embedded Christian morality also present in her taste for premonitions ('I will die of breast cancer'). Feelings of guilt are at the root of her motherly rescue fantasies towards seemingly fragile men. They are also behind her masochistic romance with Serginho, the apparent weakest person who turns out to be the strongest. Geni, a vital force, becomes the main victim in the plot of Herculano's decaying family. Her ambition to replace the family mother leads her to perdition. Her depiction is a kind of displaced, tropical version of the gothic scenario in which a woman imprisoned in a morbid household becomes the victim of forces from the past. At the same time, her sad story is akin to another, more positive, scenario in conventional melodrama, that of the redemption of the *femme fatale*, the tart with a heart of gold. Either way, Geni is defeated by the death forces embedded in the archaic moral code. Nonetheless, she attracts our sympathy and exits the narrative with dignity.

The same, however, cannot be said of Herculano. His penchant for compromise and self-deception places him in a conundrum between an archaic morality he has neither the force nor the legitimate authority to represent, and a modern sex life he is afraid to embrace. Under pressure, he chooses to mask his contradictions in a game of appearances, perversely manipulated by his own son, which ends with the unexpected revelation of the lies that had hitherto sustained his good fortune. After a hard struggle and the apparent removal of all barriers, the self-assured father and ruler of the domestic sphere meets failure and humiliation where he thought there would be happiness. The deceptions revealed by the taped message are not dwelt on in the

Figure 17.5 *Toda nudez será castigada* ends with a close-up shot of Geni's face, who is now dead.

film. Instead of Herculano facing the theatre audience as the main victim of Serginho's departure with the Bolivian thief, as in the original play, the entire final sequence concentrates on the dramatic force of Geni's traumatic last day. The film ends with a close-up of her dead face as she lies on the stairs, from which she can hear her own taped message that Herculano finds as she finally dies (Figure 17.5).

Herculano has not been able to reconcile the patriarchal law with his transgressive passion, but this unresolved contradiction does not make him a tragic hero. The major concern of the narrative is to expose his weakness and the moral family structure that ruins his life and kills Geni, all to the sound of Piazzola's modern tango.

O CASAMENTO

In order to see the *paterfamilias* moving beyond collapse and humiliation, we have to wait for *O casamento* (1975), a film in which another 'fallen' father figure, the protagonist Sabino, is given time at the end to make the radical choice of the Christian path of repentance and purification. Like Herculano, he is afflicted by a contradiction between his sex drives and moral values.

Sabino (played by the same actor, Paulo Porto) is a mirror image of the *Toda nudez* protagonist, no stronger than him and no less ridiculous in his difficult moments, despite his final radical step. Sabino's difference lies in his readiness for action, clearly demonstrated by his lucrative career in the property business, a corrupt sector co-responsible for the chaotic and disastrous urban growth in modern Brazil. Once again, Jabor's film displays the vicissitudes of a conservative father obsessed by his passion, this time a much more transgressive one, given that its coveted object is his own daughter, Glória. She is about to get married, a terrible fact that Sabino cannot bear and drives him out of control.

The film follows the development of Sabino's dramatic experiences the day before his daughter's wedding, a hectic chain of events involving Sabino's employees, who, in turn, find a solution for their own suffering and frustration in crime and suicide. The plot, like that of the original serial novel, is extremely convoluted and compressed. As such, it well suits the film medium, given its editing property that allows for the speedy combination of parallel events. Here, the different subplots create a mirror effect around the protagonist. Sabino is a bourgeois in crisis who, although troubled by the imminent marriage of his daughter, strives for the wedding ceremony to be performed with perfection because a government minister is expected to attend. It is an essential part of Sabino's strategy to seduce powerful men in order to obtain social visibility, but on this occasion his inner distress will lead to his social alienation, as we will see.

The opening scene takes place on the morning of the wedding day. Sabino is still lying in bed, assailed by nightmares. A carefully chosen opening sequence has already connected public and private spheres, providing a social framework for the family affair. Before showing Sabino in bed, a long credit sequence displays a series of images taken from one of Rio de Janeiro's summer floods, annual instances of social tragedy and death which are not unrelated to the real-estate business, private profits and political corruption. This opening sequence sets the tone for the entire film, and establishes, with its images of mud, dirt, rats, pestilence and human suffering, the central metaphor of 'overflow' which will permeate both the narrative and the characters' uncontrolled behaviour (Figure 17.6). A specific filmic property – here, the expressive visual configuration of the main characters' behaviour – allows for a synthetic representation of conservative thought and its political reverberations. Among the events in Sabino's nightmare is the memory of his father's last words to him before he died: 'be a man of honour'. Sabino wakes up and starts walking around his huge apartment. Looking in a mirror, he repeats the words, 'man of honour', while his face suggests a clear awareness of the unfulfilled promise. He goes to his daughter's bedroom and looks at her exposed

Figure 17.6 A lost doll in a Rio de Janeiro summer flood at the opening of O *casamento*.

body while she feigns sleep. In the living-room, the white bridal gown reveals the source of Sabino's crisis and, from the image of this disturbed man, the film takes us back in time to the events leading to the present state of things. The action concentrates on the day before, and the film alternates Sabino's experiences and Glória's recollections until, at sunset, they get together for a revealing scene on a deserted beach.

The flashback starts with Sabino in the back seat of his chauffeur-driven car, harassing his driver and complaining about the slowness of their journey, while the camera captures pedestrians occasionally looking at Sabino on the back seat of his car bossing his driver about. The tension caused by the surrounding crowd is the result of the extreme economic gap separating Sabino from the people on the street, creating on his part a feeling of claustrophobia akin to the famous opening sequence of Fellini's *8½* (1963). Sabino's arrival at his office brings him temporary relief, but very soon Noêmia, his secretary, announces a visitor – Doctor Camarinha, the family gynaecologist – and the calamities of the day begin in earnest. Camarinha has come to tell Sabino that he has witnessed scenes involving his own assistant and Glória's fiancé which make him suspect that the latter is homosexual. The doctor insists that Sabino should cancel his daughter's wedding ceremony, which is due to

Figure 17.7 Sabino and his daughter in *O casamento*.

take place the next day. Divided between his social duties and unconfessed jealousy, Sabino does not receive the seemingly terrible revelation in the way one might expect. Instead of cancelling the wedding, he spends the whole day trying unsuccessfully to deal with both his compulsive sexual anxiety, caused by his own desire for Glória, and his uncontrolled urge to disclose his secrets (Figure 17.7). His first confession takes place in church, to a priest, when he falls into a fit and vomits. Among vague references to humanity's corruption, he narrates to the priest a shameful episode from his childhood: his mother masturbating grotesquely while lying in bed beside him. His second confession is to Noêmia, his secretary, who, for the first time, he invites for sex in a filthy apartment that he keeps for such occasions. Once again, he gets very upset and becomes abusive to his secretary; then he tells her about another childhood episode when he was raped by a stronger and older boy. Obsessed with virility and, like Doctor Camarinha, troubled by the 'overflow' of homosexuality, he plays out this act of self-flagellation in front of a woman who means almost nothing to him. The grotesque scene culminates with him shouting the name of Glória when climaxing. Back in the office late in the afternoon, he vows to kill Noêmia, but his daughter calls him, interrupting his verbal abuse of his secretary. He leaves the office to meet Glória.

Before this meeting with her father, Glória had undergone her own set of experiences on the eve of her wedding. In a parallel flashback, she is first seen paying a visit to her father's office, where she is received as a goddess, with him playing the role of the high priest. Flirtatious yet ambivalent, she is completely at ease with his worship. Her manner suggests some complicity with Sabino's secret desire for her, though not without a sadistic edge as when she announces that she will shortly visit Camarinha – 'the doctor wants to tell me something special. I am curious.' Glória's mind circles around her first sexual experience. She goes to Camarinha to confess her own secret: to tell him that his son, Antônio Carlos, now dead, was the man to whom she lost her virginity. At the doctor's surgery, she enacts a parody of confession, undressing herself and defying the doctor to 'attest to her chastity', a guilt-free variation of her father's humiliating impulse to blend confession and sexuality. Later on in the film, her memories go further back, to her sadistic affair with Camarinha's strange son, Antônio Carlos. On the only occasion when they had sexual intercourse, they had visited Doctor Camarinha's homosexual assistant. The latter, for his part, had chosen that day to take revenge on his homophobic father, now paralysed by a brain haemorrhage. Camarinha's assistant's plan was to be penetrated by his male lover right in front of his father. While the plan did not proceed as far as this, it was enough to cause the death of the wheelchair-bound father. And it was also enough to excite Antônio Carlos and Glória, who went off to another room to have sex. Later that day, Antônio Carlos called Glória to declare his feelings for her but she coldly rejected him. Shocked and frustrated, he committed suicide.

Glória's convoluted recollections underline her competence in hurtful erotic games. On the beach, at sunset, she outwits her father, who makes a fool of himself, betrayed by his own illusory assumptions as to the extent of his power and of her innocence. She provokes him, saying he probably never loved her mother, adding that she has never liked her mother herself; neither does she love her fiancé, but only 'the man I am forbidden to love'. Encouraged by this suggestion, Sabino imagines things are ready for his own crucial revelation of desire for her. He cannot stop himself from kissing her passionately. Stepping backwards and seeming extremely shocked, Glória runs away, followed by her humiliated father, who tries to explain himself.

This pathetic scene on the beach finds resonance in the cathartic sequence which closes the intricate story involving Sabino's principal 'mirror image' in the film: Xavier, a sentimental working-class man and the lover of Sabino's secretary, Noêmia, who is married to a woman deformed and blinded by leprosy. While Sabino is having his traumatic experience on the beach, Xavier, already upset by Noêmia's longstanding lack of enthusiasm for him, overreacts to her rejection, provoked at this point by her overblown expectations after the earlier affair with Sabino. He has come to see her at the office but she immediately orders him to leave. This he does but then returns to stab her many times, creating a blood bath in Sabino's deserted office. The sequence of horror continues back home, where Xavier kills his wife and commits suicide.

The next day, Sabino calmly takes his daughter to the church, in spite of everything, including Noêmia's death; 'it is the wedding that matters, above all', he keeps saying. At the end of the ceremony, inspired by the priest's eloquent sermon – 'we all have to acknowledge our leprosy' – Sabino quietly leaves the church and heads to the police station. As he comes upon the press, waiting there for news of the murder, he performs his final, public act of confession, claiming that he was the murderer of his lover Noêmia, the night before, in his office. He holds out his hands to be cuffed and allows himself to be arrested, with a smile on his face and his eyes turned to heaven, as if leaving all human bonds behind (Figure 17.8). After Sabino's confession, the sound of the 'Wedding March' plays over this final image of joy, reminding the spectators of the priest's ridiculous speech that inspired his spiritual illumination and the farcical scene of his arrest. By means of this

Figure 17.8 With a smile on his face, Sabino allows himself to be arrested in *O casamento*.

grotesque depiction of Sabino's 'saintly' illumination, entirely at odds with the tragic drama he sees himself in, the film directs a final critical blow at this frustrated patriarch.

Failing to inspire empathy, Sabino remains the pathetic, defeated bourgeois father, a man who finds an imaginary resolution for his dilemmas but is stricken by the same impotence that affects the other father figures in the film: Doctor Camarinha is a ruined man after his son's suicide; his assistant's suburban father dies in his wheelchair; and Xavier turns to unbridled aggression and suicide. The similarity in these characters' predicaments is elicited by means of a narrative orchestration entwining misery and male impotence. I have already referred to the late 1960s and early 1970s crisis in Brazilian patriarchal morality but, beyond this ironic treatment of conservative father figures and archaic family values, the question remains of how Jabor depicts the younger generation of sons and daughters.

The children Serginho, in *Toda nudez*, and Glória, in *O casamento*, contribute enormously to their fathers' falls. Their final move into the arms of homosexual partners brings into the family a taste of that 'overflow' of homosexuality at the heart of the *paterfamilias*'s paranoia. For the young, the final act in both dramas is an occasion for revenge; theirs is the final laugh. However, we are far from the traditional optimistic comedy which celebrates the joyous victory of the son or daughter over the autocratic father, with marriage providing a happy ending. Both Serginho and the 'Bolivian bandit' look at the camera before boarding their plane, and the latter's sarcastic smile is directed not at Serginho's father, Herculano, but at Geni, Serginho's lover. She is the victim of the aggression, a detail which connotes Serginho's escape as the last fatal blow from his morbid family which he, despite his libertarian choice, still represents. There is no hope in either of these films, which prefer, instead, to stress that the young people's strategies are mechanisms of reproducing, rather than overcoming, conservative ideology, an ongoing force of sameness with all its social and individual costs.

Conclusion

The oppositional binary between the modern, seen as a source of tension, and the archaic, seen as a source of cohesion, as posited by the father figures in these films, suggests their ideological affinity with the military regime. The regime's exaltation of traditional family values constituted an ideological strategy to seduce the middle classes, even though its own most effective social base was of a rather technocratic sort, engaged in a very modern form of capitalism. However, it would be a mistake to see the archaic–modern binary as mutually exclusive terms. Their dialectical association has been repeatedly rehearsed throughout Brazilian history, the prevalence of one or the other term and their manner of interaction altering according to specific historical conjunctures.

The allegory of the military coup d'état in Rocha's *Terra em transe* placed the patriarch, a figure from the most archaic reaches of national symbolism, right at the centre of the scheming behind the coup. I have mentioned the role played by the patriarchs' young heirs at a time in which many of them, like Herculano and Sabino, could be seen as embodiment of failures. But as a social class, the heirs of the Portuguese colonisers gave birth to a rural patriarchy of Iberian descent, considered to be still actively influential in Brazil during the 1960s despite industrialisation, the rise of the new middle classes, intense urbanisation and the increasing entry of women into different spheres of work, including the highest echelons of public administration. In Rocha's allegory of the patriarch, Porfirio Diaz also personifies a kind of father figure related to tradition and the Christian family. He is the leader who orchestrates the conservative victory, displaying in his triumphal parade the grotesque physiognomy of a fascinating fascism under the critical eye of Cinema Novo.

The post-*Terra em transe* trend towards the production of dramas of bourgeois decadence – epitomised, as we have seen, by *Toda nudez*, with its revision of Rocha's opening tracking shot – corresponds to a desire to undermine part of the ideological tenets of the military regime. This is achieved by means of a clever operation entailing the recurrent representation of weak and self-pitying father figures in decline, in order to sabotage the values associated with the symbolic figure of the strong father. After *Terra em transe*, such ironic 'family trials' emerged not only in cinema, but in Brazilian cultural production in general, as best represented by the Tropicalist movement in theatre and popular music.[2] Patriarchy became Tropicalism's key target due to its central role in the legitimisation of censorship and other repressive measures adopted by the military regime. Filmmakers were, at the time, equally engaged in a critical left-wing programme aimed at revealing the backward, provincial nature of the regime's ideological enterprise, all the while pointing at what they saw as the continuum of patriarchal power, from the public, political sphere through to the private, domestic realm.

I have singled out Jabor since, among other reasons, I would argue that his approach was the most successful among filmmakers at the time in drawing attention to social sectors and experiences where it was still possible to detect the survival of the archaic amid the modern, as in the films examined here.[3] Perhaps nobody has ever articulated a pessimistic view of Brazil as eloquently as Jabor, in *Toda nudez* and *O casamento*, by means of the total dismissal not only of the patriarchs but also of the younger generations and their potential for change.[4] The cinematic criticism of patriarchal values gained in dramatic strength precisely when filmmakers like Jabor adapted the work of playwright Nelson Rodrigues for the screen. Although Rodrigues defended the coup d'état and sarcastically called himself a reactionary and a pious Catholic, his best plays and serial narratives could not be reduced to a direct expression of his political convictions, as is often the case with artworks. Rodrigues's resistance to modernisation, before and after 1964, was translated into works which depict a world of vanities and resentments, and of individuals frustrated by not attaining a state of moral perfection that, in fact, is not hampered by modernity. They are solitary figures who unite in their suffering and self-destruction, not because they find themselves in the 'most cynical age', as Rodrigues used to say. In the 1940s and 1950s, Rodrigues was the artist in Brazil who most insistently dissected masculine failure, by means of the figures of guilty fathers and feeble husbands, the heads of households who partake in the dissolution of values and remain incapable of fulfilling the role tradition had in store for them. There is an interesting debate to be held concerning the specific contribution of Rodrigues's plays because their agility, perceptiveness and modern language define a space of ambiguity in works that largely exceed the expression of the author's ideology. Filmmakers associated with Cinema Novo consciously reworked this ambiguity in their interpretations of his dramas. Jabor translated Rodrigues's acute criticism of the present as observed from the point of view of a moralist and, in his screen adaptations, turned the genres of theatrical melodrama and serial novel into a tool for ideological unmasking.

The dialectics of the archaic and the modern become, then, a means for this cinema to recognise Brazil's distinctive modernity. Through critical distance, films such as *Toda nudez* and *O casamento* cast a new light on Rodrigues's theatre and launch a bold new reading of Brazil's technical–economic modernisation under the military.

Notes

1. This chapter is a thoroughly revised version of Ismail Xavier (1993), 'Pais humilhados, filhos perversos: Jabor filma Nelson Rodrigues', *Novos Estudos* – CEBRAP, 37, São Paulo, pp. 59–81.
2. Tropicalism emerged at the end of 1967, first in the plastic arts, popular music and theatre, then in film, partially as a response to *Terra em transe*. Its overall strategy produced a significant shift in the articulation of basic questions concerning cultural nationalism, political art, the avant-garde and underdevelopment. It directed a radical critique at the 'dualist view' of Brazil, eliminating the distinction between pure national folklore and 'corrupt' urban culture, blending modern and archaic

techniques and adopting with good humour or bitter irony the syncretic nature of the Brazilian identity.
3. Another similar example of this trend is Joaquim Pedro de Andrade's adaptation of Dalton Trevisan's short stories in his bitter comedy *Guerra conjugal* (*Conjugal War*, 1975). Once more, the parodic incursion into domestic drama, with the brothel acting as a counterpoint, is guided by a gradual deconstruction of male sexual power through a series of episodes which subvert the so-called *pornochanchada*, an erotic-comedy genre very popular in Brazil during the 1970s.
4. There is no space here to analyse in detail Jabor's *Tudo bem* (*It's All Right*, 1978), with its humiliated protagonist, Juarez, an even more fragile father figure than Herculano and Sabino, and its transgressive figures from the younger generation who, like Serginho and Glória, encourage neither spectatorial identification nor optimism for the future.

Reference

Donzelot, Jacques (1997), *The Policing of Families*, translated by Robert Hurley. Baltimore: Johns Hopkins University Press.

Other Works Consulted

Bentley, Eric (1964), *The Life of Drama*. New York: Atheneum.
Brooks, Peter (1985), *The Melodramatic Imagination: Balzac, Henry James, Melodrama and the Mode of Excess*. New York: Columbia University Press.
Bruno, Giuliana (2002). *Atlas of Emotion: Journeys in Art, Architecture and Film*. New York: Verso.
Heilman, Robert (1968), *Tragedy and Melodrama: Versions of Experience*. Seattle: University of Washington Press.

CHAPTER 18

Intermedial Territories: Maps and the Amazonian Moving Image
Gustavo Procopio Furtado

In a key moment of Carlos Diegues's *Bye bye Brasil* (*Bye Bye Brazil*, 1980), the troupe of travelling performers that comprise 'Caravana Rolidei' and an indigenous family that has hitchhiked a ride with them have an anticlimactic arrival at the Amazonian town of Altamira. Located on the shores of the Xingu river in the state of Pará, Altamira was nationally relevant in the 1970s as a landmark for the westward expansion of the Transamazon Highway, the centrepiece of the military regime's project of national integration through the construction of roadways into the forest and aggressive settlement of the region. Immediately after their arrival, we see the members of the troupe and their fellow travellers inside an Altamira bar (Figure 18.1). They are positioned as disappointed spectators, standing in front of a wall that holds

Figure 18.1 Following their anticlimactic arrival in Altamira, *Bye bye Brasil*'s troupe and their indigenous passengers gather in front of a map of Brazil and a television set, establishing an 'intermedial figuration'.

a television set and a map of Brazil. The TV shows nothing but coloured lines – a detail that functions as an ironic twist underscoring the troupe's disappointment with Altamira, as well as making the TV set stand not for any particular televisual content but rather for the medium itself. The map, the largest element in the field of vision, is also reduced to the bare bones of cartographic representation and amounts to a blunt affirmation of the nation's territorial unity, emphasised by the high contrast of the country's geographical contours against a monochromatic background. This bar, along with the map and the television, are, in all likelihood, found objects incidentally discovered in Altamira by Diegues and his crew as they, much like the fictional troupe, ventured through the Brazilian interior in 1979. These elements, however, are aptly appropriated by the film to produce an 'intermedial figuration' (Pethő 2011: 2), by which I mean a spatialised citation of media in the mise-en-scène, which is deployed here to reflect the film's concern with the transformation of national space as well as with cinema's relationship to television in the wake of the latter's consolidation as a hegemonic audiovisual medium.

Although the significance of this intermedial figuration performed at an Altamira bar can and should be mapped out in relation to the narrative of Diegues's film, it can also serve as a point of entry into an underexplored and eclectic constellation of audiovisual works made in the Amazon during the 1970s and 1980s by filmmakers like Andrea Tonacci, Jorge Bodanzky, Wolf Gauer, Maureen Bisilliat, Lúcio Kodato, Hermano Penna, Adrian Cowell, Jean-Pierre Dutilleux, Yves Billon and Vincent Carelli, to name but a few. Constituting an international and multigenre corpus of works of cinema, television and video—as well as films that are self-consciously situated on the blurred borders between these media and their stylistic conventions (as we will see below in relation to Tonacci's 1980–2 *Os Arara*) – these films fall outside the scope of the prevailing genre- and nationality-based frameworks that organise film history and criticism. Yet these diverse films are fundamentally related in their shared geographies of on-site production and in their attention to questions about borders and territorialities that pertain both to Amazonian space and to the place of film in an increasingly multimedia audiovisual environment.

This chapter cannot provide an overview of this corpus of films but it hopes to exemplify a comparative approach that focuses on the significance of intermedial figurations, particularly the incorporation of maps in the mise-en-scène. Intermediality is a useful concept in the analysis of territorial films because of its inherently spatial connotation – which is not shared by related terms such as 'remediation' (Bolter and Grusin 1999). While the latter is conditioned by the temporality of the prefix 're', denoting repetition, the 'inter' of 'intermediality' conceives the relationship between media in terms of spatial frontiers that mark both the possibility of separation and the reality of contact between domains – 'border zones' where we and the films 'can test and experiment with a plethora of different strategies' (Rajewsky 2010: 65). Although rarely discussed in the scholarship on intermediality, the inclusion of maps in the visual field offers privileged moments for critical analysis. Through these inclusions films locate their diegesis in geographical space as well as positioning themselves in relation to maps as a relatable medium for spatial representation, thus inviting reflection about cinema's own cartographic dimensions. As Tom Conley argues, 'a map in a film is an element at once foreign [and] of the same essence as the film', meaning that a film is, in effect, a map insofar as it consists of a form of 'locational imaging' with a language of its own (2007: 1–2). Film, states Giuliana Bruno, going a step further with this analogy, 'is modern cartography' (2002: 71). To put it in different terms, films combine the geo-indexical possibilities of the medium (that is, its capacity to record visual inscriptions of actual locales accurately) with the formal, narrative and discursive possibilities available to the medium. This allows films to construct meaning-laden representations of space as well as to establish relationships between places, including the 'here' of the viewer and the 'there' of the world viewed (Ivakhiv 2013: 8–9). It is worth recalling that, for the vast majority of people, vital and oft-discussed places on our planet, such as the Amazon, exist primarily at the level of imagistic ideation, the cumulative result of circulating images that construct these places as cogent geographical entities and position viewers in relation to them. If we understand 'territory' to mean the symbolic as well as the material appropriation of sections of our planet by individuals and social groups, films are well-equipped accessories to such appropriations and are able to contribute to, reflect on and even disrupt them.

A number of critics working in the subfield that Les Roberts (2012) has called 'cinematic cartography' emphasise the distinctive possibilities of audiovisual cinematic mappings in contrast to territorial maps – in particular the way in which films can 'map' affects, memories, corporeal sensations and innumerable narratives and subjective perspectives in what some have called, suggestively, 'deep mappings' (Pearson and Shanks 2001; Les Roberts 2016). The appearance of territorial maps in films made in the Amazon, however, tends to place the inchoate possibilities of cinematic cartography in relation to a specific history of imperial and colonial conquest of a region and conquest's extension by the capitalist nation-state into the twentieth century. It is worth recalling that Brazil's transition from a Portuguese colony to an independent state did not represent the end of colonialism. Rather, this transition entailed colonialism's reconfiguration. The colonial project of conquering indigenous territories and peoples that was initiated by the Portuguese in the sixteenth century was continued, after Brazilian independence in 1822, by Brazilians themselves (Leonardi 1996: 99). At the time when Brazil became a republic in 1889, much of the Amazon region, which constitutes over 50 per cent of the national territory, was still unmapped and, for all practical purposes, outside the administrative control of the state. Relatively large indigenous populations, a diverse group representing over 300 distinct languages and cultures, were still living in partial or complete isolation in central Brazil and in the Amazon. During the twentieth century, the Amazon remained an internal frontier territory that was subjected to waves of settlement and colonisation programmes, as well as to myriad expeditions that in effect sought to bring the Amazon and its people into the Brazilian national map.

Drawing on the work of Michael Taussig, Luciana Martins observes that the drawing of territorial maps with clearly delineated borders in effect creates an interior to be visualised, explored and possessed – leading to expeditions that will fill in the empty spaces in the map (Martins 2013: 45–6). Cinema is no stranger to the yearning to see, map and possess (if only through visual capture) unexplored spaces. As a form of seeing and organising space, the cinematic *topos* of exploratory travel, which began shortly after cinema's invention, has been asserted to inherit the functions of imperial cartography (Stam and Shohat 1994: 147) and to be the bearer of a 'territorializing impulse' associated with colonial projects, scientific and commercial ventures, and the spatial consolidation of the nation-state (Castro 2009: 10). While the presence of specific maps in a film may suggest a difference between the media of film and cartography, it can also point to similarities and collaborations between their respective functions and visualising procedures.

Films produced in the Amazon by agents of the Brazilian state often betray their affinity with the strategies of territorial maps. For instance, the pioneering work of filmmaker and Amazonian explorer Luiz Thomaz Reis, as illustrated by *Ao redor do Brasil* (1932), incorporates maps as locational devices to situate its voyages of exploration in a national geography, as well as to position the camera as an instrument of knowledge that can provide detailed visual information that is missing from the national map, thus extending both the nation's and the map's appropriative spatial claims. Decades later, the somewhat cruder and more propagandistic filmic efforts of government newsreels such as *A integração da Amazônia* (1974), shot west of Altamira on the Transamazon Highway, also incorporate maps as part of a visual rhetoric of territorial integration. What mattered in the 1970s, though, was not as much the acquisition of visual knowledge as the imposition of the state's cartographic vision on space. In an inversion that is typical of many ambitious modernisation projects (Bauman 1998: 41; Scott 1998: 103–4), here the map precedes the territory and serves as a blueprint guiding the construction of the road and of grid-like, geometrically configured land partitions and settlements that appear indifferent to the specificity of local, social and environmental realities of the states of Pará and Rondônia. In his outstanding TV series *Decade of Destruction* (1990), Adrian Cowell would travel to some of the same locales presented in the newsreels and include a variety of maps and blueprints, while revealing a world of intense agrarian conflicts and disputes between the incompatible territorialising visions of disparate socio-cultural groups.

I careen briefly through these filmic examples to show that examination of this Amazonian corpus can connect works across geographies of audiovisual production and cartographic representation that exhibit multiple spatial understandings of the Amazon while also offering nuanced explorations of the relationship between film and territorial mapping. One could take an Icarian view and in effect map out film production in the Amazon, establishing territorial relations and comparative frameworks across a diversity of national and international films. Yet I would argue that the filmic use of maps, as represented by the intermedial figuration of the *Bye bye Brasil* bar scene, also invites us to zoom in on the details of these films and the ways in which they position themselves in relation to media and territorialities. A comparative analysis of intermedial figurations can shed new light on familiar films and invite re-evaluations of rarely discussed works—as demonstrated below in a comparative examination of the incorporation of maps in *Bye bye Brasil* and Andrea Tonacci's *Os Arara*.

Although *Bye bye Brasil* is a well-funded Embrafilme production and a classic of national cinema and *Os Arara* is an unfinished television series made for the Bandeirantes Network (only two out of the three intended episodes were completed and aired), these contemporaneous films travel the same territory along the Transamazon Highway in order to reflect critically on the issue of national integration and its consequences. They are also works that consciously navigate historic changes in audiovisual media – exploring the relationships between cinema, television and (in the case of *Os Arara*) video. Their differences are mutually illuminating because they highlight the range of filmic possibilities vis-à-vis the ideal of territorial integration manifested, in both cases, by the incorporation of maps in the mise-en-scène. As I will argue, while *Bye bye Brazil*'s spatial critique is accompanied by a cinematic version of cartographic integration, *Os Arara* enacts a refusal of totality by dwelling in the border territories between film, television and video, and also by remaining suspended in a perennial state of incompleteness.

Mapping Media and Territory in *Bye bye Brasil*

Though only two maps appear in *Bye bye Brasil*, they are crucially placed to bracket the film's voyage to Altamira along the Transamazon – which places the troupe on the map, as it were, of the national integration and development projects that transformed the state of Pará. The maps serve precisely to present the perspective of the state in visual form and thus to position the film's own reflections in relation to it. Attention to the visual elements and mise-en-scène of these moments of intermedial figuration reveal dimensions of the film's spatial thinking. The first map appears when Lorde Cigano decides that the troupe must go to Altamira, a place he imagines has not yet been reached by the ubiquitous 'fishbones' ('espinhas de peixe'), as he calls television antennae. Altamira is cast by Lorde as a prelapsarian tropical paradise in a parodic evocation of discourses of conquest and discovery ('A land so rich, no one needs to work. [. . .] It's such a green land'). These allusions to previous discourses about tropical paradises do not represent just a recycling of old clichés. Rather, they function to place the film's journey in relation to previous voyages and to situate the project of national integration at the conclusion of centuries of conquest and colonisation of this region, which has historically been as alluring as it is resistant to appropriation by outside agents. Immediately after Lorde decides to head to Altamira the film cuts to a frontal shot of the troupe's truck with one door open. Hidden from view but audible, Lorde is in the cab searching for a map of Brazil. The comical misplacement of this locational device and Lorde's complaints ('I know I have one. [. . .] How could a map of Brazil disappear?') indicate that the nomadic group has never actually used the map. Meanwhile, the long take showing the open truck door invites contemplation of other visual elements that, viewed during the map-search scene, can be seen in relation to cartography as alternate ways to represent and even to experience space. The door itself displays a painting of Rio's Sugar Loaf mountain—a rendering that, in contrast with cartographic representations, is an impressionist, suggestive allusion to a place rather than an accurate depiction. Providing an even more interesting (and overlooked) visual detail, the truck's windshield sports countless adhesive stickers showing human hands pressing against the glass (Figure 18.2). Though these hands pressed against the screen-like transparency of the windshield may seem like an inconsequential detail, I would argue that in this map-centred scene they function to evoke a relationship with space grounded not on the distance of visuality or the accurate graphic representation of space but on a corporeal, tactile reality and a sort of moment-by-moment tactical improvisation.

Representing another relationship with space, the missing map fulfils at a symbolic level the nation's imagined claim to and mastery over a territorial

Figure 18.2 While Lorde searches for a map, a shot displays the painted mountain on the vehicle's door and the stickers of hands pressed against its windshield, suggesting alternative forms of representing and experiencing space.

totality. As a *road* map, moreover, it refers specifically to the model of integration through road construction – which imposes its own logic of mobility over this land of rivers. The road map stands not just for the ideal of a territorial totality that unifies vast and diverse regions under the gaze of a single perspective but also for a radically distinct model of spatial organisation and mobility that was imposed upon the Amazonian fluvial geography during the 1970s. The map search concludes with Lorde finding the map and reading aloud the names of towns along the Transamazonian route to Altamira. Next, figure movement and a cut that reframes the shot produce a reorganisation of the space of the mise-en-scène – a reorganisation that is not unrelated to the reorganisation of space by the cartographic logic of road construction: in the scene, the map moves forward and takes precedence over the other visual elements such as the impressionistic painting on the truck's door and the palms pressed against the windshield, which we can no longer see. This scene signals the troupe's entry into the spatial order of the state and its project of national integration, an entry that is a harbinger of trouble for the nomadic group as the voyage to Altamira will be not only a letdown but also nearly their undoing (as they will lose all their belongings and be partially disbanded).

While maps may offer a sense of certainty about the organisation of space, its appearance here and the troupe's arrival at the Transamazon will lead to conflicting senses of location and dislocation, orientation and disorientation – upsetting even the otherwise smug Lorde Cigano. Spatiality is no longer a given but becomes a source of conflicting desires and confusion. This is most evident in the troupe's encounter with an indigenous group that is also headed to Altamira. This encounter evokes previous Amazonian voyages and one of these voyages' most emblematic events – the encounter between travellers and indigenous people. This indigenous group, post-contact native Amazonians who have become exilic wanderers due to the territorial transformations and settlement of the region, confounds the troupe's sense of space and orientation. Causing confusion about their location deep within Brazilian territory, an elderly woman in the indigenous group asks: 'Are you from Brazil?' An elderly indigenous man asks about the wellbeing of Brazil's president, as if he was asking about one of the troupe's family member. Moreover, the indigenous group perceives their westward journey differently from the troupe. Starting their Amazon voyage from the Brazilian coast, the troupe understands their travel as a movement away from civilisation and into the Amazon jungle. This vision draws from the duality and tension between 'litoral' and 'sertão' (the coast and the backlands of the interior) that informs much of Brazilian culture and history, and reflects the orientation of the colonisation process itself. This post-contact indigenous group, however, is headed deeper into the Amazon forest not to escape the reach of civilisation (as is the hope of the troupe), but to confront it. In Altamira they hope 'to pacify the whites', their leader says, as well as to fly in a plane. The latter proposition vexes Lorde: 'This is the Amazon forest. Have you ever heard about it?' Adding an important visual component, the indigenous children carry toy television sets made of wood. The inclusion of these objects reiterates the film's and the troupe's preoccupation with television. Even as they flee the medium's reach by travelling through the forest, they encounter indications of its far-reaching penetration into Amazonian space, here symbolically represented by the toys. This incorporation also plays with the relation between visuality and tactility that emerged in the contrast between hands and map. Here the visual technology most representative of late twentieth-century modernity and mass culture is rendered as a friendly, tactile object of play for indigenous children, the same children who will later be seen staring at the television set in the Altamira bar with expressions of puzzlement.

The appearance of the map and the troupe's subsequent entry into the cartographic space of the Transamazon Highway result in a disorientation that contradicts the map's assertion of territorial unity and cogency. The this-ness of spatial referentiality becomes disconnected from spatial experience. This process culminates with their arrival at Altamira. 'That's Altamira and the Xingu river,' says Lorde pointing from a hill on the road – but their arrival upends his preconceptions. 'Fishbones' are spotted as soon as the troupe sees the bustling town. At this point, the hands that were pressed against the windshield in the earlier shot are no longer there. The second map, at the Altamira bar (Figure 18.1), appears immediately after their arrival and functions to underscore the troupe's sense of dislocation in this landmark town for national integration. Unlike the road map, the map seen here is not a navigational device meant to be used but, as mentioned above, the bearer of a blunt visual rhetoric of territorial unity – of the nation as an unfragmented totality. This map includes only a few features, but they are crucial ones, such as the Federal District in the central plateau and two Amazonian highways, one representing the east–west span of the Transamazon and another a north–south road—probably the Cuiabá–Santarém, another ambitious Amazonian road that intersects the Transamazon west of Altamira. The shape formed by these intersecting roads on the map is vaguely suggestive of the 'fishbone' shape of TV aerials – and it is worth noting that the expression 'fishbone' is often used to describe roads like the Transamazon, which include short extensions that reach into the forest at regular intervals, producing a 'fishbone' pattern. Though this visual connection remains latent and unmentioned in the film, the relationship between television and national integration does not. The film reflects on the near omnipresence of television and its placement next to the map is an apt illustration of the fact that the medium performs its own effective work of national integration.

The film's displaying of maps at the critical juncture of the troupe's Amazonian voyage should invite us to consider the film's own cartographic dimension. Despite maps' inclusion as discrete visual objects incorporated in the film's mise-en-scène, what might be most remarkable about *Bye bye Brasil* is its capacious mapping impulse, its desire to incorporate and signify a vast array of geographical elements within its visual and narrative framework, producing its own cinematic version of the cartographic totality represented by the map in the Altamira bar. This impulse is in part represented by the film's ambitious geographical coverage of the Brazilian backlands from the northeastern coast to the Amazon and on to Brasília; while the painting of Rio's Sugar Loaf mountain on the truck door suggests a non-cartographic form of spatial representation, it also adds to the film's geo-inclusive scope by referring to Brazil's former capital city on the southeastern coast.

The film's cinematic cartography, however, is a function not just of geography but also of the way it provides a spatialised representation of the history of cinema and television, and how it locates itself as an audiovisual work in relation to these media. The film's spatial trajectory performs an oblique mapping of the history of Brazilian cinema. While the shots of local markets at the beginning evoke regional documentaries, the passage through the *sertão* revisits the emblematic setting of 'cinema novo' (Vieira 2003: 166–7). Even earlier periods in cinema's history are incorporated in the voyage, as in the troupe's encounter with the projectionist Zé da Luz, who screens Gilda de Abreu's *O ébrio* (*The Drunkard*, 1946), making reference to the Lumière brothers as well as to the productions of Cinédia. Meanwhile, the film's voyage is narratively motivated by the newly consolidated hegemony of the television, whose widespread reach is illustrated along the way by the television sets that steal Caravana Rolidei's audience. Critics have noted that Lorde Cigano stands in as a surrogate for filmmakers (Stam et al. 1995: 422) who are on a quest 'for the wide audiences that patronized the chanchadas', audiences that 'by the 1960s migrated en masse to the television' (Vieira 2003: 167). As Sara Brandellero (2013: 60) notes in a brilliant reading of the film that is attentive to gender issues, Lorde can also be identified with 'the patriarchal, political project of the time', as when he takes ownership of Salomé's body in a moment of sensuous cartographic description: 'No teu norte está seu rosto, no teu centro o teu umbigo, no teu sul todo o meu gosto, meu feijão e meu abrigo' ('In your north is your face, in the centre your navel, in your south all my pleasure, my food and my shelter'). As he caresses Salomé's body, Lorde in effect charts it in an act of symbolic possession that connects mapping and colonial power over the female body. Beyond being Salomé's travelling companion and partner, Lorde will at times also send her out as a prostitute and serve as her pimp – displaying an exploitative relationship that mirrors the relationship of the Brazilian state with the Amazon.

To some extent, the film as a whole also becomes complicit with the map and with television as instruments of national integration even as it appears to place them in a critical light. At the end of the film, the reconstituted troupe is headed to another Amazonian frontier of national integration, the state of Rondônia, which will become another major front of road construction and settlement during the 1980s (with catastrophic consequences, as documented by Adrian Cowell in *Decade of Destruction*). Like the nation and its project of integration, the film has an encompassing geographical impulse to reach every remaining frontier. In relation to television and its effects, *Bye bye Brasil* is less oppositional than complicitous. The film forges a clever collaborative pact by casting telenovela stars José Wilker and Betty Faria as its protagonists, signalling cinema's future cooperation with the competing medium and foreshadowing future developments like Globo Filmes.

Border Territories in *Os Arara*

Andrea Tonacci's obscure televisual documentary *Os Arara* offers a compelling counterpoint to *Bye bye Brasil*. An unfinished three-part series made for the Bandeirantes TV network and shot in a combination of 16mm and video, *Os Arara* documents the efforts of a group of indigenists from the National

Indian Foundation who go on a mission to establish contact with the Arara, an isolated group whose territory was traversed by the Transamazon Highway. Due to the patient methods of these indigenists (led by Sydney Possuelo), contact was slow in occurring, ultimately frustrating televisual time expectations. After two years supporting the work, Bandeirantes aired two episodes and cancelled the series before contact took place. Tonacci would film scenes of contact with the Arara shortly after but would leave these images unedited until the end of his life – a choice indicative of the film's relationship with the achievement of territorial integration, as I will argue.

The film's incorporation of maps, which are shown alongside images of visual materials such as print media and photographs, occurs at the beginning of each episode and recurs intermittently thereafter, functions as a visual motif that punctuates the film and reflects its concern with both spatial and media territories. The first sighting takes place one minute into the film and shows maps and other materials spread out on a flat surface. The camera pans slowly from right to left to display the items, the first of which appears to be a satellite image of a landscape rich in geographical features and bodies of water, presumably the Amazonian area relevant to the film. The camera then reveals a map displaying rivers, roads and state lines, as well as a pile of newspapers that are handled by the filmmaker's hands, which intervene in the visual field. The newspapers themselves display more images, including another map. From the papers, we glean references to rubber tappers, migrant colonists demanding small plots of land from the state, representatives of agribusiness demanding large tracts of land for their projects, and, most important, a headline about the elusive Arara. The hands then remove these materials from view and the camera focuses on the map, which shows the states of Pará and, to the south, Mato Grosso. Placing the viewer in a specific geography, this map at first appears to function in accordance with the conventional use of maps as locational devices in the documentary tradition (Roberts 2012: 72). Yet its use exceeds this function. In this opening sequence, the combination of visual elements places the territorial cohesion purported by the map in tension with the fractured territoriality of a region subject to the contending claims and territorialities of the groups mentioned in the headlines. Of special significance in the film, the Arara's own territorial perspective is entirely outside the logic of maps and fixed land demarcations, as Sidney Possuelo will mention later in the film while standing at the provisional border of the Arara territory, an invisible and arbitrary line of division surely incomprehensible to its beneficiaries.

It is significant that the inclusion of maps in the film does not occur through editing, as a map insert shown full-screen in the conventional manner of TV documentaries, but through a mise-en-scène that places maps and other media materials in interaction with the filmmaker's hands. This method locates the map, characterised by the fixity and authoritativeness of cartography's territorial representation, within a fluid space and temporality characterised by a performative and tactile engagement with the filmmaker. Though embedded in the documentary, these map segments are related less to the conventions of the documentary tradition than to the style of videoart from the 1970s. Thus, precisely at the moments of the map's inclusion, the film drifts subtly into another audiovisual territoriality. Brazilian 1970s art video, which represents the appropriation of televisual video technology for entirely different expressive ends, often consisted of long takes of corporeal performances, 'like the act of going up the steps of a staircase, or drawing on a mirror or sheet of paper' (Cruz 2007: 9). In a particularly relevant example, Anna Bella Geiger's *Mapas elementares* (1976–7) shows an artist's hand sketching maps of the world and of South America. As an over-the-shoulder close-up of hands and paper, the framing is almost identical to the framing of the map segments of *Os Arara*. *Mapas* is a whimsical appropriation of cartography as a performance that posits maps as objects in the making rather than as fixed representations of pre-established knowledge and develops an alternative cartography defined as an embodied means of thinking about the relation between body, culture and territory (Shtromberg 2016: 137).

Unfettered by documentary concerns, Geiger surely enacts a more radical appropriation of cartography than Tonacci. Yet *Os Arara* also posits maps as objects in the making, as illustrated by the hand that repeatedly draws on and alters a fluvial map, at one point adding lines to represent the Arara's moving territory and the path of the Transamazon Highway with its road extensions—which, by a fortuitous graphic coincidence, look rather similar to the fishbone aerials dreaded by Lorde Cigano in *Bye bye Brasil*. While the map asserts a fixed spatial totality, the film's tactile inclusions place this spatial representation and the film itself on uncertain terrain, in intermedial borders between the documentary and video performance surreptitiously played out within the constraints of a television programme. Distinct from *Bye bye Brasil*'s effective mingling of cinema and television into a collaborative arrangement through the casting of telenovela stars, this blurring of media boundaries is the expression of a formalised resistance to integration and territorial totality that leads the film to dwell on media and spatial borders.

The film has a conflicted relationship with national integration. On the one hand, it construes the full incorporation of the Amazon region by the nation as an unmitigated disaster. This view is especially evident in one of the map segments that consists of a panning shot that shows a sequence of adjacent maps. These maps intend to synthesise the history of Brazil in five stages/maps, respectively captioned 'discovery', 'commerce', 'colonisation', 'independence' and 'integration'. The 'discovery' map shows a sliver of land covered with trees. It is a reproduction of Cantino's Planisphere map from 1502, the earliest Portuguese cartographic representation of Brazil, in which a vaguely shaped land appears as a source of timber. The 'commerce' map, reproducing Lopo Homem's 1519 *Miller Atlas*, shows indigenous people harvesting brazilwood, the country's first export product. Indigenous people do not appear on the 'colonisation' map, which shows the country divided into the fourteen captaincies that partitioned Brazilian territory during the sixteenth century. The 'independence' map shows a Brazil divided into state-like provinces but not yet displaying its current size and shape (notably, much of the Amazon was not yet part of Brazilian territory at the time of independence). Completing this teleologic sequence, 'integration' shows a map much like the one seen in the Altamira bar in *Bye bye Brasil* and includes the two largest Amazonian roads as well as five other highways crisscrossing the national space and implying an car-centred model of integration. Brazilians from the 1970s would recognise this display of maps as the back of the 500 cruzeiros bill issued in commemoration of 150 years of independence. Tying colonial discovery to the latest projects of development and incorporating currency as a visual medium, this panning shot is followed by shots of wrecked cars piled in a roadside scrapyard and tractors bulldozing their way into the forest, thus rendering the historic progression of territorial integration represented by the maps as a catastrophe.

On the other hand, the quest for contact with an isolated group, the ostensible goal of the expedition and of Tonacci's film, is part and parcel of the fulfilment of the nation's territorial claim. It amounts to bringing into the national fold the remnant of a radical, unassimilated cultural alterity. The film, however, ultimately stages a refusal to embrace the completion of this task. The temporality of the two finished parts is one of permanent deferral as it represents a quest for contact that, despite having already occurred in historical time, never comes to pass in the duration of the episodes. Given the visual absence of the Arara, what is, in effect, made visible in these two episodes is our own culture's desire to bring the unseen indigenous into our visual and epistemic frameworks (Machado 1993: 246). Although the initial failure to establish contact with the Arara was circumstantial, the fact that Tonacci never edited the contact footage is not. After the television series was cancelled, *Os Arara* was publicly screened and circulated among film scholars and cinephiles with the finished episodes followed by the unedited footage – making of its incompleteness a constitutive formal component. Presented in unedited form along with the two completed episodes, the contact footage is preserved as an unassimilated record – untouched by the edited logic of the film's two finished parts even if the Arara themselves did not remain untouched by the nation's expansion into the interior.

The performative map segments interspersed within the two completed episodes can be understood as reflexive pauses in the quest for indigenous contact. Occurring not in the forest but in an interior enclosed space, these segments serve as a retreat from the contact frontier and function as reflections on territoriality and media. Especially revealing of this intention, the final map sequence displays a Brazilian national map beneath a photograph of an indigenous person working with print and visual materials at a table while looking at a glowing TV set – which, like the TV set in Altamira, stands here for television itself rather than a particular television programme (Figure 18.3). This intermedial figuration includes some of the principal elements present in the Altamira bar: the map, the TV set and the indigenous spectator. But here the arrangement of these elements cannot be neatly tethered to the film's narrative or argument but instead stands alone, offering myriad interpretive possibilities. Who is the person in the photo? Why is he looking at the television set? What are the materials on the table? We lack enough information to

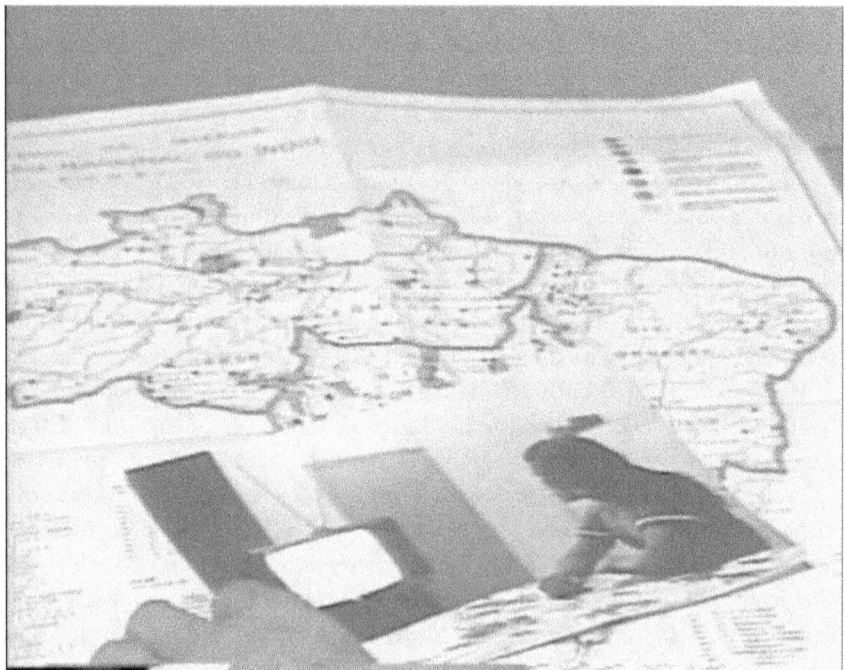

Figure 18.3 Tonacci's indigenous contact film establishes a reflexive dialogue between several media including the national map, photography and the television, thus placing itself in an intermedial territory.

decode composition confidently. Given that *Os Arara*'s ostensible purpose was to deliver the image of the Arara to television audiences, however, it is significant that what we see is not an isolated Indian but a post-contact indigenous person who is indirectly represented in the film through another medium. With his face turned away from us, the indigenous person here is less an object of vision than a viewing subject himself, a television spectator as well as a cultural producer of some sort, perhaps a *bricoleur* reordering the materials of visual culture spread before him. His position at the table mirrors the filmmaker's own placement during the map segments, which are illustrated by this very shot of materials displayed at his table. We could zoom out, at this point, to imagine a broader mapping of the Amazonian moving image. This shot and Tonacci's conflicted relationship with the contact project overall foreshadow the launch of indigenous videomaking projects in the mid-1980s, particularly Vídeo nas Aldeias. Partly inspired by Tonacci (Carelli 2004: 22), this project aimed to foster the appropriation of image-making technology by indigenous people at a moment when the indigenous were struggling to regain their territorial rights. Here, however, we remain in an intermedial figuration orchestrated by the filmmaker's hand, which places the intimation of future indigenous audiovisual agency against the background of the national map.

REFERENCES

Bauman, Zygmunt (1998), *Globalization: The Human Consequences*. New York: Columbia University Press.

Bolter, Jay David and Richard Grusin (1999), *Remediation: Understanding New Media*. Cambridge, MA: MIT Press.

Brandellero, Sara (2013), '*Bye bye Brasil* and the Quest for the Nation', in Sara Brandellero (ed.), *The Brazilian Road Movie: Journeys of (Self) Discovery*. Cardiff: University of Wales Press, pp. 49–68.

Carelli, Vincent (2004), 'Moi, un indien', in *Mostra Vídeo nas Aldeias*. Rio de Janeiro: Centro Cultural Banco do Brasil, pp. 21–32.

Castro, Teresa (2009), 'Cinema's Mapping Impulse: Questioning Visual Culture', *The Cartographic Journal*, 46:1, pp. 9–15.

Conley, Tom (2007), *Cartographic Cinema*. Minneapolis: University of Minnesota Press.

Cruz, Roberto Moreira S. (2007), 'Cortes e recortes eletrônicos', in Arlindo Machado (ed.), *Made in Brazil: Três Décadas do Cinema Brasileiro*. São Paulo: Iluminuras, pp. 9–14.

Ivakhiv, Adrian J. (2013), *Ecologies of the Moving Image: Cinema, Affect, Nature*. Waterloo, ON: Wilfrid Laurier University Press.

Leonardi, Victor (1996), *Entre árvores e esquecimentos: história social nos sertões do Brasil*. Brasília: Editora Universidade de Brasília.

Machado, Arlindo (1993), *Máquina e imaginário: o desafio das poéticas tecnológicas*. São Paulo: Editora da Universidade de São Paulo.

Martins, Luciana (2013), *Photography and Documentary Film in the Making of Modern Brazil*. Manchester: University of Manchester Press.

Pearson, Mike and Michael Shanks (2001), *Theatre/Archaeology*. London: Routledge, 2001.
Pethő, Ágnes. (2011), *Cinema and Intermediality: The Passion for the In-Between*. Newcastle-Upon-Tyne: Cambridge Scholars Publishing.
Rajewsky, Irina O. (2010), 'Border Talks: The Problematic Status of Media Borders in the Current Debate about Intermediality', in Lars Elleström (ed.), *Media Borders, Multimodality and Intermediality*. New York: Palgrave.
Roberts, Les (2012), 'Cinematic Cartography: Projecting Place Through Film', in Les Roberts (ed.), *Mapping Cultures: Place, Practice, Performance*. New York: Palgrave Press, pp. 68–84.
Robert, Les (ed.) (2016), *Deep Mapping*. Basel: MDIP AG.
Scott, James (1998), *Seeing Like a State: How Certain Schemes to Improve the Human Condition Have Failed*. New Haven, CT: Yale University Press.
Shtromberg, Elena (2016), *Art Systems: Brazil and the 1970s*. Austin: University of Texas Press.
Stam, Robert and Ella Shohat (1994), *Unthinking Eurocentrism: Multiculturalism and the Media*. New York: Routledge.
Stam, Robert, João Luiz Vieira and Ismail Xavier (1995), 'The Shape of Brazilian Cinema in the Postmodern Age', in Randal Johnson and Robert Stam (eds), *Brazilian Cinema*. New York: Columbia University Press, pp. 387–472.
Vieira, João Luiz (2003), '*Bye bye Brasil/Bye bye Brazil*', in Alberto Elena and Maria Díaz López (eds), *The Cinema of Latin America*. New York: Columbia University Press, pp. 161–8.

CHAPTER 19

An Intermedial Reading of Glauber Rocha's Cosmogony[1]

Lúcia Nagib

> He was unable to sign the noble pact
> Between the bloody cosmos and his pure soul.
> A gladiator defunct, but intact.
> (So much violence, yet so much tenderness).[2]
>
> Mário Faustino

The verses above, famously cited in Glauber Rocha's *Terra em transe* (*Entranced Earth*, 1967), offer two important clues to the director's work as a whole. In the first place, they encapsulate his cosmic ambition, announced in the poem as much as in the iconic aerial shots of the rounded, all-encompassing sea that open the film. Second, they expose intermediality as a key procedure in the director's mode of filmmaking. Poetry, in diegetic and extradiegetic form, is the language adopted by *Terra em transe*'s protagonist, poet-cum-journalist Paulo Martins, whose extended sacrificial death atop white sand dunes is combined with his voiceover, reciting:

> I'm dying now, at this time.
> My blood and tears are shedding.
> Oh Sara, they'll say I'm crazy,
> A romantic, an anarchist, as ever
> I don't know, oh Sara . . .

The pathos contained in these words, themselves a poem by Rocha, are further emphasised by the dramatic Prelude (Ponteio) of Villa-Lobos's 'Bachianas Brasileiras no. 3' on the soundtrack. The poet's tragedy is bigger than the failed revolution symbolised by the rifle he raises against the sky, bigger than the political turmoil of his allegorical country of Eldorado, bigger than his love for the revolutionary Sara: it is the primordial detachment from the cosmic whole, the irreversible banishment from paradise now tainted with his blood.

As much as a cosmic yearning, Faustino's verses reflect Rocha's voracious

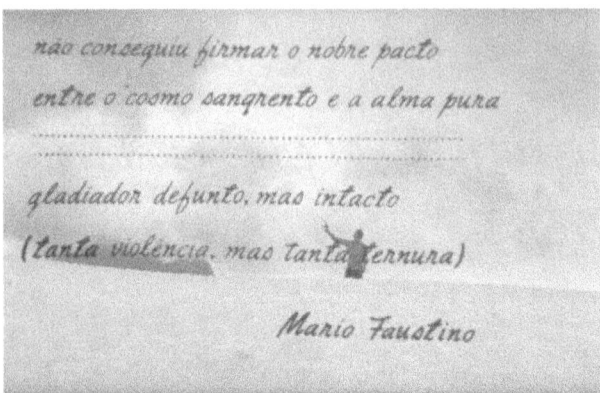

Figure 19.1 Faustino's verses appear *as* poetry: that is, as handwriting on the white page of the sand dunes.

appropriation of poetry to patch over the film medium's deficiencies in dramatic expression. Appearing *as* poetry – that is, as handwriting on the white page of the sand dunes (Figure 19.1) – they join a whole plethora of arts and media that constitute the director's output. In so doing, they place intermediality on a par with the cosmogonic impetus that propels the director's work. The aim of this chapter will be to demonstrate the radical aesthetic and historical consequences of this fact.

As is well known, Rocha was extremely proficient in poetry, fiction writing, theatre, drawing, journalism and television, all of which found expression in his cinema. As Ismail Xavier (2011: 16) has aptly summarised, art, for Rocha, 'is a foundational experience, a gesture of rupture that responds to a historical (and cosmic) condition in its totality. The artist's work is an act that mobilises all senses'. In *Terra em transe*, this totalising artistic endeavour is epitomised by the operatic tone dominating the entire film, including excerpts of the operas *O Guarani* (Carlos Gomes) and *Othello* (Giuseppe Verdi). As such, Rocha's work could be seen as the fulfilment of Wagner's utopia of the *Gesamtkunstwerk*, or total artwork, which has often been discussed within the framework of intermediality (see Jensen 2016; Breivik 2016; Clüver 2009, among others). For Wagner, the total artwork finds its utmost expression in opera, which he framed as the realm where the 'sister-arts' of drama, painting, poetry and music harmonically complement one another. Though presented as the 'artwork of the future', the total artwork, in Wagner's vision, is mobilised by an archaic romantic artist 'of the noblest manhood', who regains his lost connection with 'nature' by diving into the 'ocean of harmony' so as to give 'himself once more, refreshed and radiant, to the light of day' (Wagner 1895: 19). In a further echo of Rocha's totalising approach to cinema, the surface of the Wagnerian ocean is depicted as a 'sun-bright mirror' (36), just like the majestic, rounded, metallic sea flooding the frame in the opening of *Terra em transe*.

But Rocha's cosmogony is as much salvation as it is damnation, the 'hell of Eldorado', as Paulo Martins also proclaims in poetic form. Thus the cosmogonic sea finds its flipside in the never-ending scorched earth in the aerial shots that opens *Deus e o diabo na terra do sol*, Rocha's major breakthrough and Cinema Novo's pièce de résistance, which changes the *sertão* (the arid backlands) and its thorny *caatinga* vegetation, in the impoverished northeast of Brazil, into a representation of the planet. As such it offers itself as the ideal stage for the battle between god and the devil announced much more eloquently in the original title of the film, 'God and the devil in the land of the sun', than in its commercial English translation (*Black God, White Devil*), in which god and the devil are given racial connotations entirely absent in the film. In it, the protagonist, peasant Manuel, rises above his outcast condition to murder the exploitative landowner. He then attempts to find redemption from hunger and misery by following alternately the paths of religion and banditry. Because it is only carnage and destruction that awaits him at the end of both, the film could be read, once again, against the backdrop of Wagner's musical and philosophical proposals, or rather, in the way those have been read by Adorno. Revising his own previous condemnation of Wagner, Adorno (2002: 259) reaffirms the composer's continuing relevance in his day in the following terms:

> One can raise all imaginable sorts of objections to the Wagnerian mythology, exposing it as cheap and phony, as a romanticism of false beards and bull's-eye windows. Nevertheless, in comparison to all more moderate, detachedly realistic or classicist art, his work – especially the *Ring* – retains its decisive truth in this mythological moment: that in it violence breaks through as the same law that it was in the prehistoric world. In these thoroughly modern works, prehistory persists as modernity itself.

Because in Rocha's work, as in Wagner, 'myth is catastrophe in permanence' (Adorno 2002: 599), it features high within the modern canon, thanks to the director's promotion of 'the interaction of opposites, the mixture of styles and the reinvention of theatre in cinema' (Xavier 2011: 25).

Nonetheless, my approach to Rocha's cosmogony will veer away from the championing of the totalitarian superman that pervades Wagner's writings, as well as the philosophy of his erstwhile friend turned archenemy, Nietzsche. It is undoubtedly tempting and, to an extent, justifiable to interpret Rocha's heroes as his alter ego, and the director himself as the embodiment of the sacrificial artist, who predicted his own death at forty-two, in a reversed mirror, as he used to say, of the passing at twenty-four of his fellow Bahia countryman, the romantic poet Castro Alves. Whilst highlighting his undeniable personal talent and vision, I shall frame Rocha's cosmogony as a historical phenomenon, entirely in tune with the political movements of his time and the privileging of fragmentation and collage pervading contemporaneous artistic movements, such as Tropicália. As such, it stands in direct opposition to Wagner's unifying total artwork that drowns all artforms in a sea of harmony.

Even though Brazil and national identity have always been the focus of Rocha's films, they are also attempts at universalising the national experience into the condition of the entire Earth. This is notably the case in what became known as his '*trilogia da terra*', or 'Earth trilogy', including the aforementioned *Deus e o diabo na terra do sol* and *Terra em transe*, as well as his last film *A idade da Terra* (*The Age of the Earth*, 1981). In all three the reiteration of the term '*terra*', meaning both 'Earth' and 'land' in Portuguese, announce their planetary ambition. Focusing on the former two, as they mark the rise and fall of the 1960s revolutionary hopes through radically innovative aesthetics, this chapter will analyse cosmogonic intermediality in Rocha's work according to two totalising and strongly intermedial figures. The first is the motif of the cross, which resonates with Sergei Eisenstein's 'vertical' and 'horizontal' montage principles. In line with the abundance of crosses in the films' iconography, forming what has been called Rocha's 'Christology',[3] a recurrent up-and-down camera movement connects heaven and earth, life and death, good and evil, god and the devil. This in turn intersects with the horizontal, straightforward camera sweeps, which Xavier (1997: 31ff) famously defined as the 'teleology of history' and which juxtapose the Brazilian geography with the main phases of its history. What distinguishes both movements is the recourse to extrafilmic mediums for their completion, most notably oral and written literature.

The second figure is trance, which disrupts the finality and symmetry of the cross motif. It is elicited by what I will call here the 'unleashed camera', which roams the profilmic space like a disoriented *flâneur*, an entranced character like all the others, which supplies the film with a poetic passage to the irrational. Drawing an arc that marks the rise and fall of the cosmic revolutionary utopia from *Deus e o diabo na terra do sol* to *Terra em transe*, these figures will allow me to identify and describe the vertiginous synthesis of Brazil's political and artistic history promoted in Rocha's work.

INTERMEDIAL CROSSINGS

Deus e o diabo is structured on the basis of narrative and aesthetic binarisms. On the level of the fable, the film is an epic display of the equivalence and reversibility of opposite poles. Cowherd Manuel sees his cattle dwindle in the *sertão*'s unrelenting drought. Cheated by the landowner, Coronel Morais, in the division of the surviving livestock, Manuel stabs him to death and flees the farm with his wife, Rosa. They first turn to 'god', in the person of messianic preacher Sebastião, who entices the *sertão*'s miserable masses to the top of Monte Santo, or the Holy Mount, with the promise that 'the *sertão* will turn into sea and the sea into *sertão*'. Meanwhile, the landowners and the church hire Antônio das Mortes, the notorious killer of *cangaceiros* (northeastern social bandits), to exterminate Sebastião and his followers. Surviving the massacre, Manuel and Rosa find refuge under the wings of the 'devil', in the person of *cangaceiro* Corisco, who, with the few surviving members of his gang, wreaks havoc in the *sertão* to avenge the killing of his companion, the legendary *cangaceiro*, Lampião. Promising the *sertão*–sea reversal just like Sebastião had done, Corisco is soon tracked down and slaughtered by Antônio das Mortes, sending Manuel and Rosa on the run again, this time towards the mythic, revolutionary sea that closes the film, while in the background the music announces: 'The land belongs to man, not to god or the devil.'[4]

This binary narrative scheme finds visual expression, in the first place, in the motif of the cross (Figures 19.2–19.6). The Christian cross is a constant target for the camera, which captures it everywhere: on top of the grave of Manuel's mother, murdered by Coronel Morais's hitmen; decorating churches and homes; carried in the hands of Sebastião and his devotees; hanging on the characters' necks. Even cacti are often photographed as natural crosses in the arid *sertão*. In tune with this pervading visual trope, Waldemar Lima's dynamic, often handheld camerawork 'designs' the cross with its moves, not least along the vertical and horizontal lines of the crosses themselves. It thus becomes the embodiment of the *caméra stylo*, or 'camera-pen', that Alexandre Astruc (1948) famously identified in art cinema in its evolution towards the expressivity of painting and literature. Stressing the characters' ambiguities, the camera's vertical gestures split them in two, as in the famous shot of Corisco that leaves half of his face off frame, as he impersonates, in an extraordinary performance by Othon Bastos, his deceased companion, Lampião, in dialogue with himself (Figure 19.7).

Though a symbol of hope, the cross, in the film, is repeatedly weaponised, serving Sebastião to pin down sinners to the ground (Figure 19.8) and alternating in his hand with the dagger with which he kills an innocent newborn;

Figures 19.2 to 19.6 Cross iconography prevails in *Deus e o diabo na terra do sol*.

Figures 19.2 to 19.6 (Continued)

Antônio das Mortes and his rifle are also constantly captured against the backdrop of a cross (Figure 19.9). Comparing the cross to firearms, machetes and the sharp blade of Corisco's sword, in vertical and horizontal sweeps, the camera inserts violence into the very heart of the Christian myth, and in so doing, accomplishes the modern programme that Adorno had ascribed to Wagner's violent mythology.

Cross iconography is primarily a film-specific device, often resorted to in German and Soviet silent cinemas to signify the oppressive power of the church and social class divide. Cross-shaped camerawork served the mise-en-scène in the organisation of ornamental masses, for example, in Fritz Lang's *Metropolis* (1926) or Eisenstein's *Bronenosets Potyomkin* (*Battleship Potemkin*, 1925), the latter inflecting, later on, the Soviet-funded *Soy Cuba* (*I Am Cuba*,

Figure 19.7 The camera's vertical gesture splits Corisco in two.

Mikhail Kalatozov, 1964), which, as I have argued elsewhere (Nagib 2011: 125ff), presents astonishing similarities with *Terra em transe*. In Rocha, too, the cross is an instrument of power that changes the masses into automata coalesced around ruthless tyrants. Organisational and schematic though it may be, it is no less a disruptive device, which unveils the extrafilmic media entwined in the film's fabric. In *Deus e o diabo*, vertical and horizontal gestures dictate the film's orchestral organisation and polyphonic structure. In this respect, the film resonates strongly with Eisenstein, who, in his pioneering film theorising, defined vertical montage intermedially, by analogy with orchestral music:

> Everyone is familiar with the appearance of an orchestral score. There are several staffs, each containing the part for one instrument or a group of like instruments. Each part is developed horizontally. But the vertical structure plays no less important a role, interrelating as it does all the elements of the orchestra within each given unit of time. Through the progression of the vertical line, pervading the entire orchestra, and interwoven horizontally, the intricate harmonic musical movement of the whole orchestra moves forward. (1957: 74)

Eisenstein goes on to compare this mechanism with the polyphonic structure of his own silent films, 'where shot is linked to shot . . . through a simultaneous advance of a multiple series of lines, each maintaining an independent

Figures 19.8 and 19.9 The cross is weaponised in *Deus e o diabo na terra do sol*.

compositional course and each contributing to the total compositional course of the sequence' (75).

A similar vertical polyphony, combining simultaneous independent horizontal compositional lines, distinguishes the narrative construction of *Deus e o diabo* from the very beginning. The film opens with a series of horizontal aerial long takes of the never-ending arid *sertão*, mentioned above. With the initial credits still showing on the images, we are then presented with two close-ups of the rotting muzzle of a dead cow covered with flies, followed by a close-up of protagonist Manuel squatting next to it, visibly distraught by the loss of his cattle. He mounts his donkey and rides away in the *caatinga*. The next sequence starts with the camera now describing a vertical movement, aiming high at the scorching sun and tilting all the way down to capture, on the barren land, preacher Sebastião leading a group of ragged peasants. Sebastião holds in his hand a rudimentary wooden cross, made of a long vertical stick and a much shorter one crossing it at the top, materialising within the film's iconography the vertical and horizontal lines drawn by the camera movements up until now.

At that point non-diegetic music irrupts, consisting of guitar and a male voice singing the following verses:

> Manuel and Rosa lived in the sertão
> Working the land with their own hands.
> Until the day, for better or worse,
> That Saint Sebastião came into their lives,
> Bringing kindness in his eyes,
> Jesus Christ in his heart.[5]

These verses were written by Rocha himself in the style of *cordel* literature[6] and set to music by *bossa nova* composer Sérgio Ricardo, who also sings them. *Cordel* are popular narrative poems, usually illustrated by woodblock prints and contained in booklets, which are sold in street fairs and markets across the northeastern states of Brazil (Figure 19.10). *Cordel*-informed singing will recur throughout the film, marking its pace and serving as transition between the various narrative stages. However, rather than explaining what is shown

Figure 19.10   *Cordel* booklets hang on strings in dedicated shops.

Figure 19.11 Sebastião forces his followers into gruelling acts of penitence.

on the screen, *cordel* adds a new horizontal layer of meaning, often in frank disaccord with the images.

Take the first iteration of *cordel* cited above: the verses mention Manuel's wife, Rosa, but she is not shown to us until later, and at no point do we see the couple working the land. As for Sebastião, we are given no close-ups to demonstrate 'the kindness in his eyes and Jesus Christ in his heart', but only long shots of him surrounded by his followers, who kneel down, then continue their march across the cacti-strewn land, singing their prayers. Manuel on his donkey circles the group a few times then gallops away. Later in the film, Sebastião will give proof, not of kindness, but of utter cruelty, by forcing his devotees into gruelling acts of penitence such as carrying heavy stones on their heads while climbing up the steps of Monte Santo on their knees, with Manuel given the heaviest stone of all (Figure 19.11); beating Manuel into believing his *sertão*-sea prophecy; and stabbing to death a newborn whose blood he uses to 'cleanse Rosa's soul'.

Xavier (2007: 117ff) describes the independence of sound and image in *Deus e o diabo* in light of Eisenstein's vertical montage, but also Brechtian alienation effects, which are undoubtedly elicited here, insofar as the procedure calls for the spectator's critical thinking in deciding what version of the story to believe. In terms of intermediality, the effect of this and other disruptive *cordel* interventions in the film is consistent with what Werner Wolf famously defined as 'overt intermediality': that is, when a medium other than the dominant one makes an appearance with its 'typical and conventional signifiers', remaining 'distinct and quotable separately' (1999: 43). Indeed, here, the clash between non-diegetic *cordel* and diegetic film narrative allows for both mediums to be identified as such and be quoted separately.

The disentangling of the various horizontal narrative layers is also promoted with regard to Villa-Lobos's 'Bachianas Brasileiras', which are used throughout the film. The 'Bachianas' are based on similarities identified by Villa-Lobos between Bach and certain Brazilian musical forms, such as the arioso and the sentimental inflections of the Brazilian *modinha*. For this reason, each movement of the 'Bachianas' has two titles, one in classical terms (prelude, aria, toccata and so on), and another in Portuguese (*modinha, choro, ponteio* and so on). The grandiose opening of the vast *sertão*, at the beginning, for example, is accompanied by the second movement of 'Bachianas Brasileiras no. 2', which has the double title of 'Aria' and 'Canto da nossa terra' (Song of Our Land). This is followed, on the non-diegetic track, by the *cordel* singing noted above, as if the folkloric tune embedded in the 'Bachiana no. 2' had been set loose and had taken its own independent course. Later, when the action moves to the top of the Holy Mount, we hear a movement of Bach's 'Toccata and Fugue' for organ, as if to enlighten the spectator, in the pedagogical style of Brecht's epic theatre, on the concurrent source of Villa-Lobos's music, this time of an erudite pedigree. This procedure breaks entirely from Wagner's ocean of the total artwork, whose aim is to efface individuality in a collective harmony; instead, dissonance, ambiguity and difference are laid bare, in tune with the perennial state of doubt, confusion and torment prevailing among the characters.

Horizontal intermedial layering also occurs, in the film, in a 'covert' manner, which Wolf (1999: 43) illustrates with

> abstract modernist works by Wassily Kandinsky, Paul Klee, Georges Braque and others that constitute a kind of musicalized painting: while the result is still painting, music (its rhythm, certain non- or self-referential patterns) is the avowed structuring principle of the artefact.

In *Deus e o diabo*, literature, in covert form, informs the entire plot. The informed viewer will not fail to identify among its primary sources Euclides da Cunha's canonical book *Os sertões*, first published in 1902 and admirably translated into English by Samuel Putnam as *Rebellion in the Backlands*, in 1944. The book chronicles in epic style and minute detail Brazil's greatest peasant rebellion, the Canudos war, led by the messianic leader Antônio Conselheiro and quashed by military troops in 1897. It includes the prophecy registered in an apocryphal notebook, which Cunha found among the debris of the war, that 'the *sertão* will turn into seacoast and the seacoast into *sertão*' (Cunha 1995: 193). Rocha strategically replaced 'seacoast' – that is, the wealthy part of Brazil – with 'sea', which has no such connotation, but offered him the opportunity to display the cosmogonic visual motif of the sea that closes the film.

The events narrated in *Os sertões* are referred to by several characters in the film, in particular by Cego Júlio (Blind Júlio), who roams the cattle fairs and markets with a guitar on his back, as a typical northeastern *violeiro* or minstrel. Cego Júlio may at first seem to function as an anchor, in the diegesis, of the non-diegetic *cordel* singing; however, he never plays or sings. There is, nonetheless, a point where he becomes the conveyor of Cunha's literature, during a conversation with Antônio das Mortes. Both are sitting next to each other on a low stone wall, in a ruined village on the top of a hill (Figure 19.12). As the camera captures them from behind, looking out at the vast, barren landscape in front of them, the following dialogue takes place:

> Júlio: Mr Antônio, what can you see right in front of your eyes?
> Antônio: It is the vast *sertão* of Canudos.
> Júlio: Precisely... In this vast *sertão* I can see, in the distance, the earth red with Conselheiro's blood. Four governmental expeditions perished there... This I can see better in my darkness....[7]

Xavier (1997: 35) has brilliantly analysed the 'basic movement of expansion and contraction that characterizes [the] molding of time' in *Deus e o diabo na terra do sol*, which makes 'ordinary activities emblematic of a whole mode of existence' (36), such as the introduction of Antônio das Mortes, shooting

Figure 19.12 Júlio, in his blindness, is able to 'see', in the real landscape, the whole history of the *sertão*.

randomly in jump cuts, that summarises his profession as *cangaceiro* killer. What happens in the dialogue between Cego Júlio and Antônio das Mortes, however, shows another mode of compression of time, which again recalls Eisenstein's horizontal montage. Júlio, in his blindness, is able to 'see', in the real landscape, the whole history of the *sertão* harking back to the war of Canudos and reaching up to today. This resonates with the horizontal disposition of historical periods Eisenstein (1985: 260) had found on the geography of Mexico, when filming *Que Viva Mexico!* in 1930, where 'a matriarchal society [was situated] next to provinces that almost achieved Communism in the revolution of the first decade of this century', allowing him to retell this history in synthetic landscape shots.

In fact, rather than a faithful rendering of Cunha's book, or even of the events of Canudos, the film is a patchwork of references to the Brazilian literary canon, which, for their implausible coexistence, indicate their extrafilmic origins. The character of the messianic leader Sebastião incorporates features of Antônio Conselheiro as much as those of other figures, such as José Lourenço, who led a revolt in Caldeirão de Santa Cruz do Deserto, in the state of Ceará, in the 1920s; and, more importantly, of Sebastião, the leader of the Pedra Bonita sect (cited nominally by Rosa in the film) in Pernambuco, which also ended in a bloodbath in 1838. The Pernambucan Sebastião is a character in the novel *Pedra Bonita* (first published in1938), by José Lins do Rego, from which Rocha drew a number of episodes, including the sacrifice of a child. With this, the frontiers of the *sertão*, in *Deus e o diabo*, extend from Bahia further north to Pernambuco and Ceará, and retroact in time to encompass the early nineteenth century.

The real *cangaceiro* Corisco, in turn, was killed in 1940, and therefore could have never been a contemporary of either the real Conselheiro or Sebastião. Moreover, Rocha's *sertão* stretches down south, and closer to the present day, when it comes to another canonical book among its sources, the epic novel *Grande sertões: veredas* (first published in 1956 and translated into English as *The Devil to Pay in the Backlands*), by João Guimarães Rosa, whose work Rocha revered and emulated in his own and sole novel, *Riverão Sussuarana* (1978). In Guimarães Rosa, the *sertão* is not at all located in the Brazilian northeast, but in the hinterlands of Minas Gerais, in the southeast, presenting its own vegetation, topography and human characteristics. Having hardly anything in common with the storyline in this novel, *Deus e o diabo* overlaps with it entirely as regards the conception of the *sertão* as a totalising and objective as well as subjective cosmos, with no fixed territory or date. Proverbial phrases, such as 'the *sertão* is everywhere' and 'the *sertão* lacks a lock', as found in the novel, could be read as subtitles to the film from its legendary opening images of the endless *sertão*.

The covert use of literature is thus the means through which *Deus e o diabo* promotes a horizontal compression of time in the film's real settings, enabling Rocha to summarise to the viewer the entire history of social injustice in Brazil, even if for this he has to relent on all realistic acting and mise-en-scène: that is, turn his back on the specificity of cinema.

INTERMEDIAL TRANCE

Horizontal montage, as naturally found in the landscape in *Deus e o diabo*, is likewise a structuring device in *Terra em transe*, serving splendidly the film's cosmogonic and intermedial ambitions. Presenting itself as the aftermath or the flipside of *Deus e o diabo*, the film focuses on the land of plenty, the lush paradise of Eldorado. This is introduced by long and slow aerial takes of the sea illuminated by the sun's metallic glow, occupying the totality of the frame (Figure 19.13). The camera, on a horizontal sweep from left to right, captures the sea's rounded surface as if it were the globe itself. Credits are superimposed on the images, while the camera glides over mountains covered with dense forest, over which appears the title in parentheses: (Eldorado, inner country, Atlantic). This solemn presentation of Eldorado, suggesting the dawn of planet Earth, is then abruptly interrupted by various action sequences located in the present day, retelling the coup led by Porfírio Diaz. This is followed by the protracted scene in which Paulo Martins, mortally wounded, recalls his life in poetic form as described at the beginning of this chapter.

Martins's recitation unleashes a flashback which starts with dictator Porfírio Diaz's triumphal parade in an open car, holding, in one hand, a black flag and, in another, a crucifix, in an allegory of Brazil's 1964 military coup that curtailed the revolutionary hopes upheld in *Deus e o diabo* in the form of Manuel's

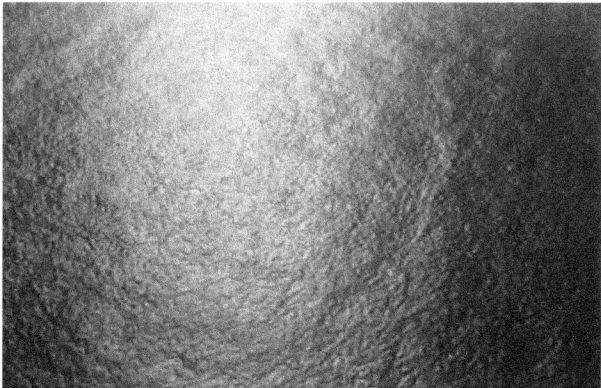

Figure 19.13 The cosmogonic sea at the opening of *Terra em transe*.

Figure 19.14 The re-enactment of Brazil's legendary First Mass, in 1500, in *Terra em transe*.

final race towards the sea. Diaz arrives at a deserted beach, where he meets a priest, a monarch (representative of the colonial power) and a native Brazilian Indian. Together, they re-enact, in front of a wooden cross, a ceremony redolent of Brazil's legendary First Mass in 1500 (Figure 19.14). The latter two characters are dressed in extravagant outfits – the monarch with richly decorated crown and cape, the Indian with a tall feather headdress – like those employed in the composition of historical allegories during carnival in Brazil (the monarch is actually performed by Clóvis Bornay, a famous champion of carnival costume contests). Thus, horizontal montage, carried out in the objective world as in *Deus e o diabo*, enables the compression of history and geography, encapsulating in one single space–time unit the dawn of the planet, the mythical Eldorado and Brazil's discovery and First Mass celebrated by the Portuguese in the sixteenth century, the whole interspersed with scenes of a contemporary world. Contravening the dynamism typical of cinema, the staging of this potted history relies on stasis, with the characters on the beach posing silently and stony-faced to the camera as if for still photographs, in carnivalesque costumes but bearing serious demeanours, as if they were decorative props on an opera stage. This is how, from the outset, *Terra em transe* evidences the intermedial nature of its totalising ambition (Figures 19.15 and 19.16).

As Xavier (1997: 15) has noted, the allegorical world of *Terra em transe* 'condenses an endless number of questions and experiences into a few individual characters whose life courses, nevertheless, represent a national fate, the destiny of an ethnic group or of a class'. Thus Paulo Martins, the film's (anti) hero, is at once a poet and a journalist redolent of a real-life journalist, Carlos Lacerda, whose articles are deemed to have effectively contributed to the military coup. On the other hand, as a poet, he can be seen as the filmmaker's

Figures 19.15 and 19.16 Characters in carnivalesque costumes pose stony-faced, as if they were decorative props on an opera stage.

self-reflexive alter-ego, whose voice, weaving in and out of the diegesis, carries the narrative forward. Ambiguous by definition, he is committed to the elites, including the media tycoon Julio Fuentes and the multinational company Explint (Compañia de Explotaciones Internacionales). At the same time, he joins the Communist party in their support for the populist leader Felipe Vieira, seen as a facilitator of social change. Vieira, in turn, is a conflation of João Goulart (known as Jango) and other populist figures in Brazilian history, such as the dictator Getúlio Vargas (President of Brazil between 1930 and 1945, then again from 1951 until his suicide in 1954), with his demagogic speeches and empty promises to the masses. Like Jango, Vieira opposes no resistance when his power is usurped by Diaz. Martins, a former friend and later traitor to Diaz, is the only one to take up arms and resist, but ends up being killed in a shootout with the police.

The transitory, multifaceted nature of all characters contaminates the film form, which, as a whole, is situated within the transience of the hero's crisis: that is, his passage to death as, mortally wounded, he recollects his life. Accordingly, the camera soon relents on the precision of horizontal and vertical sweeps, becoming instead transitional, a bewildered wanderer among contradictory characters. One could call it an 'unleashed camera', echoing the '*entfesselte Kamera*' used in *Der letzte Mann* (*The Last Laugh*, F. W. Murnau, 1924) by legendary cinematographer Karl Freund, who removed the then bulky equipment from the tripod and strapped it onto his own body, changing it into a living being (see Eisner 1965: 212ff).[8] This is precisely what Regina Mota (2001: 49–50) intuited, when she likened the use of the camera, in this film, to Dziga Vertov's 'live camera':

> The 'live camera', introduced by Vertov and rediscovered by direct cinema... can be found in some sequences of the film *Terra em transe*, in which Rocha, glued to the body of Dib [Lutfi, cinematographer], choreographs the camera-character, stripping the narrative of cuts and changing the scene into a ballet. The camera dances, pulses, loses and finds itself again in the setting, free from the limits of the frame.

As Mota rightly points out, once unleashed, the camera breaks the limits of cinema to become painting, ballet, music. It becomes intermedial and entirely germane to the idea of 'trance' that governs the film. An entranced camera could already be observed in sections of *Deus e o diabo*, most notably during Rosa and Corisco's adulterous embrace, in which the camera spins around the couple to the sound of the Aria (Cantilena) of Villa-Lobos's 'Bachianas no. 5', bringing the film to its erotic climax. In *Terra em transe*, the camera falls into further uncontrolled movements, as it joins the characters in their mental and physical paroxysms, often of a sexual nature, wandering around and between them, as if disturbed by the strident soundtrack, combining jazz, samba, Villa-Lobos and operas by Verdi and Carlos Gomes, which alternate and overlap with unmotivated gunshots and sirens. All colludes against logic and favours the exposure of the irrational element inherent in the state of trance.

Bentes (1997: 26) identifies trance as 'the first figuration of Rocha's thought and cinema':

> 'Trance' means transition, passage, possession, the process of becoming. In order to fall into a crisis or trance, one needs to be penetrated or possessed by the other. Glauber turned 'trance' into a form of experimentation and experience. [For him] to fall into a trance is to be in phase with an object or situation, to experience it from inside.

A mark of Rocha's work as a whole as it may be, the concept of trance is also entirely in tune with the artistic movements of the 1960s. Like so many libertarian artists of his time, Rocha was seduced by altered states as a creative tool with totalising potential. Trance was constitutive, for example, of the work of Hélio Oiticica, the originator of Tropicália. Like Rocha, he embraced a cosmic vision of the arts, as expressed in his installations *Cosmococas* (1970), a combination of 'cosmos' and 'cocaine', where the drug's white powder permeates and 'explodes' the perception of daily objects, configuring a holistic environment of 'pure nitro-glycerine', as poet Waly Salomão has put it (Buchman and Cruz 2013: 3–4). Having known and worked with Oiticica, who features in his film *Câncer* (*Cancer*, 1968), Rocha was also an adept of altered states as a disorganising mechanism that opened up for the expression of the irrational. He was himself partial to psychoactive substances, as he once declared in poetic form, shortly before his death: 'C'est l'herbe qui me tue ... Mon corps se fragmente comme Guernica de Picasso.'[9]

He remained, however, resistant to the humour and playfulness typical of Oiticica's installations, using trance, instead, as a harbinger of tragedy and death. This is noticeable from his very first feature film, *Barravento* (*The Turning Wind*, 1961), set in a fishing village in Bahia, inhabited by Afro-Brazilians, in which mystic trance induced by *candomblé*[10] drumming and singing brings the story to a head and defines its tragic outcome. Likewise, the music that accompanies the cosmic sea, at the beginning of *Terra em transe*, is a trance-inducing *candomblé* piece in honour of the orisha Euá,[11] which is followed by Paulo Martins's protracted agony, through which trance changes into poetry.

The flashback unleashed by Martins's slow death takes place convulsively, in the form of lumps of memory in fairly random order, starting from the end: that is, from the coup that deposes Vieira, followed by him with his bourgeois lover, Sílvia, and mentor, Diaz, as they drink and dance in the latter's marbled palace; with his Communist lover, Sara, and Vieira in a winter garden, concocting their political alliance; with the press tycoon Júlio Fuentes and his depressive newspaper colleague Álvaro, both of whom he also meets at orgiastic parties where they luxuriate in alcohol, jazz and group sex. These fragmentary recollections, charged with synecdochic value, are in direct relation to the film's poetic language, which combines verses by Mário Faustino, Castro Alves, the Argentine epic poem *Martín Fierro* and poetry by Rocha himself, sprinkled with sentences in Spanish to suit the film's pan-American aspirations.

Thus, thanks to its association with trance, the film performs a decisive intermedial leap to become the 'cinema of poetry' argued for by Pasolini and Eisenstein, both of whom ranked high in Rocha's pantheon. Pasolini defined cinema as a 'language of poetry' because of its 'fundamentally irrational nature' (Pasolini 2005: 172). Eisenstein, in turn, sided with Russian formalists, such as Khlebnikov and Kruchenykh, who defended the concept of *zaum*, or a 'transrational language', to signify poetry and incorporate an irrational element through which the word becomes 'broader than its meaning' (Steiner 1984: 144ff). Though most evident in *Terra em transe*, the role played by poetry's enigmatic excess is also key to all other Rocha films, which focus on the blinding, entrancing power of religion in order to expose the irrational roots of politics itself. In his famous article 'Aesthetics of Dream', Rocha (2019: 123) goes as far as defining revolution as fundamentally irrational:

> Revolution is the *anti-reason* which communicates the tensions and rebellion of the most *irrational* of all phenomena which is *poverty* ... Poverty is the principal self-destructive burden of any man and it has such psychiatric repercussions which transform the poor man into a two-headed creature. One head is fatalist and submits to reason which exploits him as a slave; the other, as a result of the fact that the poor man cannot explain the absurdity of his own poverty, is naturally mythical.

We have seen in *Deus e o diabo* how the submissive masses blindly follow Sebastião into self-destruction. In *Terra em transe*, improvised crowds from the reality of the Rio streets applaud, embrace and cheer Vieira, entranced by someone they deem to be a real politician; samba schools play and dance for him, offering shocking evidence in the phenomenological world of the reality of Paulo Martins's delirium. By embracing trance, with unique radicalism, as the (dis)organising principle of *Terra em transe*, Rocha rode the line of in-betweenness, which is the very definition of intermediality according to Pethő (2020). In so doing, he blurred the orchestral layers at the base of Eisenstein's vertical montage and exploded the harmony of Wagner's total artwork, offering instead a unique and staggeringly accurate assessment of our real cacophonous world.

Notes

1. This chapter expands on ideas contained in Nagib (2011), Chapters 1 and 3.
2. 'Não conseguiu firmar o nobre pacto / Entre o cosmos sangrento e a alma pura. / Gladiador defunto mas intacto / (Tanta violência, tanta ternura).' These verses are part of the poem 'Epitáfio para um poeta' ('An Epitaph to the Poet'), contained in the collection of poems *O homem e sua hora* (*Man and His Time*), by Mário Faustino.
3. Mateus Araújo Silva has been working on Glauber Rocha's 'Christology' for many years; however, I was unable to find this thesis in published form.
4. 'A terra é do homem, não é de deus nem do diabo.'
5. 'Manuel e Rosa vivia no sertão / Trabalhando a terra com as própria mão. / Até que um dia, pelo sim, pelo não / Entrou na vida deles o santo Sebastião. /

Trazia a bondade nos olho, / Jesus Cristo no coração.' The grammar mistakes in Portuguese are inherent in the original.
6. The initial credits call it 'romance', or poetic composition focusing on the folklore. The name '*cordel*' (meaning a thin *corda* or string) derives from the way the booklets are hung on lines in dedicated stalls. Despite being distributed in printed form, *cordel* preserves its oral character, since it is intended to be read or sung out loud by the author, the seller or a purchaser before a semi-literate audience. Tales of *cangaceiros* and miracle workers are considered the most exclusive Brazilian addition to this literature, whose origins go back to the Portuguese leaflets and manuscripts which, since the end of the sixteenth century, have travelled the length and breadth of the Brazilian hinterlands.
7. 'Júlio: Seu Antônio, tá vendo bem aí adiante dos seus olhos? / Antônio: É o sertão grande de Canudos. / Júlio: Apois ... Nesse sertão grande eu enxergo, no fundo, a terra vermelha do sangue de Conselheiro. Morreu quatro expedição do Governo ... Isso eu vejo melhor no meu escuro.' The grammar mistakes in Portuguese are inherent in the original.
8. The English translation of this book uses the term 'mobile camera'.
9. 'It's grass that is killing me ... My body is fragmenting like Picasso's *Guernica*.' These phrases were uttered by Glauber Rocha in a video interview with Patrick Bauchau, in 1981. Fragments of this interview can be seen in Silvio Tendler's documentary *Glauber o filme, labirinto do Brasil* (2003) and in Paula Gaitán's *Diário de Sintra* (2008).
10. Afro-Brazilian religion, whose rituals are aimed at inducing trance and spiritualist communication with deities called *orixás* (orishas).
11. Euá or Ieuá (in Yoruba Yèwá) is a female orisha in the Yoruba (called Nagô, in Brazil) religious pantheon. Her name derives from the Yèwá river, in the state of Ogun, Nigeria. The 'mother of character', she is worshipped, in the state of Bahia, in the Temple of Gantois (Terreiro do Gantois), referred to, in the Nagô dialect, as *Ilé Iyá Omi Àse Iyamasé*, or in the local pronunciation, *Ilê lá Omim Axé lá Massê*.

REFERENCES

Adorno, Theodor W. (2002), 'Wagner's Relevance for Today', in *Essays on Music*, selected, with Introduction, Commentary and Notes by Richard Leppert; new translations by Susan H. Gillespie. Berkeley, Los Angeles and London: University of California Press, pp. 603–11.

Bentes, Ivana (1997), 'Introdução', in Glauber Rocha, *Cartas ao mundo*, edited by Ivana Bentes. São Paulo: Companhia das Letras.

Breivik, Magnar (2016), 'From Operatic "Urform" to a "New Opera": On Kurt Weill and Musical Theatre', in Jens Arvidson, Mikael Askander, Jørgen Bruhn and Heidrun Führer (eds), *Changing Borders: Contemporary Positions in Intermediality*. Lund: Intermedia Studies Press, pp. 95–108.

Buchmann, Sabeth and Max Jorge Hinderer Cruz (2013), *Hélio Oiticica and Neville D'Almeida: Block-Experiments in Cosmococa – Program in Progress*. London: Afterall Books.

Clüver, Claus (2009), 'Interarts Studies: An Introduction', in Stephanie A. Glaser (ed.), *Media inter Media: Essays in Honour of Claus Clüver*. Amsterdam: Brill/Rodopi, pp. 497–526.

Cunha, Euclides da (1995), *Rebellion in the Backlands*, translated by Samuel Putnam. Basingstoke: Picador.

Eisenstein, Sergei (1957), *The Film Sense*, edited and translated by Jay Leyda. New York: Meridian Books.

Eisenstein, Sergei (1985), *Immoral Memories: An Autobiography*, translated by Herbert Marshall. London: Peter Owen.

Eisner, Lotte (1965), *The Haunted Screen: Expressionism in the German Cinema and the Influence of Max Reinhardt*. London: Thames and Hudson.

Jensen, Klaus Bruhn (2016), *Intermediality*, available at <https://onlinelibrary.wiley.com/doi/abs/10.1002/9781118766804.wbiect170> (last accessed 25 March 2021).

Mota, Regina (2001), *A épica eletrônica de Glauber: um estudo sobre cinema e TV*. Belo Horizonte: Editora UFMG.

Nagib, Lúcia (2011), *World Cinema and the Ethics of Realism*. New York and London: Continuum.

Pasolini, Pier Paolo (2005), *Heretical Empiricism*, translated by Ben Lawton and Louise K. Barnett. Washington, DC: New Academia Publishing.

Pethő, Ágnes (2020), *Cinema and Intermediality: The Passion for the In-Between*, 2nd enlarged edn. Newcastle-Upon-Tyne: Cambridge Scholars Publishing.

Rocha, Glauber (2019), *On Cinema*, edited by Ismail Xavier, general coordination by Lúcia Nagib, final text and notes by Cecília Mello, translation by Stephanie Dennison and Charlotte Smith. London and New York: I. B. Tauris.

Steiner, Peter (1984), *Russian Formalism: A Metapoetics*. Ithaca, NY, and London: Cornell University Press.

Wagner, Richard (1895), 'The Artwork of the Future', translated by William Ashton Ellis, available at <http://users.skynet.be/johndeere/wlpdf/wlpr0062.pdf> (last accessed 25 March 2021).

Wolf, Werner (1999), *The Musicalization of Fiction: A Study in the Theory and History of Intermediality*. Amsterdam and Atlanta, GA: Rodopi.

Xavier, Ismail (1997), *Allegories of Underdevelopment: Aesthetics and Politics in Modern Brazilian Cinema*. Minneapolis and London: University of Minnesota Press.

Xavier, Ismail (2007), *Sertão Mar: Glauber Rocha e a estética da fome*. São Paulo: CosacNaify.

Xavier, Ismail (2011), 'A invenção do estilo em Glauber Rocha e seu legado para o cinema político', in Peter W. Schulze and Peter B. Schumman (eds), *Glauber Rocha e as culturas na América Latina*. Frankfurt am Main: TFM, pp. 15–26.

Index

Note: *italic* indicates figure; n indicates note

Abrahão, Benjamin, 146
Abreu, Gilda de
　Alma de palhaço (*Clown Soul*), 231
　Ébrio, O (*The Drunkard*), 8, 228–30, 231–9, *233*, *234*, *236*, *237*
Abreu, Silvio de: *Mulher objeto* (*Object Woman*), 277
Acabaram-se os otários (*Gone Are the Morons/No More Suckers*) (Barros), 189, 208–9
Acidente (*Accident*) (Guimarães and Lobato), 39
Adele Fátima, 284n4
Adorno, Theodor W., 325, 329
Adriano, Carlos, 107n6
　Remanescências (*Remainiscences*), 95, 97–100, *97*, 106
adventure films, 215–16
Agamben, Giorgio, 95, 98, 103, 106
Aglio, Agostino: lithograph of the 'Modern Mexico' exhibition, London (1824), *21*
Aguenta, Felipe! (*Hang in There, Felipe!*), 180
Aïnouz, Karim: *Madame Satã*, 42, 275
Alcantara, João André, 154
Aldrich, Robert: *Kiss Me Deadly*, 45
Alencar, José de: *Ubirajara*, 180
Alencastro, Luiz Felipe de, 75
allegory, 3, 54–5, 64, 288, 290, 304, 337, 338
Alma Sertaneja (*Country Soul*) (Barros), 180, 182, 183
Almeida, Aracy de, 248
Almeida, Neville de, 221, 223
Alô, alô, Brasil (*Hello, Hello, Brazil*) (Downey, Barro and Ribeiro), 245, 248
Alô, alô, carnaval (*Hello, Hello, Carnival*) (Gonzaga), 134, 205, 245, 248, 249

Altamira, 307–8, 314–15
Altman, Rick, 177, 182, 235
Alves, Francisco, 160, 167, 169, 204–5, 248
Amado, Jorge, 277
Amaral, Justino do, 206
Amaral, Nestor, 7, 131–2, 134–5, *136*
Amazon: maps and mapping, 10, 309, 310–11
América do Sul (music video), 148
Amor, plástico e barulho (*Love, Plastic and Noise*) (Pinheiro), 151, 155
Amorim, Ottilia, 180
An 01, L' (Resnais, Doillon and Rouch), 52
Ancine (National Film Agency), 225
Ancoradouro de pescadores na Baía de Guanabara (*Fishing Pier at Guanabara Bay*) (Salles), 96–7, *97*
Andarilho (*Drifter*) (Guimarães), 45–7
Andermann, Jens, 48
Andrade, Joaquim Pedro de: *Guerra conjugal* (*Conjugal War*), 306n3
Andrade, Mário de, 41
André, Paulo, 47
Andrews, Hannah, 167
Angels With Dirty Faces (Curtiz), 64
animated pictures, 29; *see also* moving pictures
Ankito (actor), 251, 255
Annibal, Augusto, 180
anos dourados da sacanagem, Os (*The Golden Years of Pornography*) (Antonione), 59–60, *60*, 62
Antonil, André João, 35n5
Antonione, Paulo: *Os anos dourados*

da sacanagem (*The Golden Years of Pornography*), 59–60, *60*, 62
Ao redor do Brasil (Reis), 310
Aprile, Dina, 182
Aquarius (Mendonça Filho), 72, 73, 81–90, *83*, *85*, *86*, *88*, *90*, *91*
Aragão, Renato, 220, 224
Arara, Os (*The Arara*) (TV series), 316–21, *318*
Araújo, José: *Sertão das memórias* (*Landscapes of Memory*), 41
Araújo, Luciana, 153
Araújo, Vicente de Paula, 4, 244
Archambeau, Alice, 228
Areda, Laís, 206
Areias escaldantes (*Scalding Sands*) (Paula), 8, 221, *221*, 222–3, 224
Arena, Rodolfo, 228
Arena Theatre troupe, 289
Árido Movie, 7, 144, 145, 151, 155
Ariella (Herbert), 275, 276, 282, 283–4
Aristotle, 108n11
Arnaud, Arly, 83, *83*
Arnaz, Desi *see* Desi Arnaz Orchestra
Arruda, Genésio, 189
art
  comic books as, 55–6
  critical, 80
  and enfolding, 100
  'fore-edge' painting, 20
  and perception, 106
  Pop, 99
  poster, 56
  and technology, 94
  total artwork, 324
  see also transartistic commons theory
art cinema: *caméra stylo* ('camera-pen') in, 327, *330*
Asdrúbal Trouxe o Trombone (theatre troupe), 223
Assis, Cláudio *see* Pontual, Adelina, et al.
Associação Brasileira de Phonographia e Rádio, 212n22
Astruc, Alexandre, 327
Atlântida Cinematográfica company, 53, 115–16, 117, 124
Audiovisual Law, 145
Augusto Annibal quer casar! (*Augusto Annibal Wants to Get Married!*) (Barros), 180–1
aula de Charleston, Uma (*Charleston's Class*), 75, *76*
Auler, William
  Paz e amor, 182–3
  viúva alegre, A (*The Merry Widow*), 182
authenticity, 163, 224, 238
avant-garde, 3, 168, 305n2
Avellar, José Carlos, 67n15
Aviso aos navegantes (*Calling all Sailors*) (Macedo), 113, 117–29, *122*, 164, 251
Azevedo, Alinor, 255
Azevedo, Carmen, 186

b . . . profunda, A (*Deep Ass*) (Dominó), 66n6
Ba-ta-clan (revue company), 180–1
Babás (*Nannies*) (Lins), 72, 73, 74–81, *76*, *79*
Babilônia 2000 (Coutinho), 264, 265
Babo, Lamartine, 141n7, 249
Bacall, Lauren, 131
Bach, Johann Sebastian, 334
Badiou, Alain, 63, 65
Baile perfumado (*Perfumed Ball*) (Caldas and Ferreira), 41, 144, 145, 146, 148
Baker, Robert, 19
Baltar, Mariana, 265, 270
Bambozzi, Lucas, 44
Band Wagon, The (Minnelli), 128
Bandeirantes TV network, 311, 316, 317
bandes dessinées, 52
Bandido da Luz Vermelha, O (Sganzerla), 67n14
Bando da Lua (musical ensemble), 7, 135
Banvard, John, 23
baptisado de Paulo, O (*Paulo's Baptism*), 75, *76*
Barbarella (Forest), 54–5, *55*
Barbosa Júnior, 248
Barkleys of Broadway, The (Walters), 128
Barnabé tu és meu (*Barnabé You're Mine*) (Burle), 252
Barnard, Timothy, 3
Barravento (*The Turning Wind*) (Rocha), 341
Barreto, Bruno: *Dona Flor e seus dois maridos* (*Dona Flor and Her Two Husbands*), 215, 275, 277–8
Barreto, Romeu Muniz, 208
Barro, João de, 248, 249; *see also* Downey,

Wallace, Barro, João de and Ribeiro, Alberto
Barros, Luiz 'Lulu' de
  artistic career, 8, 177–8, 189–90
  film prologues: *Orphans of the Storm*, *185*
  films: *Acabaram-se os otários* (*Gone Are the Morons/No More Suckers*), 189, 208–9; *Alma Sertaneja* (*Country Soul*), 180, 182, 183; *Augusto Annibal quer casar!* (*Augusto Annibal Wants to Get Married!*), 180–1; *Capital Federal, A* (*The Federal Capital*), 180, 181–2; *Carnaval* (*Carnival*), 183; *Coração de gaúcho* (*Gaucho's Heart*), 180; *derrocada, A* (*A vingança do peão*) (*The Downfall: The Peasant's Revenge*), 180; *Perdida* (*Misguided*), 178, 179; *Rosa de sangue* (*Blood Rose*), 183; *Ubirajara*, 180; *Vivo ou morto* (*Dead or Alive*), 179
  set design, 187
  variety shows, 184
Barroso, Ary, 121, 122, 136
Barroso, Cláudio and Queiroz, Bidu: *O mundo é uma cabeça* (*The World is a Head*), 151–2
Barthes, Roland, 77–8
Bastos, Othon, 327, *330*
Batguano (Teixeira), 275
Batista, Linda, 118
Battleship Potemkin (Eisenstein), 329, 330
batuques, 133
Baucus, Joseph, 18
Baumgarten, Alexander Gottlieb, 109n24
Bazin, André, 2, 3, 72, 97–8, 104–5, 229, 261, 264
Beatles, The, 216
Beaty, Bart, 59
Beaumont, Harry: *Broadway Melody*, 246
Bela Época (*Belle Époque*), 177, 182, 190, 244
Belém: Teatro da Paz, 27
Bellour, Raymond, 71, 85, 101, 229
Ben-Hur, 31
Benedetti, Paulo, 206
Bengell, Norma, 57
Bentes, Ivana, 149, 340
Berg, Jordana, 265
Berkeley, Busby, 121
  The Gang's All Here, 135, 136

  see also Curtiz, Michael and Berkeley, Busby
Bernardet, Jean-Claude, 1–2, 177–8, 190, 268
Bernat, Julia, 83, *83*
Beugnet, Martine, 4
Beyond the Sea (Spacey), 166
Bigelow, Kathryn: *Strange Days*, 108n20
Bill, Tom, 189
Billon, Yves, 308
biopics, 166, 167
Bisilliat, Maureen, 308
Blom, Ivo, 5
Bodanzky, Jorge, 308
Bogart, Humphrey, 131
Bolsonaro, Jair, President, 225n1, 264
Bolter, Jay David, 17, 102, 255
Borba, Emilinha, 118, 120, 121, 128
Bordwell, David, 51
Bornay, Clóvis, 338
Botelho, Alberto, 180, 183, 248, 249
Bouquiaux, Laurence, 106
Braga, Rubem: *Homem no mar* (*Man at Sea*), 105–6
Braga, Sônia, 82, *83*, *88*, 277
Branco sai, preto fica (*White Out, Black In*) (Queirós), 226n12
Brandellero, Sara, 316
Brás Cubas (Bressane), 164–5
Brasil ano 2000 (*Brazil Year 2000*) (Lima Junior), 288
brasilidade (Brazilianness), 169
Brazil (Stanley), 121
Brazilian Association of Phonography and Radio *see* Associação Brasileira de Phonographia e Rádio
Brazilian Film Revival, 145
Brecht, Bertolt, 333, 334
Brenez, Nicole, 98
Bressane, Júlio, 168
  Brás Cubas, 164–5
  Cara a cara (*Face to Face*), 54
  Matou a família e foi ao cinema (*Killed the Family and Went to the Movies*), 288
Brewster, David, 23
Britto, Jomard Muniz de, 153
Broadway Melody (Beaumont), 246
brodagem ('brotherhood'), 154
Brougher, Kerry, 108n13

Bruno, Giuliana, 309
Brunow, Dagmar, 162–3, 166
Brutalidade (*Brutality*) (play), 179–80
Bull, Lucien, 107n6
Bullock, William, 20, 21
Burford, Robert, 20
Burle, José Carlos, 115
  Barnabé tu és meu (*Barnabé You're Mine*), 252
  Quem roubou meu samba (*Who Stole My Samba*), 253–5, *254*
Butler, Alison *see Screen* journal dossier: 'Intermediality in Brazilian Cinema'
Butler, Judith, 276, 279
Bye bye Brasil (*Bye bye, Brazil*) (Diegues), 10, 307–8, *307*, 311–16, *313*, *318*
Byington Jr., Alberto, 133, 135

Cabra marcado para morrer (*Twenty Years Later*) (Coutinho), 262–3
Cabral, Sérgio, 172n3
cafajestes, Os (*The Unscrupulous Ones*) (Guerra), 57
Cagney, James, 64
Caldas, Klecius, 255
Caldas, Paulo, 11n4, 146, 149, 151, 160
  Morte no Capibaribe, 153
Caldas, Paulo and Ferreira, Lírio
  Baile perfumado (*Perfumed Ball*), 41, 144, 145, 146, 148
  Sangue de bairro, 149, 151
Callegaro, João, 49, 51
  O pornógrafo, 61–2, 63–5, *65*, 66
Callegaro, João, Lima, Antônio and Reichenbach, Carlos: *As libertinas*, 61
Calvino, Italo: *Mr. Palomar*, 104, 105
Camargo, Alzirinha (singer), 134, 141n7
cameras
  caméra stylo ('camera-pen'), 327
  'live camera', 340
Caminha, Alcides Aguiar *see* Zéfiro, Carlos
Campogalliani, Carlo, 183
  A esposa do solteiro (*The Bachelor's Wife*), 183
Camus, Marcel: *Orfeu negro* (*Black Orpheus*), 163, 164, 171
canções, As (*Songs*) (Coutinho), 9, 261, 265, 266, 269–71
Candburg company, 29
Candeias, Ozualdo: *A Margem*, 67n14

candomblé, 341
cangaceiros, 146, 327
Capital Federal, A (*The Federal Capital*) (Barros), 180, 181–2
Cara a cara (*Face to Face*) (Bressane), 54
'Caranguejos com cérebro' (Crabs with Brains) manifesto, 144–5, 156
Carballo, Cuquita, 119, 252
Cardoso, Erika, 67n10
Cardoso, Fernando Henrique, 145
Cardoso, Ivan: *O segredo da múmia* (*The Secret of the Mummy*), 54
Carelli, Vicente, 308
Carequinha (actor), 251, 252–3
Carmichael, Hoagy, 131
carnival
  films about, 245–6; *Alô, alô, Brasil* (*Hello, Hello, Brazil*) (Downey, Barro and Ribeiro), 248; *Alô, alô, carnaval* (*Hello, Hello, Carnival*) (Gonzaga), 134, 205, 245, 248, 249; *Carnaval* (*Carnival*) (Barros), 183; *carnaval cantado, O* (*The Sung Carnival*) 183; *Carnaval no fogo* (*Carnival in Flames*) (Macedo), 123, 275; *Carnival in Costa Rica* (Ratoff), 136; *Rio, carnaval da vida* (*Rio, Carnival of Life*) (Hirszman), 169–70, *170*, 171; *voz do carnaval, A* (*The Voice of Carnival*), 247
  historical allegories of, 338
  see also marchinhas
Carrão, Humberto, 91n5
cartography *see* maps and mapping
Cartola (samba singer and composer), 159–60, *159*, 162, 164, 165, 166, 167, 168, 169, 170–1, *170*
Cartola – música para os olhos (*Cartola – Music for the Eyes*) (Ferreira and Lacerda), 156–61, 162, 163, 164–9
Carvalho, Beth, 167
Carvalho, Victa de, 108n21
Casa de caboclo (CNE), 205–6
casamento, O (*The Wedding*) (Jabor), 290, 297–303, *299*, *300*, *302*
Casares, Adolfo Bioy, 104
Casé, Regina, 223
Cassino Atlântico, 249
Castellar, Heloisa, 231
Castellar, José, 231

Castro, Flávia, 74
Castro Alves, Antônio Frederico de, 326, 341
Cataracts of Iguassu (Holmes), 27
catecismos, 52–3, 57–60, *60*, 61, 62, 65–6
Catherwood, Frederick, 20
Cavalcanti, Armando, 255
Cavaquinho, Nelson, 67n9, 170
Cavell, Stanley, 73–4, 104
Celestino, Vicente, 8, 186, 206, 228, 230–1, 232, *233*, *234*, 235, *237*, 238, 239, *240*
Cena Muda, A (*The Silent Scene*) (magazine), 123–4
censorship, 57, 186, 238, 278
Central do Brasil (*Central Station*) (Salles), 41
Chaco Indians, 25
chanchadas (musical comedies), 11n1, 113, 114–29, 134, 183, 189, 216, 243, 245
  definition of, 244
  and queerness, 275
  and television, 252–7
  see also Quem roubou meu samba
Chekhov, Anton: *Three Sisters*, 268, 269
Cheuiche, Jacques, 267
Chico Science & Nação Zumbi (band), 146, 149, 151–2
children *see* juvenile audiences
Chion, Michel, 147
Chiozzo, Adelaide, 118, 119, 120, 124
chorinhos, 133
Cinearte magazine, 147, 187, 188
Cinédia Studios, 228, 244, 247, 248
Cinema cafajeste, 61
cinema fallado ('talking films'), 203
Cinema Marginal, 3, 52, 53–7
Cinema Novo, 2–3, 52, 243, 245, 257, 288–305, 315
cinema on stage, 183–4
Cinema-troça (*Cinema-mockery*) (play), 179
Cinéma-Vérité, 290
Cinematógrafo Rio Branco, 182
Cinématographe, 18, 33
cinemímica, 183
cineteatros, 181
Circuito Nacional de Exibidores (CNE; National Exhibition Circuit), 205, 206
Citizen Kane (Welles), 56
Coisas nossas (*Our Things*) (Downey), 7, 133, 246–7

Colares, Raymundo, 56
Colbaz Orchestra, 133
Coleto, Zoraide, 82, *83*
colonialism, 309–10
colonisation, 313, 314
Columbia Records, 133
comedians, 248
comedies, musical *see chanchadas*
comic books
  as art, 55–6
  and cinema, 51–7; *see also* Cinema Marginal
  development of, 53
  horror, 54
  and poster art, 56
  see also catecismos
Companhia Películas de Luxo da América do Sul, 185
Conde, Eduardo, 220
Conde, Maite, 11n1
Conjunto Regional da Rádio Mayrink Veiga, 134
Conley, Tom, 309
Conselheiro, Antônio, 334
Copacabana (Green), 135
Copacabana me engana (*Copacabana Deceives Me*) (Fontoura), 288
Coração de gaúcho (*Gaucho's Heart*) (Barros), 180
cordel literature, 332, *332*
Corpani, Marcelo, 150
Correia, Carlos Alberto Prates: *Perdida* (*A Lost Woman*), 163, 164
Correio da Manhã (newspaper), 141n6, 206
Corrigan, Timothy, 74
Cortázar, Julio: *Continuidad de los parques* (*The Continuity of Parks*), 161
Costa, Antonio, 104
Courage, Tamara, 11n3
Coutinho, Eduardo, 3, 261–72
  Babilônia 2000, 264, 265
  Cabra marcado para morrer (*Twenty Years Later*), 262–3
  canções, As (*Songs*), 261, 265, 266, 269–71
  dia na vida, Um (*A Day in Life*), 9, 261, 262, 264, 266
  Edifício Master (*Master Building*), 264, 265

Coutinho, Eduardo (*cont.*)
  fim e o princípio, O (*The End and the Beginning*), 9, 261, 265
  Jogo de cena (*Playing*), 9, 261, 265, 266–8, 270
  Moscou (*Moscow*), 9, 265, 266, 268–9
  Peões (*Metalworkers*), 265
  Santo forte (*The Mighty Spirit*), 265
  Últimas conversas (*Last Conversations*), 265
Cowell, Adrian, 308
  Decade of Destruction, 310, 316
Crary, Jonathan, 41
cross-dressing, 275
cross iconography *see under* Rocha, Glauber
Cruz, Roberto Moreira S., 318
culpa, A (*Guilt*) (Oliveira), 288
Cummings, Irvin: *That Night in Rio*, 142n14
Cunha, Euclides da: *Os sertões*, 334
Cunha, Paulo, 146
Curi, Ivon, 118, 119, 124
Curtiz, Michael: *Angels With Dirty Faces*, 64
Curtiz, Michael and Berkeley, Busby: *Romance on the High Seas*, 136

Dalí, Salvador, 161
Daney, Serge, 263
D'Arco, Tina, 179
Darwin (female impersonator), 181
Davis, Whitney, 95
Day, Doris, 136
de Palma, Brian, 89
Decade of Destruction (TV series) (Cowell), 310, 316
Deleuze, Gilles, 63, 65, 108n11, 108n22
Denegri, Antonia, 180
Dennison, Stephanie, 11n1, 57, 84, 87, 125
Deporte, Edgardo, 127
derrocada, A (*A vingança do peão*) (*The Downfall: The Peasant's Revenge*) (Barros), 180
descobrimento do Brasil, O (*The Discovery of Brazil*) (Mauro), 164
desforra da titia, A (*Auntie's Revenge*) (Quirino and Pinheiro), 67n13
Desi Arnaz Orchestra, 142n16
Deus e o diabo na terra do sol (*Black God, White Devil*) (Rocha), 10, 41, 217, 325, 326–36, *328, 329, 330, 331, 333, 335,* 342
Deutschland bleiche Mutter (*Germany Pale Mother*) (Sanders-Brahms), 163
Devotos do Ódio (band), 152
dia na vida, Um (*A Day in Life*) (Coutinho), 9, 261, 262, 264, 266
Diário de Pernambuco (newspaper), 153
Diário de um detento (*An Inmate's Diary*) (video), 150
Dias, Antonio, 56
Dias, Júlia, 228
Diaz, Enrique, 268, 269
Didi-Huberman, Georges, 96
Diegues, Carlos: *Bye bye Brasil* (*Bye bye, Brazil*), 10, 307–8, *307,* 311–16, *313, 318*
digital technology, 154
Dioramas, 28, 108n18; *see also* Polyoramas
Discovery of Brazil, The (Mauro), 172n7
Disney films, 135
*dispositif*s, 95, 100–1, 102, 103, 104, 106, 107n2
dissensus, 80, 81
DJ Dolores, 153, 155
Doane, Mary Ann, 77, 282–3
documentaries, 261, 262
  music, 11n3, 169
Doillon, Jacques, 52
Dolores and Morales, 145–6
domestic servants, 75, 83, 84–6, 87
Dominó, Geraldo *see* Moya, Álvaro de
Dona Flor e seus dois maridos (*Dona Flor and Her Two Husbands*) (Barreto), 215, 275, 277–8
Donzelot, Jacques, 291–2
Dornelles, Juliano, 154
Downey, Wallace
  Coisas nossas (*Our Things*), 7, 133, 246–7
  Estudantes (*Students*), 248
Downey, Wallace, Barro, João de and Ribeiro, Alberto: *Alô, alô, Brasil* (*Hello, Hello, Brazil*), 134, 245, 248
drama na Tijuca, Um (*A Drama in Tijuca*) (Leal), 32, 34
Duarte, Anselmo, 118
Dumovich, Otto, 222
Dutilleux, Jean-Pierre, 308
Dyer, Richard, 134, 238, 245

'*É de chuá*' (*It's Super*) (Lima), 253
Ébrio, O (*The Drunkard*) (Abreu), 8, 228–30, 231–9, *233*, *234*, *236*, *237*
Ébrio, O (*The Drunkard*) (TV soap opera), 238–9
Eça, Maurício, 150
Edifício Master (*Master Building*) (Coutinho), 264, 265
Edison, Thomas Alva
  Black Maria Studio, 18
  Kinetoscope, 18
  moving pictures, 29
Edwards, Cliff, 147
Eisenstein, Sergei, 34, 150, 326, 341, 342
  Bronenosets Potyomkin (*Battleship Potemkin*), 329, 330
  Que Viva Mexico! 336
Eisner, Will: *The Spirit*, 56
Elduque, Albert, 11n3; *see also* Screen journal dossier: 'Intermediality in Brazilian Cinema'
Ele Ela (magazine), 61
Eles não usam black-tie (*They Don't Wear Black-Tie*) (Hirszman), 289
Elsaesser, Thomas, 197, 209
Em família (*Inside the Family*) (Porto), 289
embolada music, 150–1
Embrafilme, 8, 144, 215, 222, 311
Empresa Cinematográfica Pathé, 208
Empresa F. Serrador (company), 179
enfolding, 99, 100
entreimages, 101
Enxet Indians, 26
ephemera, 23
Epstein, Jean, 107n7
Erasmo Carlos, 217
Erogotoshitachi (*The Pornographers*) (Imamura), 62
erotic films, 275; *see also pornochanchadas*
esposa do solteiro, A (*The Bachelor's Wife*) (Campogalliani), 183
essay films, 74
estranguladores, Os (*The Stranglers*) (Leal), 18, 32, *32*, 34
Estudantes (*Students*) (Downey), 248
experimental cinema, 98

Fabris, Annateresa, 24
families: and social change, 288, 289, 304
Fantástico (TV show), 223
Fantômas (Feuillade), 31
Faria, Betty, 316
Faria, Reginaldo, 216–17
Farias, Roberto, 219
  Roberto Carlos em ritmo de aventura (*Roberto Carlos at Adventure Rhythm*), 8, 216, 219, 224
fascism, 264, 304
fashion, 35n14
father figures, 292, 296–304, 305; *see also* patriarchal morality
Fatos e Fotos (magazine), 62
Faustino, Mário, 341
  verses, 323–4, *324*
Feiffer, Jules, 52
Feist, Felix E.: *The Man Behind the Gun*, 142n15
Fenelon, Moacyr, 208–9
Ferguson, Norman, et al.: *The Three Caballeros*, 135–6
Ferreira, Jairo, 64
Ferreira, Lírio, 149
  O homem que engarrafava nuvens (*The Man Who Bottled Clouds*), 172n9
  see also Caldas, Paulo and Ferreira, Lírio
Ferreira, Lírio and Lacerda, Hilton: *Cartola – música para os olhos* (*Cartola – Music for the Eyes*), 156–61, 162, 163, 164–9
festas juninas, 248
Feuer, Jane, 116, 128
Feuillade, Louis: *Fantômas*, 31
Ficção e filosofia (*Fiction and Philosophy*), 153
Figueirôa, Alexandre, 152–3
Figuras na paisagem (*Figures in a Landscape*) (Parente), 95, 100–4, *101*
Filho, Daniel, 219
film discs, 208
film prologues, 185–9
  The Lost World (Hoyt), *186*
filmes cantantes (sung films), 182, 183
filmusicais, 244, 248
fim do sem fim, O (*End of the Endless*) (Guimarães), 44, 45
fim e o princípio, O (*The End and the Beginning*) (Coutinho), 9, 261, 265

Fiore, Quentin *see* McLuhan, Marshall and Fiore, Quentin
First Mass (1500), 337, 338
Fitzcarraldo (Herzog), 27
flashbacks, 292
Flusser, Vilém, 94, 98
folk songs, 248
Fome de sexo (*Sex Hunger*) (Fraga), 57
Fonda, Jane, 55
Fontoura, Antônio Carlos: *Copacabana me engana* (*Copacabana Deceives Me*), 288
'fore-edge' painting, 20
Forest, Jean-Claude: *Barbarella*, 54–5, *55*
Formenti, Gastão, 205
Fox Magazine, 203
Fraga, Ody: *Fome de sexo* (*Sex Hunger*), 57
Francisco Carlos, 118, 120, 121, 122, 123–4
Franco, Itamar, 145
Franco, Wilton: *insociáveis, Os* (*The Unsociable Ones*), 218
Fred Zero Quatro, 144, 146–7, 151, 154
Freund, Karl, 340
Froes, Leopoldo, 178–9
Fullerton, John, 19
Furtado, Gustavo Procopio, 78
fuzis, Os (*The Guns*) (Guerra), 41

Gabara, Esther, 41
Galpão Troupe, 268, 269
Gance, Abel, 168
Gang's All Here, The (Berkeley), 135, 136
Gantus, Mixel, 62
Garcia, Stênio, 62, *65*
Garoto (Aníbal Augusto Sardinha), 135
Garwood, Ian, 131
Gaudreault, André, 3
Gauer, Wolf, 308
Gaya, Lindolfo, 119, 128
Gazeta de Notícias (newspaper), 134, 188
Geiger, Anna Bella, 318
gender
   boundaries of, 276
   inversion of roles, 275
   and invisibility, 78
   and pornography, 61, 62, 67n10
   and sexual revolution, 277
   see also father figures; patriarchal morality; queerness; sexism; sexual revolution; women
Genette, Gérard, 105, 161
Gentil, Romeu, 129n5
Gibbs, John, 136
Gil, Gilberto, 151–2
Globo Filmes, 224, 316
Globo Network, 148, 218, 221, 222, 223, 224, 224–5
Godard, Jean-Luc, 51–2, 263
Gomes, Marcelo, 11n4, 42, 47, 148
   Maracatu, maracatus, 152
   see also Pontual, Adelina, et al.
Gomes, Paulo Emilio Salles, 2–3, 4, 244
Gonçalves, Camila Koshiba, 201
Gonçalves, Dercy, 129n5
Gonçalves, Nelson, 271
Gonzaga, Adhemar, 228, 231
   Alô, alô, carnaval (*Hello, Hello, Carnival*), 134, 205, 245, 248, 249
Gonzaga, Adhemar and Mauro, Humberto: *A voz do carnaval* (*The Voice of Carnival*), 247
Goulart, João (Jango), 339
Goulart, Jorge, 118, 120, 121, 125
Goulart, Luis Fernando: *Muro alto* (*High Wall*), 278
gramophones, 210n3
'gramophonoradiomania', 194, 201
   comic strip, *196*
Grande Otelo (actor), 66n3, 118, 126, 257, 275
Grauman, Sid, 185
Gray, Hugh, 3
Green, Alfred E.: *Copacabana*, 135
Grubb, Wilfrid, 26
Grusin, Richard, 17, 102, 255
Guanabara-Film, 178, 179
Guerra, Ruy
   Os cafajestes (*The Unscrupulous Ones*), 57
   Os fuzis (*The Guns*), 41
Guerra conjugal (*Conjugal War*) (Andrade), 306n3
Guignard, Alberto da Veiga: *Imaginary Landscapes*, 39
Guilbert, Yvette, 29
Guillaume Tell (Lumière brothers), 30

Guimarães, Cao
  films: *Andarilho* (*Drifter*), 45–7; *O fim do sem fim* (*End of the Endless*), 44, 45; *O homem das multidões* (*Man of the Crowd*), 47–8
  and interrmediality, 49
  photography: *Gambiarras*, 42; *Paisagens reais – homenagem a Guignard* (*Real Landscapes – Homage to Guignard*), 39
  videos, 39–40, 42–4; *Drawing*, 44; *Quarta-Feira de cinzas/Epílogue* (*Ash Wednesday/Epilogue*), 43; *Sculpting*, 43–4; *Sin peso* (*Weightless*), 43; *The Tenant*, 43
Guimarães, Cao and Lobato, Pablo: *Acidente* (*Accident*), 39
Guimarães, Luiz Fernando, 223
Gullar, Ferreira, 289
Gunning, Tom, 3, 101–2
Guy, Alice: *Life and Passion of Our Lord Jesus Christ*, 29, 31, *31*

Hackford, Taylor: *Ray*, 166
Hagedorn, Friedrich, 23
Hamburger, Esther, 263
Hamilton, Richard, 108n13
Hansen, Mark, 103, 104
haptic visuality, 44, 75
Hawks, Howard
  Rio Bravo, 142n15
  To Have and Have Not, 131
Haymes, Dick, 136
Hayworth, Rita, 62–3, *63*
Heise, Tatiana, 169
Herbert, John
  Ariella, 275, 276, 282, 283–4
  Tessa, a gata (*Tessa, the Hottie*), 278
Hernández, José: *Martín Fierro*, 341
Herzog, Werner: *Fitzcarraldo*, 27
Higgins, Dick, 3
High Noon (Zinnemann), 189, 284n3
Hirszman, Leon
  Eles não usam black-tie (*They Don't Wear Black-Tie*), 289
  Rio, carnaval da vida (*Rio, Carnival of Life*), 169–70, *170*, 171
Hitchcock, Alfred
  Spellbound, 161
  Vertigo, 88

Hokusai, Katsushika: *The Great Wave off Kanagawa*, 107n4
Hollywood
  musicals, 116, 121, 128, 131, 203, 205, 245
  parodies of, 220
  universality of, 244
Hollywood Revue of 1929 (Reisner), 141n6, 147
Holmes, Burton, 26–7
  Cataracts of Iguassu, 27
Holmes, Oliver Wendell, 23
homem das multidões, O (*Man of the Crowd*) (Guimarães), 47–8
homem que engarrafava nuvens, O (*The Man Who Bottled Clouds*) (Ferreira), 172n9
Homero o junkie (Dolores and Morales) 145–6
homoeroticism, 274
homosexuality, 299–300, 301, 303; *see also* lesbianism; queerness
Hooker, Johnny, 154
Hoyt, Harry O.: *The Lost World*, 186–9, *186*
Huhtamo, Erkki, 19, 23
Hutcheon, Linda, 279
Huygens, Christiaan, 19, 25

I Want to Go Home (Resnais), 52
idade da Terra, A (*The Age of the Earth*) (Rocha), 10, 246, 326
Ignez, Helena, 54, *55*
Iguaçu Falls, 27
Imamura, Shohei: *Erogotoshitachi* (*The Pornographers*), 62
Imitation of Life (Sirk), 71
immediacy: and hypermediacy, 102
impure cinema
  Bazin and, 3
  Coutinho and, 9, 261–72
  O Ébrio, 229
Incredible Hulk, The (Lee), 220–1
incrível monstro trapalhão, O (*The Incredible Goofy Monster*) (Stuart), 8, 220, 224
indigenous populations, 310, 314, 317, 319, 320
Ingold, Tim, 40–1, 46
Inmates, The (Resnais), 52
innovation, 17
insociáveis, Os (*The Unsociable Ones*) (Franco), 218
integração da Amazônia, A (newsreel), 310

'IntermIdia' research project, 5
intermedial figurations, 308
　of social exclusion, 71–91
　　Aquarius, 81–91
　　Babás, 74–81
intermediality, 2, 3, 34, 185
　definition of, 113
　and dissensus, 81
　and interdisciplinarity, 274
　intramedial and intermedial references, 162–3
　and media borders, 161
　and remediation, 308–9
　as a research axis, 132–3
　as an 'in-between' space, 72, 229, 275–6, 342
　taxonomies on, 4
'Intermediality in Brazilian Cinema' (*Screen* journal dossier), 5
intertextuality, 162
Intervalo (magazine), 239
Irmãs Pagãs, 248
Ivakhiv, Adrian J., 309

J. Carlos, 197
Jabor, Arnaldo, 10, 289–90
　casamento, O (*The Wedding*), 290, *299, 300*, 302
　opinião pública, A (*Public Opinion*), 290
　Toda nudez será castigada (*All Nudity Shall Be Punished*), 290, 290–7, *291, 293, 294, 295, 297*; *Tudo bem* (*It's All Right*), 306n4
Jackson, Wilfred, et al.: *Saludos Amigos*, 135
Jacobs, Ken: *Tom, Tom, the Piper's Son*, 108n13
Jagose, Annamarie, 280
Janotti Jr., Jeder, 155
Jazz Columbia Orchestra, 141n6
Jercolis, Jardel, 184
Jerslev, Anne, 261
Jesuits, 25
'Joe Carioca' (Zé Carioca) (cartoon), 132
Jogo de cena (*Playing*) (Coutinho), 9, 261, 265, 266–8, 270
Johnson, Randal, 33–4, 57
Jordão, Yara, 181, 182
Jornal do Brasil (newspaper), 278
Jornal do Commercio (newspaper), 153

Joubert, Claudette, 277
Jovem Guarda (Young Wave) movement, 217, 219
juvenile audiences, 215–16, 218, 219, *235, 237*

Kalatozov, Mikhail: *Soy Cuba* (*I Am Cuba*), 329
Kendler, Moisés: *Os marginais* (*The Outsiders*), 163, 164
Khouri, Walter Hugo: *Noite vazia* (*Men and Women*), 57
Kinetoscopes, 18, 33
Kircher, Athanasius, 25
Kishi, Vinícius, *221*
Kiss Me Deadly (Aldrich), 45
Kleiman, Naum, 34
Klumb, Revert Henrique, 23
　stereographs, *23*
　stereoscopes, *24*
Kodato, Lúcio, 308
Kracauer, Siegfried, 107n7
Kubitschek, Juscelino, President, 168, 245

Lacerda, Alcir, 82
Lacerda, Benedito, 249
Lacerda, Carlos, 338
Lacerda, Hilton 148
　Tatuagem (*Tattoo*), 153–4, 154–5, 275
　see also Ferreira, Lírio and Lacerda, Hilton
Lacerda Júnior, Luiz Francisco Buarque de, 274
Lady from Shanghai, The (Welles), 62–3, *63*, 64, 65
Lampião (outlaw), 146, 147
landscape, 40–1, 48
　Guimarães, Cao and, 39, 42–9
Lane, Virgínia, 118, 124, 127
Lang, Fritz: *Metropolis*, 329
Lara, Odete, 57
Last Days of Pompeii, The, 31
Lazary, Angelo, 179
Leal, Antonio
　drama na Tijuca, Um (*A Drama in Tijuca*), 32, 34
　estranguladores, Os (*The Stranglers*), 18, 32, *32*, 34

Leal, Augusto Gomes, 74–5
Leão, Nara, 167
Lee, Stan, 52, 220–1
Leibniz, Gottfried Wilhelm, 96, 105, 106
Lenharo, Alcir, 116–17, 123
Lennon, John, 84
Leone, Sergio, 89
LeRoy, Mervyn: *Little Caesar*, 62
lesbianism, 283–4; *see also* queerness
Lester, Richard, 216
letzte Mann, Der (*The Last Laugh*) (Murnau), 339–40
Levant, Oscar, 128
Libertinas, As (Callegaro, Lima and Reichenbach), 61
Life and Passion of Our Lord Jesus Christ (Guy), 29, 31, *31*
Lima Antônio *see* Callegaro, João, Lima, Antônio and Reichenbach, Carlos
Lima, Pedro, 206
Lima, Victor: *É de chuá* (*It's Super*) (Lima), 253
Lima, Waldemar, 327
Lima Junior, Walter: *Brasil ano 2000* (*Brazil Year 2000*), 288
Linger, Daniel Touro, 58
Lins, Consuelo, 39, 40
   Babás (*Nannies*), 72, 73, 74–81, *76*, *79*
Lira, Buda, 84
literature: popular, 276–81
lithographs, *21*, 23
Little Caesar (LeRoy), 62
Lobão (singer), 222
Lobato, Pablo *see* Guimarães, Cao and Lobato, Pablo
Lopes, Oscar, 179
López, Ana M., 18, 132–3
Lost Highway (Lynch), 45
Lost World The (Hoyt), 186–9, *186*
Lourenço, José, 336
Lourenço, Sílvia, 47
Lubitsch, Ernst: *The Patriot*, 207
Lucchetti, Rubens Francisco, 54
Lumière, Antoine, 18
Lumière brothers, 27, 30, 107n8
Lumière operators, 17, 18
Lynch, David: *Lost Highway*, 45
Lyra, Carlos, 270

Macalé, Jards, 164, 222
McCloud, Scott, 65
Macedo, Eliana, 118, 119, 120, 121, *122*, 123, 124, 127, 277
Macedo, Watson
   and the Atlântida Cinematográfica, 115–17
   Aviso aos navegantes (*Calling all Sailors*), 113, 117–29, *122*, 164, 251
   Carnaval no fogo (*Carnival in Flames*), 123, 275
Machado, Arlindo, 319
Machado de Assis, Joaquim Maria, 165
   Memórias póstumas de Brás Cubas (*The Posthumous Memoirs of Brás Cubas*), 164
MacLuhan, Marshall: *Understanding Media*, 91n3
McLuhan, Marshall and Fiore, Quentin: *The Medium is the Massage*, 55
MAD (magazine), 62
Madame Satã (Aïnouz), 275
Magalhães, Beto, 44
magic lanterns, 19, 25–9
   slides, *25*
Maguire, Frank, 18
Maiolino, Anna Maria, 56
Malho, O (magazine), 194, 197, 204
Malthête, Jacques, 107n6
Man Behind the Gun, The (Feist), 142n15
Manaus: Teatro Amazonas, 27
manga, 52
Manga, Carlos, 115, 121, 219
   Matar ou Correr (*To Kill or to Run*), 284n3
Mangold, James: *Walk the Line*, 166
Manguebeat music, 7, 144, 146, 150, 151, 155
Manuel, Antonio, 56
maps and mapping, 308, 309, 310
   Arara, Os, 316–20
   Bye bye Brasil, 311–16
   road maps, 313
Maracatu de tiro certeiro (Dolores and Morales), 146
Maracatu, maracatus (Gomes), 152
Marcel, Marina, 127
marchinhas, 118, 121, 124, 141n7, 247, 253
Marey, Etienne Jules: *La Vague*, 96
Margem, A (Candeias), 67n14

marginais, Os (*The Outsiders*) (Kendler), 163, 164
Maria Bethânia, 148
Marins, José Mojica, 54, 66n2
Marks, Laura, 44, 75, 99–100
Marreco, J.: *orgasmo da serpente, O* (*The Snake's Orgasm*), 278
Martínez, Alejandro, 25–6
Martins, Luciana, 310
Marvel Comics, 54
mass culture triad (Lenharo), 116–17, 123
Matar ou Correr (*To Kill or to Run*) (Manga), 284n3
Matogrosso, Ney, 148
Matou a família e foi ao cinema (*Killed the Family and Went to the Movies*) (Bressane), 288
Mattos, Carlos Alberto, 272
Mauro, Humberto: *O descobrimento do Brasil* (*The Discovery of Brazil*), 164
Mayrink Veiga (radio station), 141n8, 247
Mazzeo, Alcione, 220
mediality, 95
  of gesture, 96–100
Méliès, Georges, 107n6
Mello, Fernando Collor de, President, 144, 145
Melo, Luis Rocha, 117
melodramas, 33, 289, 290, 292; *see also Toda nudez será castigada*
Mendonça Filho, Kleber, 42, 154
  Aquarius, 72, 73, 81–90, *83, 85, 86, 88, 90, 91*
  som ao redor, O (*Neighbouring Sounds*), 81–2
menina do cinematógrafo, A (*The Cinematograph Girl*) (operetta), 179
Mercadier (French star), 29
Merleau-Ponty, Maurice, 108n19, 109n23
Mesoamerican culture, 20, 22
Mesquitinha, 248
Mestre Ambrósio (band), 146, 147, 151
Mestre Salustiano (musician), 147, 152
Mestre Touro (Antônio Oliveira Bemvindo), 221
metalepsis, 160, 161
Methodists, 25
Metropolis (Lang), 329
migration, 245
'milieux associés', 95
military dictatorship, 290, 304, 307
Minas Gerais: Poços de Caldas church, 25, *25*
Minnelli, Vincente: *The Band Wagon*, 128
miracle workers, 343n6
Miranda, Aurora, 134, 136, 248
Miranda, Carmen, 132, 134, 135, 160, 205, 247, 249–51
Miranda, Luiz Felipe, 212n32
Miranda, Suzana Reck, 136
missionaries, 25–6
Mitchell, W. J. T., 40, 48
modernity, 94
Mombojó (band), 154
Mônica (slave), 74–5
Monster Maker, The (Resnais), 52
Moore, Juanita, 71
Moraes, Marcos, 43
Moraes, Vinícius de, 270
Moraes Neto, Geneton, 153
Moreira, Eduardo, 269
Moreno, Antônio, 274, 275
Morettin, Eduardo, et al., 11n1
Morte de Chocolat (Lumière brothers), 30
morte de um poeta, A (*The Death of a Poet*) (Raulino), 169, 170
Morte no Capibaribe (Caldas), 153
Moscou (*Moscow*) (Coutinho), 9, 265, 266, 268–9
Mota, Regina, 340
Moura, Rodrigo, 42
movietone, 203, 207, 247
moving pictures, 27–8, 29; *see also* animated pictures
Moya, Álvaro de, 55
  A b . . . profunda (*Deep Ass*), 66n6
MTV, 148, 149, 150
Muié macho sim sinhô (*Yes, Sir, I'm a Macho Woman*) (revue), 125, 126–9
mulher de todos, A (*Everyone's Woman*) (Sganzerla), 56
Mulher objeto (*Object Woman*) (Abreu), 277
Müller, Aldine, 276–84, 285n4
Müller, Jürgen, 238
multimedia installations *see Figuras na paisagem*
Mulvey, Laura, 71–2
mundo é uma cabeça, O (*The World is a Head*) (Barroso and Queiroz), 151–2

Mundo Livre S/A (band), 144, 146–7, 151, 154
Muñoz, José Esteban, 274
Murnau, F. W.: *Der letzte Mann* (*The Last Laugh*), 339–40
Muro alto (*High Wall*) (Goulart), 278
music, 131
  brega, 155
  candomblé, 291
  in *Cartola – música para os olhos*, 166–8
  cordel style, 332, 333
  in Coutinho's *As canções*, 269–70
  documentaries, 11n3, 169
  and *Ébrio, O*, 232–5, 239
  embolada, 150–1
  orchestral scores, 330
  popular, 222, 248–9
  rap, 150–1
  regional, 247
  tango, 291
  tecnobrega, 155
  see also marchinhas; singers
Música Popular Brasileira (MPB), 220; *see also* samba
musical comedies *see* chanchadas
musicals, 116, 121, 128, 131, 203, 205, 245; *see also filmusicais*; Hollywood
musicians
  and musical creation, 152
  supporting, 131–2, 136–7, 182
  and unemployment, 205
  see also singers
Musser, Charles, 178
mystery films, 32–3

Na onda do Ié-iê-ié (*In the Rhythm of Iéiêié*) (Teixeira), 219
Nader, Carlos, 264
Nagib, Lúcia, 3, 81, 150, 261; *see also* 'Intermediality in Brazilian Cinema'
Nagib, Lúcia and Paiva, Samuel: *Passages: Travelling in and out of Film Through Brazilian Geography*, 11n4, 91n4, 151
Nagime, Mateus, 274
Navarro, Edgard: *SuperOutro*, 66n8
Navas, Montejo, 43
Navitski, Rielle, *32*
neo-realism, 2

Neuenschwander, Rivane, 43
Nicolay, Faure, 28
Ninja bugei-chō (*Band of Ninja*) (Oshima), 52
Nogueira, Amanda Mansur Custódio, 146, 149
noite das taras, A (*The Night of Perversions*), 57
Noite vazia (*Men and Women*) (Khouri), 57
Nordisk (Danish company), 32–3
Nóvoa, Ricardo, 239, *240*
Novos Baianos (band), 148
Nunes, Bené, 119, 120, 121, 124, 127–8

Odeon record company, 121, 199
Oeser, Valery, 186, 187
Offenbach, Jacques: *La Vie parisienne*, 23–4, 35n14
Oiticica, Hélio: *Cosmococas* installation, 340–1
Oliveira, Aloysio de, 135
Oliveira, Dalva de, 118, 121, 127
Oliveira, Domingos de: *A culpa* (*Guilt*), 288
Oliveira, José do Patrocínio *see* Zezinho
Omniographo, 18, 33–4
opera, 324
opinião pública, A (*Public Opinion*) (Jabor), 290
Orfeu negro (*Black Orpheus*) (Camus), 163, 164, 171
orgasmo da serpente, O (*The Snake's Orgasm*) (Marreco), 278
Oricchio, Luiz Zanin, 41
Ortiz, Daniela, 87
Oscarito (actor), 66n3, 118, 119, 120, 122, 123, 124, 125, 126, *127*, 251, 275
Oshima, Nagisa: *Ninja bugei-chō* (*Band of Ninja*), 52

Pacheco, Annibal, 185
Paiva, Samuel *see* Nagib, Lúcia and Paiva, Samuel
Palatnik, Ronald, 97
'Pandegolandia', 210n1
panoramas, 19, *20*, *21*, 23, 102
Paquito, 129n5
Pará, 311, 312
Parabólica Brasil, 152
Paraguassu (singer), 208
parallax historiography, 3
Parente, André, 95
  Figuras na paisagem (*Figures in a Landscape*), 100–4, *101*

Parlophon, 199, 208
Parville, Henri de, 107n8
Pasolini, Pier Paolo, 341
   Teorema, 66n5
Passages: Travelling in and out of Film Through Brazilian Geography (Paiva and Nagib), 11n4, 91n4, 151
passion films, 31
Passos, Paula, 145
patriarchal morality, 278, 281, 283, 289, 290, 292, 293–4, 297, 303, 304, 316; *see also* father figures
Patriot, The (Lubitsch), 207
Patrocínio Filho, José do, 179
Paul, Robert, 18
Paula, Francisco de: *Areias escaldantes* (*Scalding Sands*), 8, 221, *221*, 222–3, 224
Paz e amor (Auler), 182–3
peasant actors, 263
Pederneiras, Raul, 179, 197
pedido, O (*The Request*) (Pontual), 91n4
Pedra Bonita sect, 336
Pedro II, Emperor, 23, *23*
peepshows, 19
Peixoto, Luiz, 129n5, 205, 206
Penna, Hermano, 308
Peões (*Metalworkers*) (Coutinho), 265
Perdida (*A Lost Woman*) (Correia), 163, 164
Perdida (*Misguided*) (Barros), 178–9
Pernambucan cinema, 145–6, 152, 153, 154, 156
   music videos, 145, 148
Pernambuco, 336; *see also* Recife
Pessoal da Velha Guarda, O (group), 142n18
Pethő, Ágnes, 3, 4, 72, 113, 160, 161, 229, 275–6, 308, 342
Phenakistoscopes, 108n18
Phono-Arte magazine, 203
phonographs, 199, 200, 205, 210n3
photograms, 71, 95, 97, 99, 100
photographs
   in films, 85–7, 172n10
   portrait, 77
   viewing of, 71, 73, 77; *Aquarius*, 83, 84, 86–7, 89; *Babás*, 74–5, 77, 81
photography, 19, 23, 27
   animated, 25
   and class, 83

and film, 81, 87, 99–100
and landscape, 41
and racial bias, 84
and reality, 77
and social exclusion, 71–91
Piazzola, Astor: 'Fuga 9', 291
Picado, Benjamim, 39
picture postcards, 23
Pinheiro, Reinaldo *see* Quirino, Eduardo and Pinheiro, Reinaldo
Pinheiro, Renata, 148
   Amor, plástico e barulho (*Love, Plastic and Noise*), 151, 155
Pinto, Walter, 126
Pixinguinha, 142n18
poetry: cinema of, 341
Polyoramas, 23, 28
Pontual, Adelina, 148
   O pedido (*The Request*), 91n4
Pontual, Adelina, et al.: *Punk rock hardcore*, 152
pornochanchadas, 9, 57, 59, 276–7, 284n4, 306n3
pornógrafo, O (Callegaro), 61–2, 63–5, *65*, 66
pornography: and *catecismos*, 57–60
Porto Alegre
   Teatro São Pedro, 27, 28, *28*, 29;
   programme of films (1901), *30*
Porto, Paulo, 298, *300*, *302*
   Em família (*Inside the Family*), 289
Possuelo, Sydney, 317
Post, Frans, 41
Prêmio Resgate do Cinema Brasileiro (Brazilian Cinema Rescue Award), 145
printers: optical, 98
projectors, 28
Public Enemy, The (Wellman), 62
Punk rock hardcore (Pontual et al.), 152
Purse, Lisa, 11n3
Puzzi, Nicole, 285n4

Quaranta, Letizia, 183
Quatro Ases e um Coringa (Four Aces and a Joker) (group), 120, 121
Que Viva Mexico! (Eisenstein), 336
queerness, 9, 274–6, 279, 281, 282, 284; *see also* lesbianism; homosexuality
Queiroga, Yuri, 155

Queirós, Adirley: *Branco sai, preto fica* (*White Out, Black In*), 226n12
Queiroz, Bidu *see* Barroso, Claudio and Queiroz, Bidu
Queiroz, Pedro, 83
Quem roubou meu samba (*Who Stole My Samba*) (Burle), 253–5, *254*
Quirino, Eduardo and Pinheiro, Reinaldo: *A desforra da titia* (*Auntie's Revenge*), 67n13

rabeca (fiddles), 147
Raccord (company), 160
race
 and culture, 165
 and prison system, 150
 and social exclusion, 71–2, 75, 84, 89, 90, 160; *see also* slaves and slavery
Racionais MCs (band), 150
radio, 114, 117, 131, 134–5
 and cinema, 271
 in films, 231–2, 248
 and phonographs, 200
 radiomania, 198–9
 'victrolamania', 200–2
Rádio Nacional, 138
Radio Paulista (magazine), 209
Radio Phono (magazine), 202
Rádio Tupi, 142n18
Radiocultura (magazine), 200
Radiomania magazine, 209
radiotelephony (TSF), 198
rail travel, 19
Rajewsky, Irina, 162, 163, 238, 262, 276, 309
Ramos, Fernão, 11n1
Ramos, Helena, 277
Ramos, José Mário Ortiz, 215, 216, 217
Ramos, Nuno, 170
Rancière, Jacques, 80, 81
Randall, Rachel, 78
rap do Pequeno Príncipe contra as almas sebosas, O (documentary), 150
rap music, 150–1
Ra-ta-plan Company of Sketches and Ballets, 187, 189
Ratoff, Gregory: *Carnival in Costa Rica*, 136
Raulino, Aloysio: *A morte de um poeta* (*The Death of a Poet*), 169, 170

Ray (Hackford), 166
realism
 neo-realism, 2
 and reflexivity, 267
Recife, 82, 144–5, 152, 154
 Alto José do Pinho, 152
record industry, 117, 199
records
 and cinema, 202–3, 203–5
 'illustrated', 205–6
 sale of, 201, 248
 see also 'gramophonoradiomania'
Rede Globo, 148, 218
Rego, José Lins do: *Pedra Bonita*, 336
Reichenbach, Carlos *see* Callegaro, João, Lima, Antônio and Reichenbach, Carlos
Reis, Luiz Thomaz: *Ao redor do Brasil*, 310
Reis, Mário, 248
Reisner, Charles: *Hollywood Revue of 1929*, 141n6, 147
religion: and politics, 264; *see also* Methodists; passion films
Remanescências (*Remainiscences*) (Adriano), 95, 97–100, *97*, 106
remediations, 4, 17, 31–2, 34, 102, 308–9
 rebound effect, 105
Renor, Paula de, 84
Renor, Roger de, 151
Réo, Tom, 201
Resnais, Alain, 52
Retomada do Cinema Brasileiro (Brazilian Film Revival), 2, 42, 144
Revista do Rádio, 253
revistas (revue films), 182; *see also filmusicais*
revolution, 342
Rey, Ruy, 118, 119, 120, 124–5
Ribeiro, Alberto *see* Downey, Wallace, Barro, João de and Ribeiro, Alberto
Ribeiro, Zilco, 129n5
Ribeiro Junior, Luiz Severiano, 115
Ricardo, Rodrigo, 251–2, 332
Rio, 40 graus (*Rio, 40 Degrees*) (Santos), 163–4, 253, 257
Rio Bravo (Hawks), 142n15
Rio, carnaval da vida (*Rio, Carnival of Life*) (Hirszman), 169–70, *170*, 171

Rio de Janeiro
　Alhambra theatre, 249
　Capitolio cinema, 185, 202, 207
　Cinelândia (Filmland), 185, 187
　cinematographo fallante, 202
　entertainment industry, 190, 247
　Glauce Rocha Theatre, 266
　Gloria Theatre, 129n5, 184–5, *185*, 187
　Guarani Theatre, 206
　Imperial Academy, 23
　Imperio cinema, 184–5
　National Exhibition (1866), 23, 24
　Odeon theatre, 184–5, 202, *204*
　Palacio theatre, 203, 246
　Polytheama Theatre, 206
　soundscape, 194–210
　Teatro Recreio, 126, *126*
　Victrola Ortophonica Auditorium, 202, 205
Rio, Zona Norte (*Rio, Northern Zone*) (Santos), 253, 257
Rios, Cassandra, 9
　Ariella, a Paranóica (*Ariella, the Paranoid*), 276, 278, 279–80, *280*, 281–2, 283
　Eu sou uma lésbica (*I Am a Lesbian*), 279
　Muros altos (*High Walls*), 278
　serpente e a flor, A (*The Snake and the Flower*), 278
　Tessa, a gata (*Tessa, the Hottie*), 278
Road to Zanzibar (Schertzinger), 142n15
Roberto Carlos, 270, 271
Roberto Carlos em ritmo de aventura (*Roberto Carlos at Adventure Rhythm*) (Farias), 8, 216–18, 219, 224
Roberto Guilherme, 218
Roberts, Les, 309, 317
Rocha, Glauber
　'Aesthetics of Dream' (article), 342
　Barravento (*The Turning Wind*), 341
　'Christology' of, 326
　and cosmogony, 325, 326
　and cross iconography, 327–36, *328*, *329*, *331*, *335*, *337*, *338*
　documentaries on, 343n9
　Riverão Sussuarana, 336
　'trilogia da terra' ('Earth trilogy'), 10, 326; *Deus e o diabo na terra do sol* (*Black God, White Devil*), 41, 217, 325, 326–36, *328*, *329*, *330*, *331*, *333*, *335*, 342; *idade da Terra, A* (*The Age of Earth*), 246; *Terra em transe* (*Entranced Earth*), 245, 290, 304, 323, 324, 337–42, *337*, *338*, *339*
Rodrigues, Nelson, 289, 305
　casamento, O (*The Wedding*), 290
　Toda nudez será castigada (*All Nudity Shall Be Punished*), 9–10, 289, 296
　Vestido de noiva (*Wedding Dress*), 289
Rojas, Carlos, 274
Romance on the High Seas (Curtiz and Berkeley), 136
Rondônia, 311, 316
Rosa, João Guimarães: *Grande sertões: veredas* (*The Devil to Pay in the Backlands*), 336
Rosa, Noel, 248
Rosa de sangue (*Blood Rose*) (Barros), 183
Rossi, Reginaldo, 155
Rothafel, Samuel 'Roxy', 185
Rouch, Jean, 52, 268
Roussef, Dilma, President, 264
Russell, Catherine, 3

Sá, Daniel Serrevalle de, 53
Sadek, Isis, 41–2
Salles, João Moreira, 265, 269
　Santiago, 91n1
Salles, José Roberto Cunha: *Ancoradouro de pescadores na Baía de Guanabara* (*Fishing Pier at Guanabara Bay*), 96–7, *97*
Salles, Walter: *Central do Brasil* (*Central Station*), 41
Salomão, Waly, 341
saltimbancos trapalhões, Os (*The Goofy Acrobats*) (Tanko), 215, 219–20
Saludos Amigos (Jackson et al.), 135
samba, 160, 201, 255, 270, 342
Samba esquema noise (Dolores and Morales), 146, 154
Sampaio, Bernardo, 83
Sampaio, Sebastião, 207
Sanders-Brahms, Helma: *Deutschland bleiche Mutter* (*Germany Pale Mother*), 163
Sandrich, Mark: *Shall We Dance*, 128
Sangue de bairro (music video), 149, 151
Santiago (Salles), 91n1
Santiago, Oswaldo, 249
Santo forte (*The Mighty Spirit*) (Coutinho), 265

Santos: Cineteatro Coliseu, 189
Santos, João Francisco dos, 275
Santos, Lulu, 222, 223
Santos, Nelson Pereira dos
   Rio, 40 graus (*Rio, 40 Degrees*), 163–4, 253, 257
   Rio, Zona Norte (*Rio, Northern Zone*), 253, 257
   Vidas secas (*Barren Lives*), 41
Santos, Venilton, 255
São Paulo
   Boca do Lixo, 61, 64
   Empresas Cinematográficas Reunidas (Reunidas Film Companies), 189–90
   entertainment industry, 190
   First International Comics Exhibition (1951), 55–6
   International Film Festival, 262
   Olavo Setúbal gallery of Instituto Itaú Cultural: 'O Brasil Secreto' (Secret Brazil), 20
   Paramount Theatre, 203
Sardinha, Aníbal Augusto *see* Garoto
Sastro, Henrique: 'Grand-Prix marvellous cinematograph', 30
Sattler, Hubert, 23
Saudação à cidade de São Paulo (*Greetings to the City of São Paulo*), 207
Saúde (magazine), 61
Saving Private Ryan (Spielberg), 163
Schaefer, Murray, 194
Schelling, Vivian, 94
Schertzinger, Victor: *Road to Zanzibar*, 142n15
Schindler, Melissa, 57, 67n15
Schlotterbeck, Jess, 166
science fiction, 221–2
Screen journal dossier: 'Intermediality in Brazilian Cinema', 5
Se Zé Limeira sambasse maracatu (Dolores and Morales), 146
Segreto, Afonso, 4
Seixas, Raul, 148
Serrador, Francisco, 182, 184–5, 187, 190; *see also* Empresa F. Serrador
Sertão das memórias (*Landscapes of Memory*) (Araújo), 41
sexism, 200

sexual revolution, 277
Sganzerla, Rogério
   Bandido da Luz Vermelha, O, 67n14
   HQ: História em Quadrinhos (*Comics*), 55
   mulher de todos, A (*Everyone's Woman*), 56
Shakespeare, William: *Romeo and Juliet*, 275
Shall We Dance (Sandrich), 128
Shamoon, Deborah, 67n11
Shaw, Lisa, 11n1, 57, 125, 180, 181, 250
Shimamoto, Júlio, 54
Shipwreck of the SS Sírio, The, 29
Shirato, Sanpei: *Ninja bugei-chō* (*Band of Ninja*) (manga), 52
short films: and local TV, 151–4
Shtromberg, Elena, 318
silent film, 29
   Barros and, 177
   Eisenstein and, 330
   and race, 75
Silva, Ismael, 171n3
Silva, Maria Cristina Miranda da, 23
Silveira, Celestino, 185
Simião, Marcos Paulo, 160
Simondon, Albert, 95
Sincrocinex, 208
singers
   and race inequality, 160
   radio, 205
singing *see filmes cantantes*; *filmusicais*; *marchinhas*
Sirk, Douglas: *Imitation of Life*, 71
slaves and slavery, 74–7, 78
Soares, Elza, 167
Soares, Thiago, 147, 148, 154
social changes: and family decadence, 288, 289, 304
social exclusion: intermedial figurations of, 71–91
   Aquarius, 81–91
   Babás, 74–81
social injustice, 336
Sócrates, Lessandro, 160
Solha, W. J., 82
Solomon, Stefan, 5
som ao redor, O (*Neighbouring Sounds*) (Mendonça Filho), 81–2
Sonofilmes, 244
sound, 247, 248

sound media, 195; *see also* phonographs; radio
sound recording: electrical amplification, 199
soundscapes, 194
Souto, Gilberto, 137
Souto, Mariana, 78
Souza, José Inácio de Melo, 35n16
Soy Cuba (*I Am Cuba*) (Kalatozov), 329
Spacey, Kevin: *Beyond the Sea*, 166
spectatorship, 104
speeches: filmed, 206–7
Spellbound (Hitchcock), 161
Spencer, Fernando, 153
Spielberg, Steven: *Saving Private Ryan*, 163
Stam, Robert, 4, 42, 57, 267, 280, 316
Stanley, Joseph: *Brazil*, 121
Stephens, John Lloyd, 20
Stepple, Amin, 153
stereographs and stereography, 19, 23–5, *23*
stereopticons, 27
stereoscopes and stereoscopy, 19, 23–4, *24*, 108n18
Sterne, Jonathan, 195, 199
Sterne, Lawrence: *Tristram Shandy*, 161
Stevenson, Robert Louis: *Strange Case of Dr Jekyll and Mr Hyde*, 220–1
Stoddard, John L., 26
Strange Days (Bigelow), 108n20
Stroheim, Erich von: *The Wedding March*, 207
Stuart, Adriano, 219
  O incrível monstro trapalhão (*The Incredible Goofy Monster*), 8, 220, 224
subtitles, 248, 336
Sugar Loaf mountain, 312, 315
Super-8 format film, 44–5, 66n8, 145, 152–4, 156
Superbeldades (Tkaczenko), 68n19
SuperOutro (Navarro), 66n8
Sylphorama, 28–9

talking films *see cinema fallado*
Tanko, J. B.
  Os saltimbancos trapalhões (*The Goofy Acrobats*), 215, 219–20
  Os trapalhões na Serra Pelada (*The Goofies in Serra Pelada*), 215
Tashlin, Frank, 51

Tatuagem (*Tattoo*) (Lacerda), 153–4, 154–5, 275
Tavares, Heckel, 205, 206
Tavares, Mair, 160
Teixeira, Aurélio: *Na onda do Ié-iê-iê* (*In the Rhythm of Iêiêiê*), 219
Teixeira, Humberto, 172n9
Teixeira, Tavinho: *Batguano*, 275
telephony, 195
television, 117, 251–7
  films for, 262
  and irony, 308
  local, 151–4
  and national integration, 315, 316
  open, 262
  post-television era, 154–6
  rise of, 218
Teorema (Pasolini), 66n5
Terra em transe (*Entranced Earth*) (Rocha), 10, 290, 304, 323, 324, 326, 337–42, *337*, *338*, *339*
territorial films, 308
Tessa, a gata (*Tessa, the Hottie*) (Herbert), 278
That Night in Rio (Cummings), 142n14
theatre
  cinema on stage, 183–4
  cineteatros, 181
  pronunciation, 249–50
  teatro de revista (theatrical revue), 113–14, 180, 185, 216; *see also Muié macho sim sinhô*
theatrical culture, 178, 189
Theatrograph, 18
Thompson, Emily, 194, 210n5
Three Caballeros, The (Ferguson et al.), 135–6
Tijuana Bibles, 58
Tijuca, 23, 24, 32
Tinhorão, José Ramos, 230
Titãs, Os (band), 222, 223, 224
Tkaczenko, Konstantin: *Superbeldades*, 68n19
To Have and Have Not (Hawks), 131
Toda nudez será castigada (*All Nudity Shall Be Punished*) (Jabor), 10, 290–7, *291*, *293*, *294*, *295*, *297*
Tom, Tom, the Piper's Son (Jacobs), 108n13
Tonacci, Andrea, 308
  Os Arara (*The Arara*), 10, 311, 316–21

Torres, Fernanda, 267
'Towards an Intermedial History of Brazilian Cinema: Exploring Intermediality as a Historiographic Method' research project, 5
Transamazon Highway, 307, 310, 311, 312, 314, 315, 317, 318
transartistic commons theory (Stam), 4
Trapalhões, Os (The Goofies), 215, 218–21, 224
trapalhões na Serra Pelada, Os (*The Goofies in Serra Pelada*) (Tanko), 215
travelogues, 26–7
Trevisan, Dalton: *Guerra conjugal* (*Conjugal War*), 306n3
Triunfo, Nelson (Nelson Gonçalves Campos Filho), 151
Tro-lo-ló (revue company), 184, 187
Tropicália movement, 5, 304, 325, 340
Trusz, Alice Dubina, 27–8, 29
TSF (magazine), 209
Tudo bem (*It's All Right*) (Jabor), 306n4
Turner, Lana, 71
TV Paulista (company), 231
TV Pirata (TV show), 223
TV Record (company), 217, 218, 219
TV Viva (company), 151

Ubirajara (Barros), 180
Últimas conversas (*Last Conversations*) (Coutinho), 265
Ultraje a Rigor (band), 223
unfolding, 99
United States
  cultural influences, 54
  Good Neighbour Policy, 132, 134, 135
  see also Hollywood
Uranga, Arturo, 222
Uricchio, William, 207

Vague, La (Marey), 96
vague, the, 95, 96, 105, 107
Van Sant, Gus: *Milk*, 163
Vanusa (singer), 218, 219
Varda, Agnès, 161–2
Vargas, Getúlio, President, 141n8, 245, 339
Vargas, Herom *see* 'Caranguejos com cérebro' (Crabs with Brains) manifesto

Vasconcellos, Evandro, 182
vaudeville *see teatro de revista*
Vaz, Reto, 204
Velho, Luiz, 108n15
Vera Cruz studios, 53
Verberena, Cleo de, 231
Verga, Vittorio, 205
Vergueiro, Waldomiro, 53, 58
Verhoeff, Nanna, 19
Verne, Jules: *Eight Hundred Leagues on the Amazon* (*Huit cents lieues sur l'Amazone*), 35n14
Vertigo (Hitchcock), 88
Vertov, Dziga, 340
Veyre, Gaston, 18
Viajo porque preciso, volto porque te amo (*I Travel Because I Have to, I Come Back Because I Love You*), 42
Vianna Filho, Oduvaldo, 289
Viany, Alex, 137
victrolas, 200–2, 210n3
Vidal, Maria, 255
Vidas secas (*Barren Lives*) (Santos), 41
Vídeo nas Aldeias project, 321
videos
  art, 318
  installations, 101, 102, 104
  music, 144–56, 218, 223; and advertising, 149; digital, 154–6; in films, 147–54
  pornographic, 60
  texts, 105–6
Vieira, João Luiz, 118, 231, 316
Vieira Jr., João, 155
Vieira, Tony, 277
view-boxes, 19
Vilela, Diogo, 223
Villa-Lobos, Heitor, 333
  'Bachianas Brasileiras', 323, 333–4, 340
Villela, João Ferreira, 74–5
Vilmar, Roberto, 186, 187
Vinci, Leonardo da: *Trattato della pittura*, 107n3
virtual reality (VR), 64, 100, 102, 103–4, 105, 106, 107n2
Visconti, Luchino, 5
Visorama, 100, 106
visuality, 95
vitaphone system, 133, 202, 203, 205

viúva alegre, A (*The Merry Widow*) (Auler), 182–3
Vivencial Diversiones (troupe), 153
Vivo ou morto (*Dead or Alive*) (Barros), 179
VMB-Video Music Brasil award, 148
voiceovers, 289, 292
voz do carnaval, A (*The Voice of Carnival*) (Gonzaga and Mauro), 247

Wagner, Richard, 325, 329, 334, 342
   Gesamtkunstwerk (total artwork), 324
Waldow Films, 248
Walk the Line (Mangold), 166
Walters, Charles: *The Barkleys of Broadway*, 128
Waltz, Gwendolyn, 183–4
Warhol, Andy, 99
Warner Bros., 202
Washington Post, 145
Wedding March, The (Stroheim), 207
Welles, Orson
   Citizen Kane, 56
   Lady from Shanghai, The, 62–3, *63*, 64, 65
Wellman, William A.
   Public Enemy, The, 62
   Wings, 202
Western Electric, 202, 203
Wheatstone, Charles, 23
Wilker, José, 316
Williams, Linda, 59

Wings (Wellman), 202
Wolf, Werner, 333, 334
women
   and colonialism, 316
   as directors, 231
   and documentaries, 267–8
   invisibility of, 71, 78, 84–5, 86–8, 90
   non-normative identities of, 283
   and *pornochanchadas*, 277, 284n4
   and sexism, 200
   voiceovers by, 289, 292
   and work, 304

Xavier, Ismail, 3, 4, 263, 324, 325, 326, 333, 335, 338

Yanakiewa, Juliana, 121–2, 127–8, *127*
Yantock (Yantok), Max (Nicolau Cesarino), 194

Zalla, Rodolfo, 66n2
'Zé Carioca' (cartoon) *see* 'Joe Carioca'
Zéfiro, Carlos (Alcides Aguiar Caminha), 61
   catecismos, 52–3, 57–60, 58, *60*, 61, 62, 65–6
Zezinho (José do Patrocínio Oliveira), 7, 131–2, 133–4, 136–8, 139–41
Zica, Dona, 164, 167
Zinnemann, Fred: *High Noon*, 189, 284n3

EU representative:
Easy Access System Europe
Mustamäe tee 50, 10621 Tallinn, Estonia
Gpsr.requests@easproject.com

www.ingramcontent.com/pod-product-compliance
Lightning Source LLC
Chambersburg PA
CBHW050834230426
43667CB00012B/1999